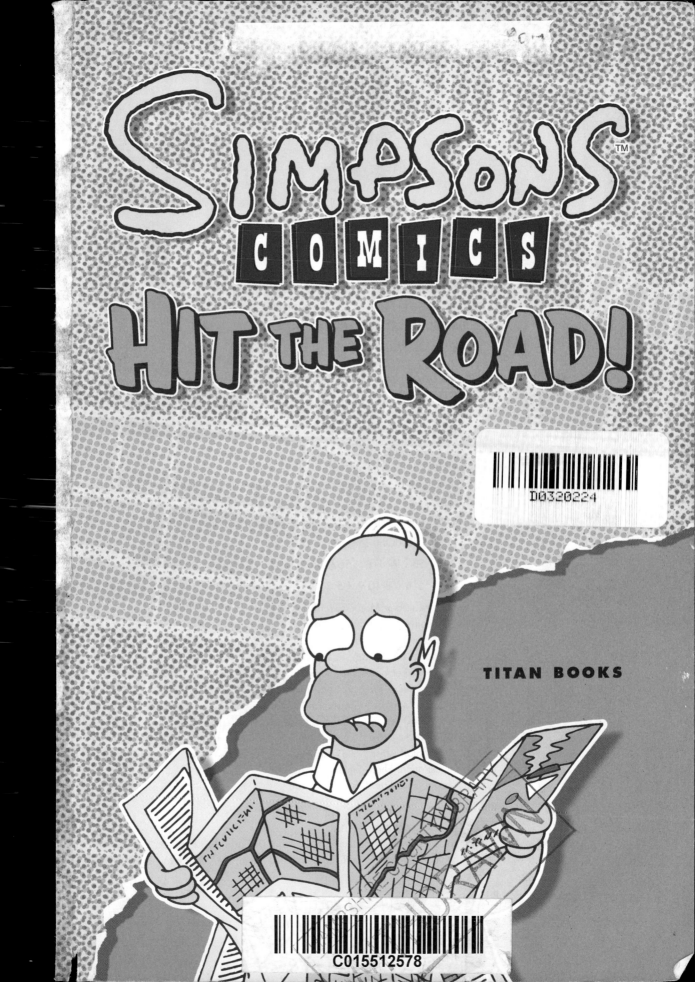

SIMPSONS™ COMICS HIT THE ROAD!

TITAN BOOKS

*Dedicated to the memory of
Douglas Patrick Whaley, our bighearted Big Daddy,
Big Brother, and Big Kahuna*

SIMPSONS COMICS HIT THE ROAD!

Collects Simpsons Comics 85, 86, 88, 89 and 90

Published in the UK by Titan Books, a division of Titan Publishing Group,
144 Southwark St., London SE1 0UP, under licence from Bongo Entertainment, Inc.

FIRST EDITION: JANUARY 2008

ISBN 9781848562271

2 4 6 8 10 9 7 5 3 1

Publisher: Matt Groening
Creative Director: Bill Morrison
Managing Editor: Terry Delegeane
Director of Operations: Robert Zaugh
Art Director: Nathan Kane
Art Director Special Projects: Serban Cristescu
Production Manager: Christopher Ungar
Assistant Art Director: Chia-Hsien Jason Ho
Production/Design: Karen Bates, Nathan Hamill, Art Villanueva
Staff Artist: Mike Rote
Administration: Sherri Smith, Pete Benson
Legal Guardian: Susan A. Grode

Trade Paperback Concepts and Design: Serban Cristescu

Contributing Artists:
Karen Bates, John Costanza, Serban Cristescu, Dan Davis, Mike DeCarlo, Luis Escobar,
Phyllis Novin, Phil Ortiz, Patrick Owsley, Ryan Rivette, Howard Shum, Art Villanueva

Contributing Writers:
Ian Boothby, Gail Simone, Mary Trainor, Patrick M. Veronne

PRINTED IN CANADA

TABLE OF CONTENTS

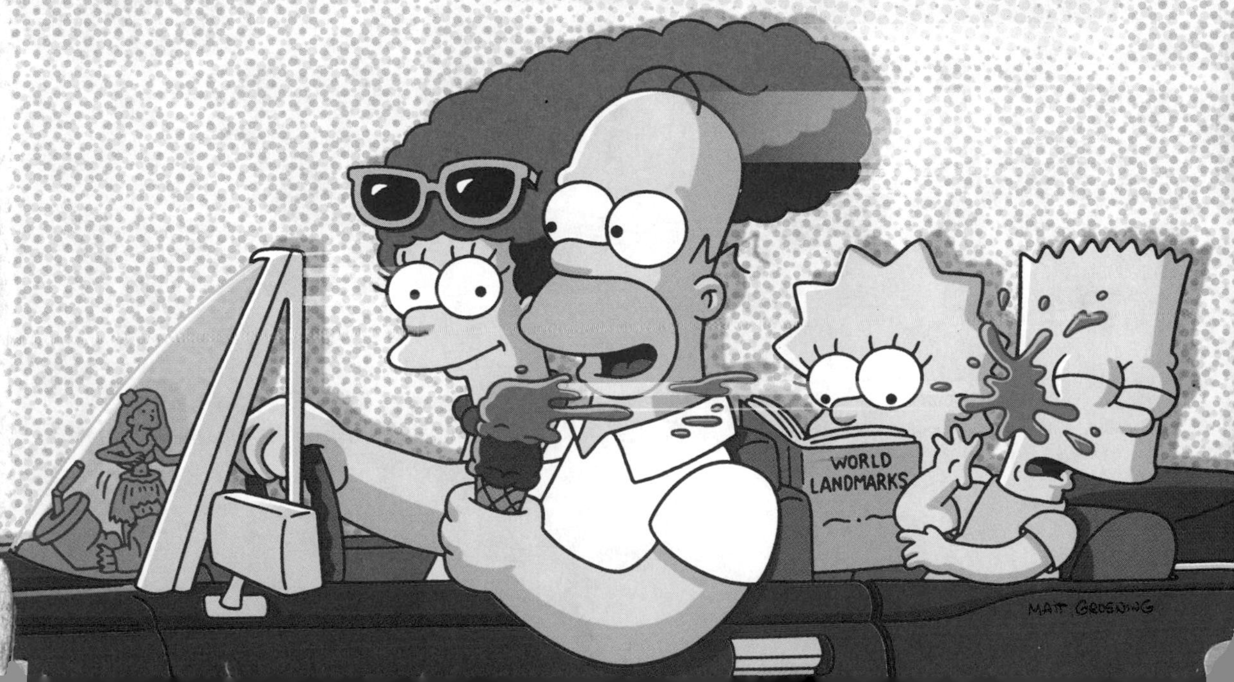

WORLD
LANDMARKS
MATT GROENING

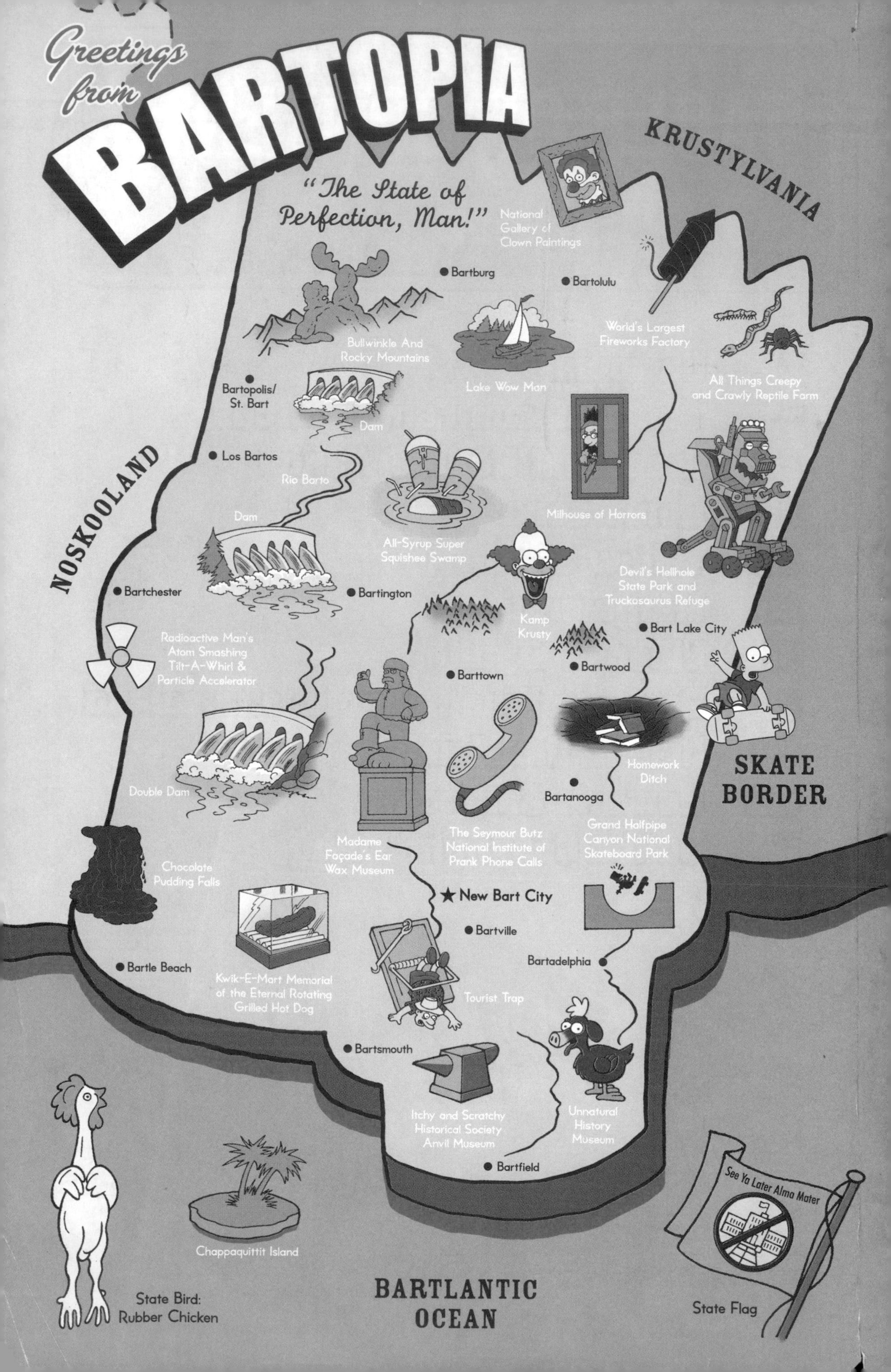
Greetings from
BARTOPIA
"The State of Perfection, Man!"
KRUSTYLVANIA
NOSKOOLAND
SKATE BORDER
BARTLANTIC OCEAN
National Gallery of Clown Paintings
Bartburg
Bartolulu
World's Largest Fireworks Factory
All Things Creepy and Crawly Reptile Farm
Bullwinkle And Rocky Mountains
Lake Wow Man
Bartopolis/ St. Bart
Dam
Los Bartos
Rio Barto
Milhouse of Horrors
Dam
All-Syrup Super Squishee Swamp
Devil's Hellhole State Park and Truckosaurus Refuge
Bartchester
Bartington
Kamp Krusty
Bart Lake City
Radioactive Man's Atom Smashing Tilt-A-Whirl & Particle Accelerator
Barttown
Bartwood
Homework Ditch
Bartanooga
Double Dam
Madame Façade's Ear Wax Museum
The Seymour Butz National Institute of Prank Phone Calls
Grand Halfpipe Canyon National Skateboard Park
Chocolate Pudding Falls
New Bart City
Bartville
Bartle Beach
Kwik-E-Mart Memorial of the Eternal Rotating Grilled Hot Dog
Tourist Trap
Bartadelphia
Bartsmouth
Itchy and Scratchy Historical Society Anvil Museum
Unnatural History Museum
Bartfield
Chappaquittit Island
See Ya Later Alma Mater
State Bird: Rubber Chicken
State Flag

MATT GROENING PRESENTS

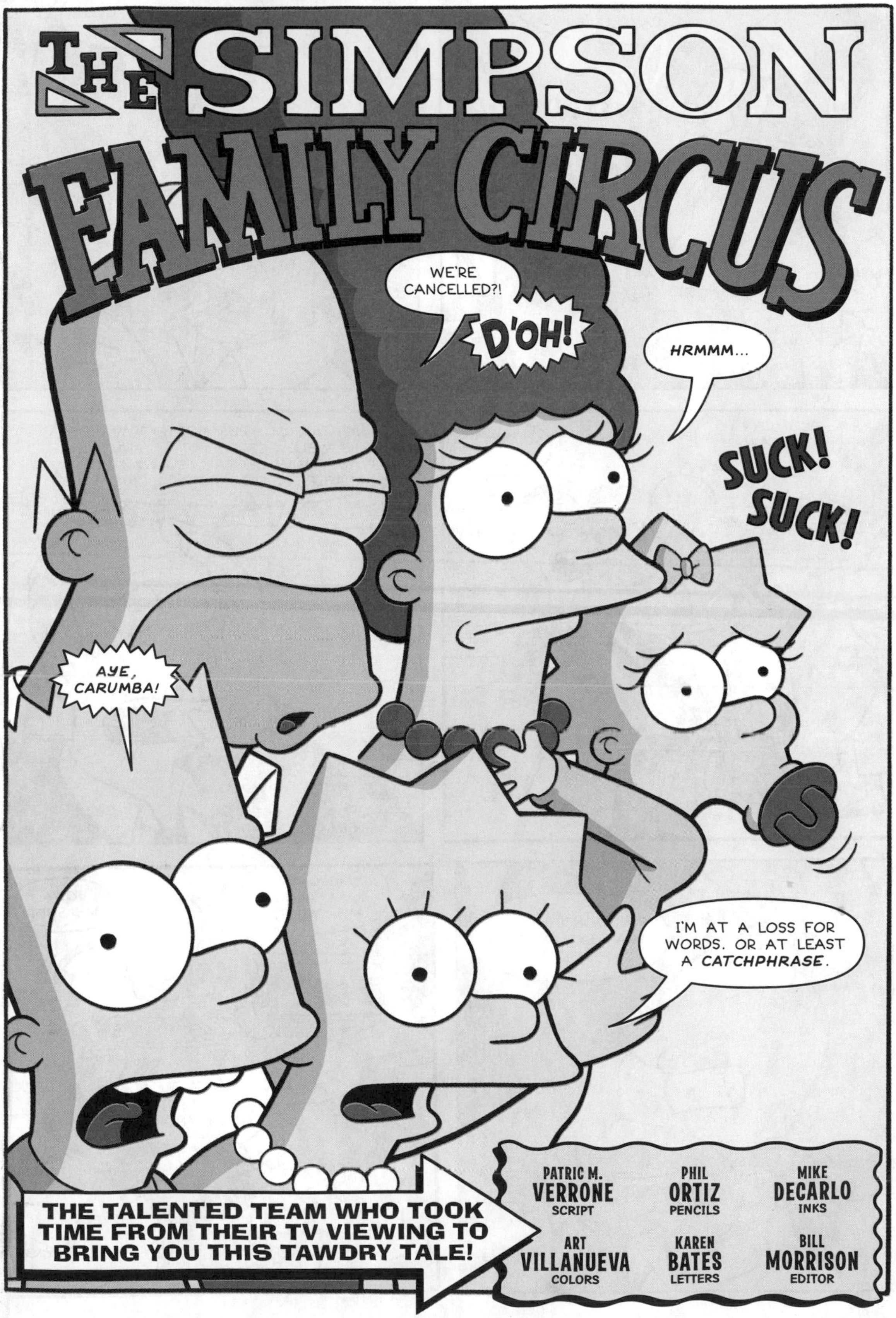
THE SIMPSON FAMILY CIRCUS
WE'RE CANCELLED?!
D'OH!
HRMMM...
SUCK! SUCK!
AYE, CARUMBA!
I'M AT A LOSS FOR WORDS. OR AT LEAST A CATCHPHRASE.
THE TALENTED TEAM WHO TOOK TIME FROM THEIR TV VIEWING TO BRING YOU THIS TAWDRY TALE!
PATRIC M. VERRONE SCRIPT
PHIL ORTIZ PENCILS
MIKE DECARLO INKS
ART VILLANUEVA COLORS
KAREN BATES LETTERS
BILL MORRISON EDITOR

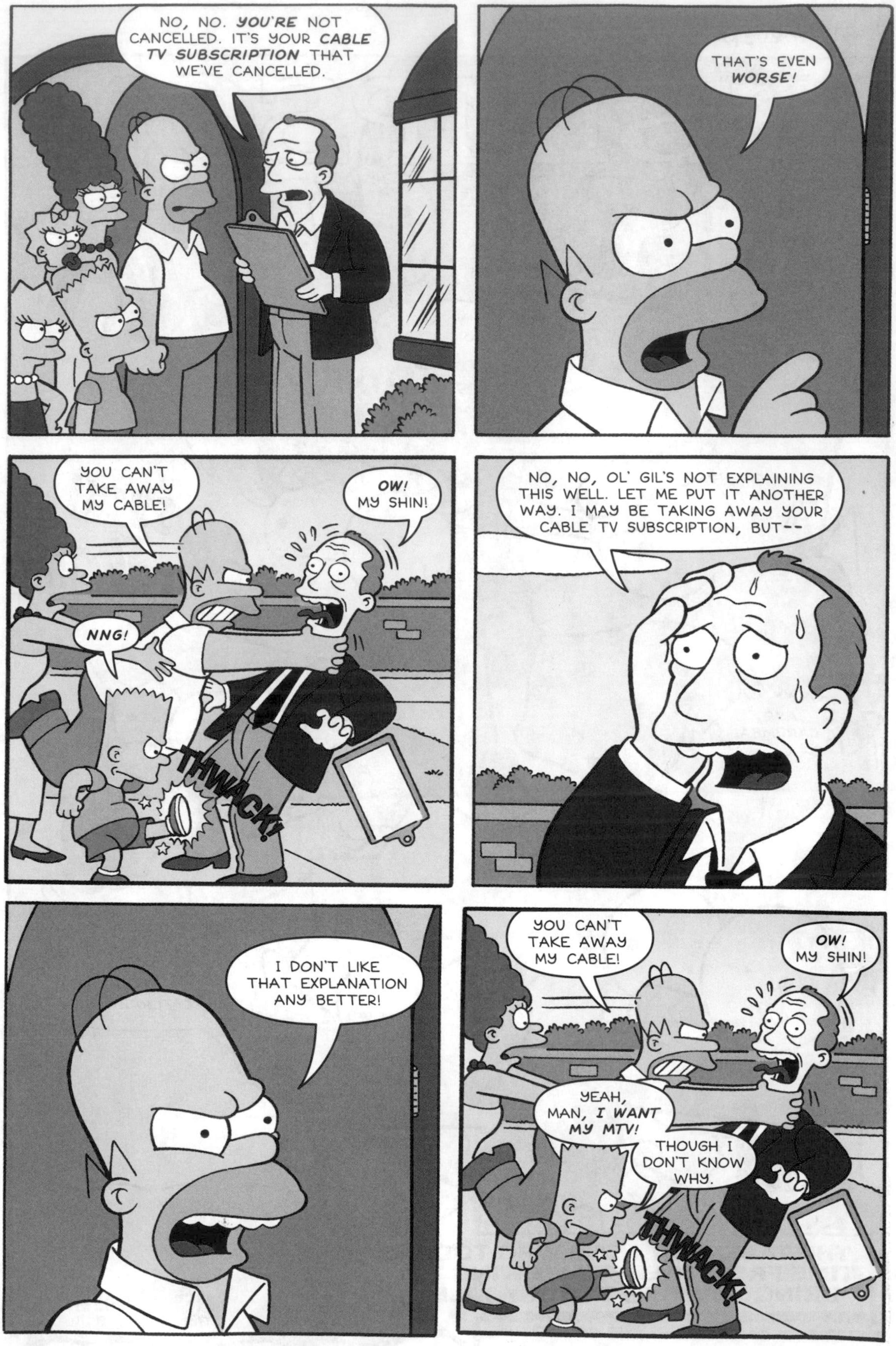
NO, NO. YOU'RE NOT CANCELLED. IT'S YOUR CABLE TV SUBSCRIPTION THAT WE'VE CANCELLED.
THAT'S EVEN WORSE!
YOU CAN'T TAKE AWAY MY CABLE!
OW! MY SHIN!
NNG!
THWACK!
NO, NO, OL' GIL'S NOT EXPLAINING THIS WELL. LET ME PUT IT ANOTHER WAY. I MAY BE TAKING AWAY YOUR CABLE TV SUBSCRIPTION, BUT--
I DON'T LIKE THAT EXPLANATION ANY BETTER!
YOU CAN'T TAKE AWAY MY CABLE!
OW! MY SHIN!
YEAH, MAN, I WANT MY MTV!
THOUGH I DON'T KNOW WHY.
THWACK!

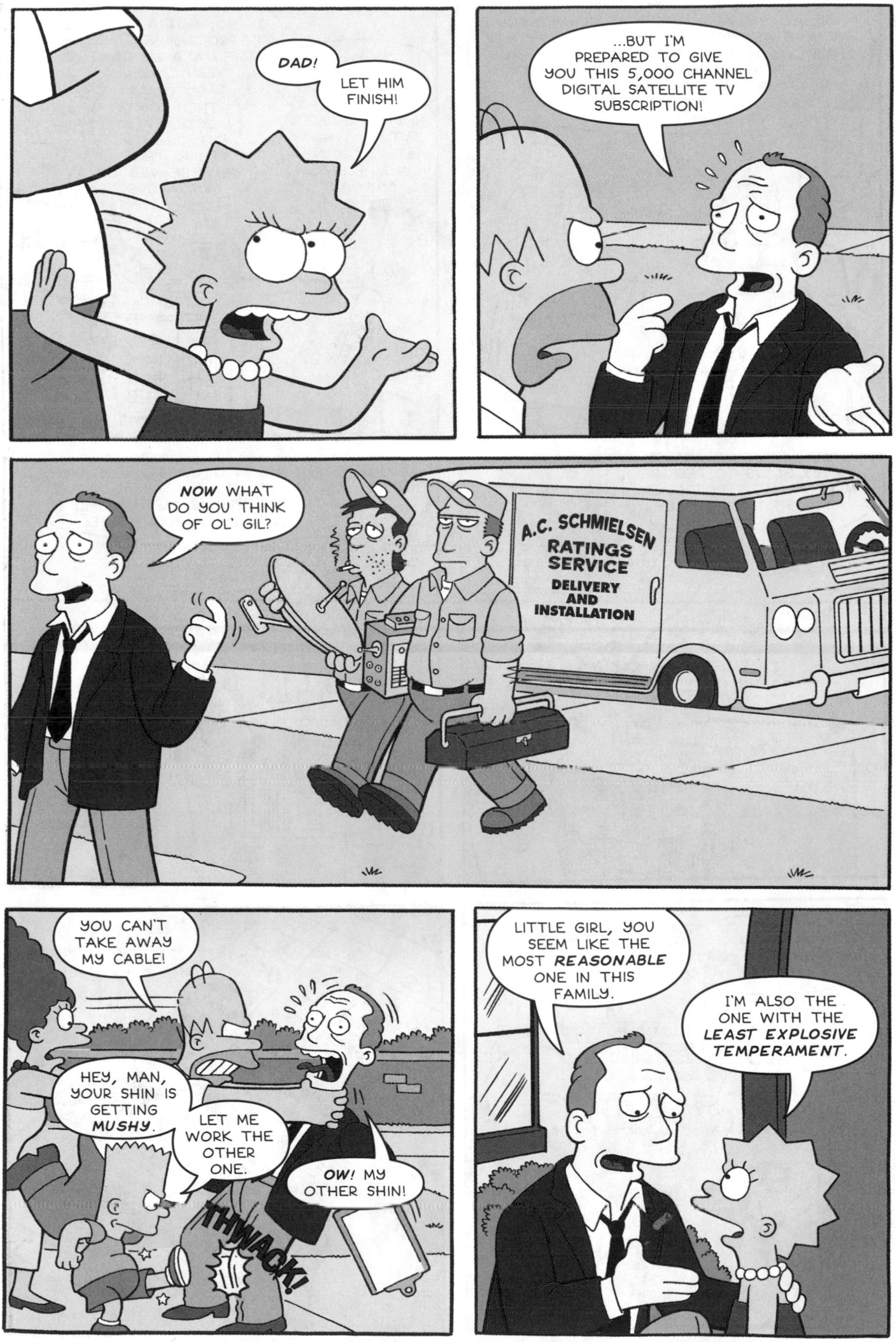
DAD!
LET HIM FINISH!
...BUT I'M PREPARED TO GIVE YOU THIS 5,000 CHANNEL DIGITAL SATELLITE TV SUBSCRIPTION!
NOW WHAT DO YOU THINK OF OL' GIL?
A.C. SCHMIELSEN RATINGS SERVICE DELIVERY AND INSTALLATION
YOU CAN'T TAKE AWAY MY CABLE!
HEY, MAN, YOUR SHIN IS GETTING MUSHY.
LET ME WORK THE OTHER ONE.
THWACK!
OW! MY OTHER SHIN!
LITTLE GIRL, YOU SEEM LIKE THE MOST REASONABLE ONE IN THIS FAMILY.
I'M ALSO THE ONE WITH THE LEAST EXPLOSIVE TEMPERAMENT.

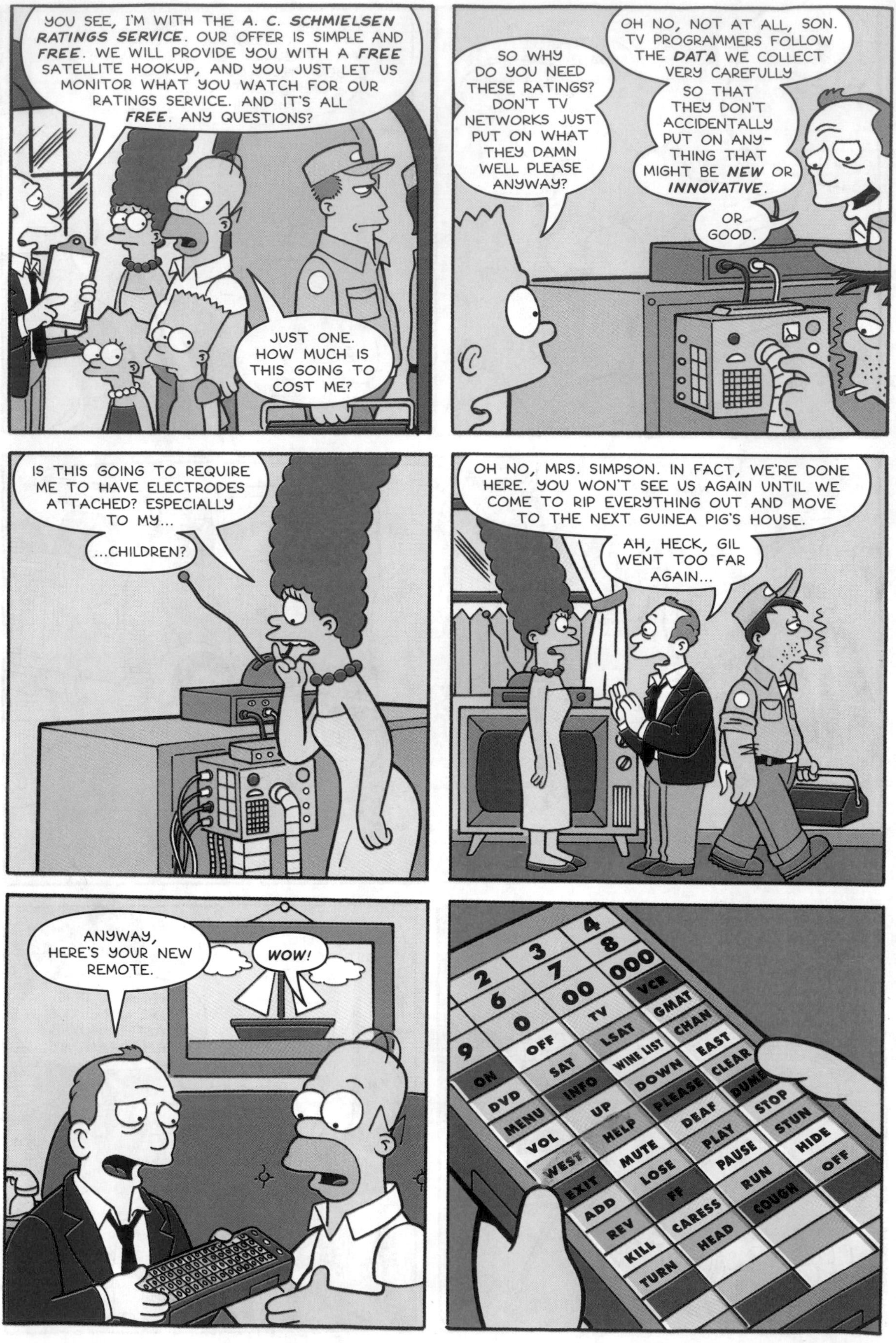
YOU SEE, I'M WITH THE A. C. SCHMIELSEN RATINGS SERVICE. OUR OFFER IS SIMPLE AND FREE. WE WILL PROVIDE YOU WITH A FREE SATELLITE HOOKUP, AND YOU JUST LET US MONITOR WHAT YOU WATCH FOR OUR RATINGS SERVICE. AND IT'S ALL FREE. ANY QUESTIONS?
JUST ONE. HOW MUCH IS THIS GOING TO COST ME?
SO WHY DO YOU NEED THESE RATINGS? DON'T TV NETWORKS JUST PUT ON WHAT THEY DAMN WELL PLEASE ANYWAY?
OH NO, NOT AT ALL, SON. TV PROGRAMMERS FOLLOW THE DATA WE COLLECT VERY CAREFULLY
SO THAT THEY DON'T ACCIDENTALLY PUT ON ANY-THING THAT MIGHT BE NEW OR INNOVATIVE.
OR GOOD.
IS THIS GOING TO REQUIRE ME TO HAVE ELECTRODES ATTACHED? ESPECIALLY TO MY...
...CHILDREN?
OH NO, MRS. SIMPSON. IN FACT, WE'RE DONE HERE. YOU WON'T SEE US AGAIN UNTIL WE COME TO RIP EVERYTHING OUT AND MOVE TO THE NEXT GUINEA PIG'S HOUSE.
AH, HECK, GIL WENT TOO FAR AGAIN...
ANYWAY, HERE'S YOUR NEW REMOTE.
WOW!
2 3 4 6 7 8 9 0 00 000
VCR GMAT TV LSAT CHAN OFF SAT WINE LIST EAST ON INFO DOWN CLEAR DVD UP PLEASE MENU HELP DEAF STOP VOL MUTE PLAY STUN WEST LOSE PAUSE HIDE EXIT FF RUN OFF ADD CARESS COUGH REV HEAD KILL TURN

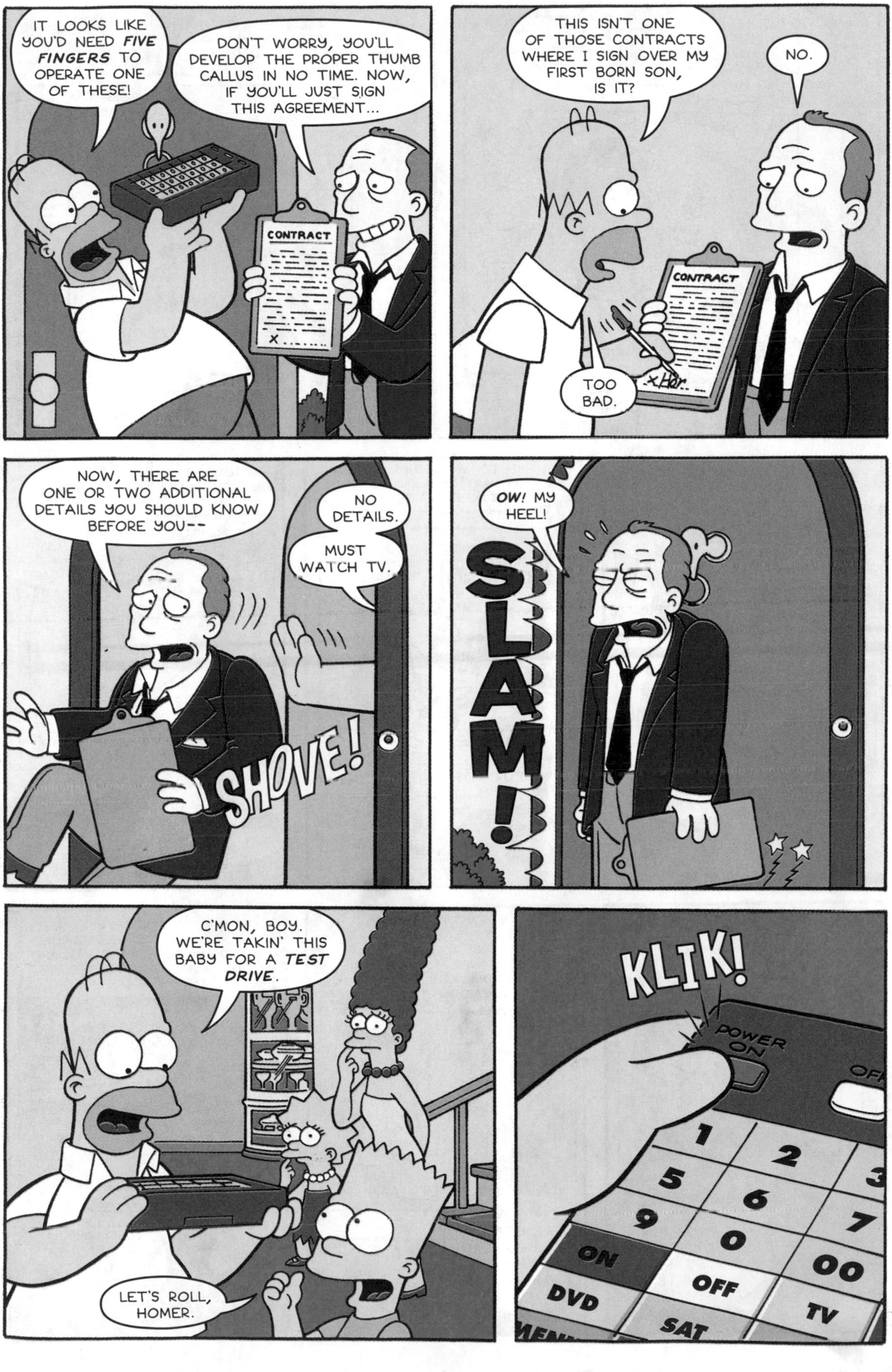
IT LOOKS LIKE YOU'D NEED **FIVE FINGERS** TO OPERATE ONE OF THESE!
DON'T WORRY, YOU'LL DEVELOP THE PROPER THUMB CALLUS IN NO TIME. NOW, IF YOU'LL JUST SIGN THIS AGREEMENT...
CONTRACT
THIS ISN'T ONE OF THOSE CONTRACTS WHERE I SIGN OVER MY FIRST BORN SON, IS IT?
NO.
TOO BAD.
CONTRACT
NOW, THERE ARE ONE OR TWO ADDITIONAL DETAILS YOU SHOULD KNOW BEFORE YOU--
NO DETAILS.
MUST WATCH TV.
SHOVE!
OW! MY HEEL!
SLAM!
C'MON, BOY. WE'RE TAKIN' THIS BABY FOR A **TEST DRIVE**.
LET'S ROLL, HOMER.
KLIK!
POWER ON
1 2 5 6 9 0 7 00
ON
OFF
DVD
TV
SAT

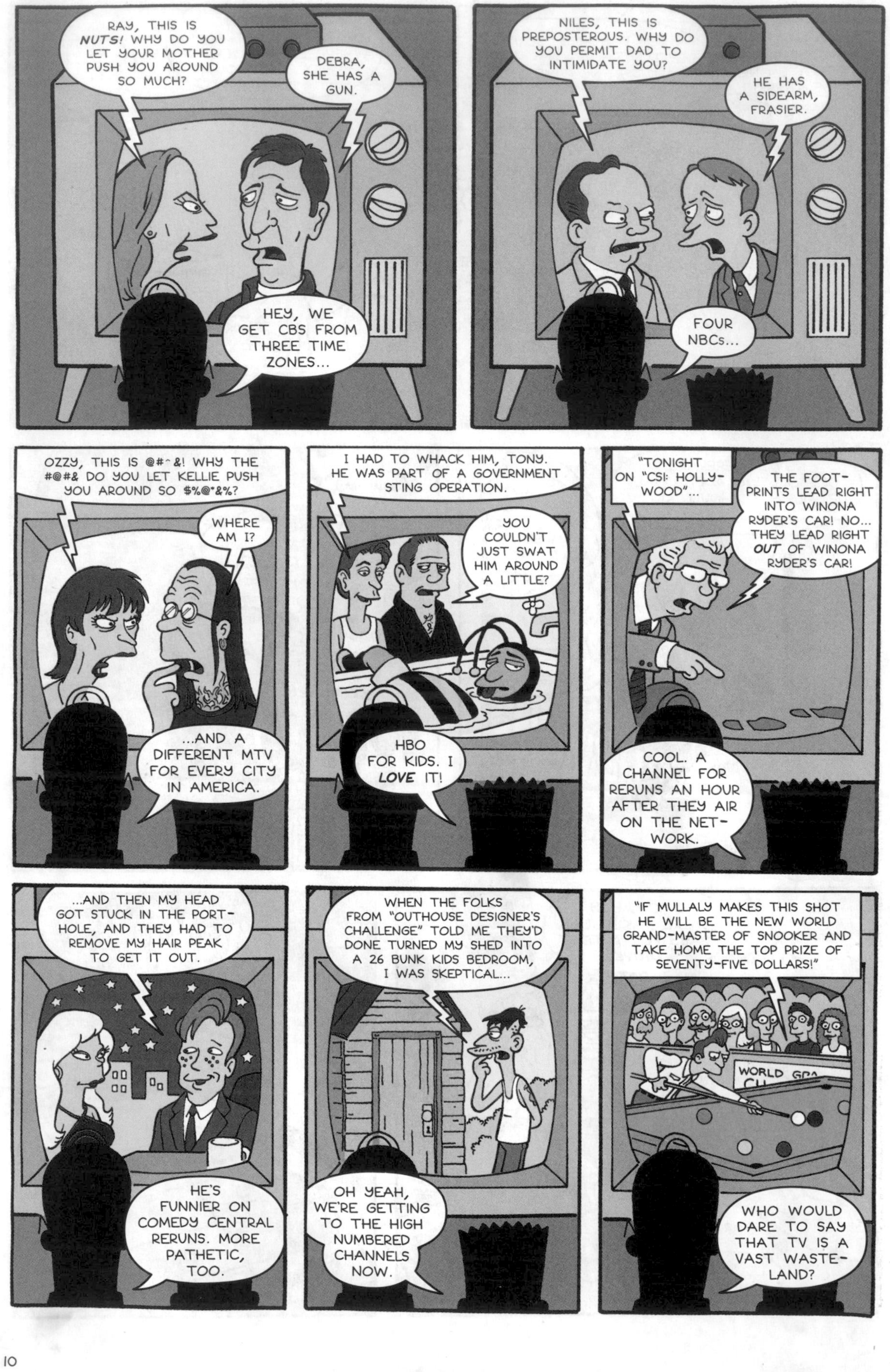
RAY, THIS IS NUTS! WHY DO YOU LET YOUR MOTHER PUSH YOU AROUND SO MUCH?
DEBRA, SHE HAS A GUN.
HEY, WE GET CBS FROM THREE TIME ZONES...
NILES, THIS IS PREPOSTEROUS. WHY DO YOU PERMIT DAD TO INTIMIDATE YOU?
HE HAS A SIDEARM, FRASIER.
FOUR NBCs...
OZZY, THIS IS @#^&! WHY THE #@#& DO YOU LET KELLIE PUSH YOU AROUND SO $%@*&%?
WHERE AM I?
...AND A DIFFERENT MTV FOR EVERY CITY IN AMERICA.
I HAD TO WHACK HIM, TONY. HE WAS PART OF A GOVERNMENT STING OPERATION.
YOU COULDN'T JUST SWAT HIM AROUND A LITTLE?
HBO FOR KIDS. I LOVE IT!
"TONIGHT ON "CSI: HOLLY-WOOD"...
THE FOOT-PRINTS LEAD RIGHT INTO WINONA RYDER'S CAR! NO... THEY LEAD RIGHT OUT OF WINONA RYDER'S CAR!
COOL. A CHANNEL FOR RERUNS AN HOUR AFTER THEY AIR ON THE NET-WORK.
...AND THEN MY HEAD GOT STUCK IN THE PORT-HOLE, AND THEY HAD TO REMOVE MY HAIR PEAK TO GET IT OUT.
HE'S FUNNIER ON COMEDY CENTRAL RERUNS. MORE PATHETIC, TOO.
WHEN THE FOLKS FROM "OUTHOUSE DESIGNER'S CHALLENGE" TOLD ME THEY'D DONE TURNED MY SHED INTO A 26 BUNK KIDS BEDROOM, I WAS SKEPTICAL...
OH YEAH, WE'RE GETTING TO THE HIGH NUMBERED CHANNELS NOW.
"IF MULLALY MAKES THIS SHOT HE WILL BE THE NEW WORLD GRAND-MASTER OF SNOOKER AND TAKE HOME THE TOP PRIZE OF SEVENTY-FIVE DOLLARS!"
WHO WOULD DARE TO SAY THAT TV IS A VAST WASTE-LAND?

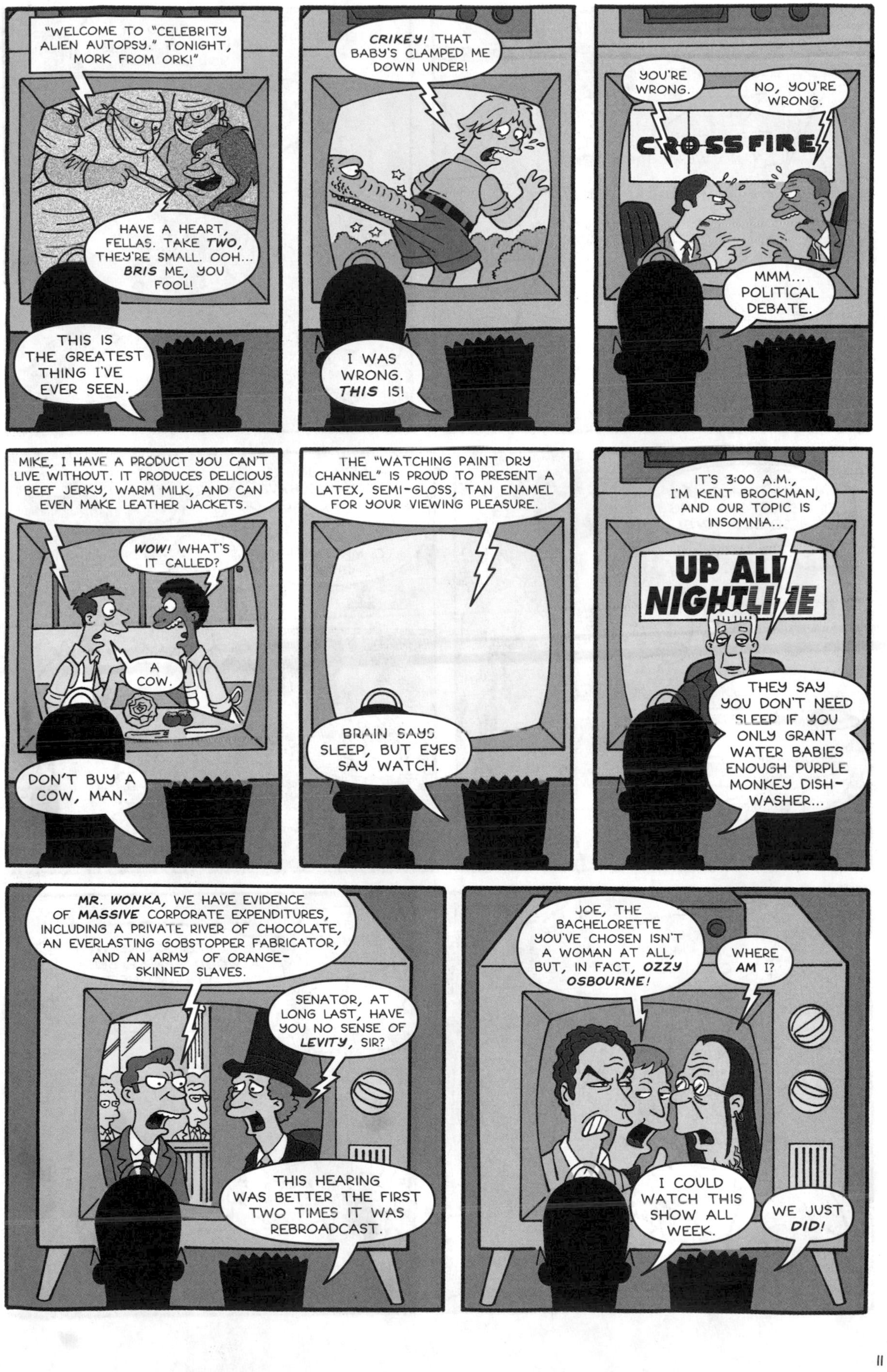
"WELCOME TO "CELEBRITY ALIEN AUTOPSY." TONIGHT, MORK FROM ORK!"
HAVE A HEART, FELLAS. TAKE **TWO,** THEY'RE SMALL. OOH... **BRIS** ME, YOU FOOL!
THIS IS THE GREATEST THING I'VE EVER SEEN.
CRIKEY! THAT BABY'S CLAMPED ME DOWN UNDER!
I WAS WRONG. **THIS** IS!
YOU'RE WRONG.
NO, YOU'RE WRONG.
CROSSFIRE
MMM... POLITICAL DEBATE.
MIKE, I HAVE A PRODUCT YOU CAN'T LIVE WITHOUT. IT PRODUCES DELICIOUS BEEF JERKY, WARM MILK, AND CAN EVEN MAKE LEATHER JACKETS.
WOW! WHAT'S IT CALLED?
A COW.
DON'T BUY A COW, MAN.
THE "WATCHING PAINT DRY CHANNEL" IS PROUD TO PRESENT A LATEX, SEMI-GLOSS, TAN ENAMEL FOR YOUR VIEWING PLEASURE.
BRAIN SAYS SLEEP, BUT EYES SAY WATCH.
IT'S 3:00 A.M., I'M KENT BROCKMAN, AND OUR TOPIC IS INSOMNIA...
THEY SAY YOU DON'T NEED SLEEP IF YOU ONLY GRANT WATER BABIES ENOUGH PURPLE MONKEY DISH-WASHER...
MR. WONKA, WE HAVE EVIDENCE OF **MASSIVE** CORPORATE EXPENDITURES, INCLUDING A PRIVATE RIVER OF CHOCOLATE, AN EVERLASTING GOBSTOPPER FABRICATOR, AND AN ARMY OF ORANGE-SKINNED SLAVES.
SENATOR, AT LONG LAST, HAVE YOU NO SENSE OF **LEVITY,** SIR?
THIS HEARING WAS BETTER THE FIRST TWO TIMES IT WAS REBROADCAST.
JOE, THE BACHELORETTE YOU'VE CHOSEN ISN'T A WOMAN AT ALL, BUT, IN FACT, **OZZY OSBOURNE!**
WHERE **AM** I?
I COULD WATCH THIS SHOW ALL WEEK.
WE JUST **DID!**

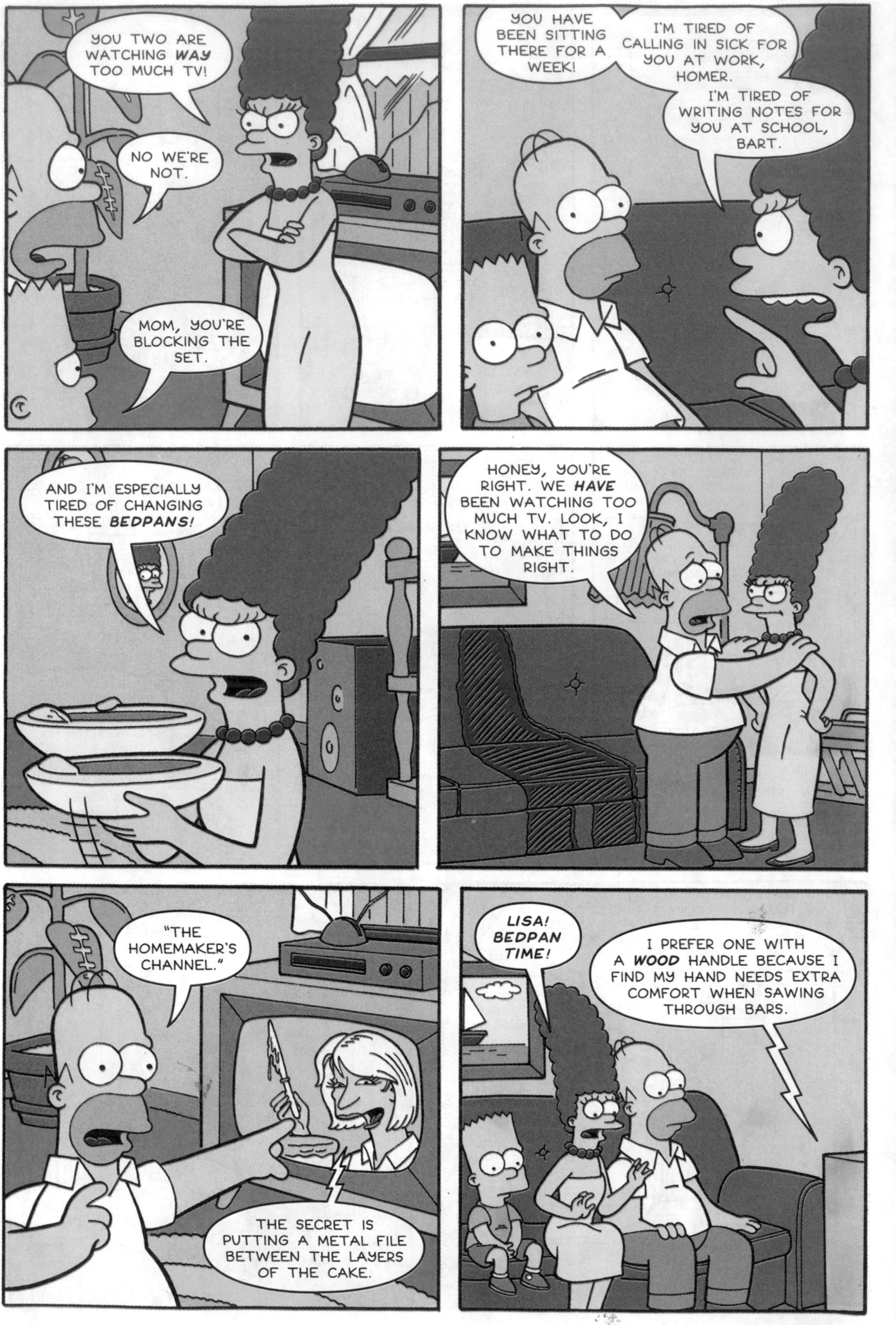

YOU TWO ARE WATCHING **WAY** TOO MUCH TV!
NO WE'RE NOT.
MOM, YOU'RE BLOCKING THE SET.
YOU HAVE BEEN SITTING THERE FOR A WEEK!
I'M TIRED OF CALLING IN SICK FOR YOU AT WORK, HOMER.
I'M TIRED OF WRITING NOTES FOR YOU AT SCHOOL, BART.
AND I'M ESPECIALLY TIRED OF CHANGING THESE ***BEDPANS!***
HONEY, YOU'RE RIGHT. WE ***HAVE*** BEEN WATCHING TOO MUCH TV. LOOK, I KNOW WHAT TO DO TO MAKE THINGS RIGHT.
"THE HOMEMAKER'S CHANNEL."
THE SECRET IS PUTTING A METAL FILE BETWEEN THE LAYERS OF THE CAKE.
LISA! BEDPAN TIME!
I PREFER ONE WITH A ***WOOD*** HANDLE BECAUSE I FIND MY HAND NEEDS EXTRA COMFORT WHEN SAWING THROUGH BARS.

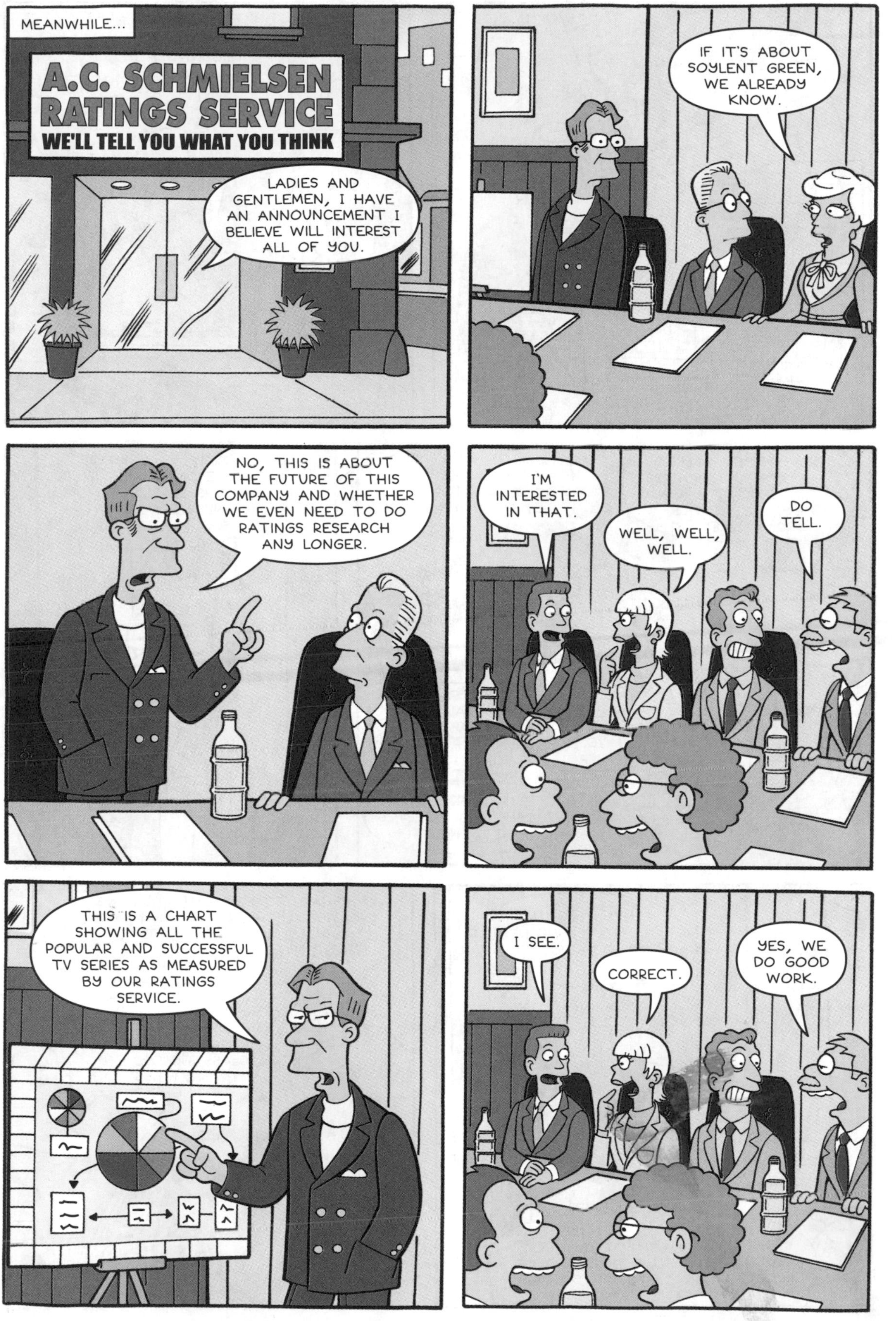
MEANWHILE...
A.C. SCHMIELSEN RATINGS SERVICE
WE'LL TELL YOU WHAT YOU THINK
LADIES AND GENTLEMEN, I HAVE AN ANNOUNCEMENT I BELIEVE WILL INTEREST ALL OF YOU.
IF IT'S ABOUT SOYLENT GREEN, WE ALREADY KNOW.
NO, THIS IS ABOUT THE FUTURE OF THIS COMPANY AND WHETHER WE EVEN NEED TO DO RATINGS RESEARCH ANY LONGER.
I'M INTERESTED IN THAT.
WELL, WELL, WELL.
DO TELL.
THIS IS A CHART SHOWING ALL THE POPULAR AND SUCCESSFUL TV SERIES AS MEASURED BY OUR RATINGS SERVICE.
I SEE.
CORRECT.
YES, WE DO GOOD WORK.

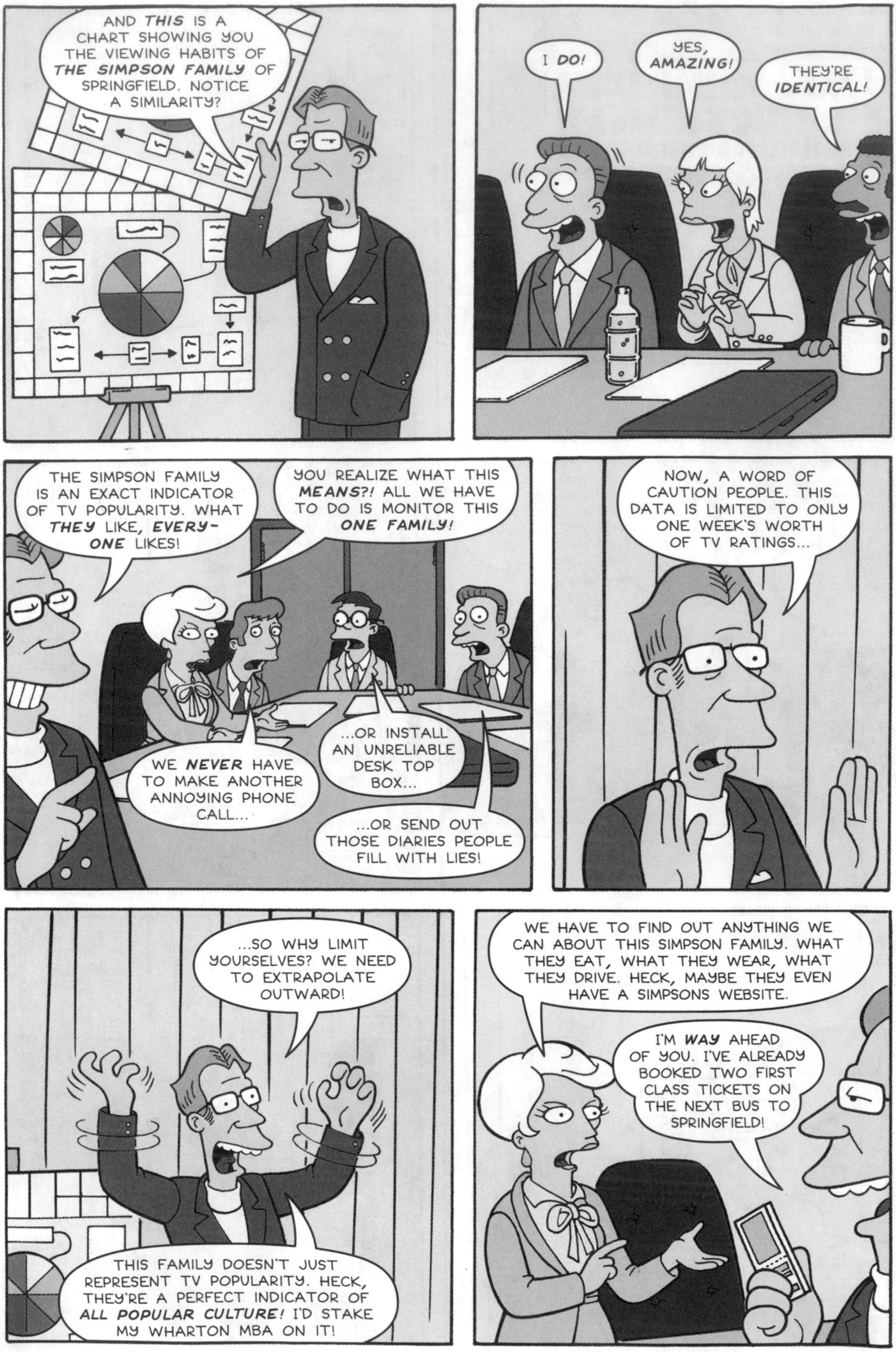
AND THIS IS A CHART SHOWING YOU THE VIEWING HABITS OF THE SIMPSON FAMILY OF SPRINGFIELD. NOTICE A SIMILARITY?
I DO!
YES, AMAZING!
THEY'RE IDENTICAL!
THE SIMPSON FAMILY IS AN EXACT INDICATOR OF TV POPULARITY. WHAT THEY LIKE, EVERY-ONE LIKES!
YOU REALIZE WHAT THIS MEANS?! ALL WE HAVE TO DO IS MONITOR THIS ONE FAMILY!
WE NEVER HAVE TO MAKE ANOTHER ANNOYING PHONE CALL...
...OR INSTALL AN UNRELIABLE DESK TOP BOX...
...OR SEND OUT THOSE DIARIES PEOPLE FILL WITH LIES!
NOW, A WORD OF CAUTION PEOPLE. THIS DATA IS LIMITED TO ONLY ONE WEEK'S WORTH OF TV RATINGS...
...SO WHY LIMIT YOURSELVES? WE NEED TO EXTRAPOLATE OUTWARD!
THIS FAMILY DOESN'T JUST REPRESENT TV POPULARITY. HECK, THEY'RE A PERFECT INDICATOR OF ALL POPULAR CULTURE! I'D STAKE MY WHARTON MBA ON IT!
WE HAVE TO FIND OUT ANYTHING WE CAN ABOUT THIS SIMPSON FAMILY. WHAT THEY EAT, WHAT THEY WEAR, WHAT THEY DRIVE. HECK, MAYBE THEY EVEN HAVE A SIMPSONS WEBSITE.
I'M WAY AHEAD OF YOU. I'VE ALREADY BOOKED TWO FIRST CLASS TICKETS ON THE NEXT BUS TO SPRINGFIELD!

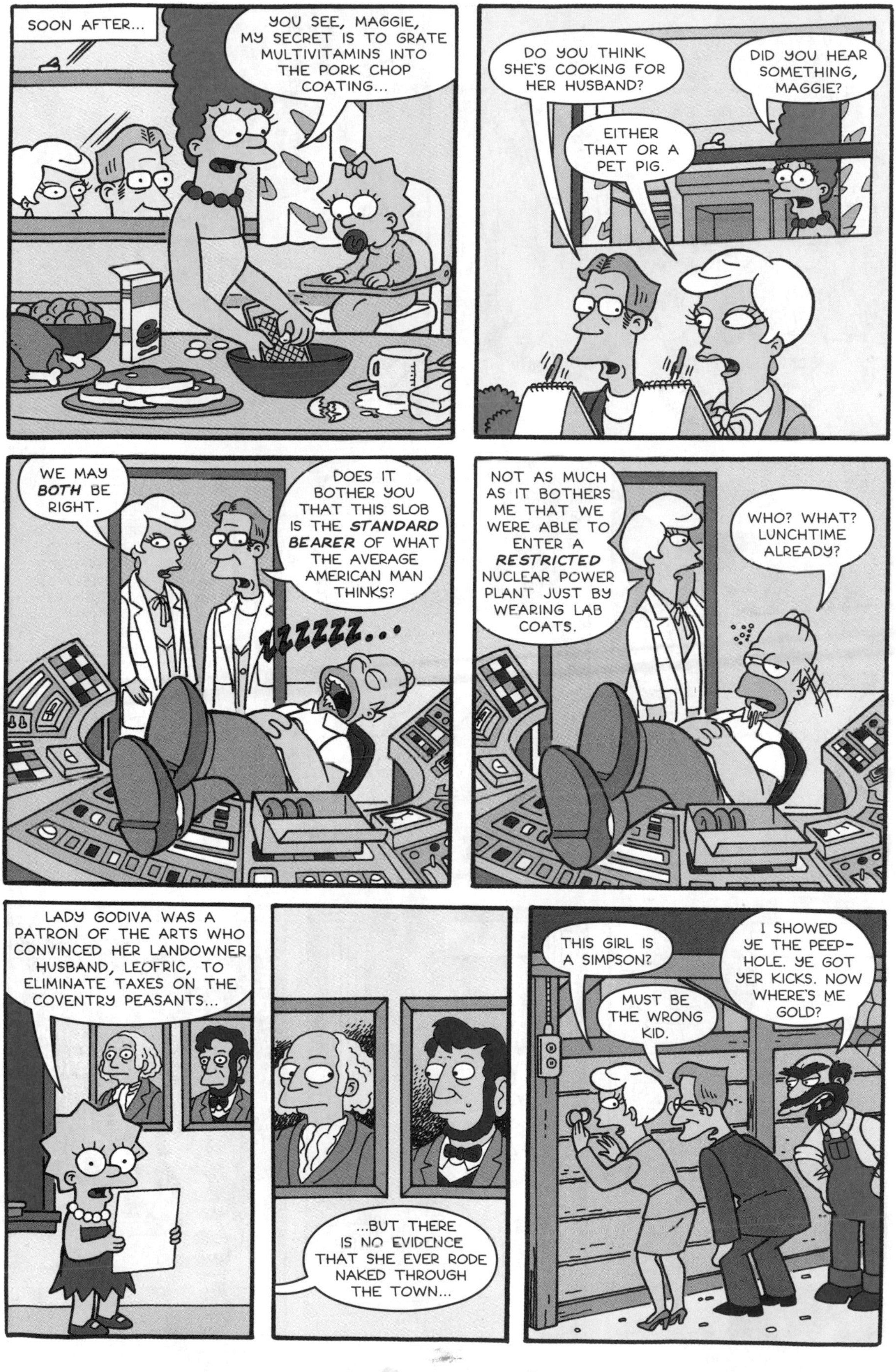
SOON AFTER...
YOU SEE, MAGGIE, MY SECRET IS TO GRATE MULTIVITAMINS INTO THE PORK CHOP COATING...
DO YOU THINK SHE'S COOKING FOR HER HUSBAND?
EITHER THAT OR A PET PIG.
DID YOU HEAR SOMETHING, MAGGIE?
WE MAY BOTH BE RIGHT.
DOES IT BOTHER YOU THAT THIS SLOB IS THE STANDARD BEARER OF WHAT THE AVERAGE AMERICAN MAN THINKS?
ZZZZZZ...
NOT AS MUCH AS IT BOTHERS ME THAT WE WERE ABLE TO ENTER A RESTRICTED NUCLEAR POWER PLANT JUST BY WEARING LAB COATS.
WHO? WHAT? LUNCHTIME ALREADY?
LADY GODIVA WAS A PATRON OF THE ARTS WHO CONVINCED HER LANDOWNER HUSBAND, LEOFRIC, TO ELIMINATE TAXES ON THE COVENTRY PEASANTS...
...BUT THERE IS NO EVIDENCE THAT SHE EVER RODE NAKED THROUGH THE TOWN...
THIS GIRL IS A SIMPSON?
MUST BE THE WRONG KID.
I SHOWED YE THE PEEP-HOLE. YE GOT YER KICKS. NOW WHERE'S ME GOLD?

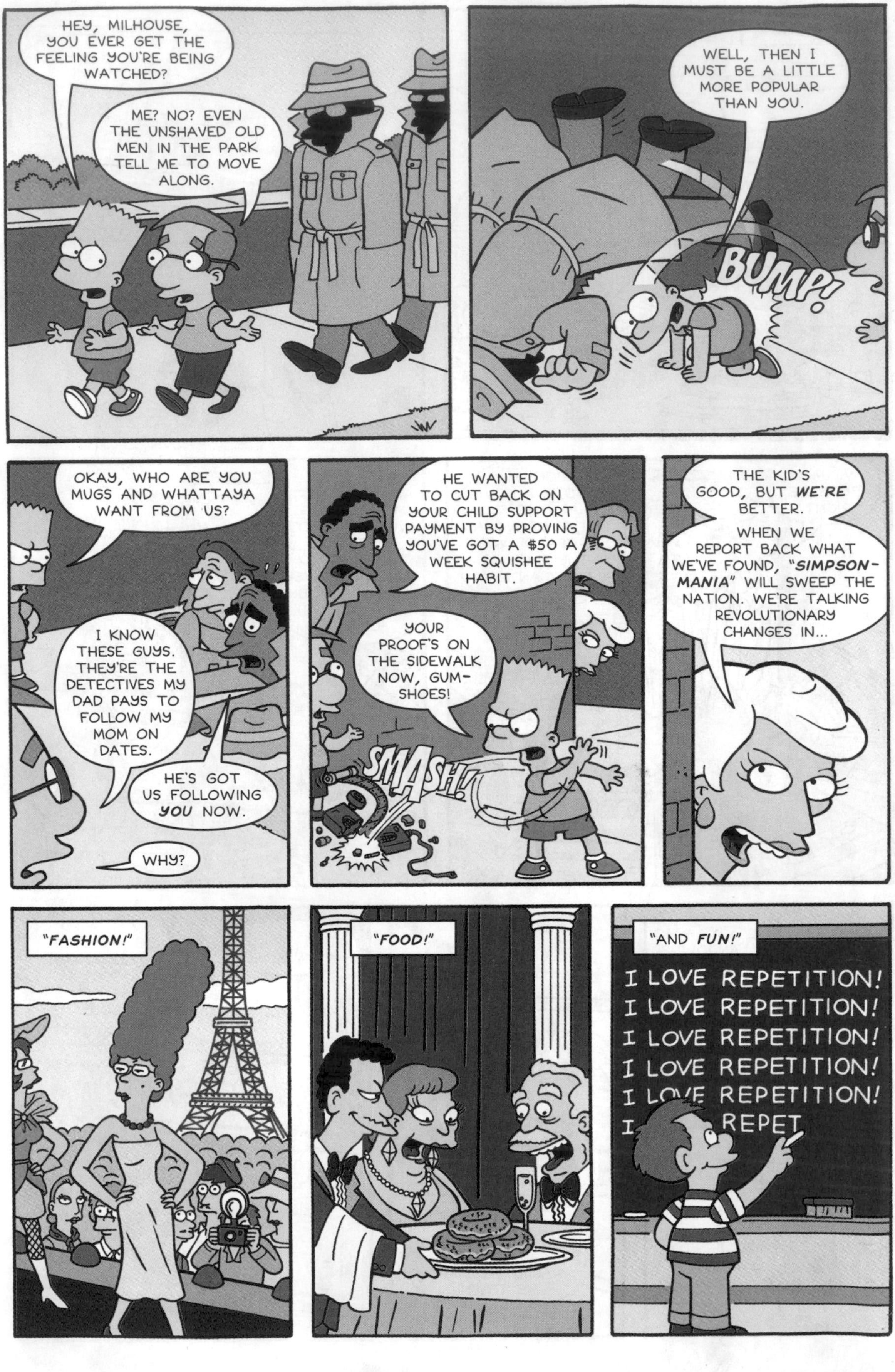
HEY, MILHOUSE, YOU EVER GET THE FEELING YOU'RE BEING WATCHED?
ME? NO? EVEN THE UNSHAVED OLD MEN IN THE PARK TELL ME TO MOVE ALONG.
WELL, THEN I MUST BE A LITTLE MORE POPULAR THAN YOU.
BUMP!
OKAY, WHO ARE YOU MUGS AND WHATTAYA WANT FROM US?
I KNOW THESE GUYS. THEY'RE THE DETECTIVES MY DAD PAYS TO FOLLOW MY MOM ON DATES.
HE'S GOT US FOLLOWING *YOU* NOW.
WHY?
HE WANTED TO CUT BACK ON YOUR CHILD SUPPORT PAYMENT BY PROVING YOU'VE GOT A $50 A WEEK SQUISHEE HABIT.
YOUR PROOF'S ON THE SIDEWALK NOW, GUM-SHOES!
SMASH!
THE KID'S GOOD, BUT *WE'RE* BETTER.
WHEN WE REPORT BACK WHAT WE'VE FOUND, "*SIMPSON-MANIA*" WILL SWEEP THE NATION. WE'RE TALKING REVOLUTIONARY CHANGES IN...
"*FASHION!*"
"*FOOD!*"
"AND *FUN!*"
I LOVE REPETITION!
I LOVE REPETITION!
I LOVE REPETITION!
I LOVE REPETITION!
I LOVE REPETITION!
I REPET

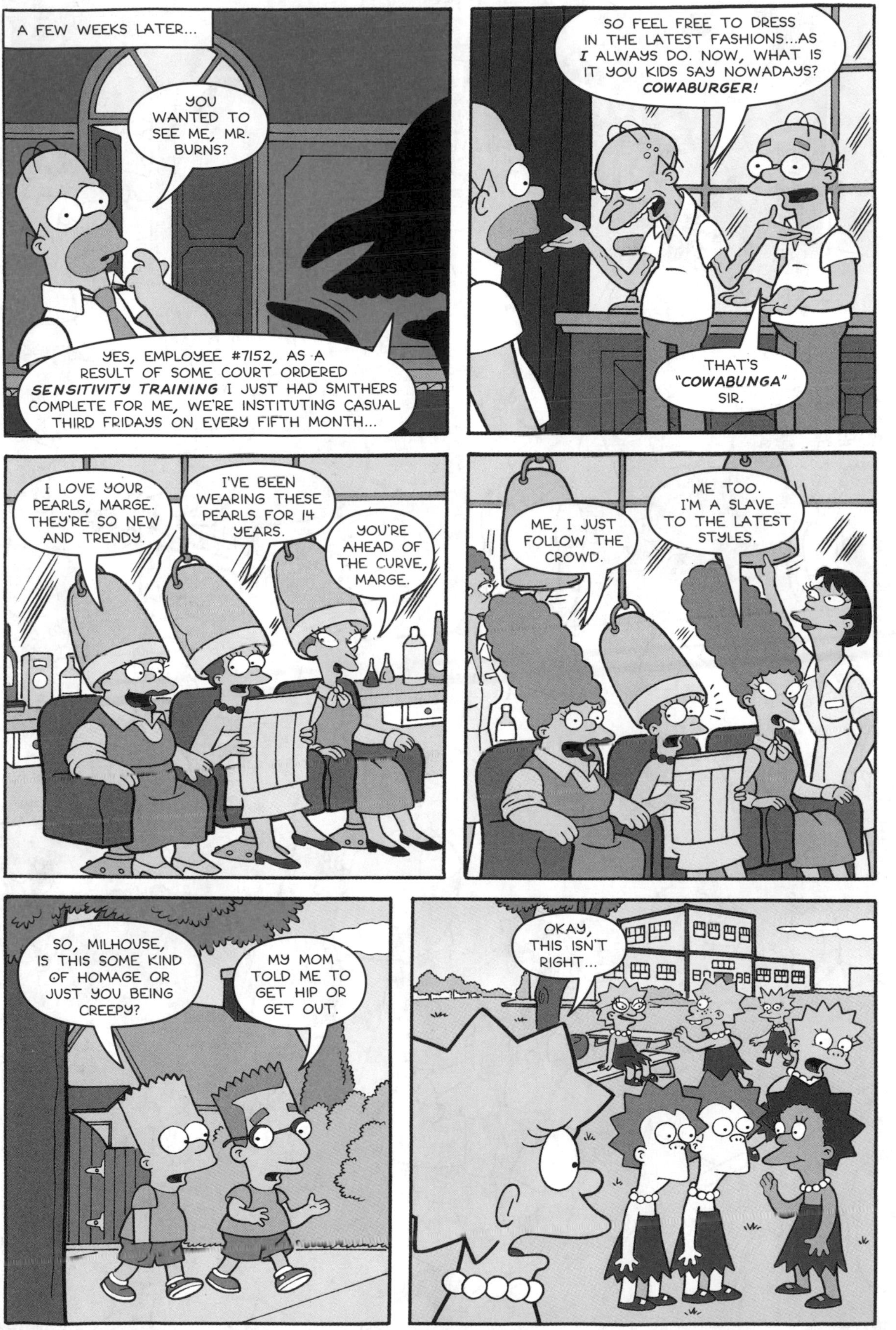
A FEW WEEKS LATER...
YOU WANTED TO SEE ME, MR. BURNS?
YES, EMPLOYEE #7152, AS A RESULT OF SOME COURT ORDERED **SENSITIVITY TRAINING** I JUST HAD SMITHERS COMPLETE FOR ME, WE'RE INSTITUTING CASUAL THIRD FRIDAYS ON EVERY FIFTH MONTH...
SO FEEL FREE TO DRESS IN THE LATEST FASHIONS...AS *I* ALWAYS DO. NOW, WHAT IS IT YOU KIDS SAY NOWADAYS? ***COWABURGER!***
THAT'S "***COWABUNGA***" SIR.
I LOVE YOUR PEARLS, MARGE. THEY'RE SO NEW AND TRENDY.
I'VE BEEN WEARING THESE PEARLS FOR 14 YEARS.
YOU'RE AHEAD OF THE CURVE, MARGE.
ME, I JUST FOLLOW THE CROWD.
ME TOO. I'M A SLAVE TO THE LATEST STYLES.
SO, MILHOUSE, IS THIS SOME KIND OF HOMAGE OR JUST YOU BEING CREEPY?
MY MOM TOLD ME TO GET HIP OR GET OUT.
OKAY, THIS ISN'T RIGHT...

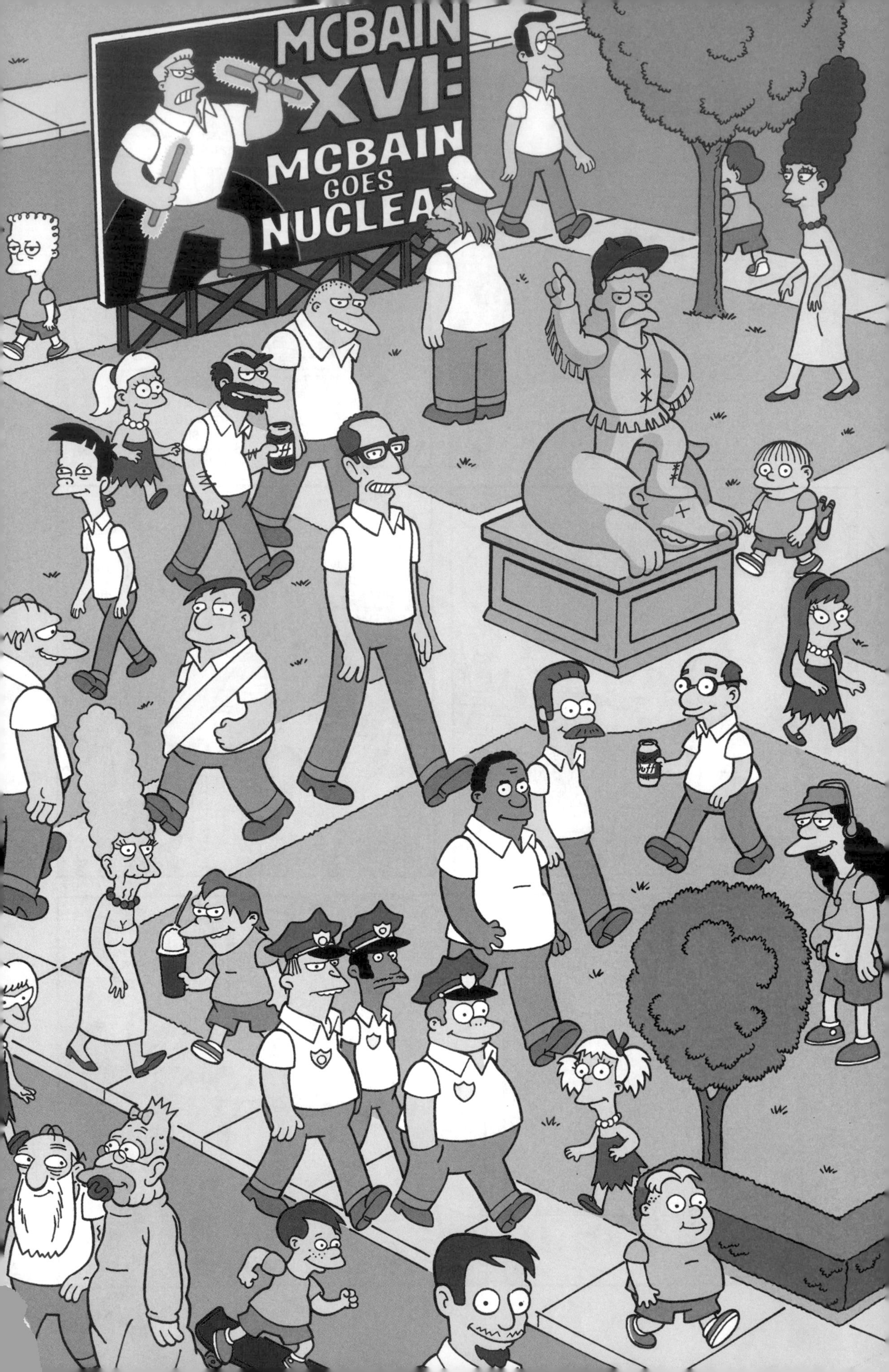
MCBAIN
XVI:
MCBAIN
GOES
NUCLEA

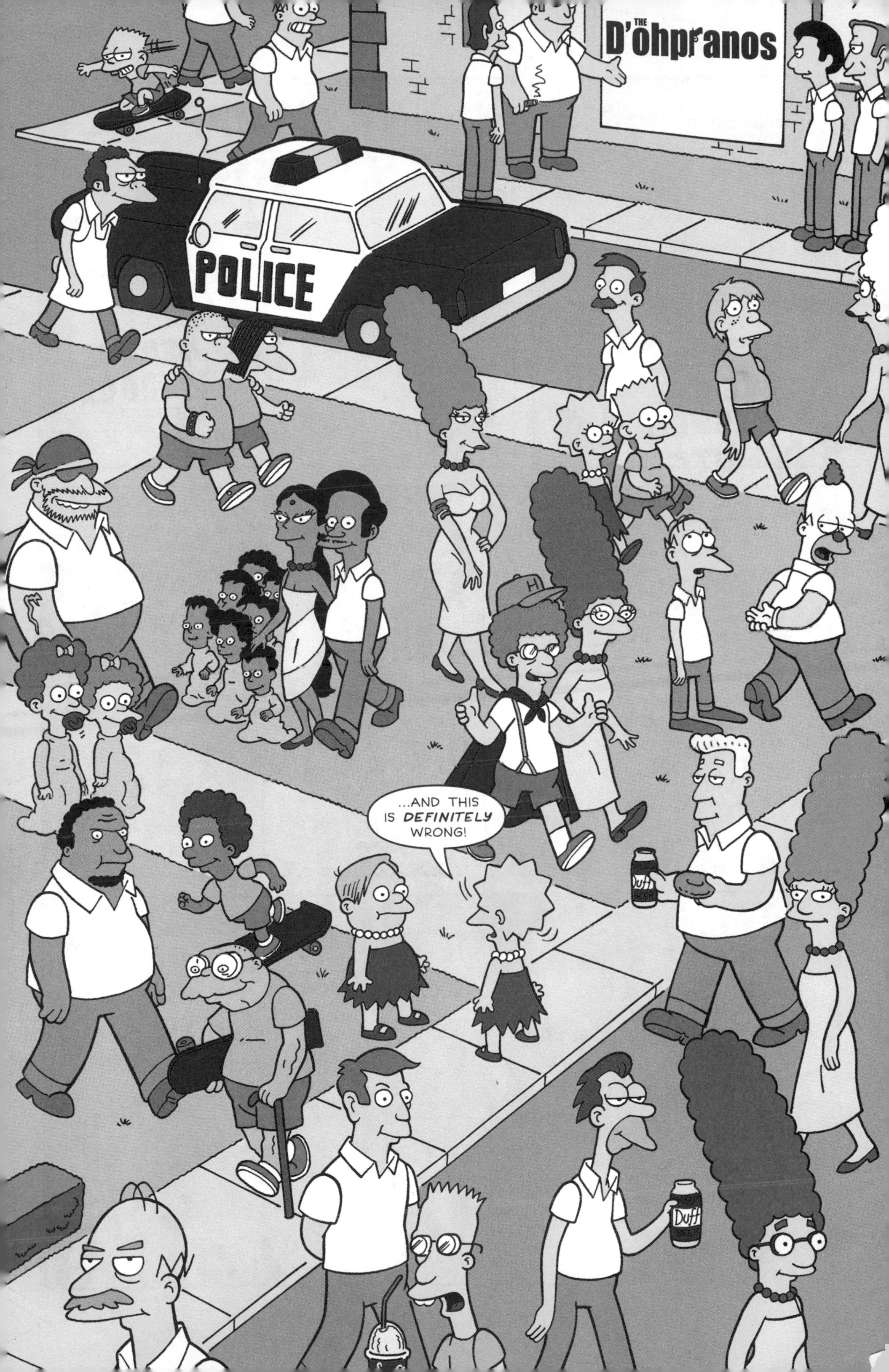
THE D'OHPRANOS
POLICE
...AND THIS IS DEFINITELY WRONG!

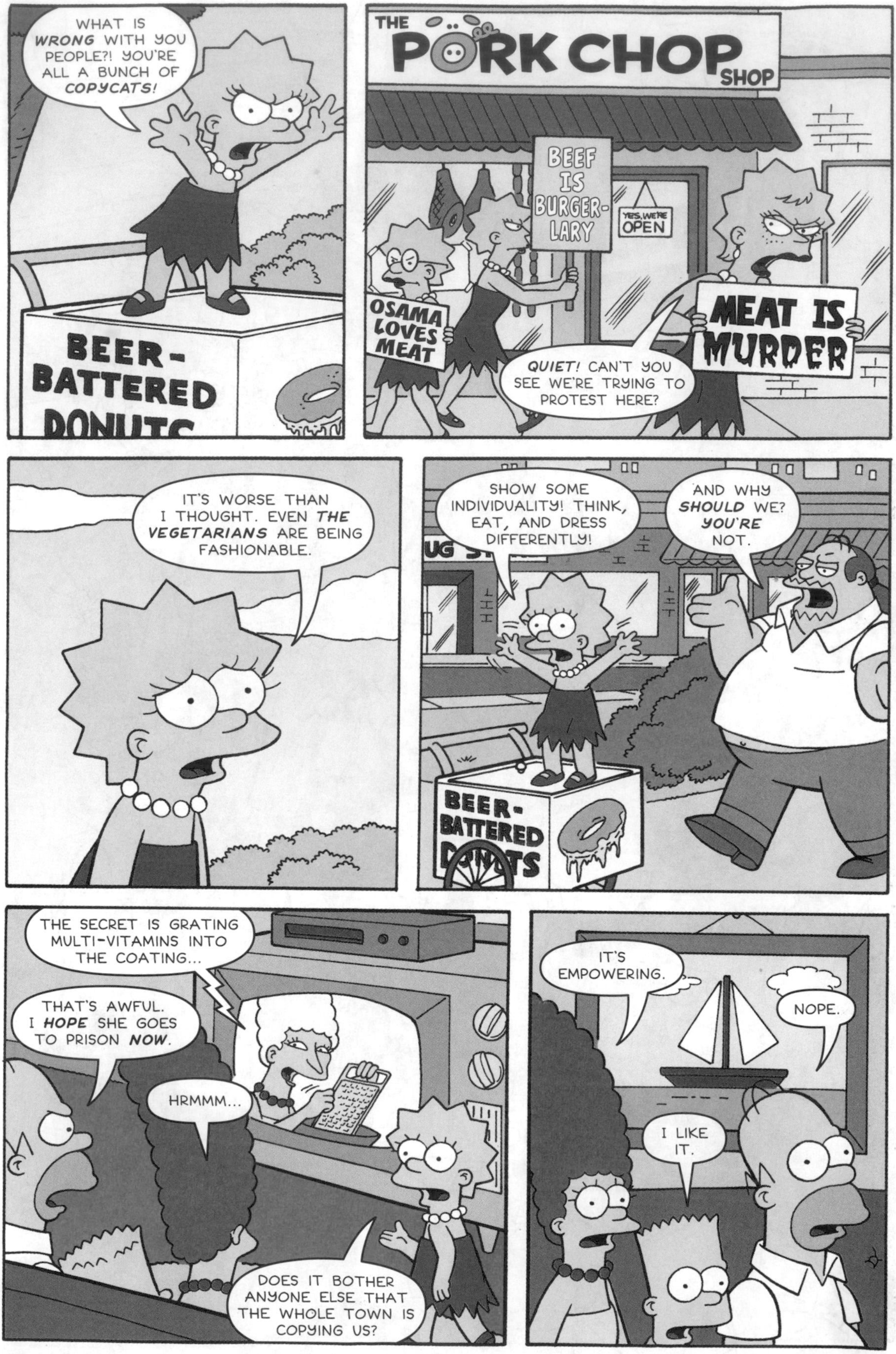
WHAT IS WRONG WITH YOU PEOPLE?! YOU'RE ALL A BUNCH OF COPYCATS!
BEER-BATTERED DONUTS
THE PORK CHOP SHOP
BEEF IS BURGER-LARY
YES, WE'RE OPEN
OSAMA LOVES MEAT
MEAT IS MURDER
QUIET! CAN'T YOU SEE WE'RE TRYING TO PROTEST HERE?
IT'S WORSE THAN I THOUGHT. EVEN THE VEGETARIANS ARE BEING FASHIONABLE.
SHOW SOME INDIVIDUALITY! THINK, EAT, AND DRESS DIFFERENTLY!
AND WHY SHOULD WE? YOU'RE NOT.
BEER-BATTERED DONUTS
THE SECRET IS GRATING MULTI-VITAMINS INTO THE COATING...
THAT'S AWFUL. I HOPE SHE GOES TO PRISON NOW.
HRMMM...
DOES IT BOTHER ANYONE ELSE THAT THE WHOLE TOWN IS COPYING US?
IT'S EMPOWERING.
NOPE.
I LIKE IT.

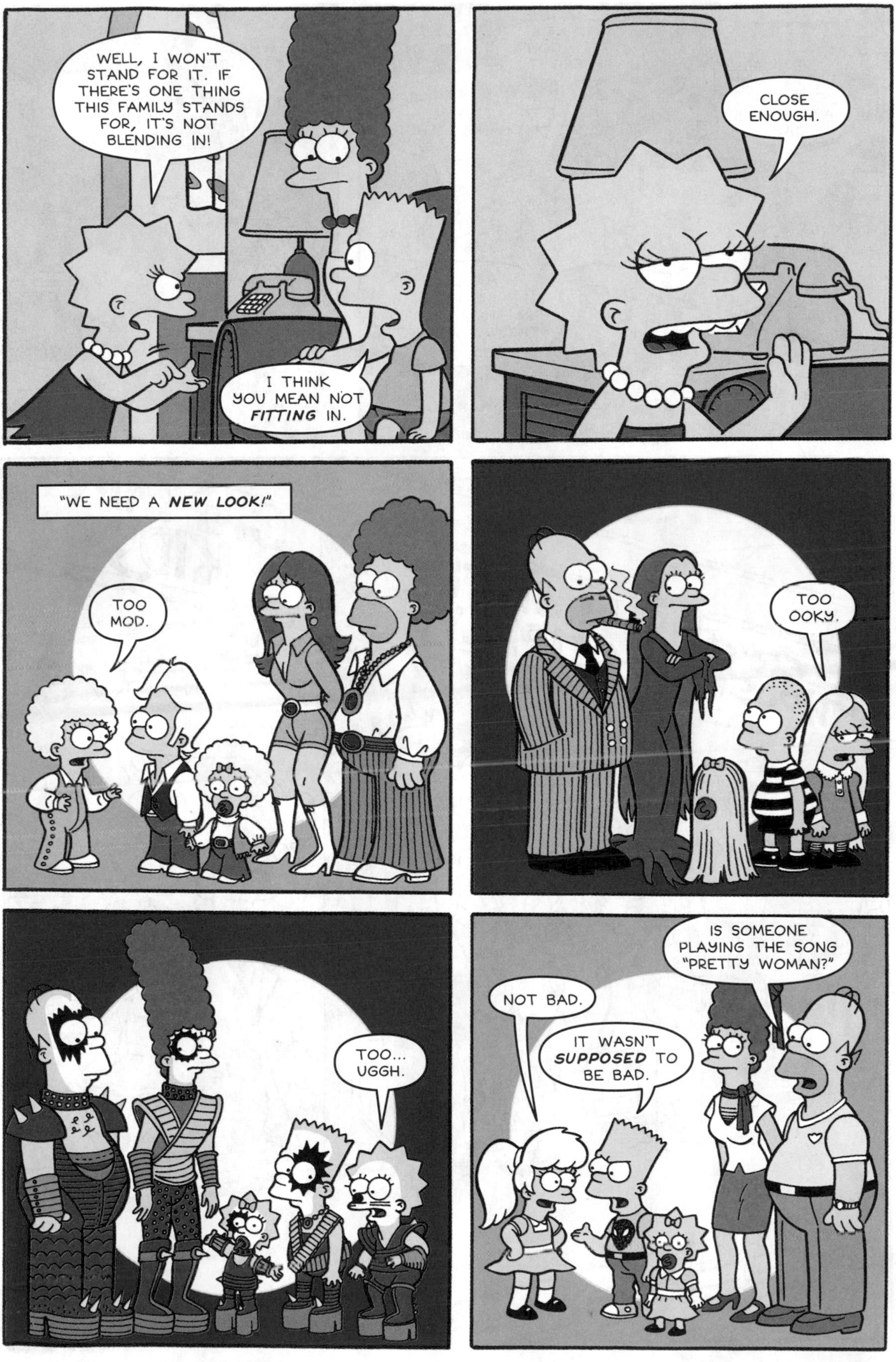
WELL, I WON'T STAND FOR IT. IF THERE'S ONE THING THIS FAMILY STANDS FOR, IT'S NOT BLENDING IN!
I THINK YOU MEAN NOT *FITTING* IN.
CLOSE ENOUGH.
"WE NEED A **NEW LOOK!**"
TOO MOD.
TOO OOKY.
TOO... UGGH.
NOT BAD.
IT WASN'T **SUPPOSED** TO BE BAD.
IS SOMEONE PLAYING THE SONG "PRETTY WOMAN?"

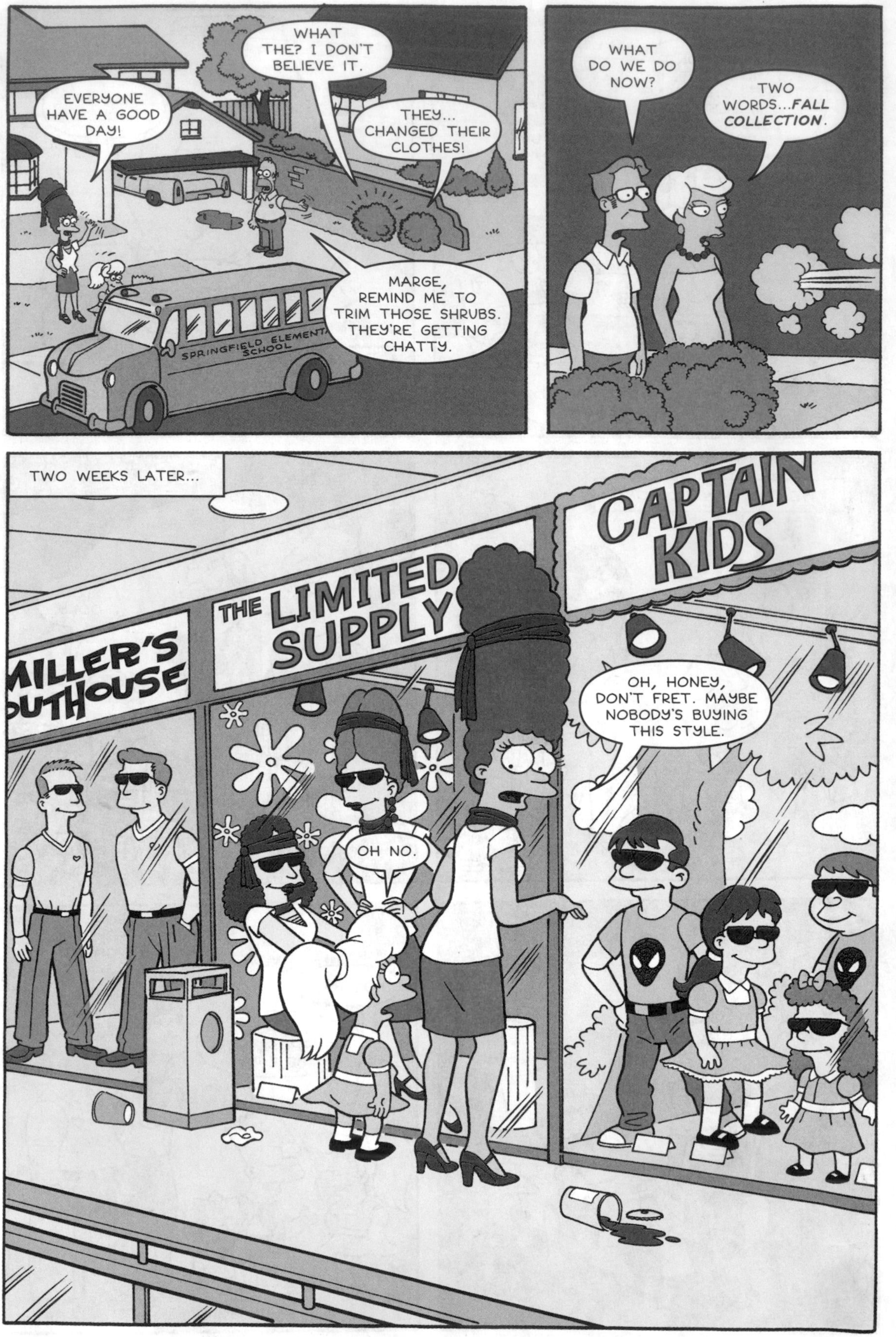
EVERYONE HAVE A GOOD DAY!
WHAT THE? I DON'T BELIEVE IT.
THEY... CHANGED THEIR CLOTHES!
SPRINGFIELD ELEMENTA SCHOOL
MARGE, REMIND ME TO TRIM THOSE SHRUBS. THEY'RE GETTING CHATTY.
WHAT DO WE DO NOW?
TWO WORDS...FALL COLLECTION.
TWO WEEKS LATER...
CAPTAIN KIDS
THE LIMITED SUPPLY
MILLER'S OUTHOUSE
OH, HONEY, DON'T FRET. MAYBE NOBODY'S BUYING THIS STYLE.
OH NO.

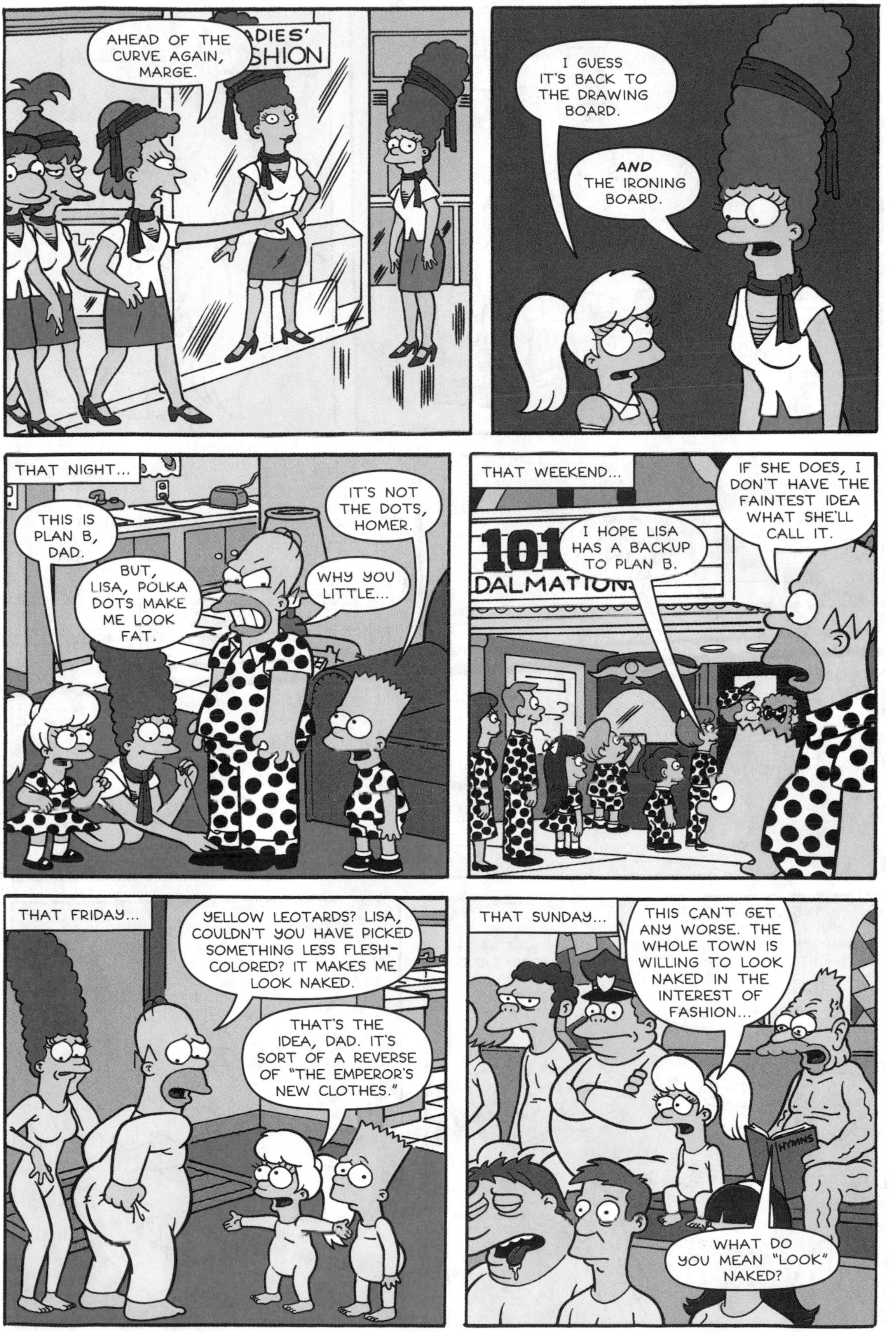
LADIES' FASHION
AHEAD OF THE CURVE AGAIN, MARGE.
I GUESS IT'S BACK TO THE DRAWING BOARD.
AND THE IRONING BOARD.
THAT NIGHT...
THIS IS PLAN B, DAD.
BUT, LISA, POLKA DOTS MAKE ME LOOK FAT.
IT'S NOT THE DOTS, HOMER.
WHY YOU LITTLE...
THAT WEEKEND...
101
DALMATIONS
I HOPE LISA HAS A BACKUP TO PLAN B.
IF SHE DOES, I DON'T HAVE THE FAINTEST IDEA WHAT SHE'LL CALL IT.
THAT FRIDAY...
YELLOW LEOTARDS? LISA, COULDN'T YOU HAVE PICKED SOMETHING LESS FLESH-COLORED? IT MAKES ME LOOK NAKED.
THAT'S THE IDEA, DAD. IT'S SORT OF A REVERSE OF "THE EMPEROR'S NEW CLOTHES."
THAT SUNDAY...
THIS CAN'T GET ANY WORSE. THE WHOLE TOWN IS WILLING TO LOOK NAKED IN THE INTEREST OF FASHION...
HYMNS
WHAT DO YOU MEAN "LOOK" NAKED?

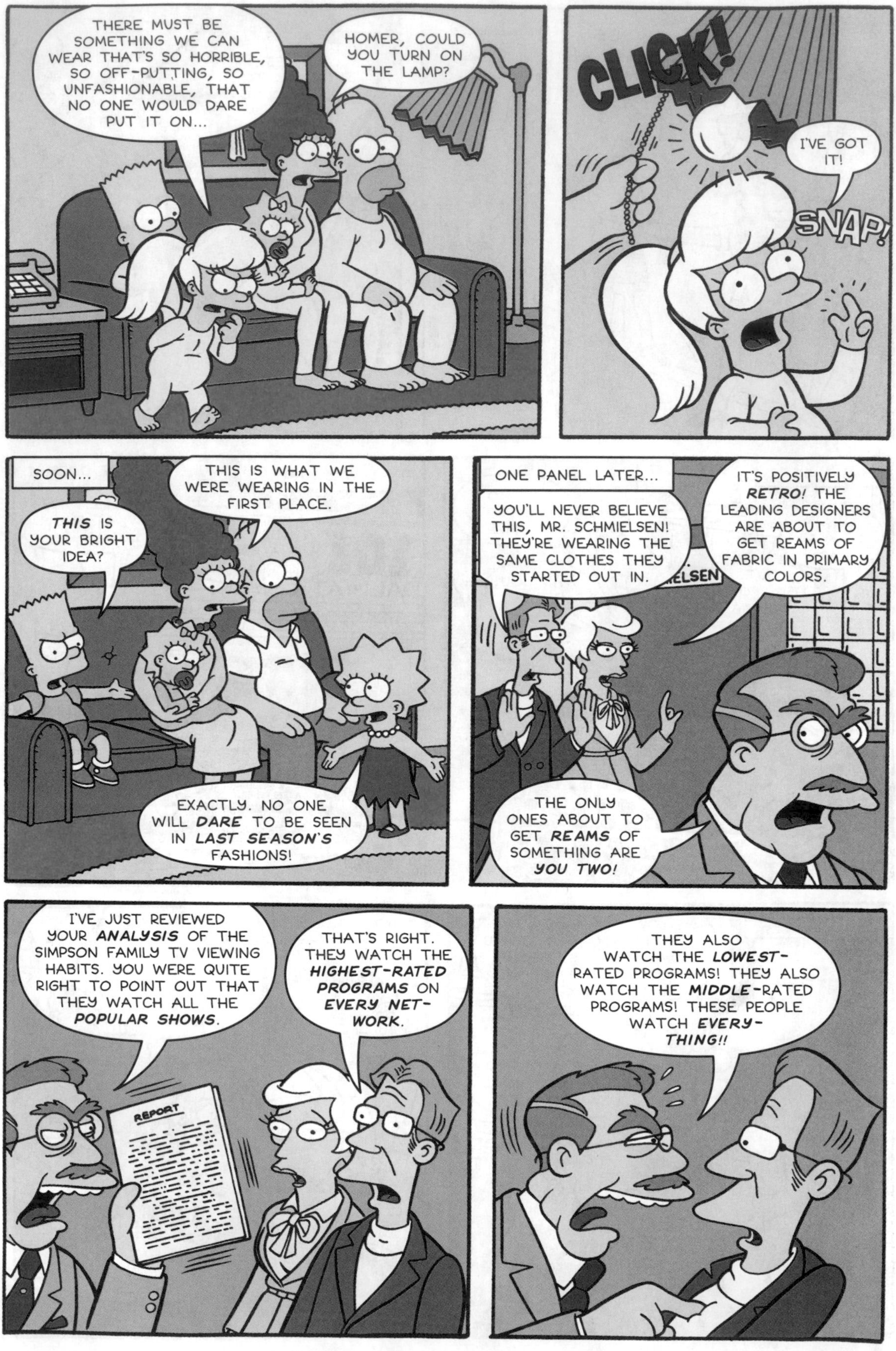
THERE MUST BE SOMETHING WE CAN WEAR THAT'S SO HORRIBLE, SO OFF-PUTTING, SO UNFASHIONABLE, THAT NO ONE WOULD DARE PUT IT ON...
HOMER, COULD YOU TURN ON THE LAMP?
CLICK!
I'VE GOT IT!
SNAP!
SOON...
THIS IS YOUR BRIGHT IDEA?
THIS IS WHAT WE WERE WEARING IN THE FIRST PLACE.
EXACTLY. NO ONE WILL DARE TO BE SEEN IN LAST SEASON'S FASHIONS!
ONE PANEL LATER...
YOU'LL NEVER BELIEVE THIS, MR. SCHMIELSEN! THEY'RE WEARING THE SAME CLOTHES THEY STARTED OUT IN.
IT'S POSITIVELY RETRO! THE LEADING DESIGNERS ARE ABOUT TO GET REAMS OF FABRIC IN PRIMARY COLORS.
THE ONLY ONES ABOUT TO GET REAMS OF SOMETHING ARE YOU TWO!
I'VE JUST REVIEWED YOUR ANALYSIS OF THE SIMPSON FAMILY TV VIEWING HABITS. YOU WERE QUITE RIGHT TO POINT OUT THAT THEY WATCH ALL THE POPULAR SHOWS.
THAT'S RIGHT. THEY WATCH THE HIGHEST-RATED PROGRAMS ON EVERY NET-WORK.
REPORT
THEY ALSO WATCH THE LOWEST-RATED PROGRAMS! THEY ALSO WATCH THE MIDDLE-RATED PROGRAMS! THESE PEOPLE WATCH EVERY-THING!!

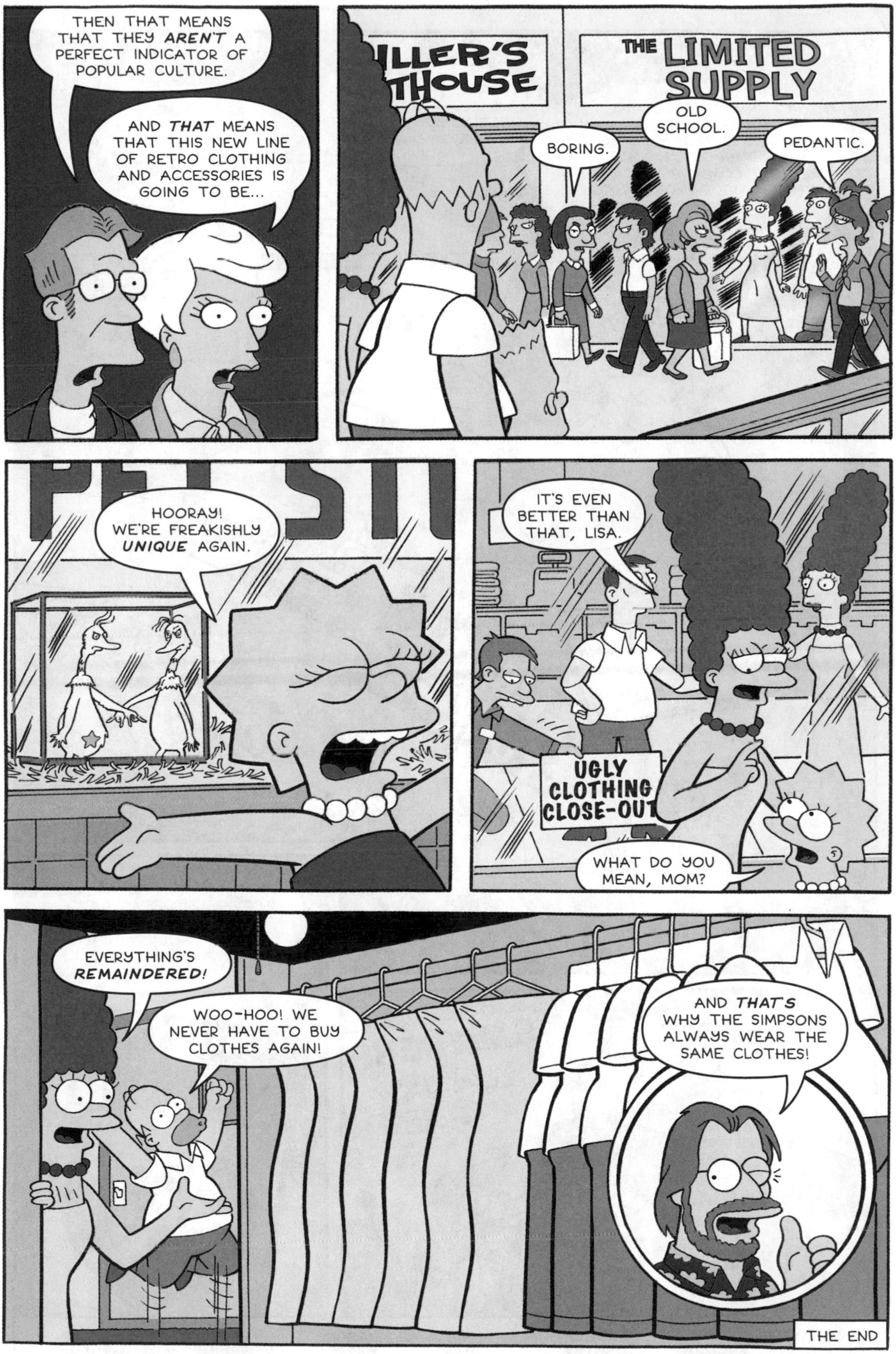
THEN THAT MEANS THAT THEY AREN'T A PERFECT INDICATOR OF POPULAR CULTURE.
AND THAT MEANS THAT THIS NEW LINE OF RETRO CLOTHING AND ACCESSORIES IS GOING TO BE...
ILLER'S THOUSE
THE LIMITED SUPPLY
BORING.
OLD SCHOOL.
PEDANTIC.
HOORAY! WE'RE FREAKISHLY UNIQUE AGAIN.
IT'S EVEN BETTER THAN THAT, LISA.
UGLY CLOTHING CLOSE-OUT
WHAT DO YOU MEAN, MOM?
EVERYTHING'S REMAINDERED!
WOO-HOO! WE NEVER HAVE TO BUY CLOTHES AGAIN!
AND THAT'S WHY THE SIMPSONS ALWAYS WEAR THE SAME CLOTHES!
THE END

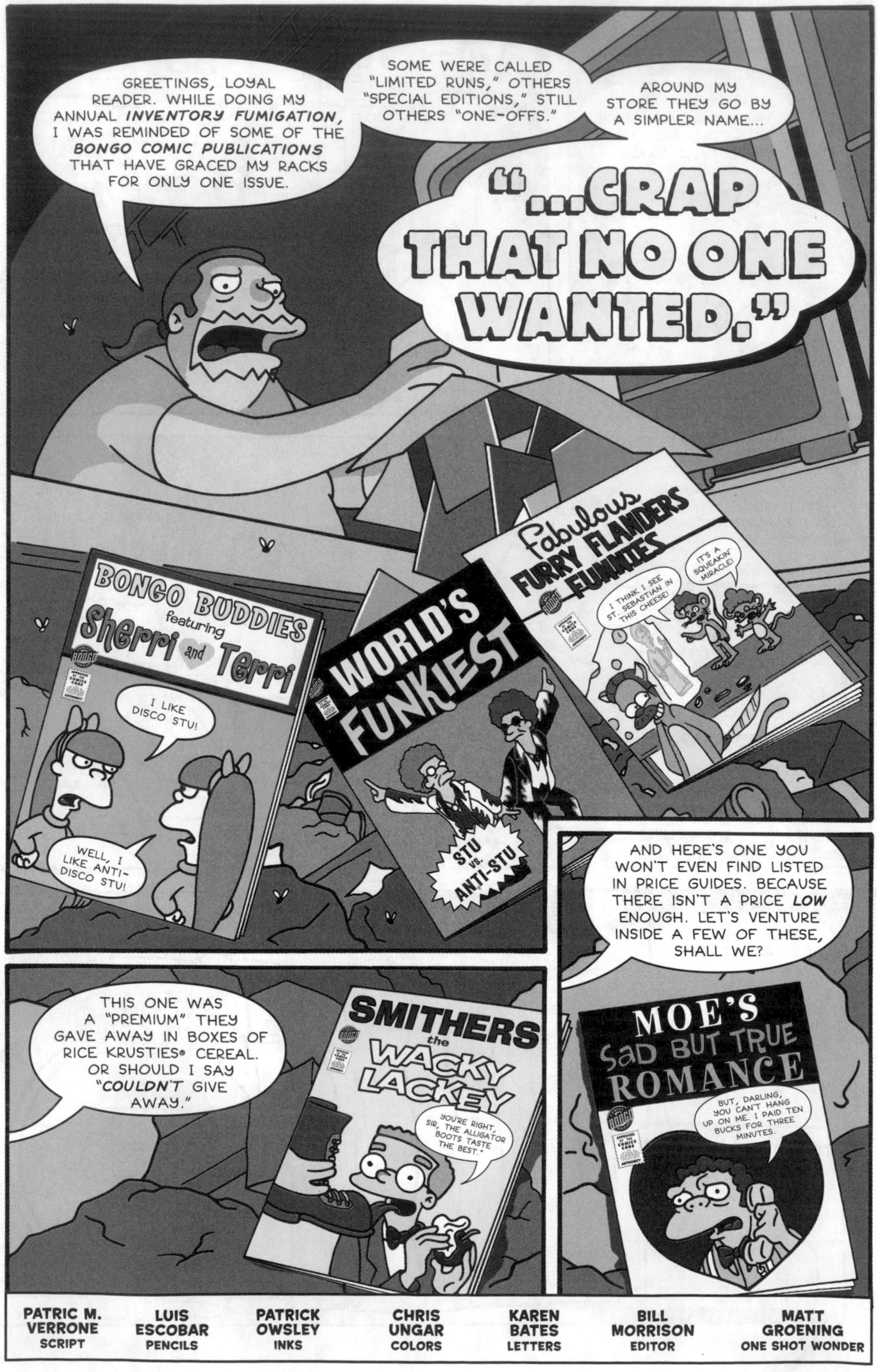
GREETINGS, LOYAL READER. WHILE DOING MY ANNUAL INVENTORY FUMIGATION, I WAS REMINDED OF SOME OF THE BONGO COMIC PUBLICATIONS THAT HAVE GRACED MY RACKS FOR ONLY ONE ISSUE.
SOME WERE CALLED "LIMITED RUNS," OTHERS "SPECIAL EDITIONS," STILL OTHERS "ONE-OFFS."
AROUND MY STORE THEY GO BY A SIMPLER NAME...
"...CRAP THAT NO ONE WANTED."
BONGO BUDDIES featuring Sherri and Terri
I LIKE DISCO STU!
WELL, I LIKE ANTI-DISCO STU!
WORLD'S FUNKIEST
STU vs. ANTI-STU
Fabulous FURRY FLANDERS FUNNIES
I THINK I SEE ST. SEBASTIAN IN THIS CHEESE!
IT'S A SQUEAKIN' MIRACLE!
AND HERE'S ONE YOU WON'T EVEN FIND LISTED IN PRICE GUIDES. BECAUSE THERE ISN'T A PRICE LOW ENOUGH. LET'S VENTURE INSIDE A FEW OF THESE, SHALL WE?
THIS ONE WAS A "PREMIUM" THEY GAVE AWAY IN BOXES OF RICE KRUSTIES® CEREAL. OR SHOULD I SAY "COULDN'T GIVE AWAY."
SMITHERS the WACKY LACKEY
YOU'RE RIGHT, SIR, THE ALLIGATOR BOOTS TASTE THE BEST.
MOE'S SAD BUT TRUE ROMANCE
BUT, DARLING, YOU CAN'T HANG UP ON ME. I PAID TEN BUCKS FOR THREE MINUTES.

PATRIC M. VERRONE SCRIPT · **LUIS ESCOBAR** PENCILS · **PATRICK OWSLEY** INKS · **CHRIS UNGAR** COLORS · **KAREN BATES** LETTERS · **BILL MORRISON** EDITOR · **MATT GROENING** ONE SHOT WONDER

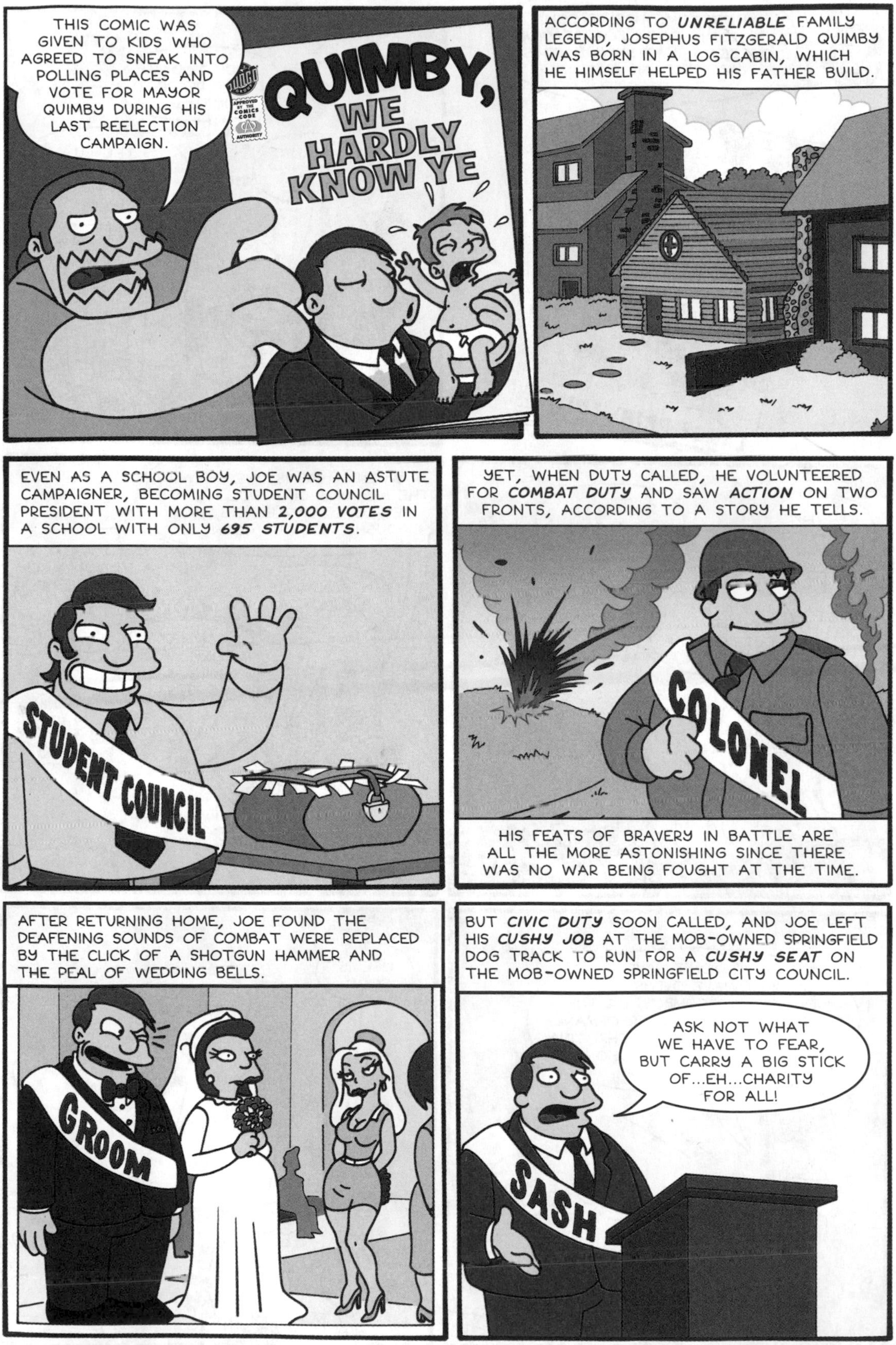

THIS COMIC WAS GIVEN TO KIDS WHO AGREED TO SNEAK INTO POLLING PLACES AND VOTE FOR MAYOR QUIMBY DURING HIS LAST REELECTION CAMPAIGN.
QUIMBY, WE HARDLY KNOW YE
ACCORDING TO UNRELIABLE FAMILY LEGEND, JOSEPHUS FITZGERALD QUIMBY WAS BORN IN A LOG CABIN, WHICH HE HIMSELF HELPED HIS FATHER BUILD.
EVEN AS A SCHOOL BOY, JOE WAS AN ASTUTE CAMPAIGNER, BECOMING STUDENT COUNCIL PRESIDENT WITH MORE THAN 2,000 VOTES IN A SCHOOL WITH ONLY 695 STUDENTS.
STUDENT COUNCIL
YET, WHEN DUTY CALLED, HE VOLUNTEERED FOR COMBAT DUTY AND SAW ACTION ON TWO FRONTS, ACCORDING TO A STORY HE TELLS.
COLONEL
HIS FEATS OF BRAVERY IN BATTLE ARE ALL THE MORE ASTONISHING SINCE THERE WAS NO WAR BEING FOUGHT AT THE TIME.
AFTER RETURNING HOME, JOE FOUND THE DEAFENING SOUNDS OF COMBAT WERE REPLACED BY THE CLICK OF A SHOTGUN HAMMER AND THE PEAL OF WEDDING BELLS.
GROOM
BUT CIVIC DUTY SOON CALLED, AND JOE LEFT HIS CUSHY JOB AT THE MOB-OWNED SPRINGFIELD DOG TRACK TO RUN FOR A CUSHY SEAT ON THE MOB-OWNED SPRINGFIELD CITY COUNCIL.
ASK NOT WHAT WE HAVE TO FEAR, BUT CARRY A BIG STICK OF...EH...CHARITY FOR ALL!
SASH

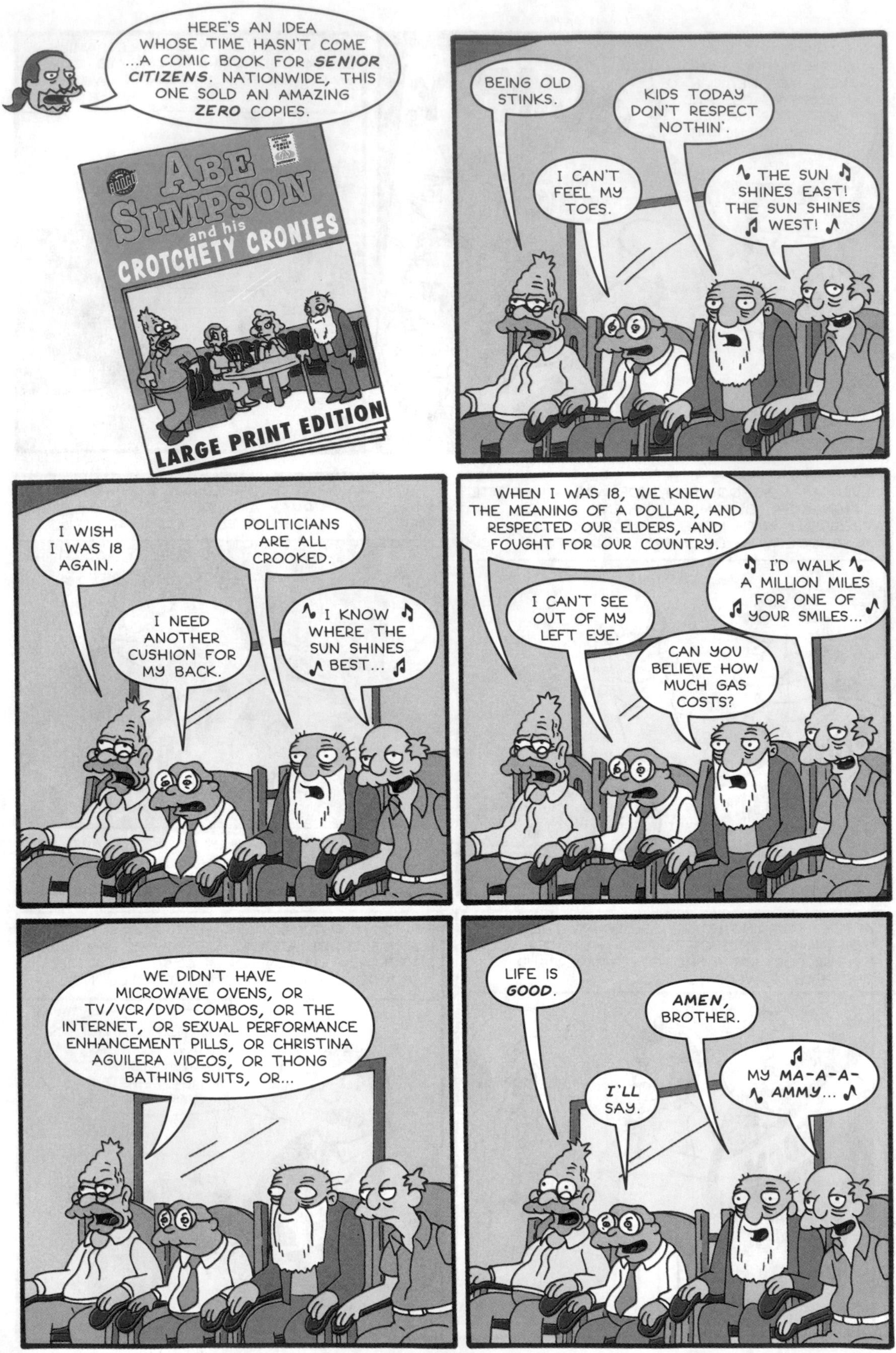
HERE'S AN IDEA WHOSE TIME HASN'T COME ...A COMIC BOOK FOR **SENIOR CITIZENS**. NATIONWIDE, THIS ONE SOLD AN AMAZING **ZERO** COPIES.
ABE SIMPSON and his CROTCHETY CRONIES
LARGE PRINT EDITION
BEING OLD STINKS.
I CAN'T FEEL MY TOES.
KIDS TODAY DON'T RESPECT NOTHIN'.
THE SUN SHINES EAST! THE SUN SHINES WEST!
I WISH I WAS 18 AGAIN.
I NEED ANOTHER CUSHION FOR MY BACK.
POLITICIANS ARE ALL CROOKED.
I KNOW WHERE THE SUN SHINES BEST...
WHEN I WAS 18, WE KNEW THE MEANING OF A DOLLAR, AND RESPECTED OUR ELDERS, AND FOUGHT FOR OUR COUNTRY.
I CAN'T SEE OUT OF MY LEFT EYE.
CAN YOU BELIEVE HOW MUCH GAS COSTS?
I'D WALK A MILLION MILES FOR ONE OF YOUR SMILES...
WE DIDN'T HAVE MICROWAVE OVENS, OR TV/VCR/DVD COMBOS, OR THE INTERNET, OR SEXUAL PERFORMANCE ENHANCEMENT PILLS, OR CHRISTINA AGUILERA VIDEOS, OR THONG BATHING SUITS, OR...
LIFE IS **GOOD**.
I'LL SAY.
AMEN, BROTHER.
MY **MA-A-A-AMMY**...

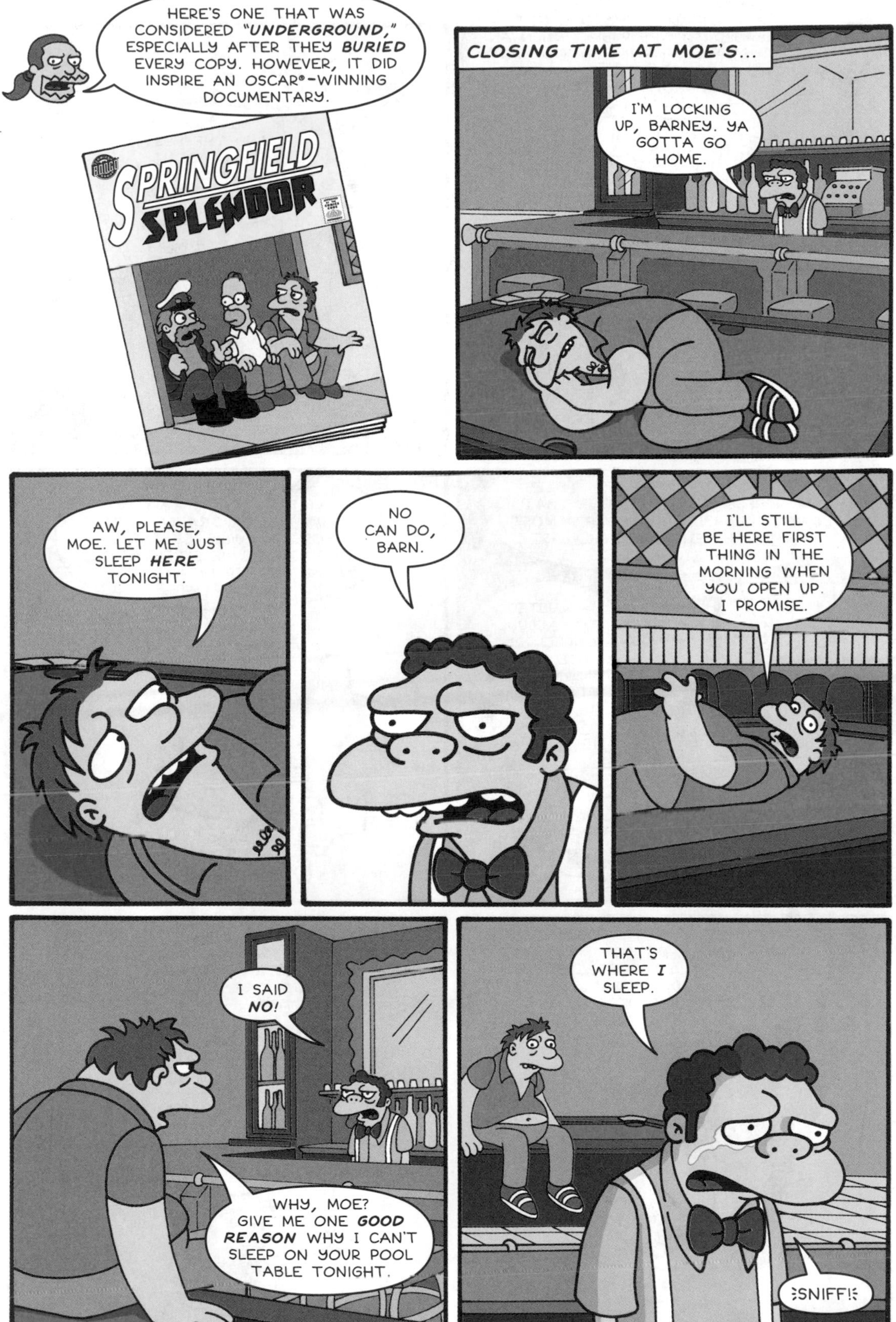
HERE'S ONE THAT WAS CONSIDERED "UNDERGROUND," ESPECIALLY AFTER THEY BURIED EVERY COPY. HOWEVER, IT DID INSPIRE AN OSCAR®-WINNING DOCUMENTARY.
SPRINGFIELD SPLENDOR
CLOSING TIME AT MOE'S...
I'M LOCKING UP, BARNEY. YA GOTTA GO HOME.
AW, PLEASE, MOE. LET ME JUST SLEEP HERE TONIGHT.
NO CAN DO, BARN.
I'LL STILL BE HERE FIRST THING IN THE MORNING WHEN YOU OPEN UP. I PROMISE.
WHY, MOE? GIVE ME ONE GOOD REASON WHY I CAN'T SLEEP ON YOUR POOL TABLE TONIGHT.
I SAID NO!
THAT'S WHERE I SLEEP.
SNIFF!

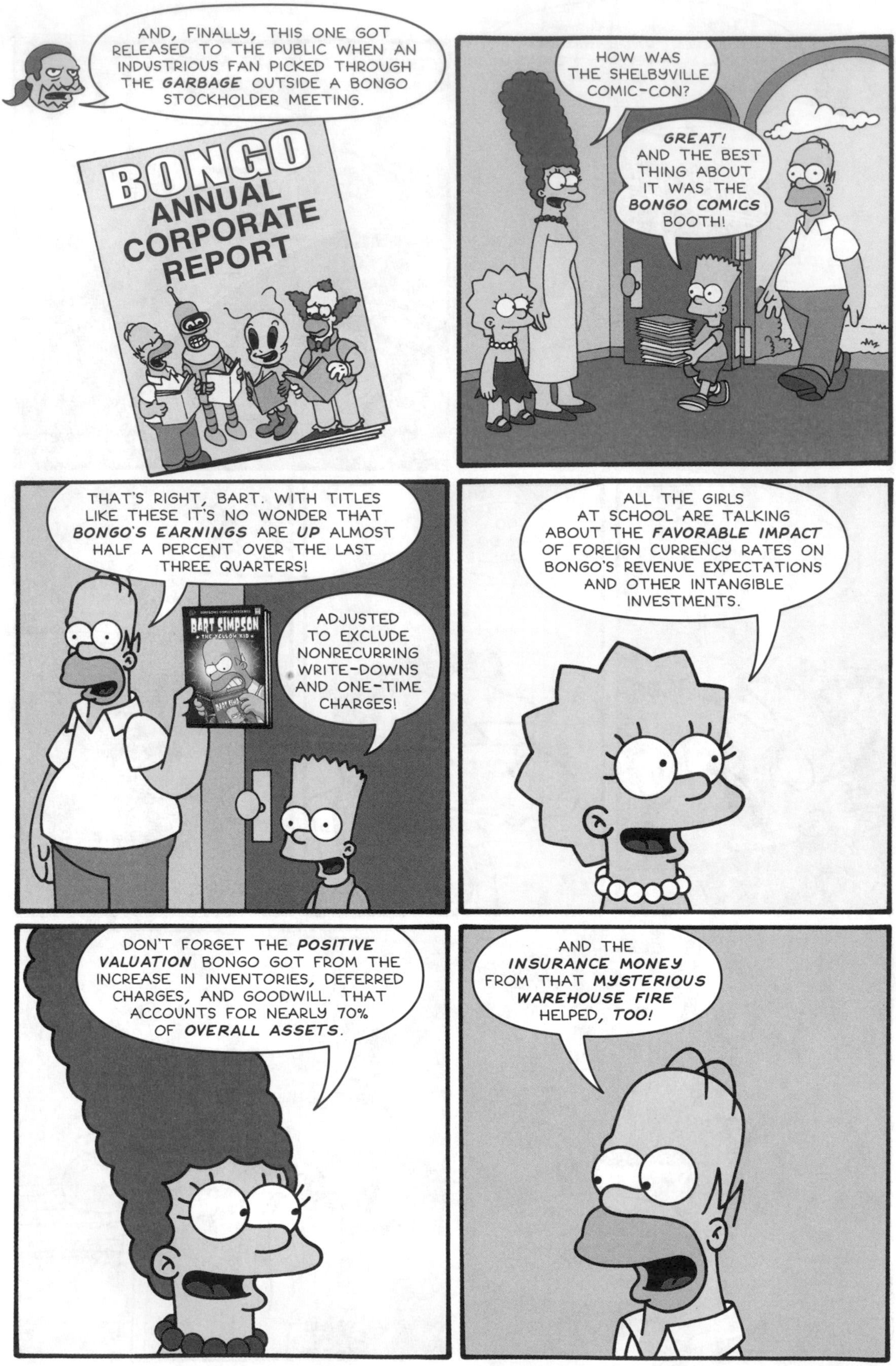

AND, FINALLY, THIS ONE GOT RELEASED TO THE PUBLIC WHEN AN INDUSTRIOUS FAN PICKED THROUGH THE GARBAGE OUTSIDE A BONGO STOCKHOLDER MEETING.
BONGO
ANNUAL CORPORATE REPORT
HOW WAS THE SHELBYVILLE COMIC-CON?
GREAT! AND THE BEST THING ABOUT IT WAS THE BONGO COMICS BOOTH!
THAT'S RIGHT, BART. WITH TITLES LIKE THESE IT'S NO WONDER THAT BONGO'S EARNINGS ARE UP ALMOST HALF A PERCENT OVER THE LAST THREE QUARTERS!
BART SIMPSON
ADJUSTED TO EXCLUDE NONRECURRING WRITE-DOWNS AND ONE-TIME CHARGES!
ALL THE GIRLS AT SCHOOL ARE TALKING ABOUT THE FAVORABLE IMPACT OF FOREIGN CURRENCY RATES ON BONGO'S REVENUE EXPECTATIONS AND OTHER INTANGIBLE INVESTMENTS.
DON'T FORGET THE POSITIVE VALUATION BONGO GOT FROM THE INCREASE IN INVENTORIES, DEFERRED CHARGES, AND GOODWILL. THAT ACCOUNTS FOR NEARLY 70% OF OVERALL ASSETS.
AND THE INSURANCE MONEY FROM THAT MYSTERIOUS WAREHOUSE FIRE HELPED, TOO!

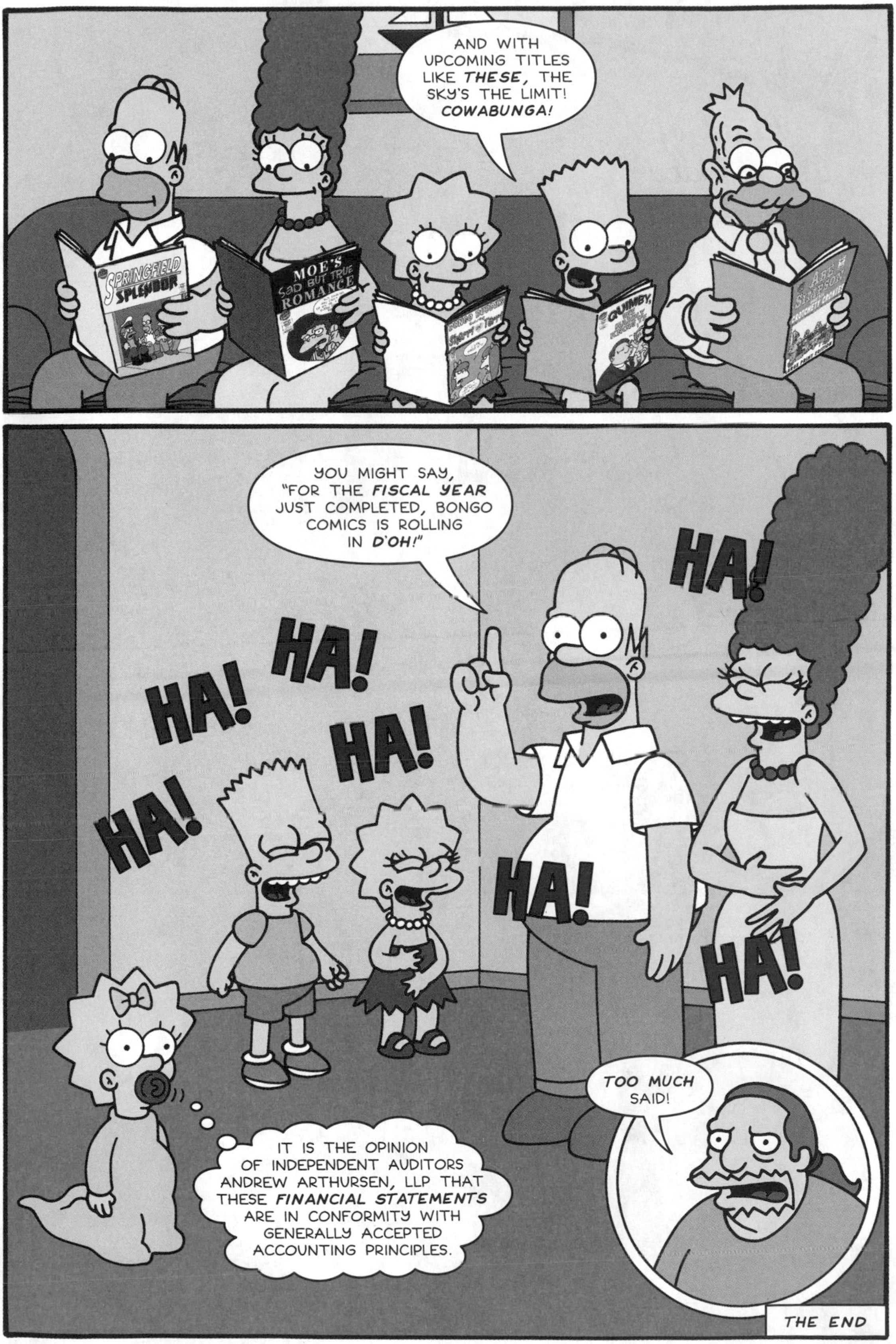
SPRINGFIELD SPLENDOR
MOE'S SAD BUT TRUE ROMANCE
AND WITH UPCOMING TITLES LIKE *THESE,* THE SKY'S THE LIMIT! ***COWABUNGA!***
YOU MIGHT SAY, "FOR THE *FISCAL YEAR* JUST COMPLETED, BONGO COMICS IS ROLLING IN *D'OH!*"
HA!
HA!
HA!
HA!
HA!
HA!
HA!
IT IS THE OPINION OF INDEPENDENT AUDITORS ANDREW ARTHURSEN, LLP THAT THESE ***FINANCIAL STATEMENTS*** ARE IN CONFORMITY WITH GENERALLY ACCEPTED ACCOUNTING PRINCIPLES.
TOO MUCH SAID!
THE END

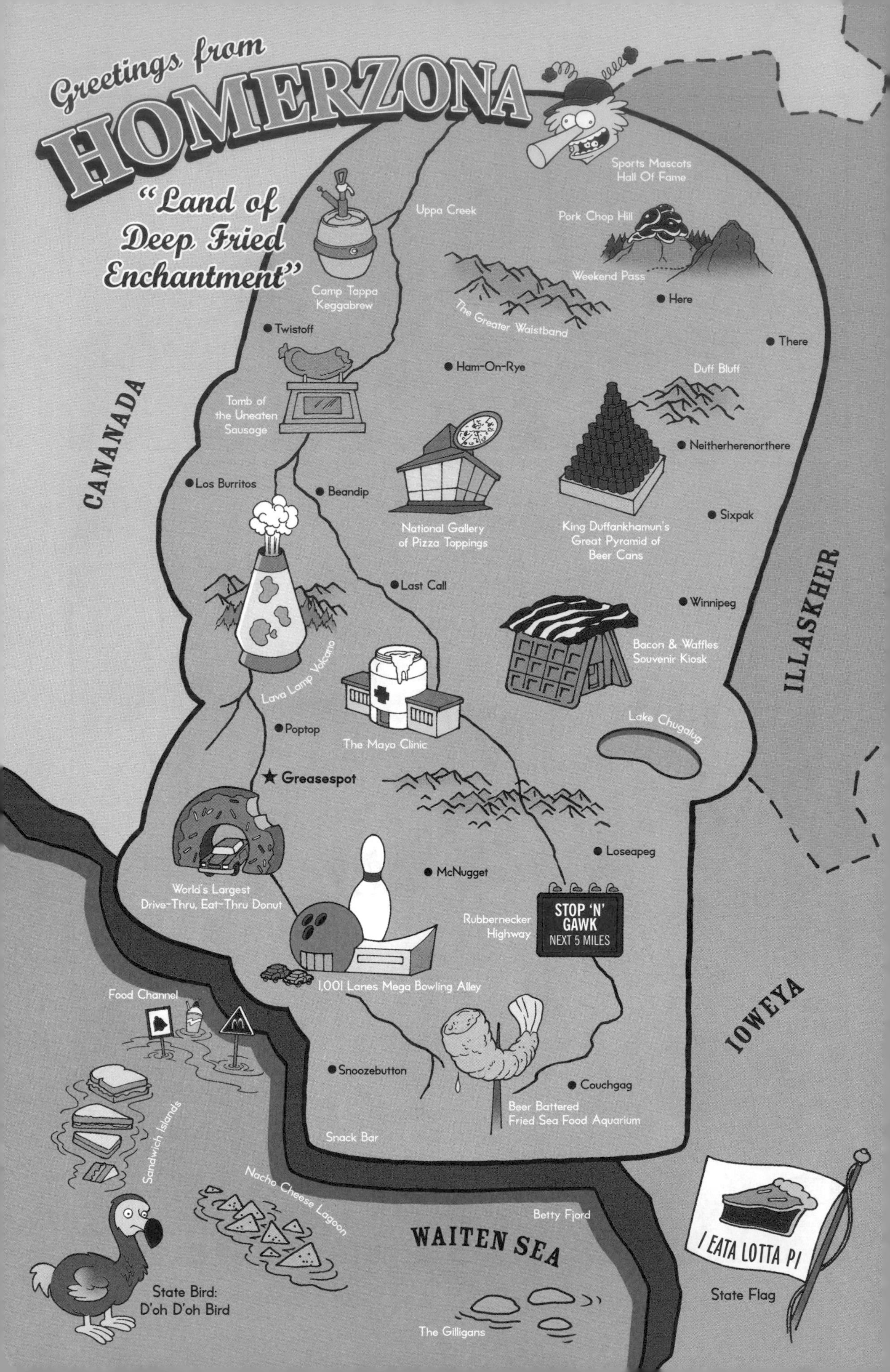

Greetings from
HOMERZONA
"Land of Deep Fried Enchantment"
Sports Mascots Hall Of Fame
Uppa Creek
Pork Chop Hill
Camp Tappa Keggabrew
Weekend Pass
Here
The Greater Waistband
Twistoff
There
Ham-On-Rye
Duff Bluff
Tomb of the Uneaten Sausage
CANANADA
Neitherherenorthere
Los Burritos
Beandip
National Gallery of Pizza Toppings
King Duffankhamun's Great Pyramid of Beer Cans
Sixpak
Last Call
ILLASKHER
Winnipeg
Bacon & Waffles Souvenir Kiosk
Lava Lamp Volcano
Lake Chugalug
Poptop
The Mayo Clinic
Greasespot
Loseapeg
McNugget
World's Largest Drive-Thru, Eat-Thru Donut
STOP 'N' GAWK
NEXT 5 MILES
Rubbernecker Highway
1,001 Lanes Mega Bowling Alley
Food Channel
IOWEYA
Snoozebutton
Couchgag
Beer Battered Fried Sea Food Aquarium
Sandwich Islands
Snack Bar
Nacho Cheese Lagoon
Betty Fjord
WAITEN SEA
I EATA LOTTA PI
State Bird: D'oh D'oh Bird
State Flag
The Gilligans

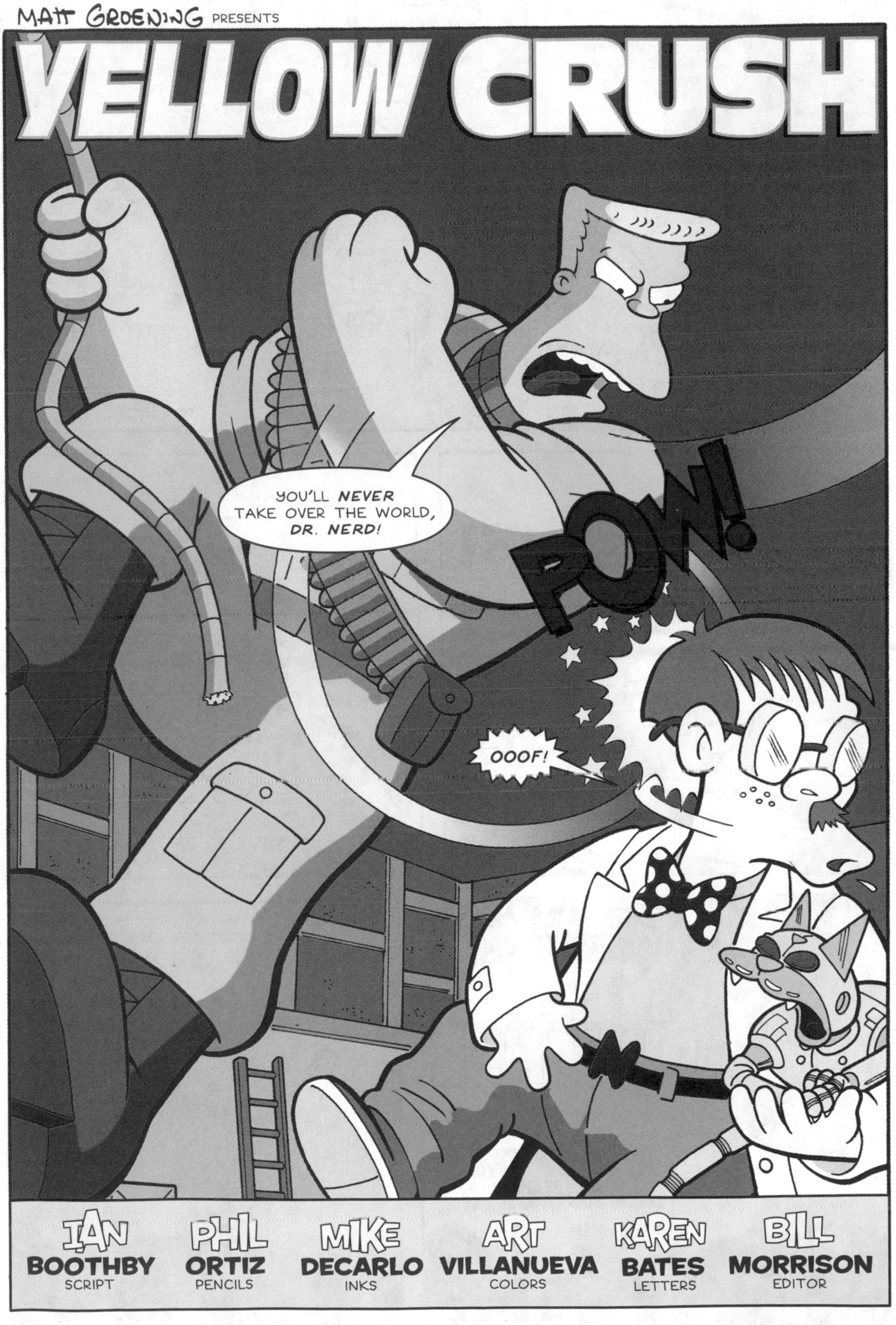
MATT GROENING PRESENTS
YELLOW CRUSH
YOU'LL NEVER TAKE OVER THE WORLD, DR. NERD!
POW!
OOOF!
IAN BOOTHBY SCRIPT
PHIL ORTIZ PENCILS
MIKE DECARLO INKS
ART VILLANUEVA COLORS
KAREN BATES LETTERS
BILL MORRISON EDITOR

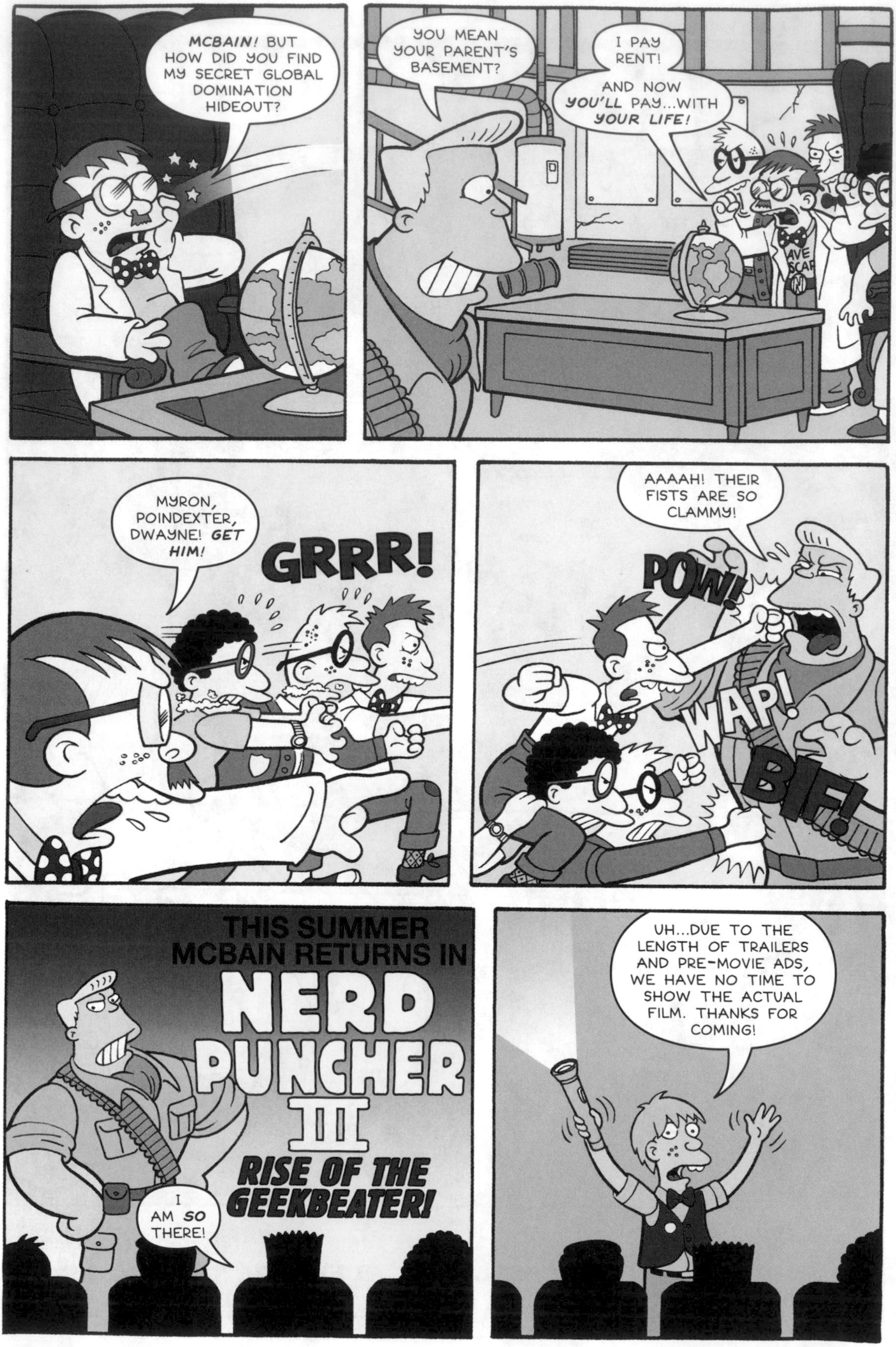
MCBAIN! BUT HOW DID YOU FIND MY SECRET GLOBAL DOMINATION HIDEOUT?
YOU MEAN YOUR PARENT'S BASEMENT?
I PAY RENT!
AND NOW YOU'LL PAY...WITH YOUR LIFE!
MYRON, POINDEXTER, DWAYNE! GET HIM!
GRRR!
AAAAH! THEIR FISTS ARE SO CLAMMY!
POW!
WAP!
BIF!
THIS SUMMER MCBAIN RETURNS IN
NERD PUNCHER III
RISE OF THE GEEKBEATER!
I AM SO THERE!
UH...DUE TO THE LENGTH OF TRAILERS AND PRE-MOVIE ADS, WE HAVE NO TIME TO SHOW THE ACTUAL FILM. THANKS FOR COMING!

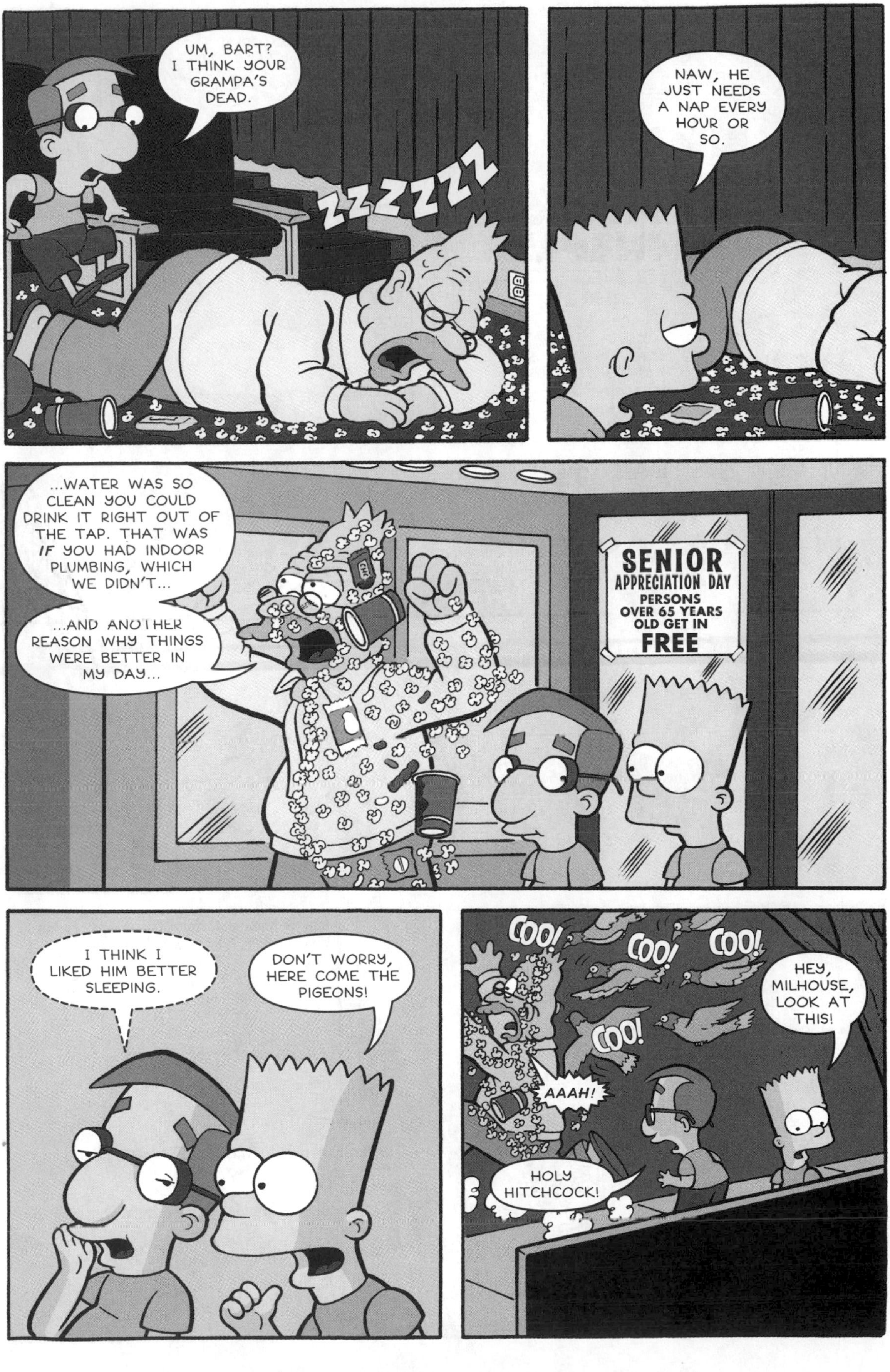
UM, BART? I THINK YOUR GRAMPA'S DEAD.
ZZZZZZ
NAW, HE JUST NEEDS A NAP EVERY HOUR OR SO.
...WATER WAS SO CLEAN YOU COULD DRINK IT RIGHT OUT OF THE TAP. THAT WAS *IF* YOU HAD INDOOR PLUMBING, WHICH WE DIDN'T...
...AND ANOTHER REASON WHY THINGS WERE BETTER IN MY DAY...
SENIOR APPRECIATION DAY PERSONS OVER 65 YEARS OLD GET IN FREE
I THINK I LIKED HIM BETTER SLEEPING.
DON'T WORRY, HERE COME THE PIGEONS!
COO!
COO!
COO!
COO!
HEY, MILHOUSE, LOOK AT THIS!
AAAH!
HOLY HITCHCOCK!

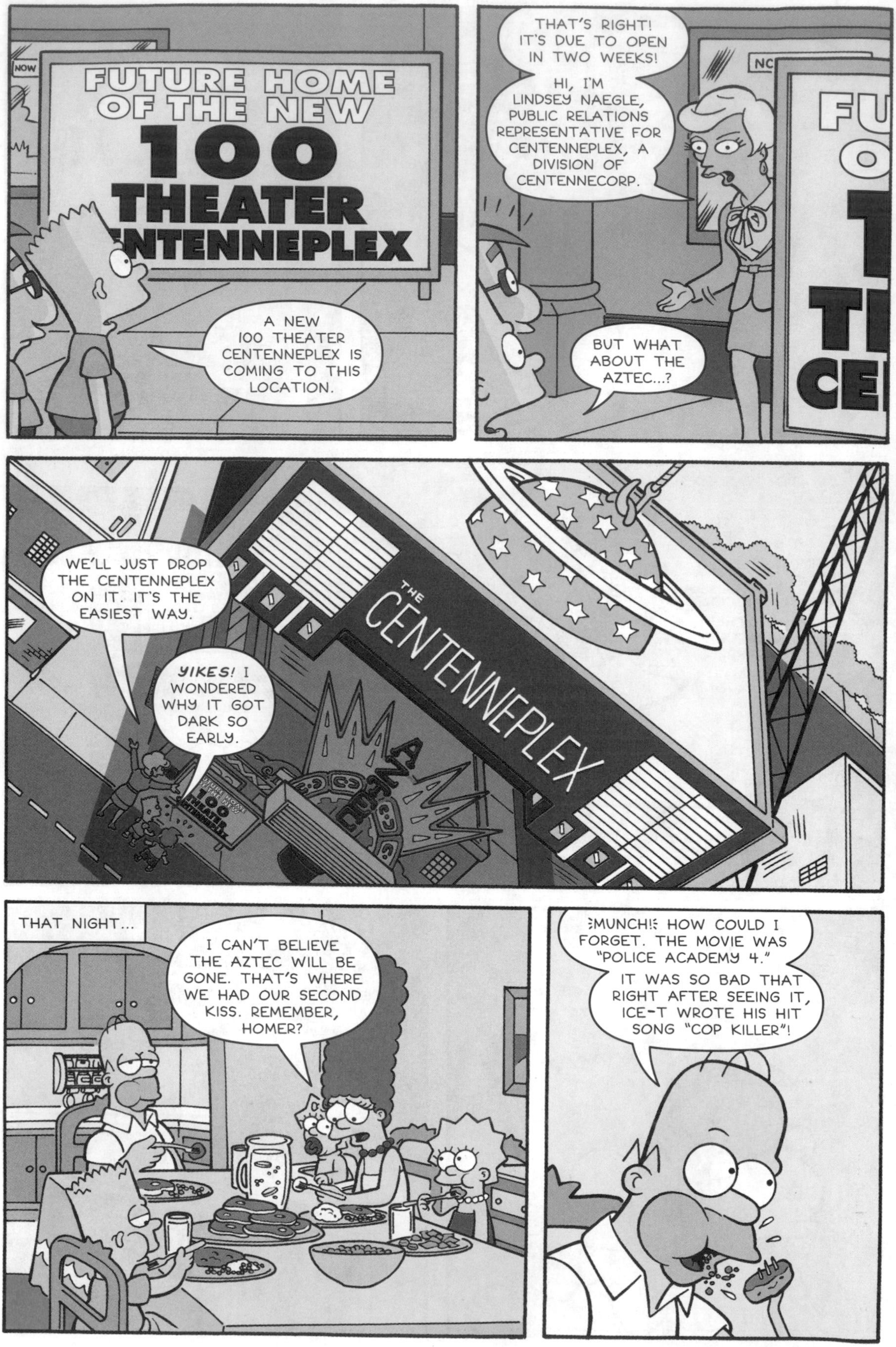
NOW
FUTURE HOME OF THE NEW 100 THEATER CENTENNEPLEX
A NEW 100 THEATER CENTENNEPLEX IS COMING TO THIS LOCATION.
THAT'S RIGHT! IT'S DUE TO OPEN IN TWO WEEKS!
HI, I'M LINDSEY NAEGLE, PUBLIC RELATIONS REPRESENTATIVE FOR CENTENNEPLEX, A DIVISION OF CENTENNECORP.
BUT WHAT ABOUT THE AZTEC...?
WE'LL JUST DROP THE CENTENNEPLEX ON IT. IT'S THE EASIEST WAY.
THE CENTENNEPLEX
YIKES! I WONDERED WHY IT GOT DARK SO EARLY.
THAT NIGHT...
I CAN'T BELIEVE THE AZTEC WILL BE GONE. THAT'S WHERE WE HAD OUR SECOND KISS. REMEMBER, HOMER?
ƎMUNCH!Ǝ HOW COULD I FORGET. THE MOVIE WAS "POLICE ACADEMY 4."
IT WAS SO BAD THAT RIGHT AFTER SEEING IT, ICE-T WROTE HIS HIT SONG "COP KILLER"!

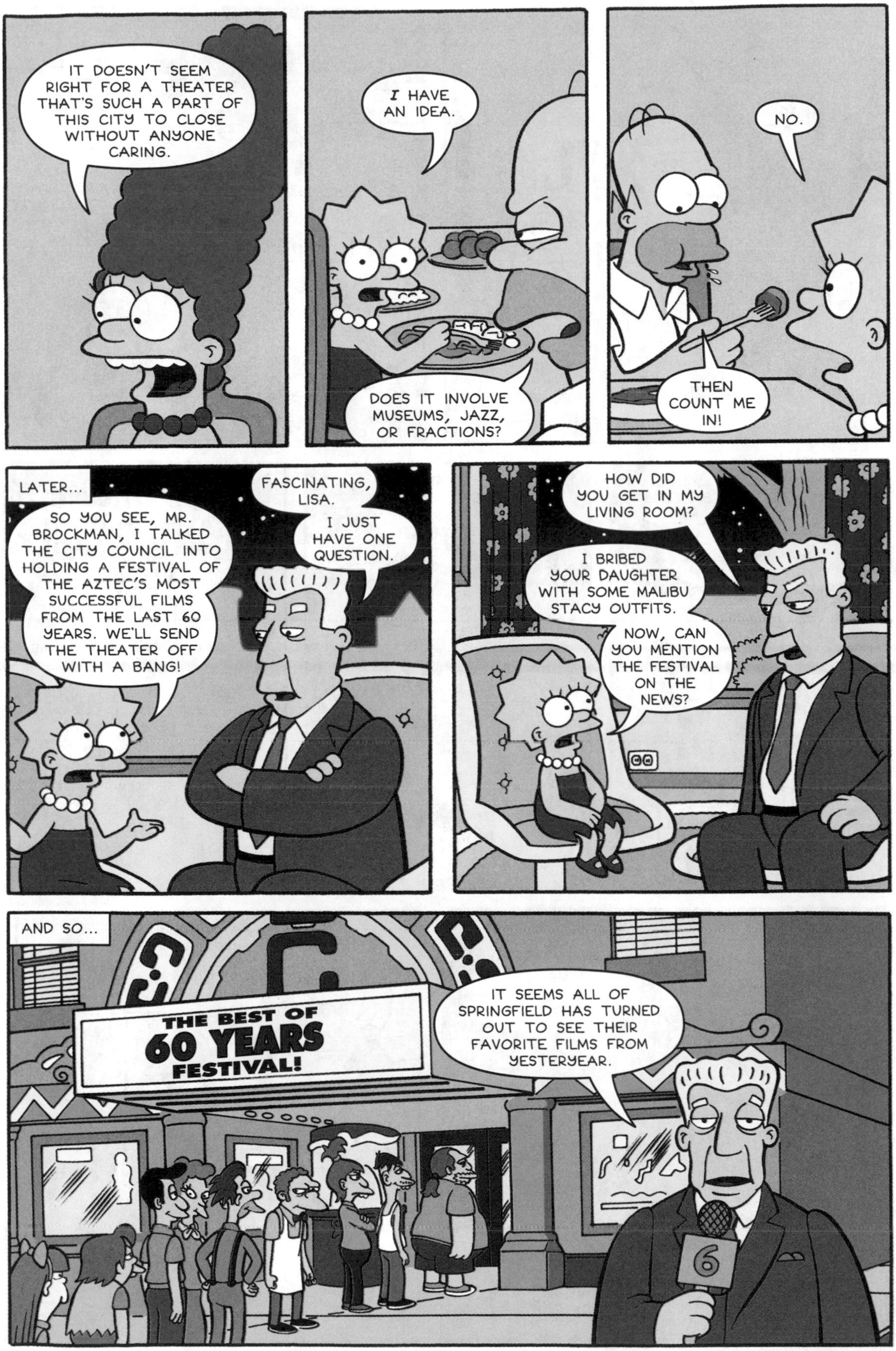

IT DOESN'T SEEM RIGHT FOR A THEATER THAT'S SUCH A PART OF THIS CITY TO CLOSE WITHOUT ANYONE CARING.
I HAVE AN IDEA.
DOES IT INVOLVE MUSEUMS, JAZZ, OR FRACTIONS?
NO.
THEN COUNT ME IN!
LATER...
SO YOU SEE, MR. BROCKMAN, I TALKED THE CITY COUNCIL INTO HOLDING A FESTIVAL OF THE AZTEC'S MOST SUCCESSFUL FILMS FROM THE LAST 60 YEARS. WE'LL SEND THE THEATER OFF WITH A BANG!
FASCINATING, LISA.
I JUST HAVE ONE QUESTION.
HOW DID YOU GET IN MY LIVING ROOM?
I BRIBED YOUR DAUGHTER WITH SOME MALIBU STACY OUTFITS.
NOW, CAN YOU MENTION THE FESTIVAL ON THE NEWS?
AND SO...
THE BEST OF 60 YEARS FESTIVAL!
IT SEEMS ALL OF SPRINGFIELD HAS TURNED OUT TO SEE THEIR FAVORITE FILMS FROM YESTERYEAR.
6

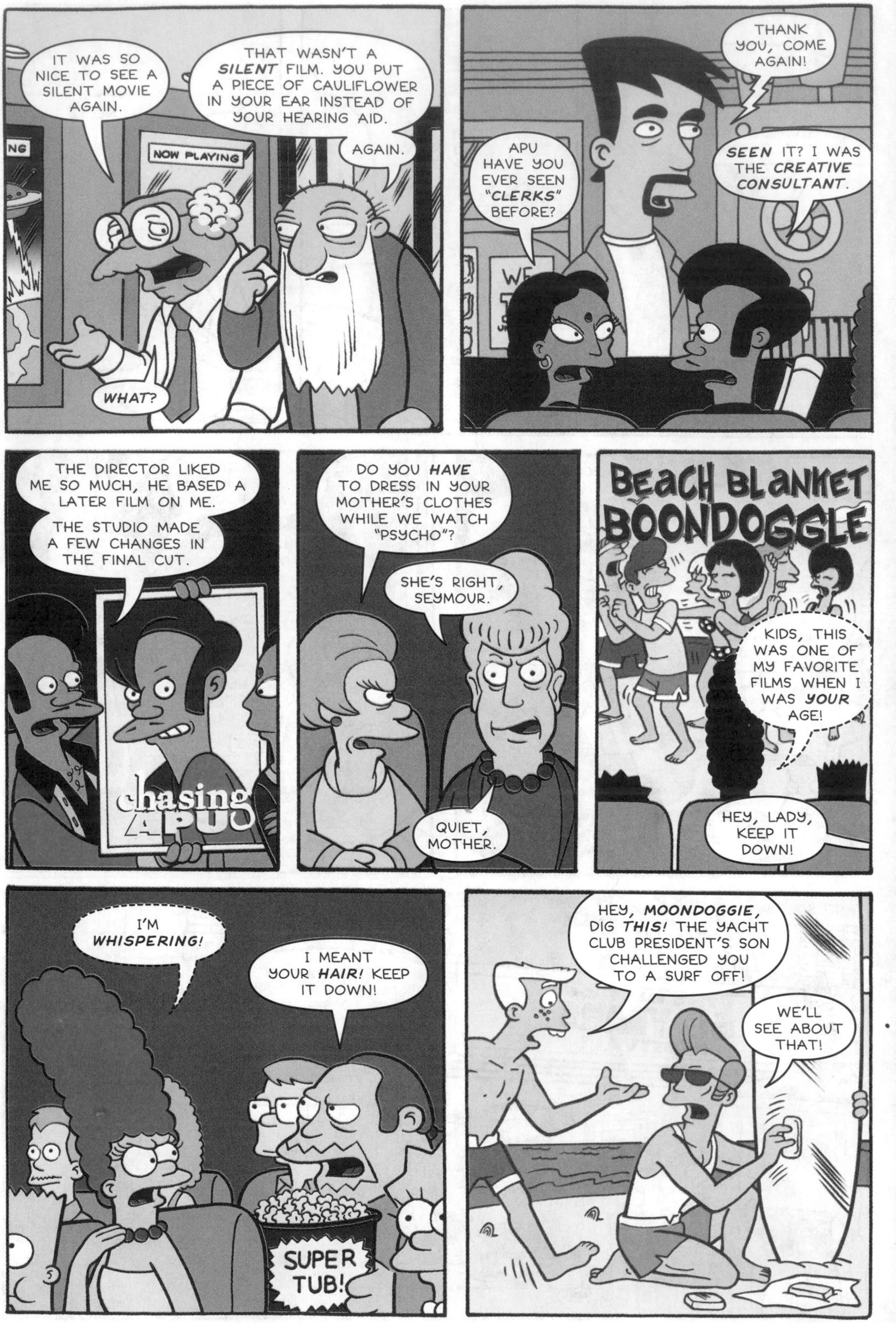
IT WAS SO NICE TO SEE A SILENT MOVIE AGAIN.
THAT WASN'T A SILENT FILM. YOU PUT A PIECE OF CAULIFLOWER IN YOUR EAR INSTEAD OF YOUR HEARING AID.
AGAIN.
WHAT?
NOW PLAYING
THANK YOU, COME AGAIN!
APU HAVE YOU EVER SEEN "CLERKS" BEFORE?
SEEN IT? I WAS THE CREATIVE CONSULTANT.
THE DIRECTOR LIKED ME SO MUCH, HE BASED A LATER FILM ON ME.
THE STUDIO MADE A FEW CHANGES IN THE FINAL CUT.
chasing APU
DO YOU HAVE TO DRESS IN YOUR MOTHER'S CLOTHES WHILE WE WATCH "PSYCHO"?
SHE'S RIGHT, SEYMOUR.
QUIET, MOTHER.
BEACH BLANKET BOONDOGGLE
KIDS, THIS WAS ONE OF MY FAVORITE FILMS WHEN I WAS YOUR AGE!
HEY, LADY, KEEP IT DOWN!
I'M WHISPERING!
I MEANT YOUR HAIR! KEEP IT DOWN!
SUPER TUB!
HEY, MOONDOGGIE, DIG THIS! THE YACHT CLUB PRESIDENT'S SON CHALLENGED YOU TO A SURF OFF!
WE'LL SEE ABOUT THAT!

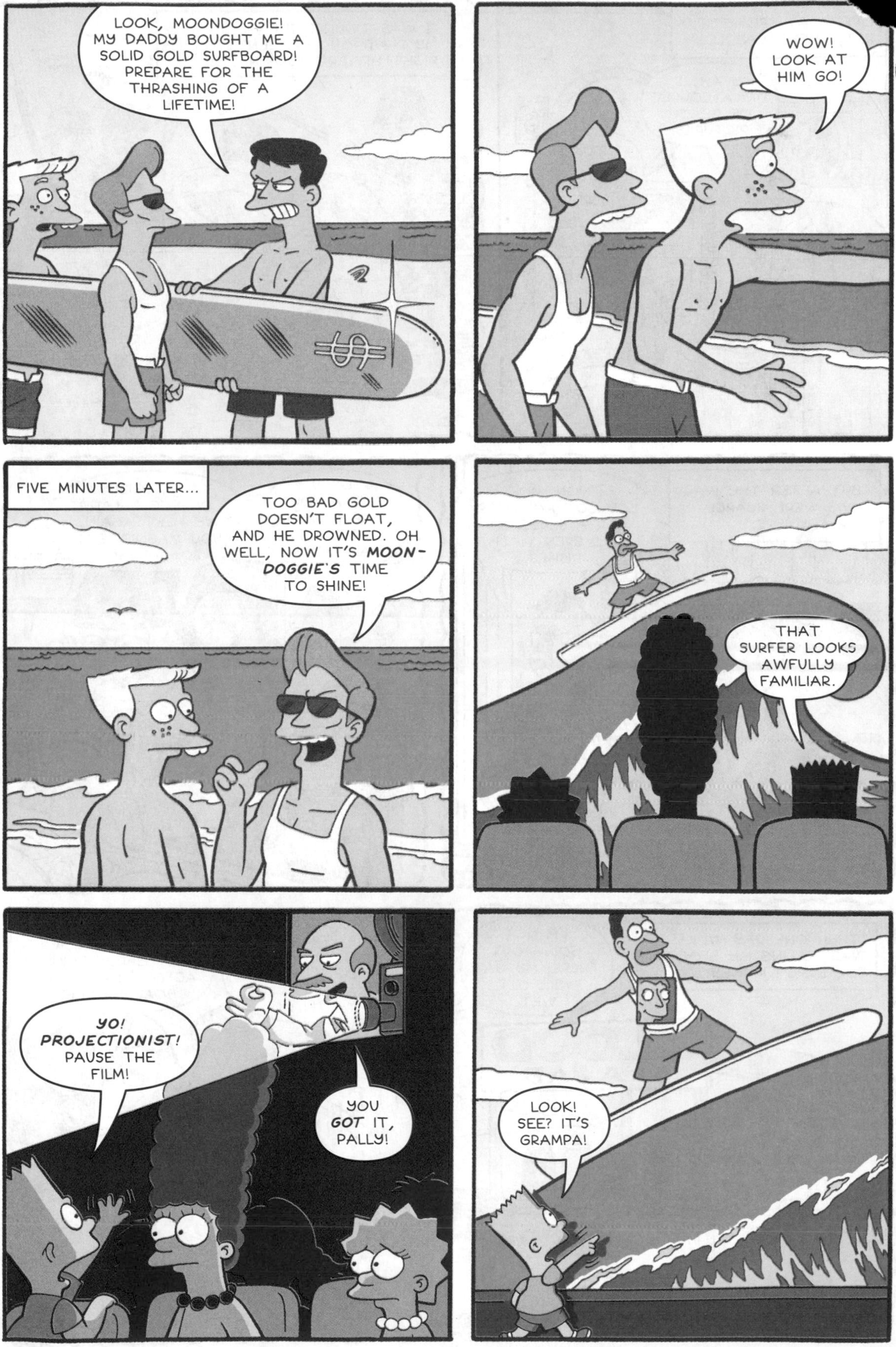
LOOK, MOONDOGGIE! MY DADDY BOUGHT ME A SOLID GOLD SURFBOARD! PREPARE FOR THE THRASHING OF A LIFETIME!
WOW! LOOK AT HIM GO!
FIVE MINUTES LATER...
TOO BAD GOLD DOESN'T FLOAT, AND HE DROWNED. OH WELL, NOW IT'S MOON-DOGGIE'S TIME TO SHINE!
THAT SURFER LOOKS AWFULLY FAMILIAR.
YO! PROJECTIONIST! PAUSE THE FILM!
YOU GOT IT, PALLY!
LOOK! SEE? IT'S GRAMPA!

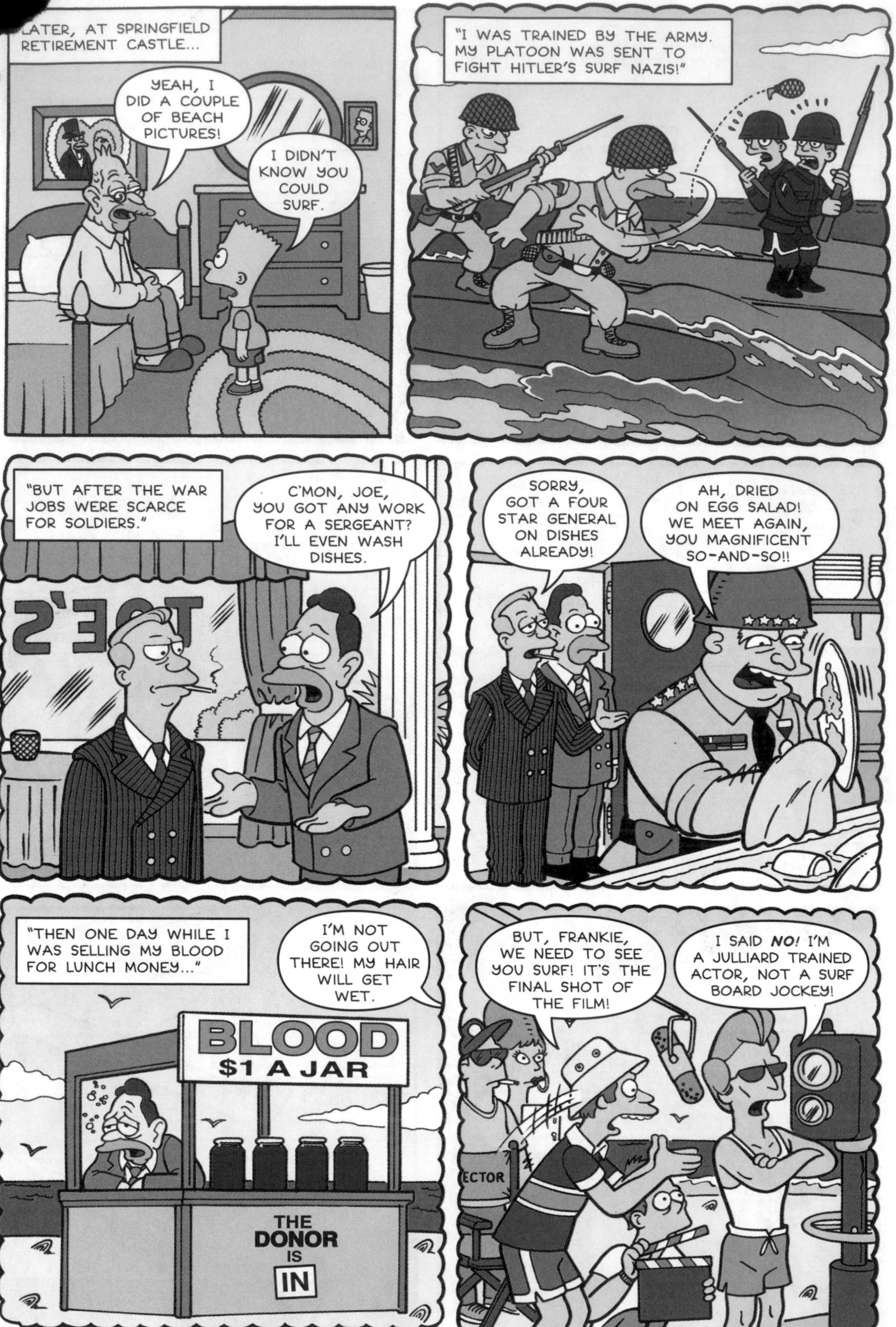
LATER, AT SPRINGFIELD RETIREMENT CASTLE...
YEAH, I DID A COUPLE OF BEACH PICTURES!
I DIDN'T KNOW YOU COULD SURF.
"I WAS TRAINED BY THE ARMY. MY PLATOON WAS SENT TO FIGHT HITLER'S SURF NAZIS!"
"BUT AFTER THE WAR JOBS WERE SCARCE FOR SOLDIERS."
C'MON, JOE, YOU GOT ANY WORK FOR A SERGEANT? I'LL EVEN WASH DISHES.
SORRY, GOT A FOUR STAR GENERAL ON DISHES ALREADY!
AH, DRIED ON EGG SALAD! WE MEET AGAIN, YOU MAGNIFICENT SO-AND-SO!!
"THEN ONE DAY WHILE I WAS SELLING MY BLOOD FOR LUNCH MONEY..."
I'M NOT GOING OUT THERE! MY HAIR WILL GET WET.
BLOOD
$1 A JAR
THE DONOR IS IN
BUT, FRANKIE, WE NEED TO SEE YOU SURF! IT'S THE FINAL SHOT OF THE FILM!
I SAID NO! I'M A JULLIARD TRAINED ACTOR, NOT A SURF BOARD JOCKEY!

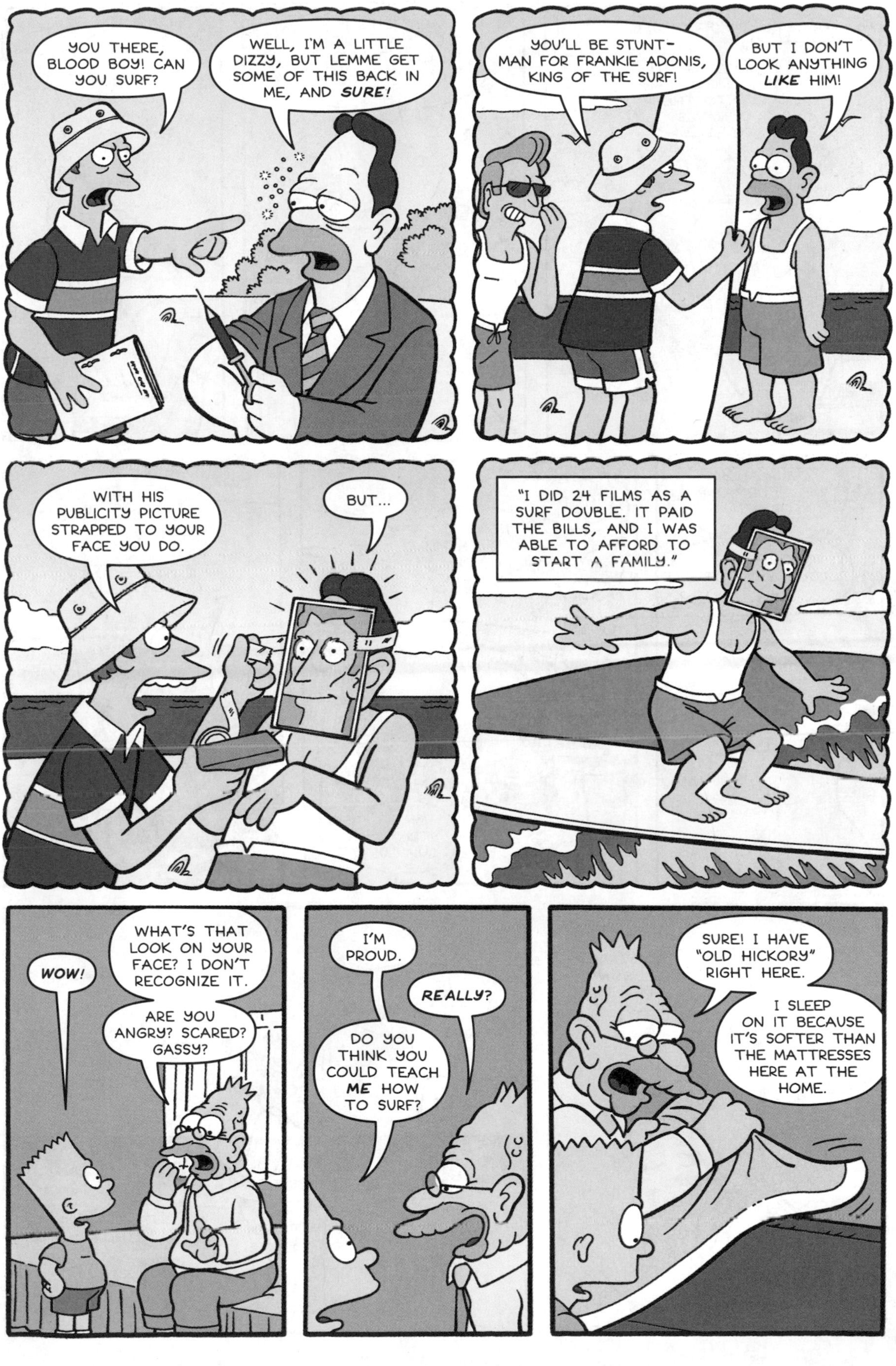
YOU THERE, BLOOD BOY! CAN YOU SURF?
WELL, I'M A LITTLE DIZZY, BUT LEMME GET SOME OF THIS BACK IN ME, AND SURE!
YOU'LL BE STUNT-MAN FOR FRANKIE ADONIS, KING OF THE SURF!
BUT I DON'T LOOK ANYTHING LIKE HIM!
WITH HIS PUBLICITY PICTURE STRAPPED TO YOUR FACE YOU DO.
BUT...
"I DID 24 FILMS AS A SURF DOUBLE. IT PAID THE BILLS, AND I WAS ABLE TO AFFORD TO START A FAMILY."
WOW!
WHAT'S THAT LOOK ON YOUR FACE? I DON'T RECOGNIZE IT.
ARE YOU ANGRY? SCARED? GASSY?
I'M PROUD.
REALLY?
DO YOU THINK YOU COULD TEACH ME HOW TO SURF?
SURE! I HAVE "OLD HICKORY" RIGHT HERE.
I SLEEP ON IT BECAUSE IT'S SOFTER THAN THE MATTRESSES HERE AT THE HOME.

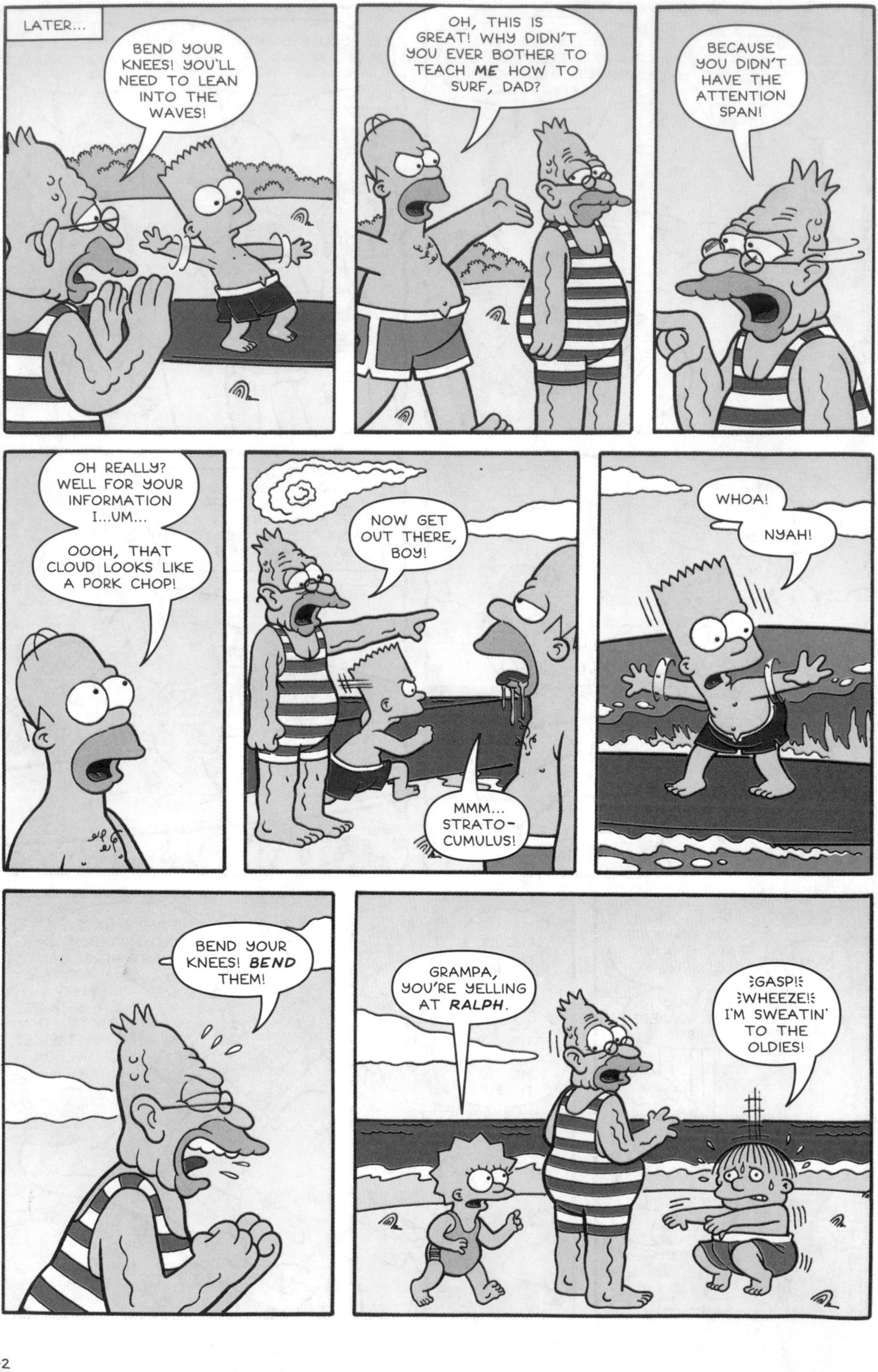
LATER...
BEND YOUR KNEES! YOU'LL NEED TO LEAN INTO THE WAVES!
OH, THIS IS GREAT! WHY DIDN'T YOU EVER BOTHER TO TEACH **ME** HOW TO SURF, DAD?
BECAUSE YOU DIDN'T HAVE THE ATTENTION SPAN!
OH REALLY? WELL FOR YOUR INFORMATION I...UM...
OOOH, THAT CLOUD LOOKS LIKE A PORK CHOP!
NOW GET OUT THERE, BOY!
MMM... STRATO-CUMULUS!
WHOA!
NYAH!
BEND YOUR KNEES! ***BEND*** THEM!
GRAMPA, YOU'RE YELLING AT ***RALPH***.
GASP! WHEEZE! I'M SWEATIN' TO THE OLDIES!

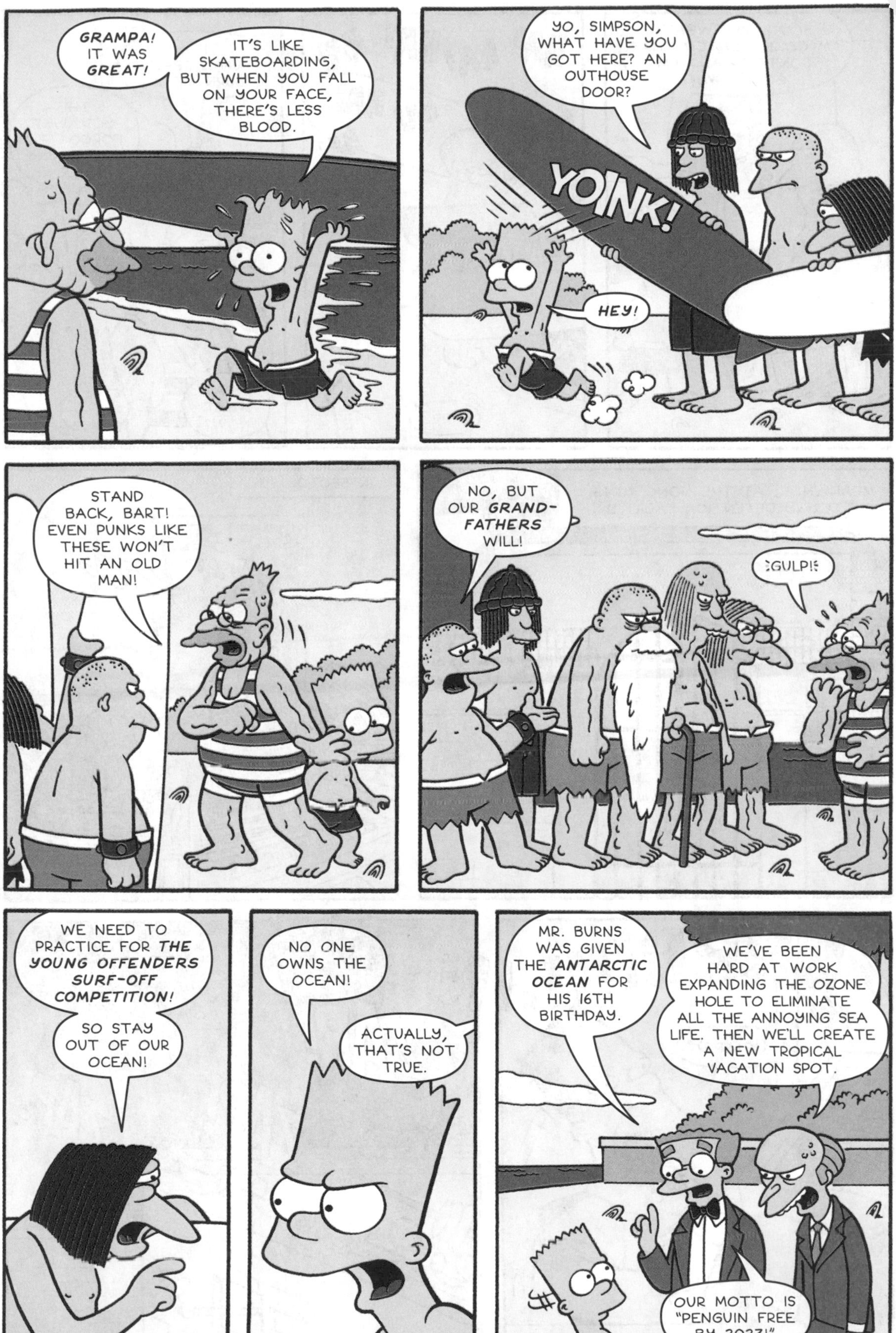
GRAMPA! IT WAS GREAT!
IT'S LIKE SKATEBOARDING, BUT WHEN YOU FALL ON YOUR FACE, THERE'S LESS BLOOD.
YO, SIMPSON, WHAT HAVE YOU GOT HERE? AN OUTHOUSE DOOR?
YOINK!
HEY!
STAND BACK, BART! EVEN PUNKS LIKE THESE WON'T HIT AN OLD MAN!
NO, BUT OUR GRAND-FATHERS WILL!
GULP!
WE NEED TO PRACTICE FOR THE YOUNG OFFENDERS SURF-OFF COMPETITION!
SO STAY OUT OF OUR OCEAN!
NO ONE OWNS THE OCEAN!
ACTUALLY, THAT'S NOT TRUE.
MR. BURNS WAS GIVEN THE ANTARCTIC OCEAN FOR HIS 16TH BIRTHDAY.
WE'VE BEEN HARD AT WORK EXPANDING THE OZONE HOLE TO ELIMINATE ALL THE ANNOYING SEA LIFE. THEN WE'LL CREATE A NEW TROPICAL VACATION SPOT.
OUR MOTTO IS "PENGUIN FREE BY 2023!"

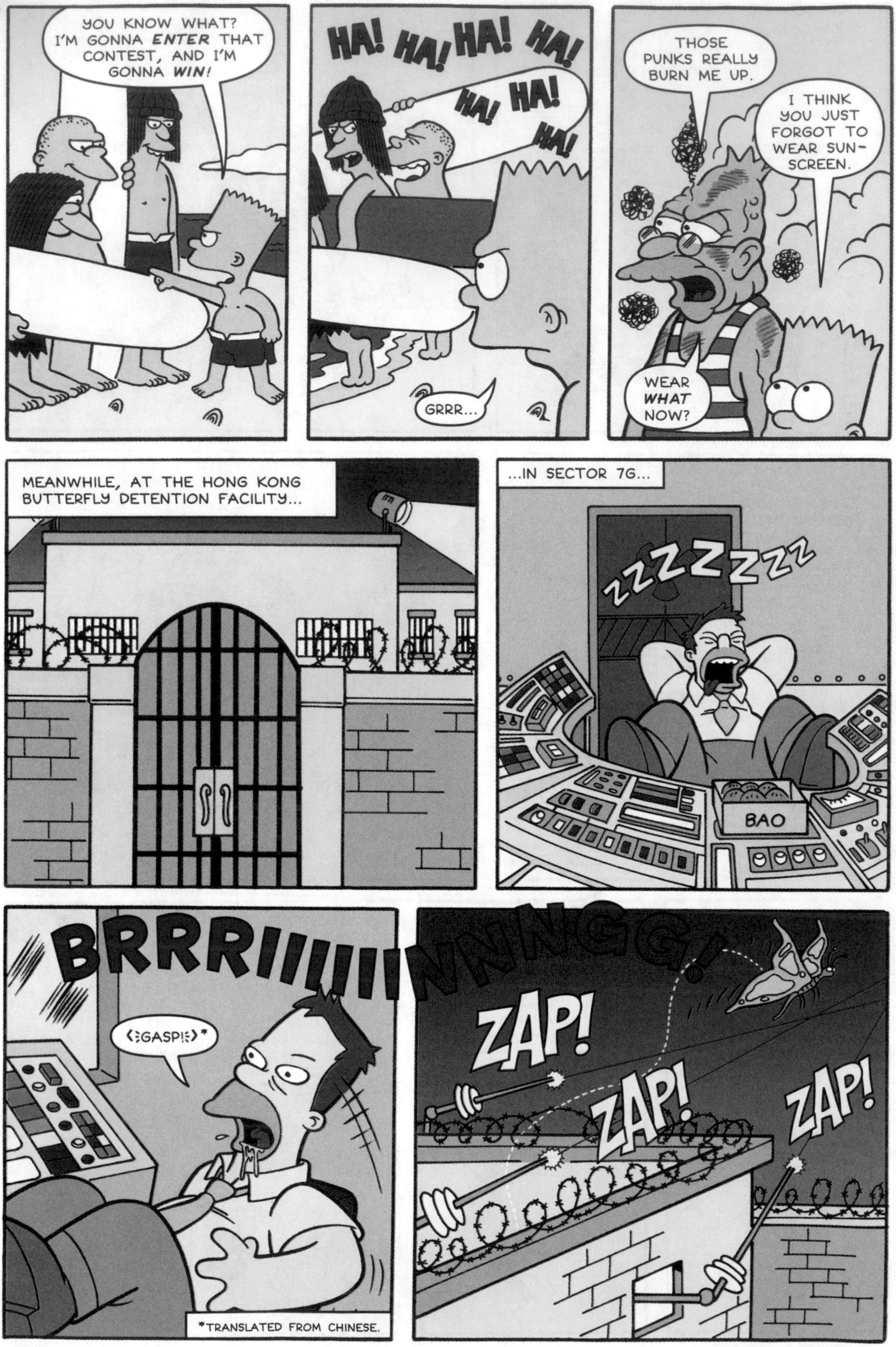
YOU KNOW WHAT? I'M GONNA ENTER THAT CONTEST, AND I'M GONNA WIN!
HA! HA! HA! HA!
HA! HA! HA!
GRRR...
THOSE PUNKS REALLY BURN ME UP.
I THINK YOU JUST FORGOT TO WEAR SUN-SCREEN.
WEAR WHAT NOW?
MEANWHILE, AT THE HONG KONG BUTTERFLY DETENTION FACILITY...
...IN SECTOR 7G...
ZZZZZZZZ
BAO
BRRRIIIIIINNNGG!
‹GASP!›*
*TRANSLATED FROM CHINESE.
ZAP!
ZAP!
ZAP!

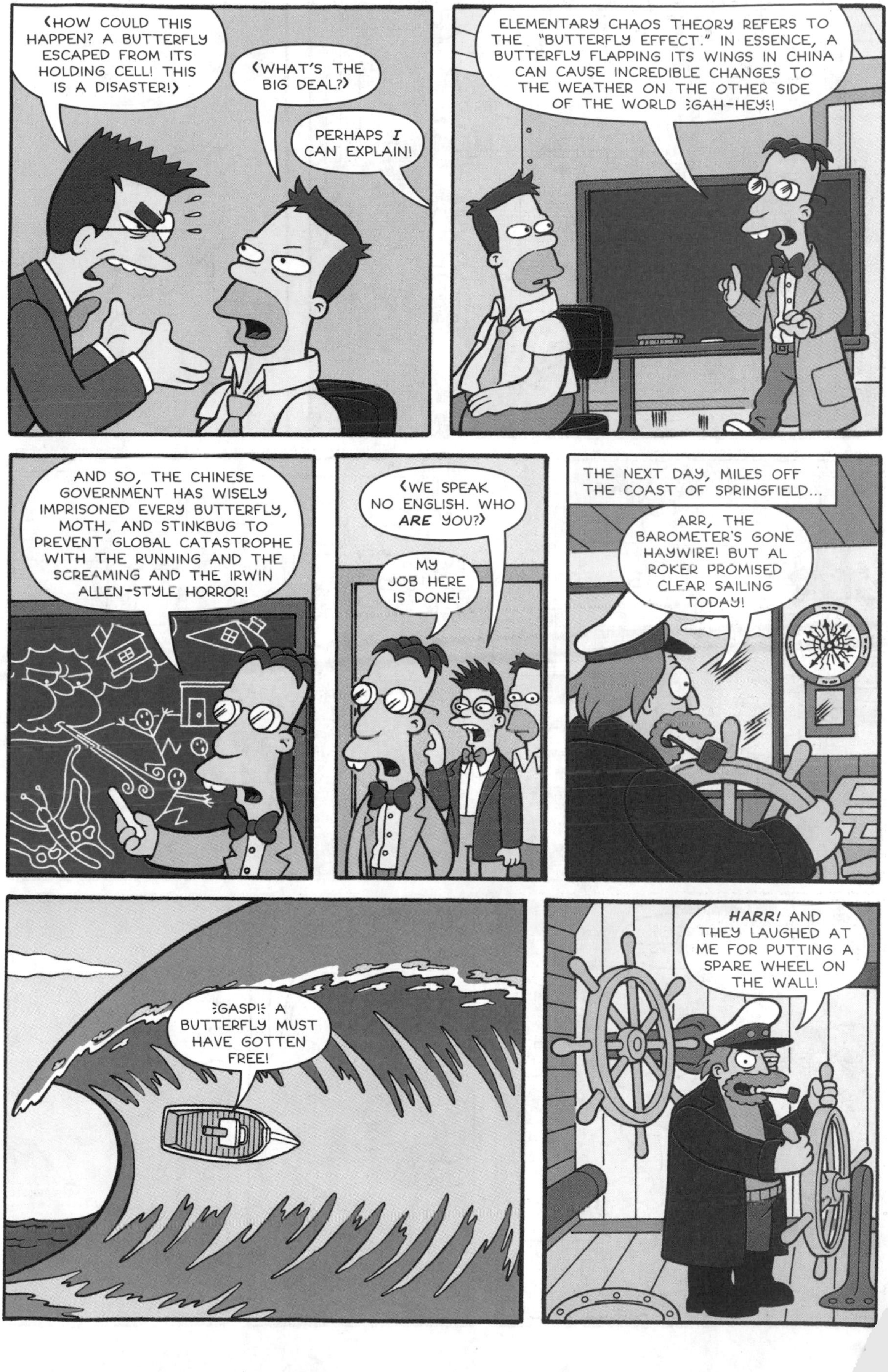
‹HOW COULD THIS HAPPEN? A BUTTERFLY ESCAPED FROM ITS HOLDING CELL! THIS IS A DISASTER!›
‹WHAT'S THE BIG DEAL?›
PERHAPS *I* CAN EXPLAIN!
ELEMENTARY CHAOS THEORY REFERS TO THE "BUTTERFLY EFFECT." IN ESSENCE, A BUTTERFLY FLAPPING ITS WINGS IN CHINA CAN CAUSE INCREDIBLE CHANGES TO THE WEATHER ON THE OTHER SIDE OF THE WORLD ⁝GAH-HEY⁝!
AND SO, THE CHINESE GOVERNMENT HAS WISELY IMPRISONED EVERY BUTTERFLY, MOTH, AND STINKBUG TO PREVENT GLOBAL CATASTROPHE WITH THE RUNNING AND THE SCREAMING AND THE IRWIN ALLEN-STYLE HORROR!
‹WE SPEAK NO ENGLISH. WHO ***ARE*** YOU?›
MY JOB HERE IS DONE!
THE NEXT DAY, MILES OFF THE COAST OF SPRINGFIELD...
ARR, THE BAROMETER'S GONE HAYWIRE! BUT AL ROKER PROMISED CLEAR SAILING TODAY!
⁝GASP!⁝ A BUTTERFLY MUST HAVE GOTTEN FREE!
HARR! AND THEY LAUGHED AT ME FOR PUTTING A SPARE WHEEL ON THE WALL!

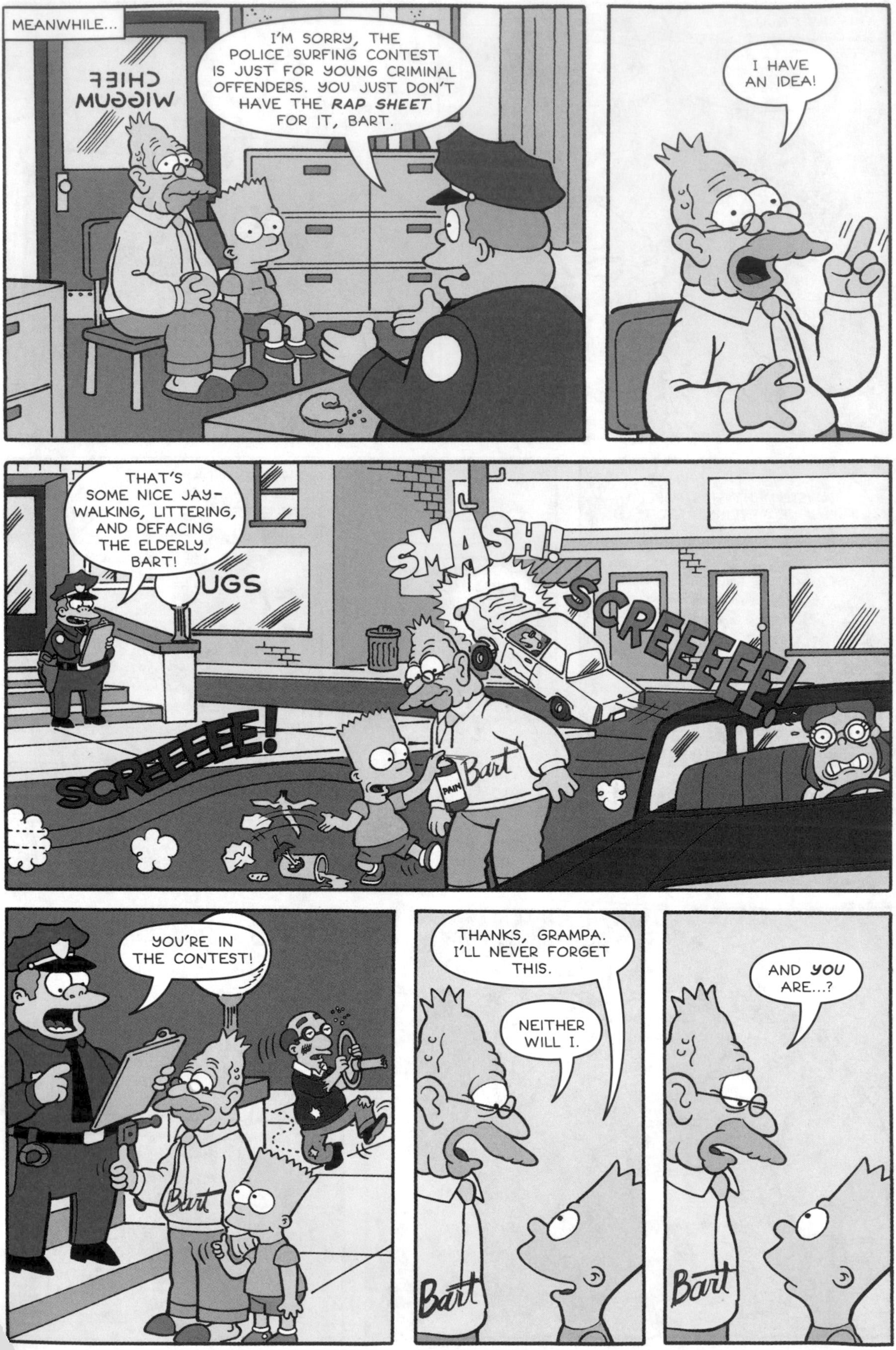
MEANWHILE...
CHIEF WIGGUM
I'M SORRY, THE POLICE SURFING CONTEST IS JUST FOR YOUNG CRIMINAL OFFENDERS. YOU JUST DON'T HAVE THE ***RAP SHEET*** FOR IT, BART.
I HAVE AN IDEA!
THAT'S SOME NICE JAY-WALKING, LITTERING, AND DEFACING THE ELDERLY, BART!
UGS
SMASH!
SCREEEEEE!
SCREEEEEE!
PAIN
Bart
YOU'RE IN THE CONTEST!
Bart
THANKS, GRAMPA. I'LL NEVER FORGET THIS.
NEITHER WILL I.
Bart
AND ***YOU*** ARE...?
Bart

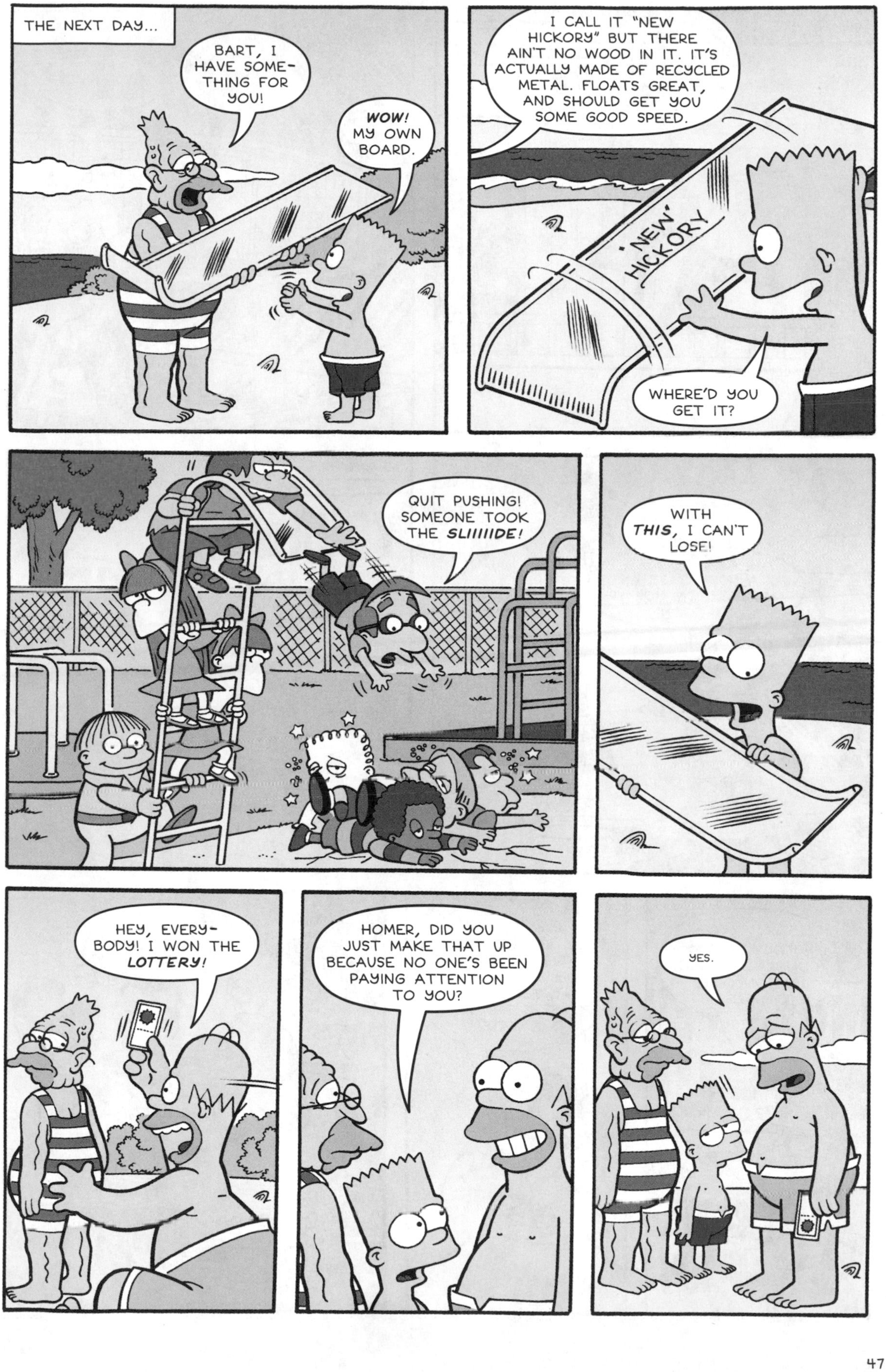
THE NEXT DAY...
BART, I HAVE SOME-THING FOR YOU!
WOW! MY OWN BOARD.
I CALL IT "NEW HICKORY" BUT THERE AIN'T NO WOOD IN IT. IT'S ACTUALLY MADE OF RECYCLED METAL. FLOATS GREAT, AND SHOULD GET YOU SOME GOOD SPEED.
'NEW' HICKORY
WHERE'D YOU GET IT?
QUIT PUSHING! SOMEONE TOOK THE SLIIIIIDE!
WITH THIS, I CAN'T LOSE!
HEY, EVERY-BODY! I WON THE LOTTERY!
HOMER, DID YOU JUST MAKE THAT UP BECAUSE NO ONE'S BEEN PAYING ATTENTION TO YOU?
YES.

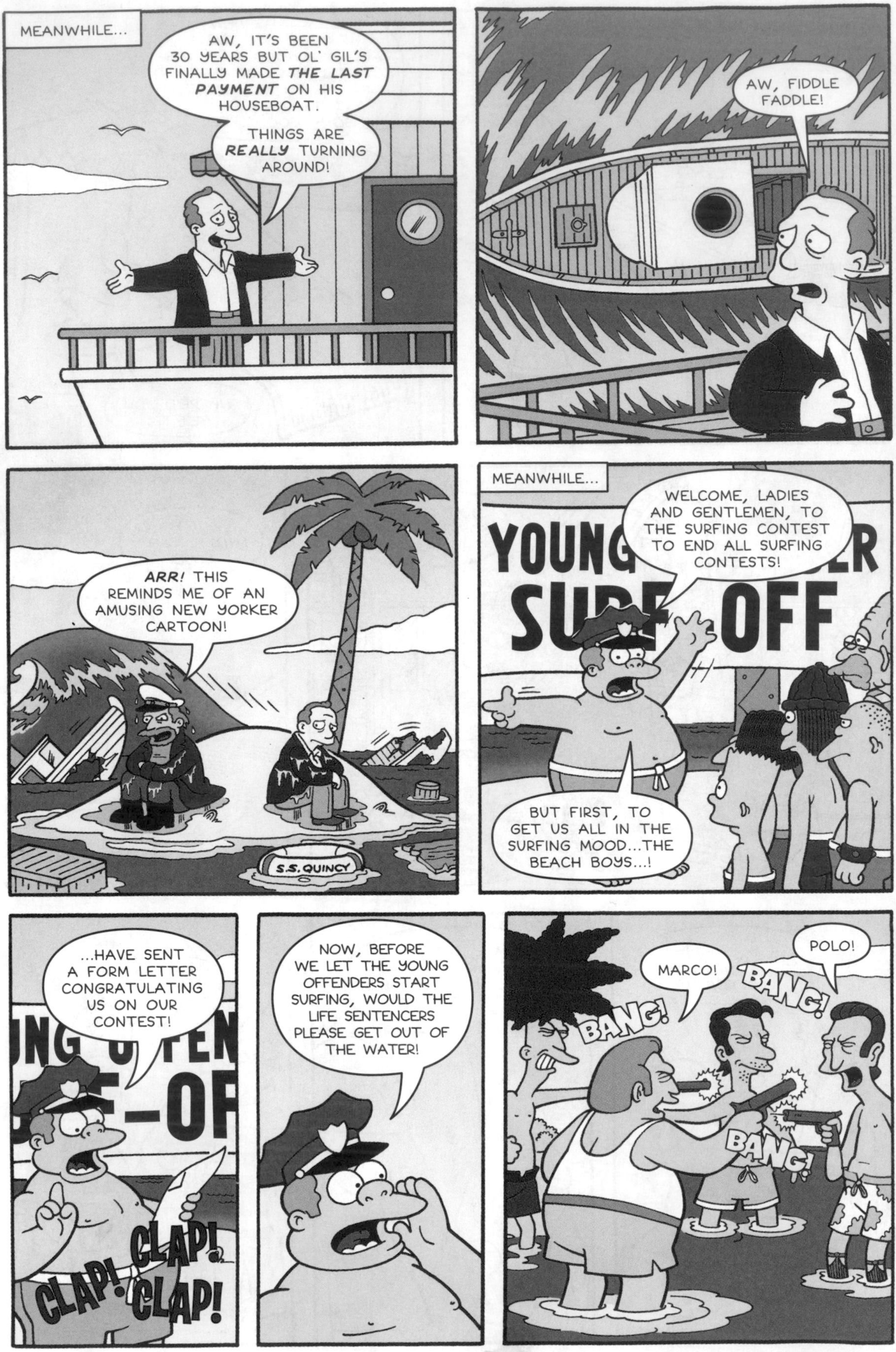

MEANWHILE...
AW, IT'S BEEN 30 YEARS BUT OL' GIL'S FINALLY MADE ***THE LAST PAYMENT*** ON HIS HOUSEBOAT.
THINGS ARE ***REALLY*** TURNING AROUND!
AW, FIDDLE FADDLE!
ARR! THIS REMINDS ME OF AN AMUSING NEW YORKER CARTOON!
S.S. QUINCY
MEANWHILE...
YOUNG
ER
SUR
OFF
WELCOME, LADIES AND GENTLEMEN, TO THE SURFING CONTEST TO END ALL SURFING CONTESTS!
BUT FIRST, TO GET US ALL IN THE SURFING MOOD...THE BEACH BOYS...!
...HAVE SENT A FORM LETTER CONGRATULATING US ON OUR CONTEST!
CLAP! CLAP! CLAP!
NOW, BEFORE WE LET THE YOUNG OFFENDERS START SURFING, WOULD THE LIFE SENTENCERS PLEASE GET OUT OF THE WATER!
MARCO!
POLO!
BANG!
BANG!
BANG!

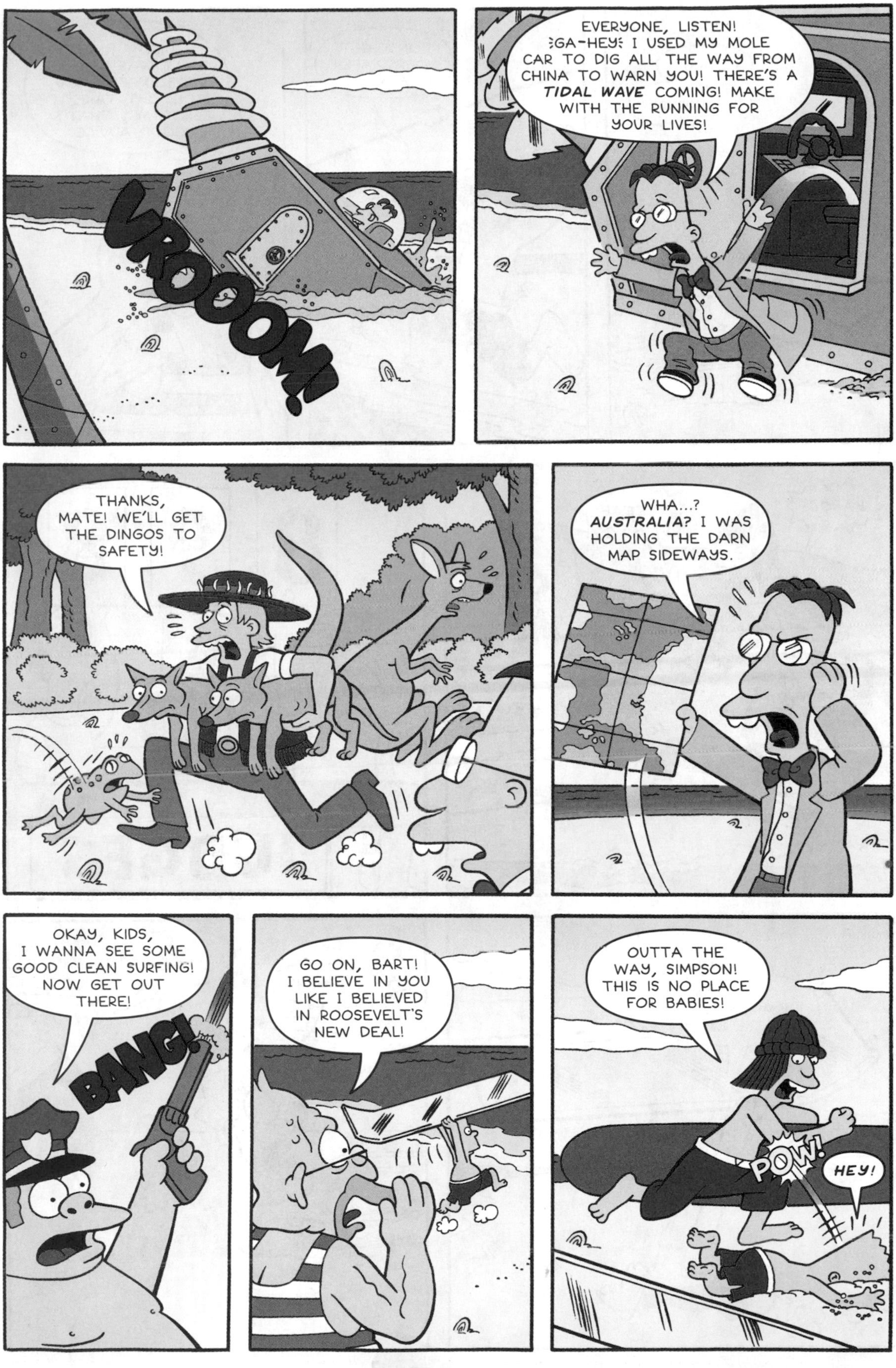
VROOOOM!
EVERYONE, LISTEN! ⁝GA-HEY⁝ I USED MY MOLE CAR TO DIG ALL THE WAY FROM CHINA TO WARN YOU! THERE'S A *TIDAL WAVE* COMING! MAKE WITH THE RUNNING FOR YOUR LIVES!
THANKS, MATE! WE'LL GET THE DINGOS TO SAFETY!
WHA...? *AUSTRALIA*? I WAS HOLDING THE DARN MAP SIDEWAYS.
OKAY, KIDS, I WANNA SEE SOME GOOD CLEAN SURFING! NOW GET OUT THERE!
BANG!
GO ON, BART! I BELIEVE IN YOU LIKE I BELIEVED IN ROOSEVELT'S NEW DEAL!
OUTTA THE WAY, SIMPSON! THIS IS NO PLACE FOR BABIES!
POW!
HEY!

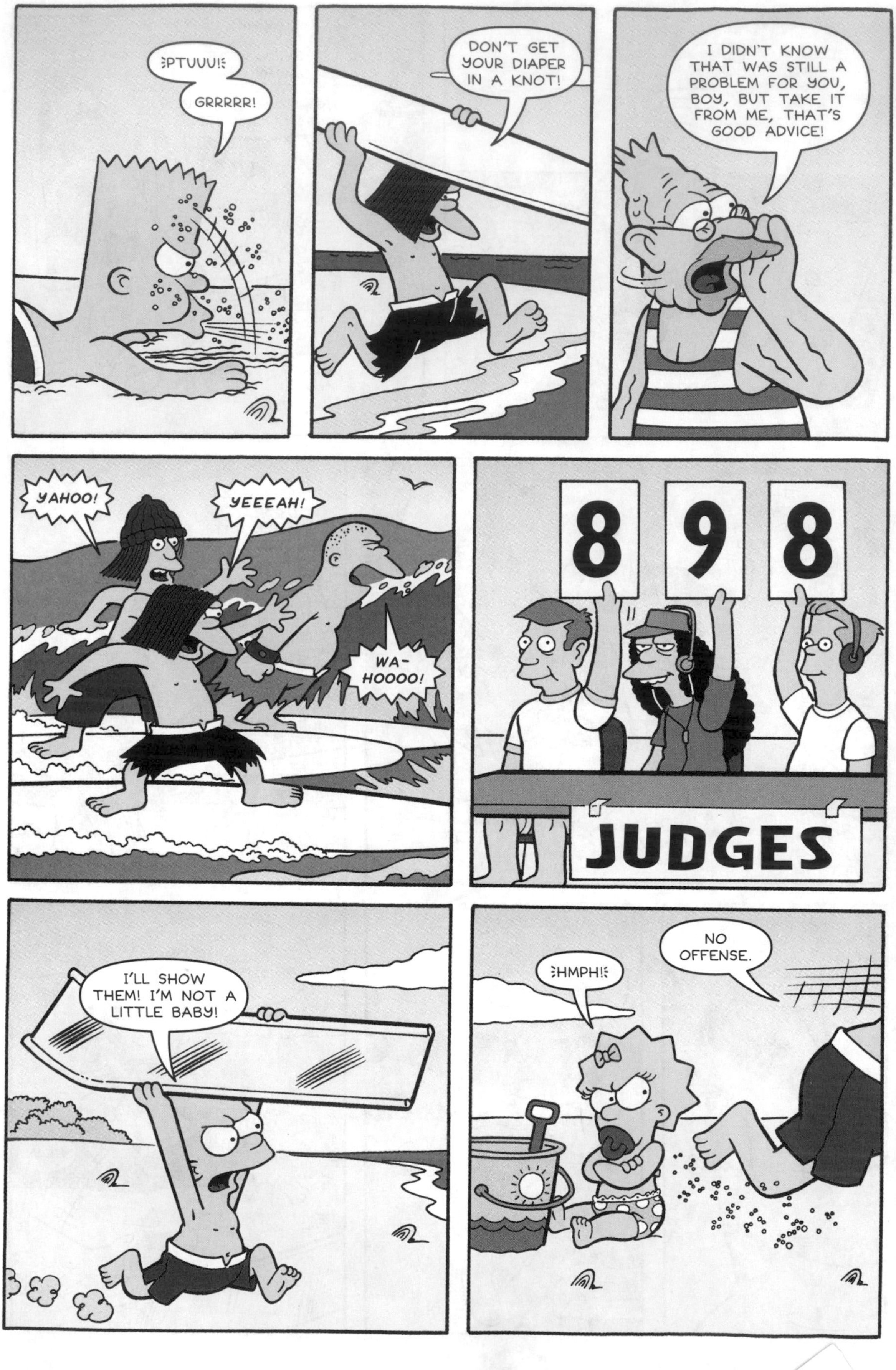
PTUUU!
GRRRRR!
DON'T GET YOUR DIAPER IN A KNOT!
I DIDN'T KNOW THAT WAS STILL A PROBLEM FOR YOU, BOY, BUT TAKE IT FROM ME, THAT'S GOOD ADVICE!
YAHOO!
YEEEAH!
WA-HOOOO!
8
9
8
JUDGES
I'LL SHOW THEM! I'M NOT A LITTLE BABY!
HMPH!
NO OFFENSE.

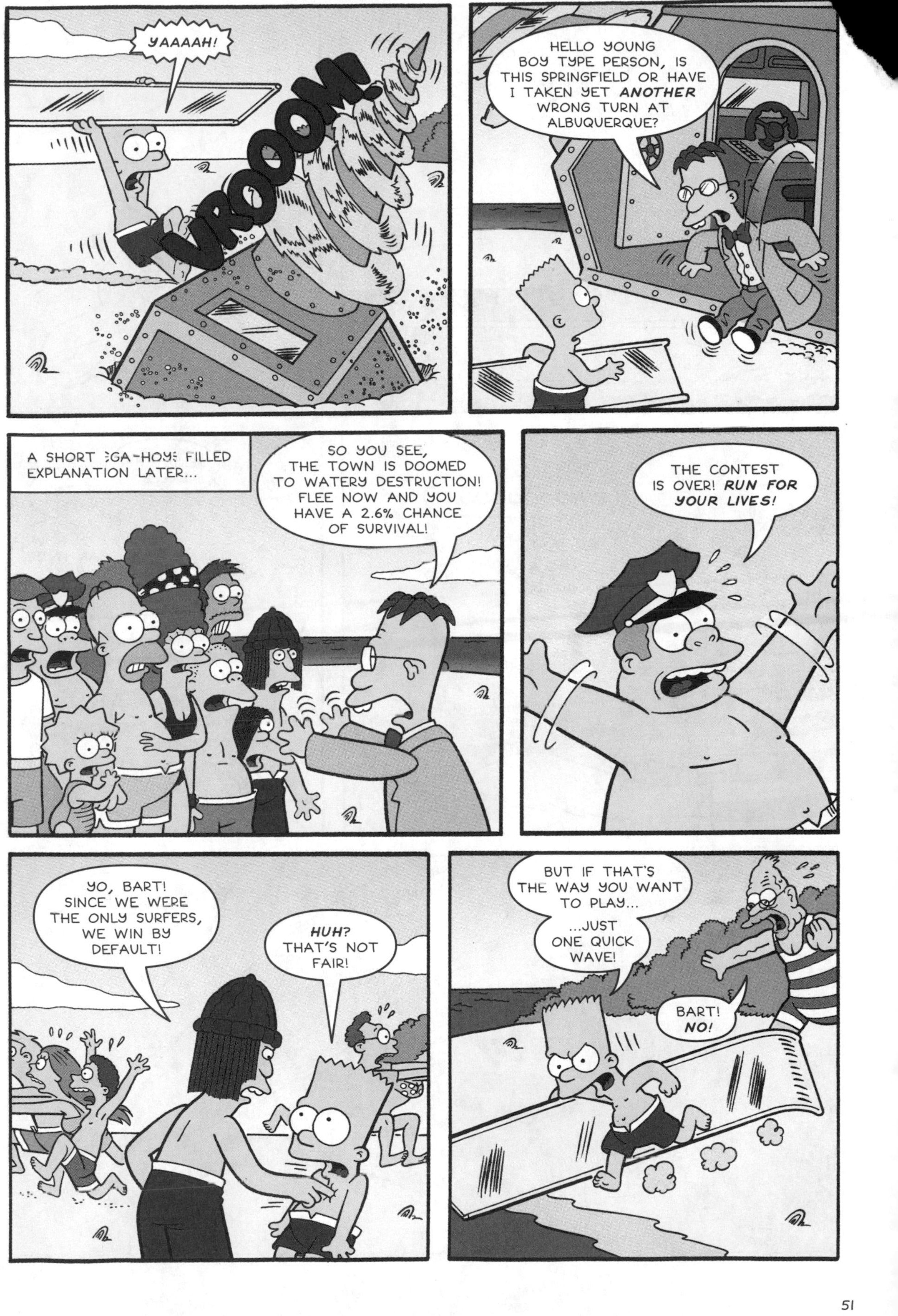
YAAAAH!
VROOOM!
HELLO YOUNG BOY TYPE PERSON, IS THIS SPRINGFIELD OR HAVE I TAKEN YET ANOTHER WRONG TURN AT ALBUQUERQUE?
A SHORT GA-HOY FILLED EXPLANATION LATER...
SO YOU SEE, THE TOWN IS DOOMED TO WATERY DESTRUCTION! FLEE NOW AND YOU HAVE A 2.6% CHANCE OF SURVIVAL!
THE CONTEST IS OVER! RUN FOR YOUR LIVES!
YO, BART! SINCE WE WERE THE ONLY SURFERS, WE WIN BY DEFAULT!
HUH? THAT'S NOT FAIR!
BUT IF THAT'S THE WAY YOU WANT TO PLAY...
...JUST ONE QUICK WAVE!
BART! NO!

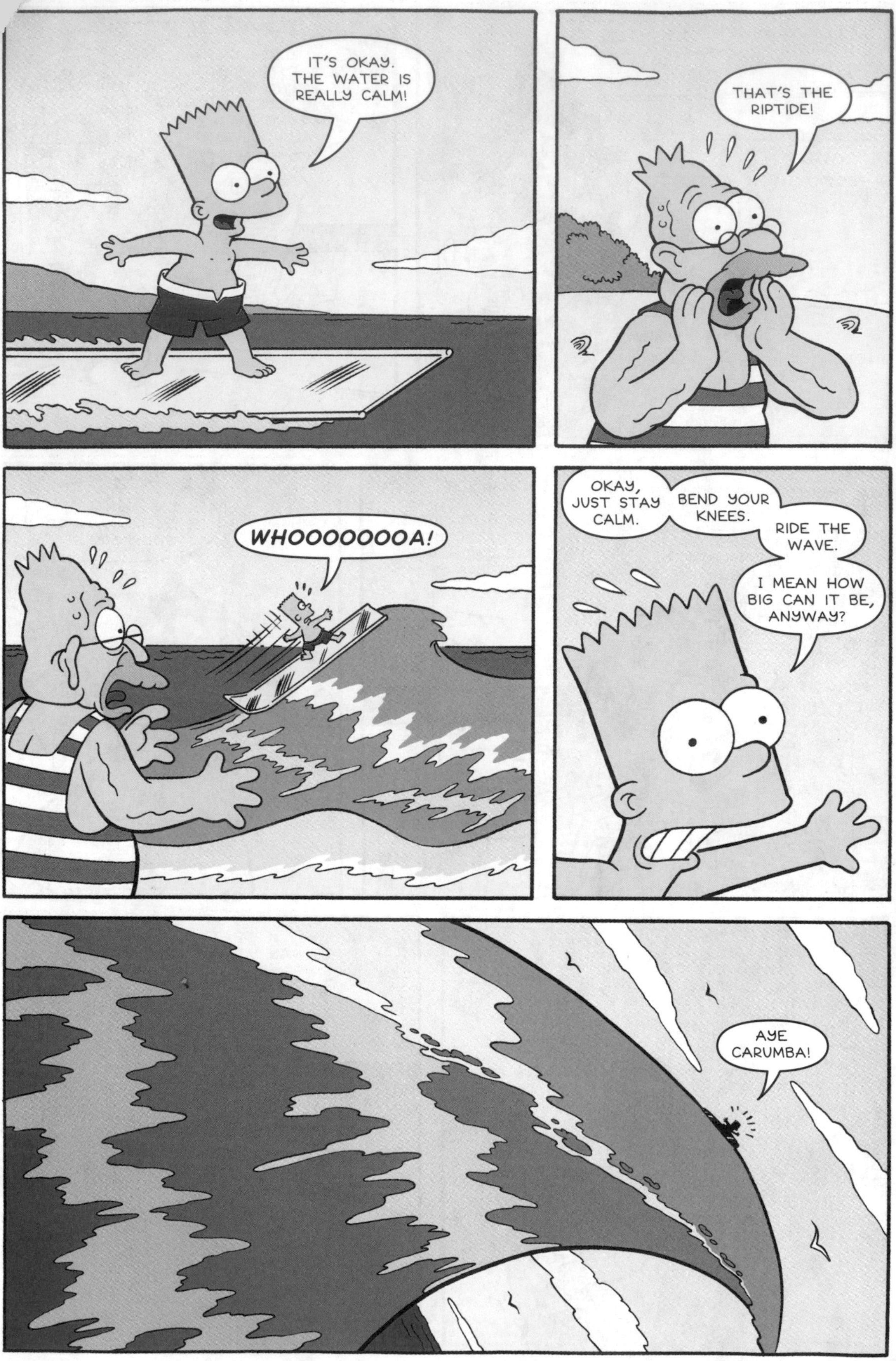
IT'S OKAY. THE WATER IS REALLY CALM!
THAT'S THE RIPTIDE!
WHOOOOOOOA!
OKAY, JUST STAY CALM.
BEND YOUR KNEES.
RIDE THE WAVE.
I MEAN HOW BIG CAN IT BE, ANYWAY?
AYE CARUMBA!

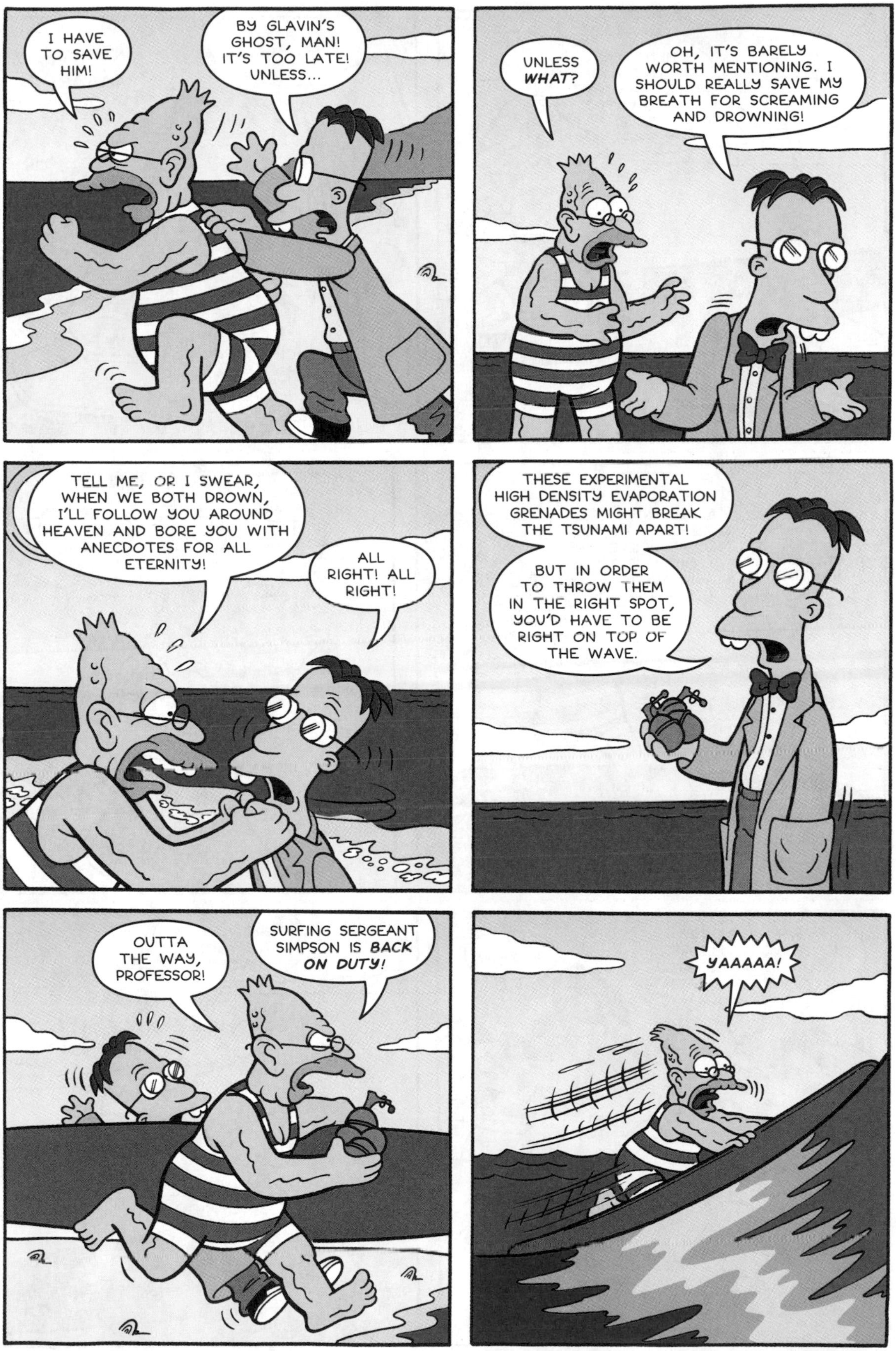
I HAVE TO SAVE HIM!
BY GLAVIN'S GHOST, MAN! IT'S TOO LATE! UNLESS...
UNLESS *WHAT*?
OH, IT'S BARELY WORTH MENTIONING. I SHOULD REALLY SAVE MY BREATH FOR SCREAMING AND DROWNING!
TELL ME, OR I SWEAR, WHEN WE BOTH DROWN, I'LL FOLLOW YOU AROUND HEAVEN AND BORE YOU WITH ANECDOTES FOR ALL ETERNITY!
ALL RIGHT! ALL RIGHT!
THESE EXPERIMENTAL HIGH DENSITY EVAPORATION GRENADES MIGHT BREAK THE TSUNAMI APART!
BUT IN ORDER TO THROW THEM IN THE RIGHT SPOT, YOU'D HAVE TO BE RIGHT ON TOP OF THE WAVE.
OUTTA THE WAY, PROFESSOR!
SURFING SERGEANT SIMPSON IS *BACK ON DUTY*!
YAAAAA!

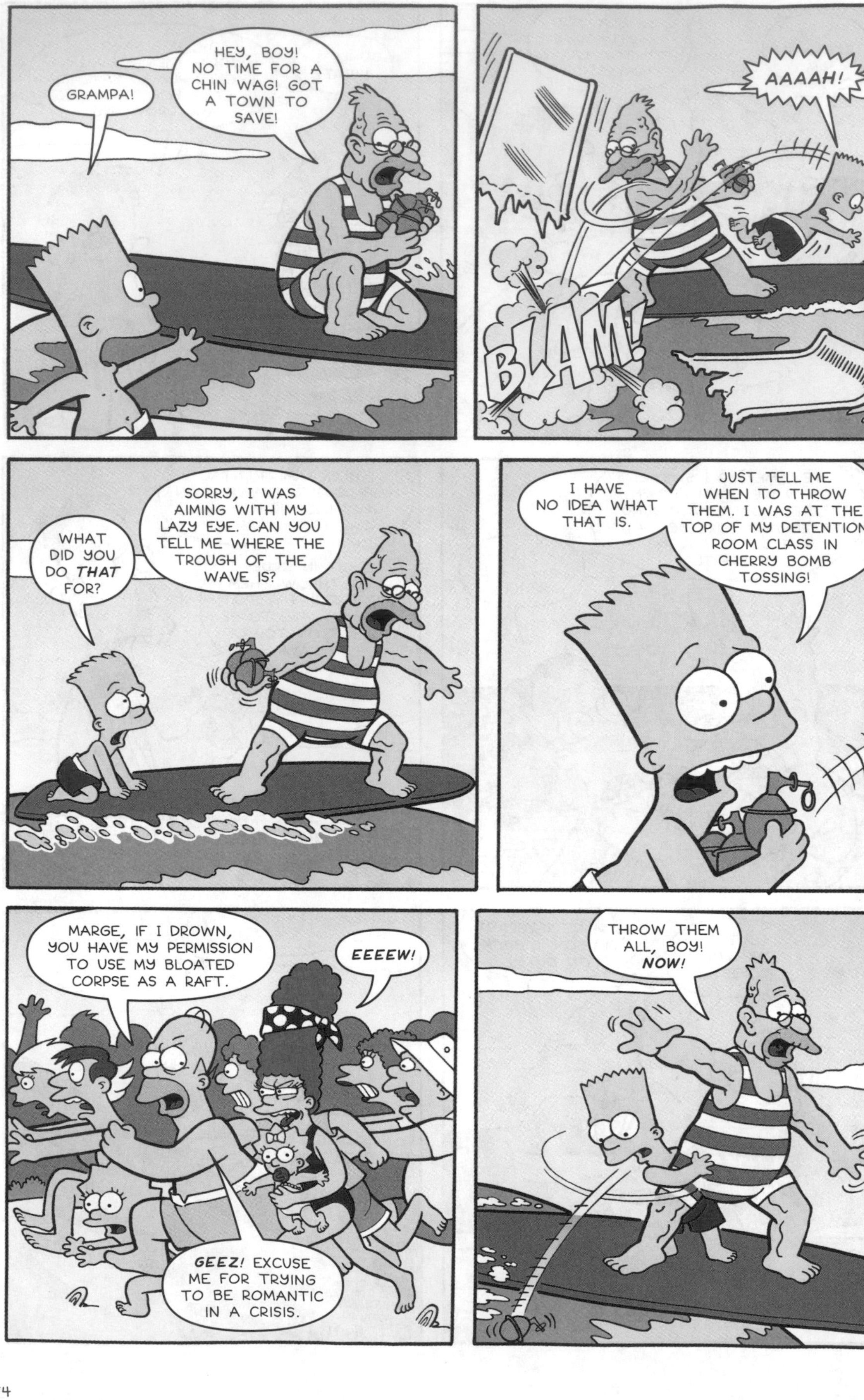
GRAMPA!
HEY, BOY! NO TIME FOR A CHIN WAG! GOT A TOWN TO SAVE!
AAAAH!
BLAM!
WHAT DID YOU DO *THAT* FOR?
SORRY, I WAS AIMING WITH MY LAZY EYE. CAN YOU TELL ME WHERE THE TROUGH OF THE WAVE IS?
I HAVE NO IDEA WHAT THAT IS.
JUST TELL ME WHEN TO THROW THEM. I WAS AT THE TOP OF MY DETENTION ROOM CLASS IN CHERRY BOMB TOSSING!
MARGE, IF I DROWN, YOU HAVE MY PERMISSION TO USE MY BLOATED CORPSE AS A RAFT.
EEEEW!
GEEZ! EXCUSE ME FOR TRYING TO BE ROMANTIC IN A CRISIS.
THROW THEM ALL, BOY! *NOW!*

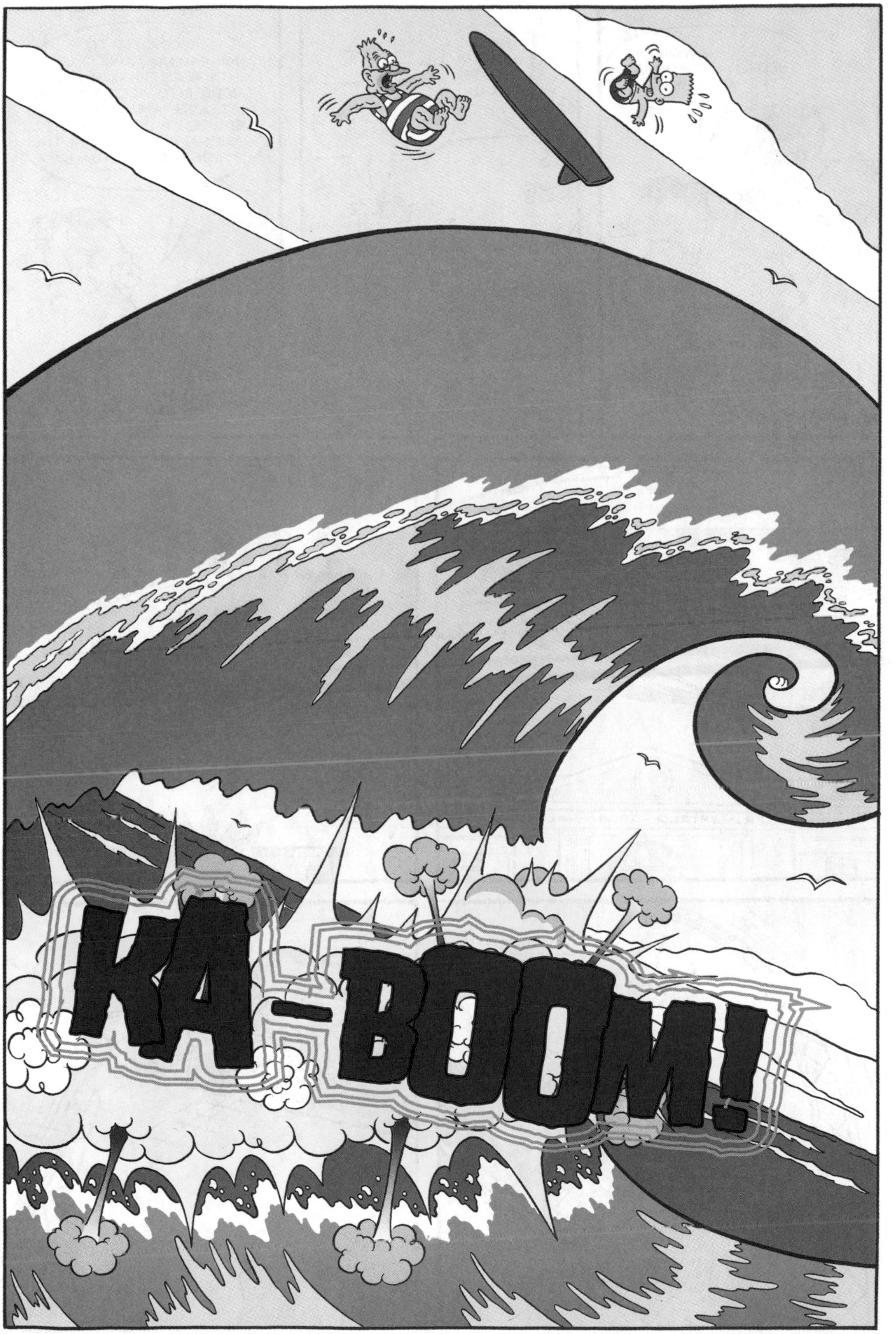
KA-BOOM!

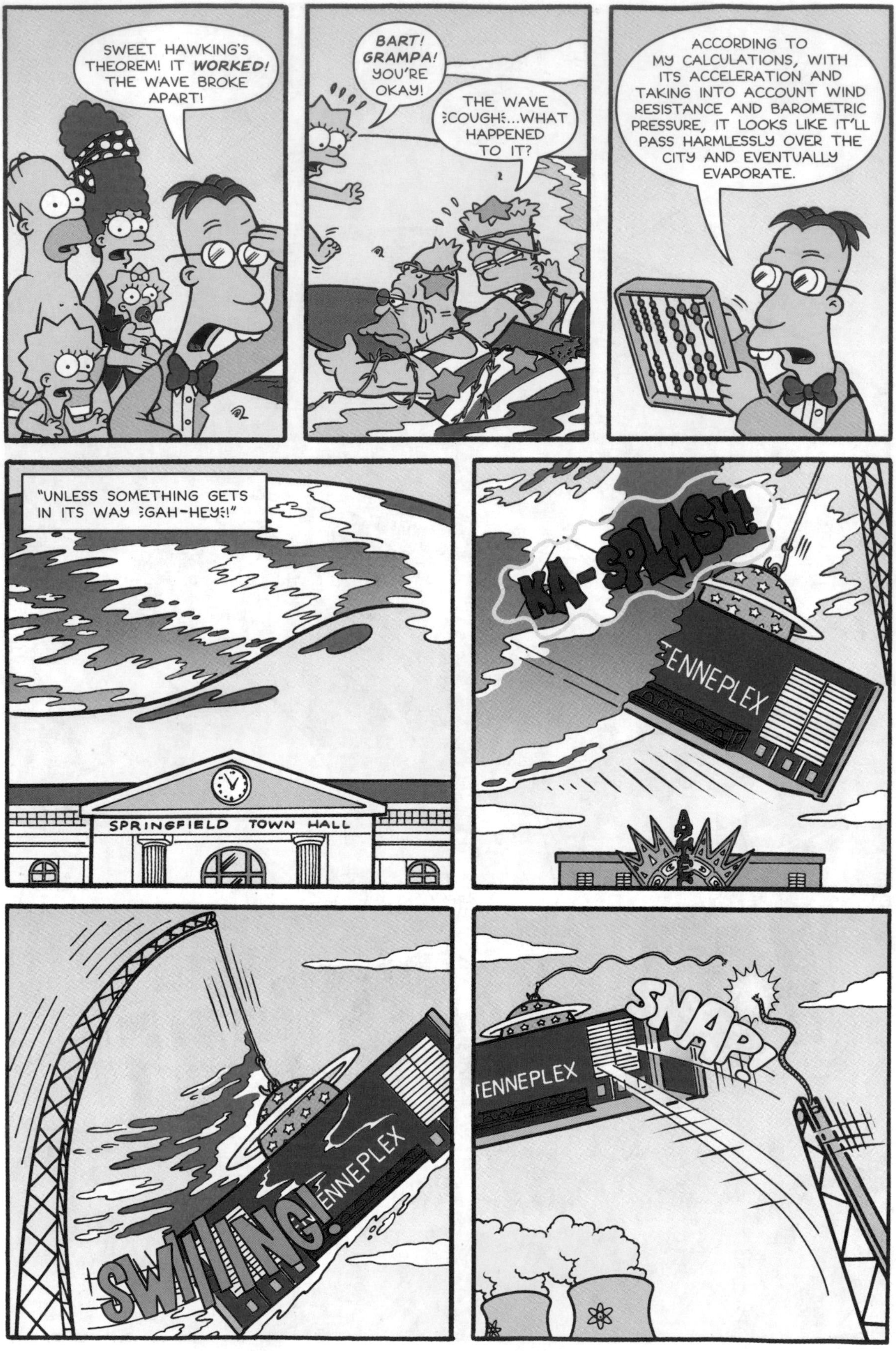
SWEET HAWKING'S THEOREM! IT **WORKED!** THE WAVE BROKE APART!
BART! GRAMPA! YOU'RE OKAY!
THE WAVE *COUGH*...WHAT HAPPENED TO IT?
ACCORDING TO MY CALCULATIONS, WITH ITS ACCELERATION AND TAKING INTO ACCOUNT WIND RESISTANCE AND BAROMETRIC PRESSURE, IT LOOKS LIKE IT'LL PASS HARMLESSLY OVER THE CITY AND EVENTUALLY EVAPORATE.
"UNLESS SOMETHING GETS IN ITS WAY *GAH-HEY*!"
SPRINGFIELD TOWN HALL
KA-SPLASH!
TENNEPLEX
SWIIIING!
TENNEPLEX
TENNEPLEX
SNAP!

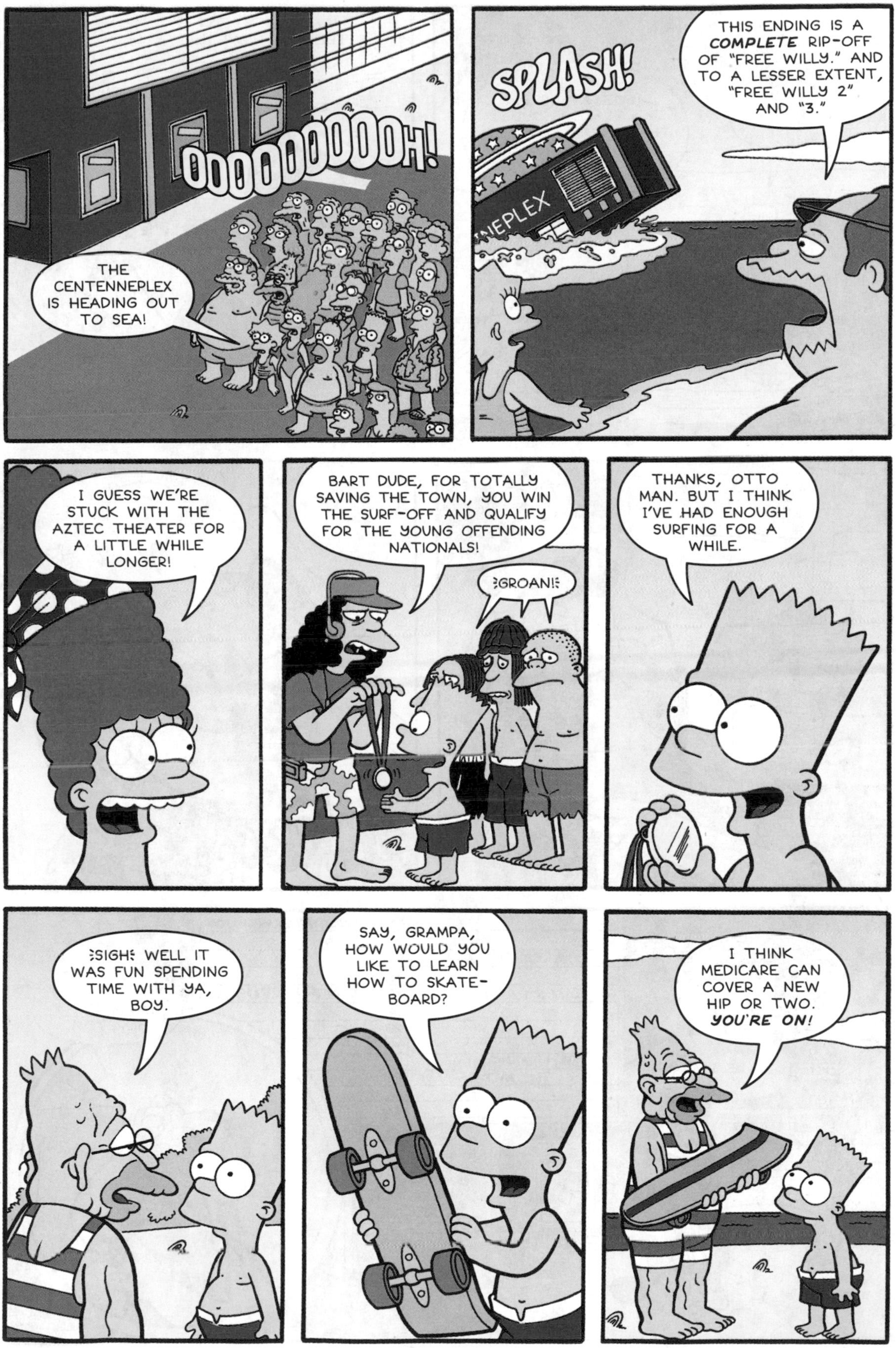
OOOOOOOOOOH!
THE CENTENNEPLEX IS HEADING OUT TO SEA!
SPLASH!
NEPLEX
THIS ENDING IS A COMPLETE RIP-OFF OF "FREE WILLY." AND TO A LESSER EXTENT, "FREE WILLY 2" AND "3."
I GUESS WE'RE STUCK WITH THE AZTEC THEATER FOR A LITTLE WHILE LONGER!
BART DUDE, FOR TOTALLY SAVING THE TOWN, YOU WIN THE SURF-OFF AND QUALIFY FOR THE YOUNG OFFENDING NATIONALS!
GROAN!
THANKS, OTTO MAN. BUT I THINK I'VE HAD ENOUGH SURFING FOR A WHILE.
SIGH WELL IT WAS FUN SPENDING TIME WITH YA, BOY.
SAY, GRAMPA, HOW WOULD YOU LIKE TO LEARN HOW TO SKATE-BOARD?
I THINK MEDICARE CAN COVER A NEW HIP OR TWO. YOU'RE ON!

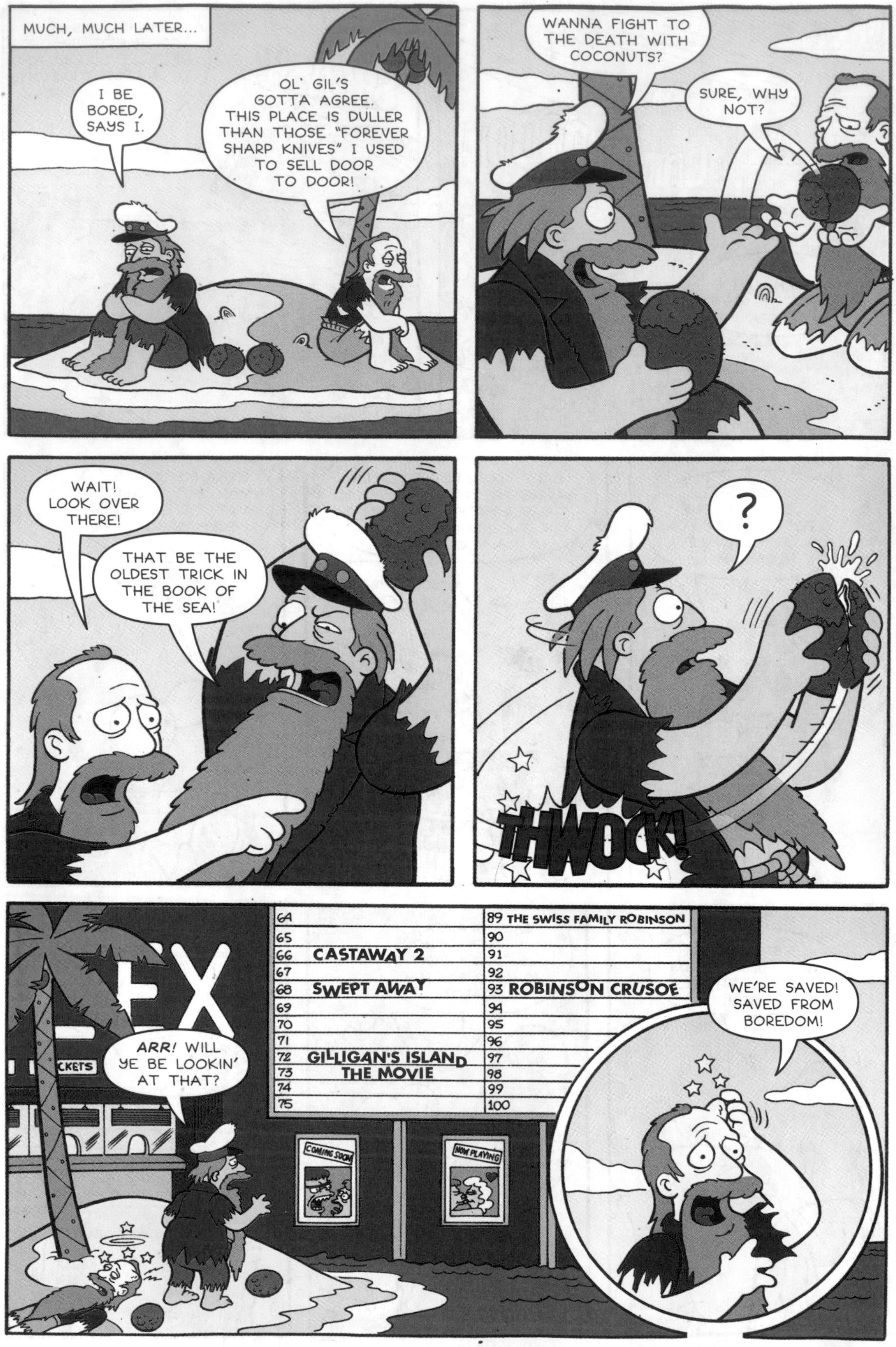

MUCH, MUCH LATER...
I BE BORED, SAYS I.
OL' GIL'S GOTTA AGREE. THIS PLACE IS DULLER THAN THOSE "FOREVER SHARP KNIVES" I USED TO SELL DOOR TO DOOR!
WANNA FIGHT TO THE DEATH WITH COCONUTS?
SURE, WHY NOT?
WAIT! LOOK OVER THERE!
THAT BE THE OLDEST TRICK IN THE BOOK OF THE SEA!
?
THWOCK!
64
65
66 CASTAWAY 2
67
68 SWEPT AWAY
69
70
71
72 GILLIGAN'S ISLAND THE MOVIE
73
74
75
89 THE SWISS FAMILY ROBINSON
90
91
92
93 ROBINSON CRUSOE
94
95
96
97
98
99
100
CKETS
COMING SOON
NOW PLAYING
ARR! WILL YE BE LOOKIN' AT THAT?
WE'RE SAVED! SAVED FROM BOREDOM!

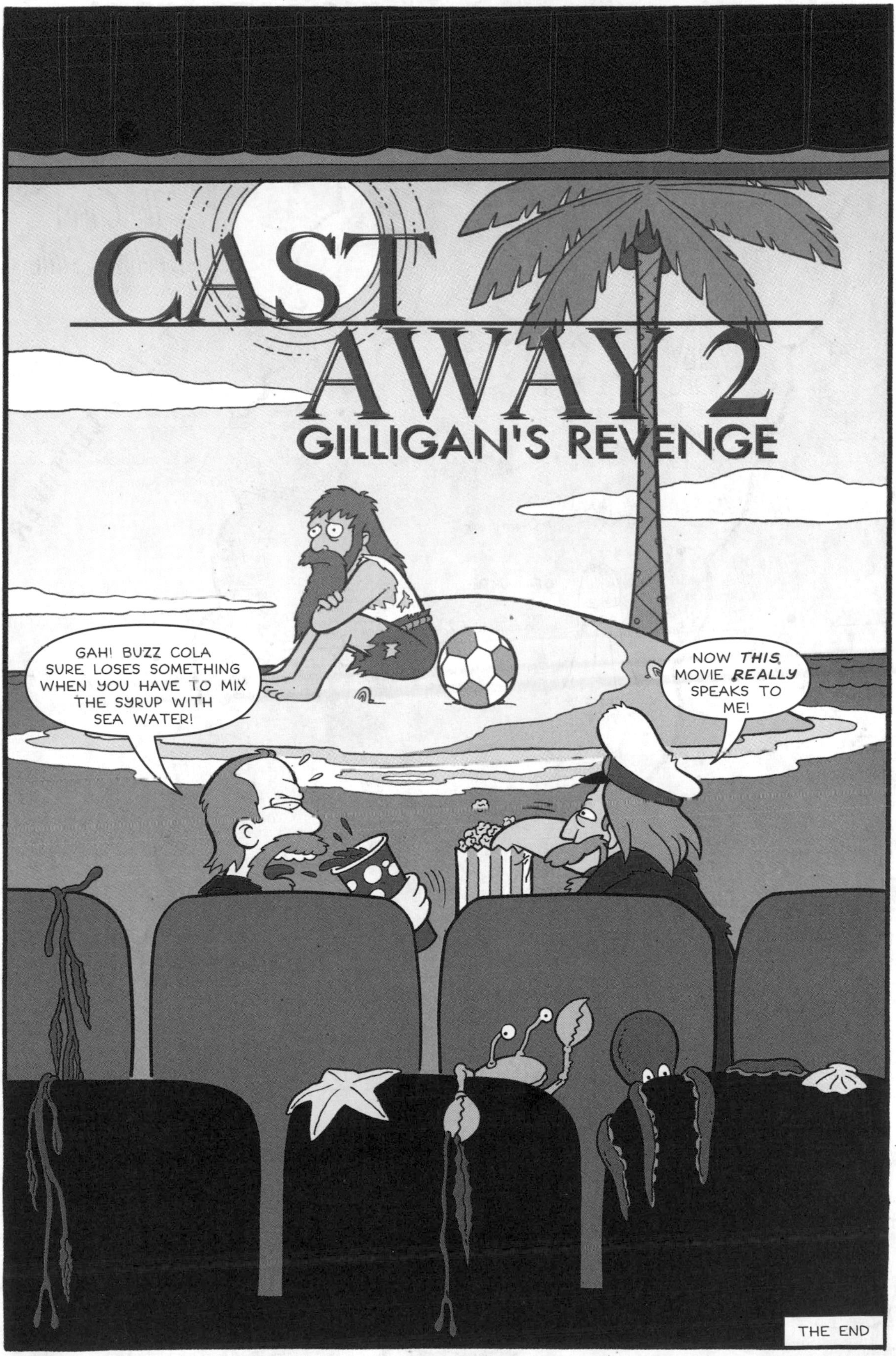
CAST AWAY 2
GILLIGAN'S REVENGE
GAH! BUZZ COLA SURE LOSES SOMETHING WHEN YOU HAVE TO MIX THE SYRUP WITH SEA WATER!
NOW THIS MOVIE REALLY SPEAKS TO ME!
THE END

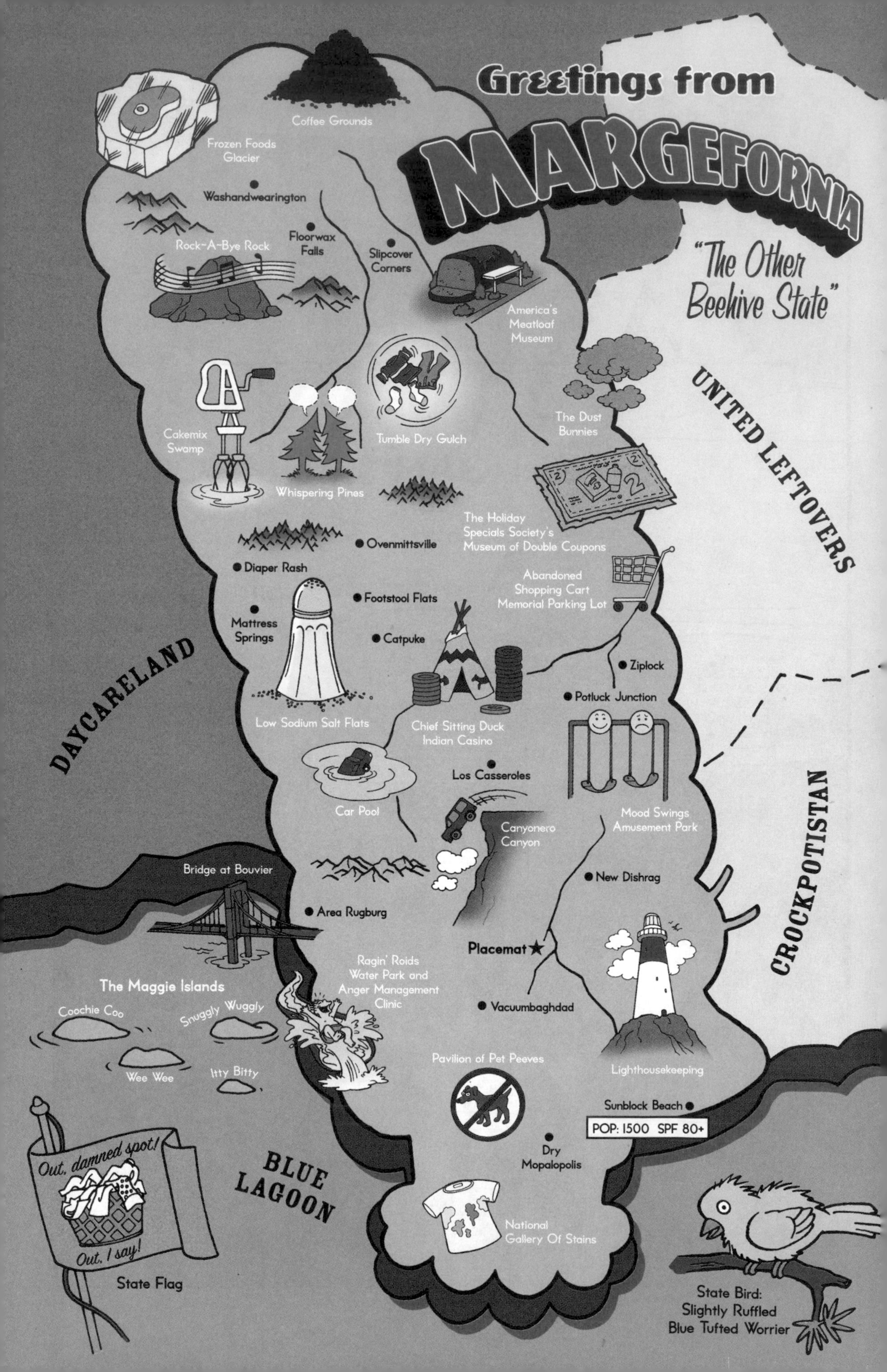
Greetings from
MARGEFORNIA
"The Other Beehive State"
Coffee Grounds
Frozen Foods Glacier
Washandwearington
Floorwax Falls
Slipcover Corners
Rock-A-Bye Rock
America's Meatloaf Museum
UNITED LEFTOVERS
The Dust Bunnies
Cakemix Swamp
Tumble Dry Gulch
Whispering Pines
The Holiday Specials Society's Museum of Double Coupons
Ovenmittsville
Diaper Rash
Abandoned Shopping Cart Memorial Parking Lot
Footstool Flats
Mattress Springs
Catpuke
DAYCARELAND
Ziplock
Potluck Junction
Low Sodium Salt Flats
Chief Sitting Duck Indian Casino
Los Casseroles
Car Pool
Canyonero Canyon
Mood Swings Amusement Park
CROCKPOTISTAN
Bridge at Bouvier
New Dishrag
Area Rugburg
Placemat
Ragin' Roids Water Park and Anger Management Clinic
The Maggie Islands
Coochie Coo
Snuggly Wuggly
Wee Wee
Itty Bitty
Vacuumbaghdad
Pavilion of Pet Peeves
Lighthousekeeping
Sunblock Beach
POP: 1500 SPF 80+
Out, damned spot!
Out, I say!
State Flag
BLUE LAGOON
Dry Mopalopolis
National Gallery Of Stains
State Bird: Slightly Ruffled Blue Tufted Worrier

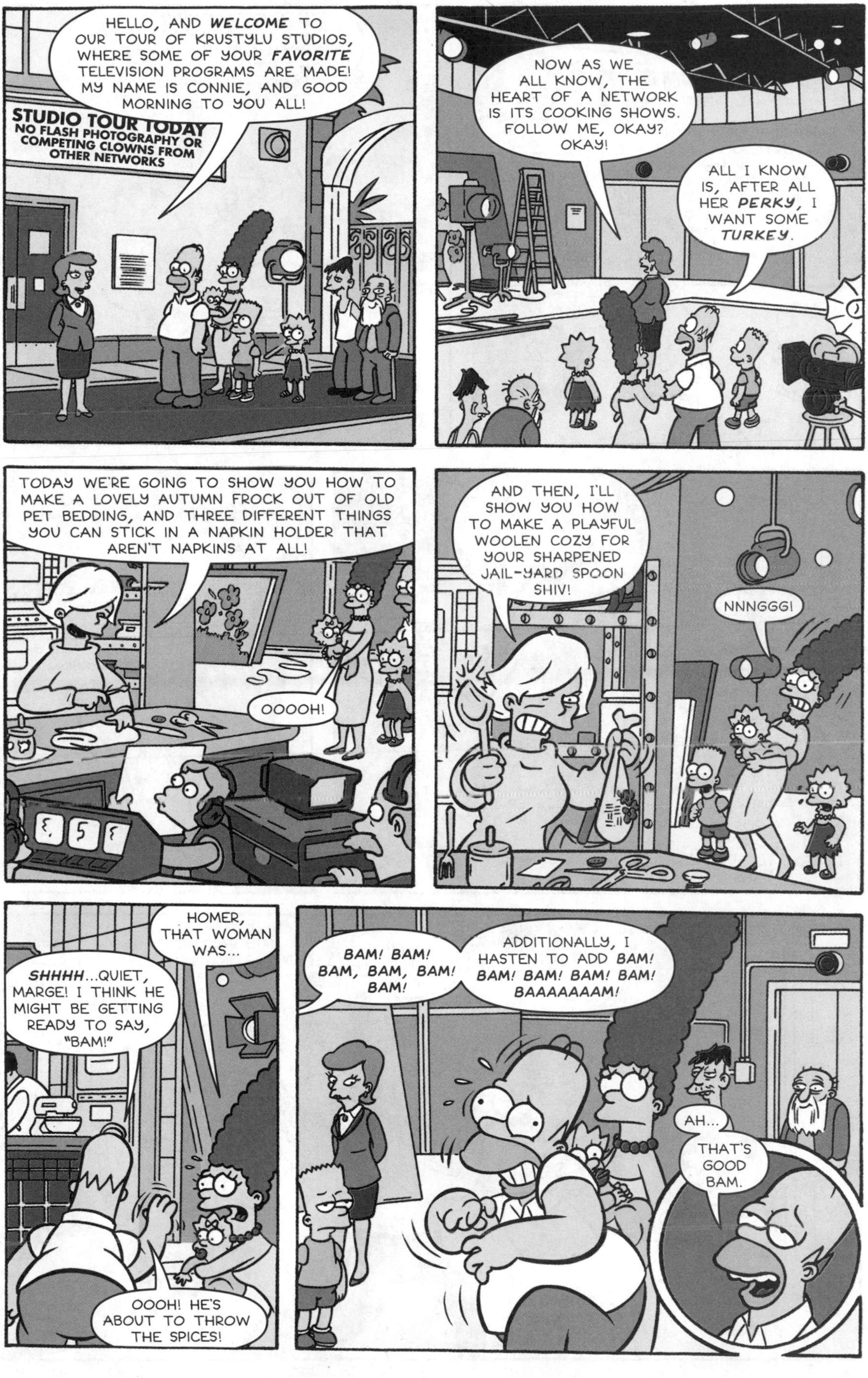
HELLO, AND WELCOME TO OUR TOUR OF KRUSTYLU STUDIOS, WHERE SOME OF YOUR FAVORITE TELEVISION PROGRAMS ARE MADE! MY NAME IS CONNIE, AND GOOD MORNING TO YOU ALL!
STUDIO TOUR TODAY
NO FLASH PHOTOGRAPHY OR COMPETING CLOWNS FROM OTHER NETWORKS
NOW AS WE ALL KNOW, THE HEART OF A NETWORK IS ITS COOKING SHOWS. FOLLOW ME, OKAY? OKAY!
ALL I KNOW IS, AFTER ALL HER PERKY, I WANT SOME TURKEY.
TODAY WE'RE GOING TO SHOW YOU HOW TO MAKE A LOVELY AUTUMN FROCK OUT OF OLD PET BEDDING, AND THREE DIFFERENT THINGS YOU CAN STICK IN A NAPKIN HOLDER THAT AREN'T NAPKINS AT ALL!
OOOOH!
AND THEN, I'LL SHOW YOU HOW TO MAKE A PLAYFUL WOOLEN COZY FOR YOUR SHARPENED JAIL-YARD SPOON SHIV!
NNNGGG!
HOMER, THAT WOMAN WAS...
SHHHH...QUIET, MARGE! I THINK HE MIGHT BE GETTING READY TO SAY, "BAM!"
OOOH! HE'S ABOUT TO THROW THE SPICES!
BAM! BAM! BAM, BAM, BAM! BAM!
ADDITIONALLY, I HASTEN TO ADD BAM! BAM! BAM! BAM! BAM! BAAAAAAAM!
AH...
THAT'S GOOD BAM.

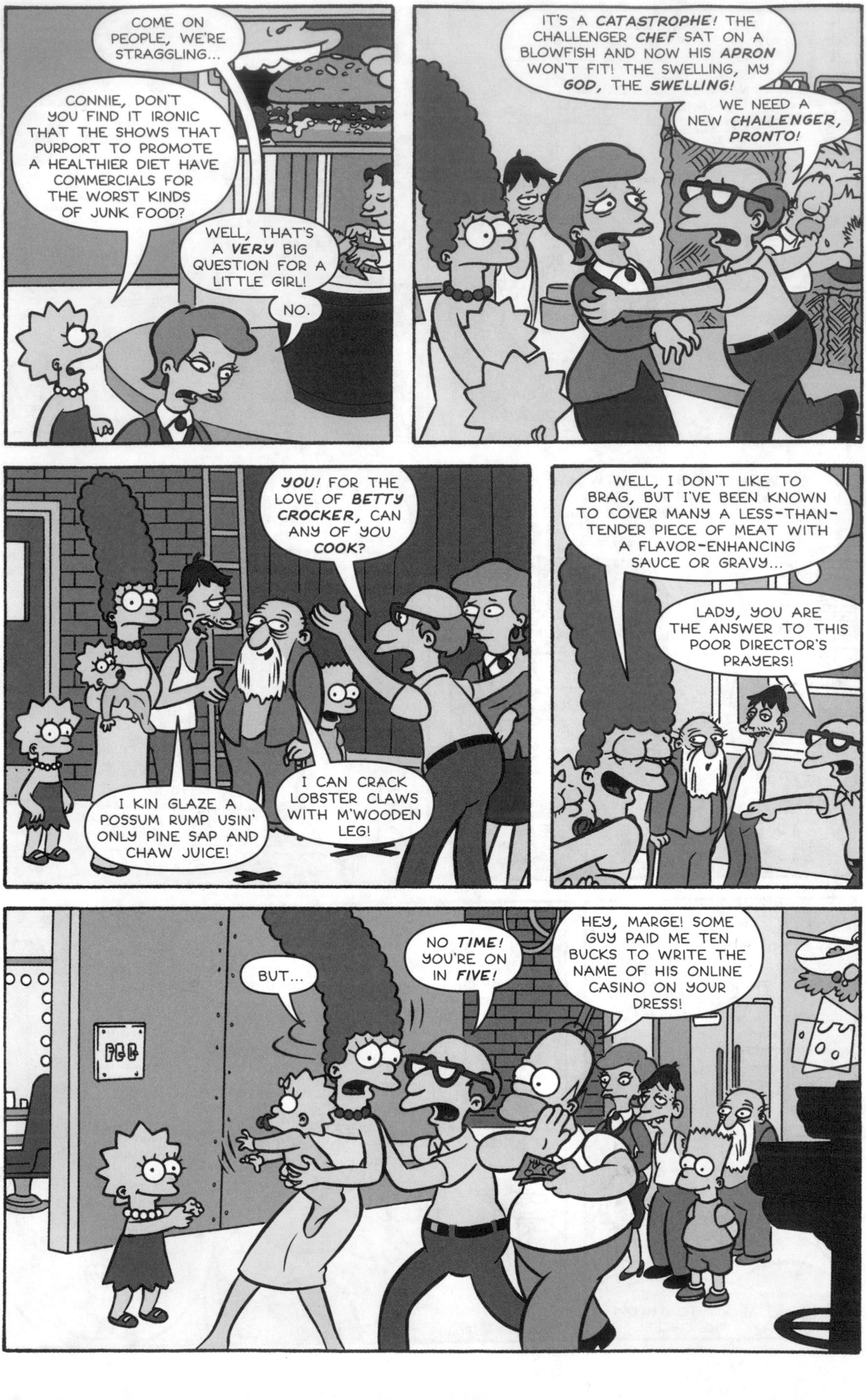
COME ON PEOPLE, WE'RE STRAGGLING...
CONNIE, DON'T YOU FIND IT IRONIC THAT THE SHOWS THAT PURPORT TO PROMOTE A HEALTHIER DIET HAVE COMMERCIALS FOR THE WORST KINDS OF JUNK FOOD?
WELL, THAT'S A VERY BIG QUESTION FOR A LITTLE GIRL!
NO.
IT'S A CATASTROPHE! THE CHALLENGER CHEF SAT ON A BLOWFISH AND NOW HIS APRON WON'T FIT! THE SWELLING, MY GOD, THE SWELLING!
WE NEED A NEW CHALLENGER, PRONTO!
YOU! FOR THE LOVE OF BETTY CROCKER, CAN ANY OF YOU COOK?
I KIN GLAZE A POSSUM RUMP USIN' ONLY PINE SAP AND CHAW JUICE!
I CAN CRACK LOBSTER CLAWS WITH M'WOODEN LEG!
WELL, I DON'T LIKE TO BRAG, BUT I'VE BEEN KNOWN TO COVER MANY A LESS-THAN-TENDER PIECE OF MEAT WITH A FLAVOR-ENHANCING SAUCE OR GRAVY...
LADY, YOU ARE THE ANSWER TO THIS POOR DIRECTOR'S PRAYERS!
BUT...
NO TIME! YOU'RE ON IN FIVE!
HEY, MARGE! SOME GUY PAID ME TEN BUCKS TO WRITE THE NAME OF HIS ONLINE CASINO ON YOUR DRESS!

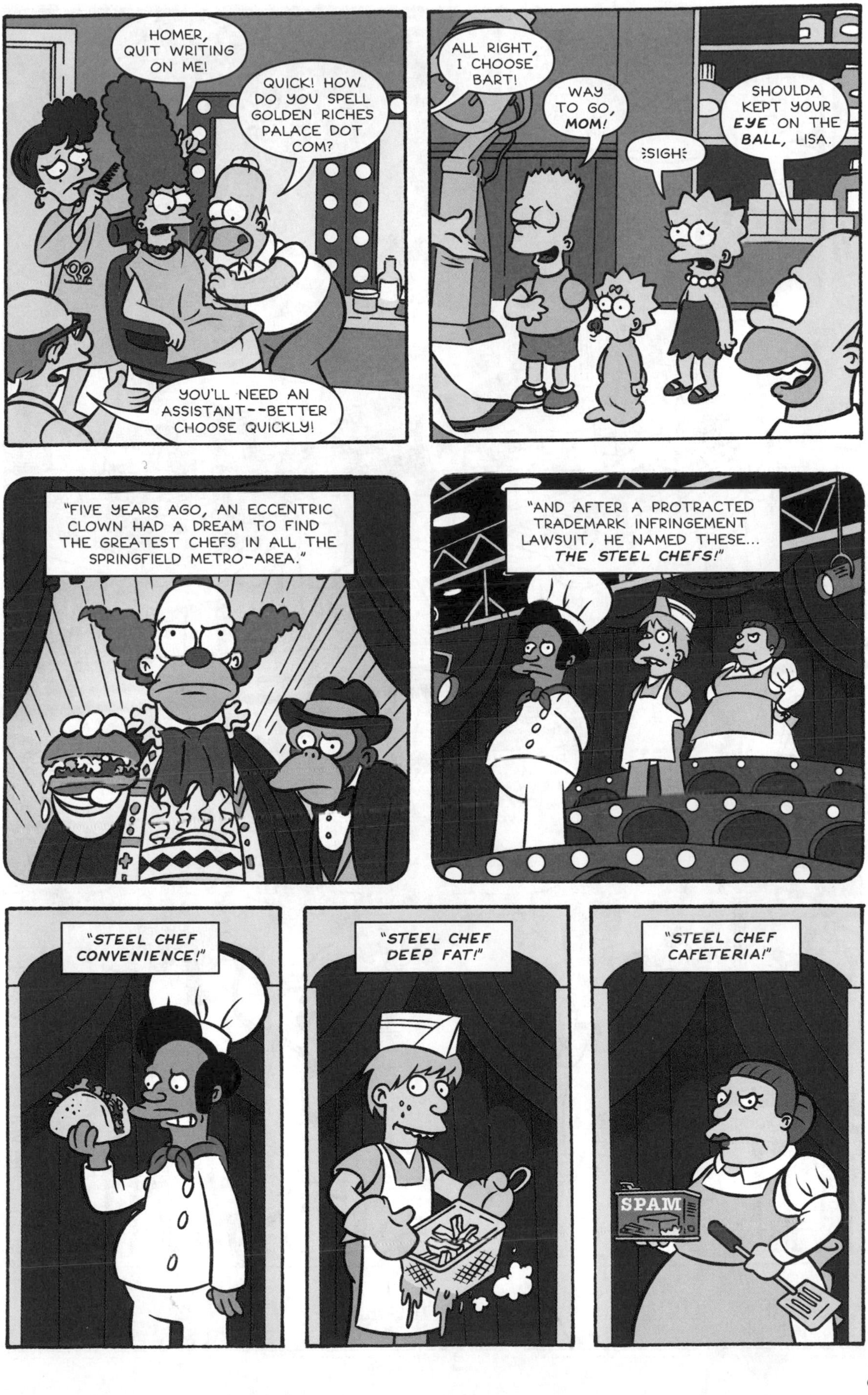
HOMER, QUIT WRITING ON ME!
QUICK! HOW DO YOU SPELL GOLDEN RICHES PALACE DOT COM?
YOU'LL NEED AN ASSISTANT--BETTER CHOOSE QUICKLY!
ALL RIGHT, I CHOOSE BART!
WAY TO GO, MOM!
SIGH
SHOULDA KEPT YOUR EYE ON THE BALL, LISA.
"FIVE YEARS AGO, AN ECCENTRIC CLOWN HAD A DREAM TO FIND THE GREATEST CHEFS IN ALL THE SPRINGFIELD METRO-AREA."
"AND AFTER A PROTRACTED TRADEMARK INFRINGEMENT LAWSUIT, HE NAMED THESE... THE STEEL CHEFS!"
"STEEL CHEF CONVENIENCE!"
"STEEL CHEF DEEP FAT!"
"STEEL CHEF CAFETERIA!"
SPAM

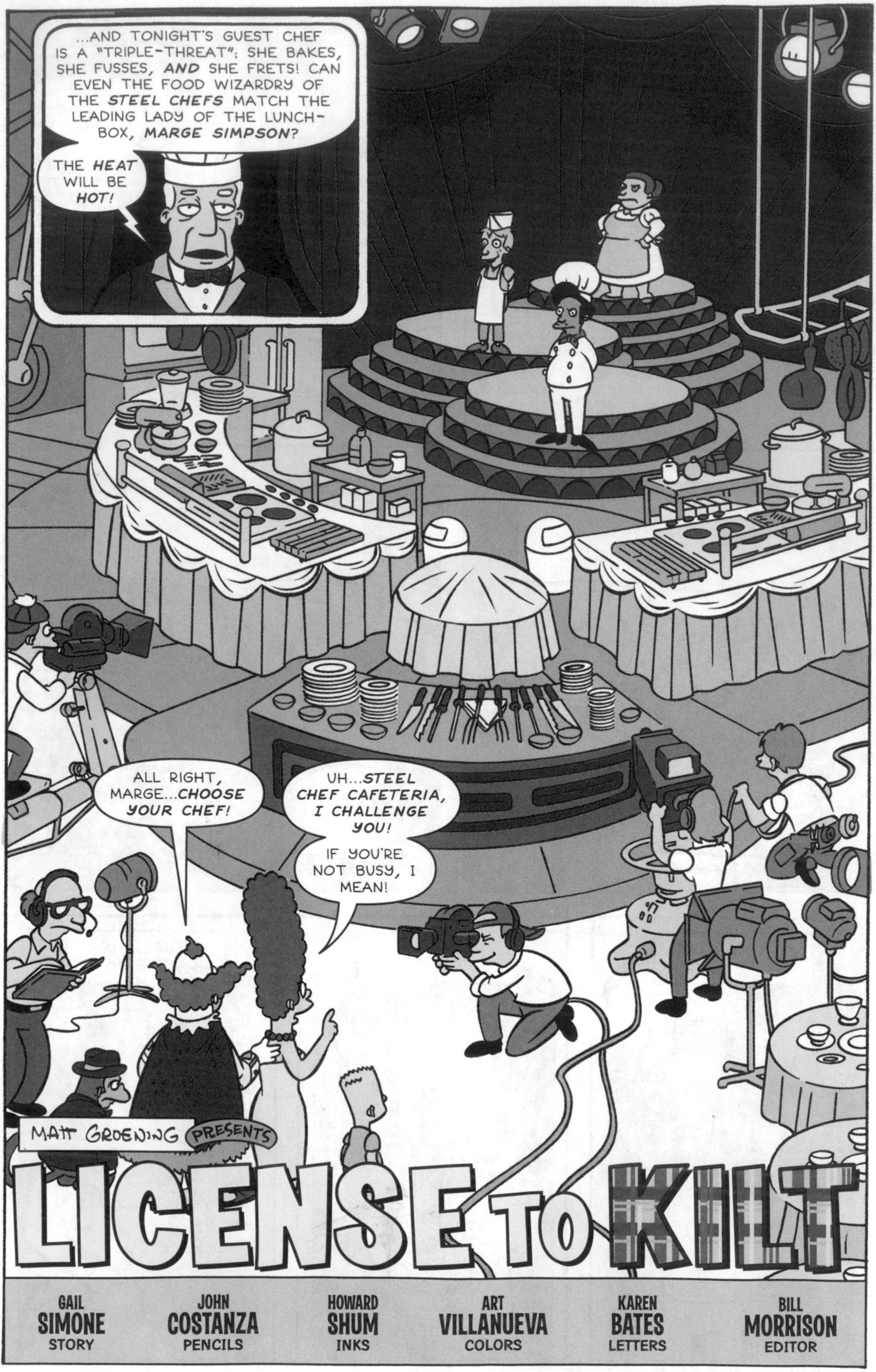
...AND TONIGHT'S GUEST CHEF IS A "TRIPLE-THREAT"; SHE BAKES, SHE FUSSES, AND SHE FRETS! CAN EVEN THE FOOD WIZARDRY OF THE STEEL CHEFS MATCH THE LEADING LADY OF THE LUNCH-BOX, MARGE SIMPSON?
THE HEAT WILL BE HOT!
ALL RIGHT, MARGE...CHOOSE YOUR CHEF!
UH...STEEL CHEF CAFETERIA, I CHALLENGE YOU!
IF YOU'RE NOT BUSY, I MEAN!
MATT GROENING PRESENTS
LICENSE TO KILT

GAIL **SIMONE** STORY | JOHN **COSTANZA** PENCILS | HOWARD **SHUM** INKS | ART **VILLANUEVA** COLORS | KAREN **BATES** LETTERS | BILL **MORRISON** EDITOR

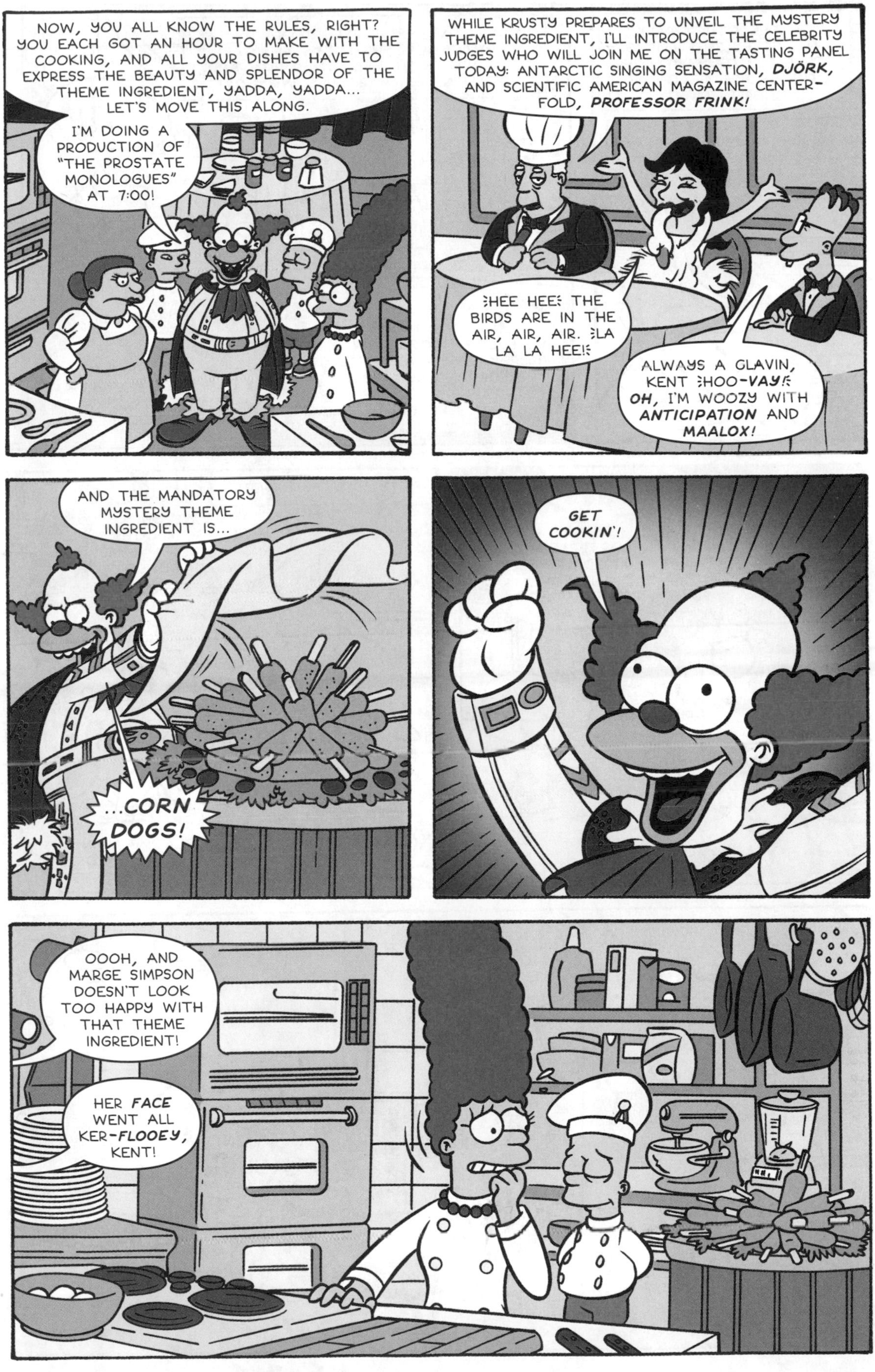
NOW, YOU ALL KNOW THE RULES, RIGHT? YOU EACH GOT AN HOUR TO MAKE WITH THE COOKING, AND ALL YOUR DISHES HAVE TO EXPRESS THE BEAUTY AND SPLENDOR OF THE THEME INGREDIENT, YADDA, YADDA... LET'S MOVE THIS ALONG.
I'M DOING A PRODUCTION OF "THE PROSTATE MONOLOGUES" AT 7:00!
WHILE KRUSTY PREPARES TO UNVEIL THE MYSTERY THEME INGREDIENT, I'LL INTRODUCE THE CELEBRITY JUDGES WHO WILL JOIN ME ON THE TASTING PANEL TODAY: ANTARCTIC SINGING SENSATION, DJÖRK, AND SCIENTIFIC AMERICAN MAGAZINE CENTER-FOLD, PROFESSOR FRINK!
HEE HEE THE BIRDS ARE IN THE AIR, AIR, AIR. LA LA LA HEE!
ALWAYS A GLAVIN, KENT HOO-VAY! OH, I'M WOOZY WITH ANTICIPATION AND MAALOX!
AND THE MANDATORY MYSTERY THEME INGREDIENT IS...
...CORN DOGS!
GET COOKIN'!
OOOH, AND MARGE SIMPSON DOESN'T LOOK TOO HAPPY WITH THAT THEME INGREDIENT!
HER FACE WENT ALL KER-FLOOEY, KENT!

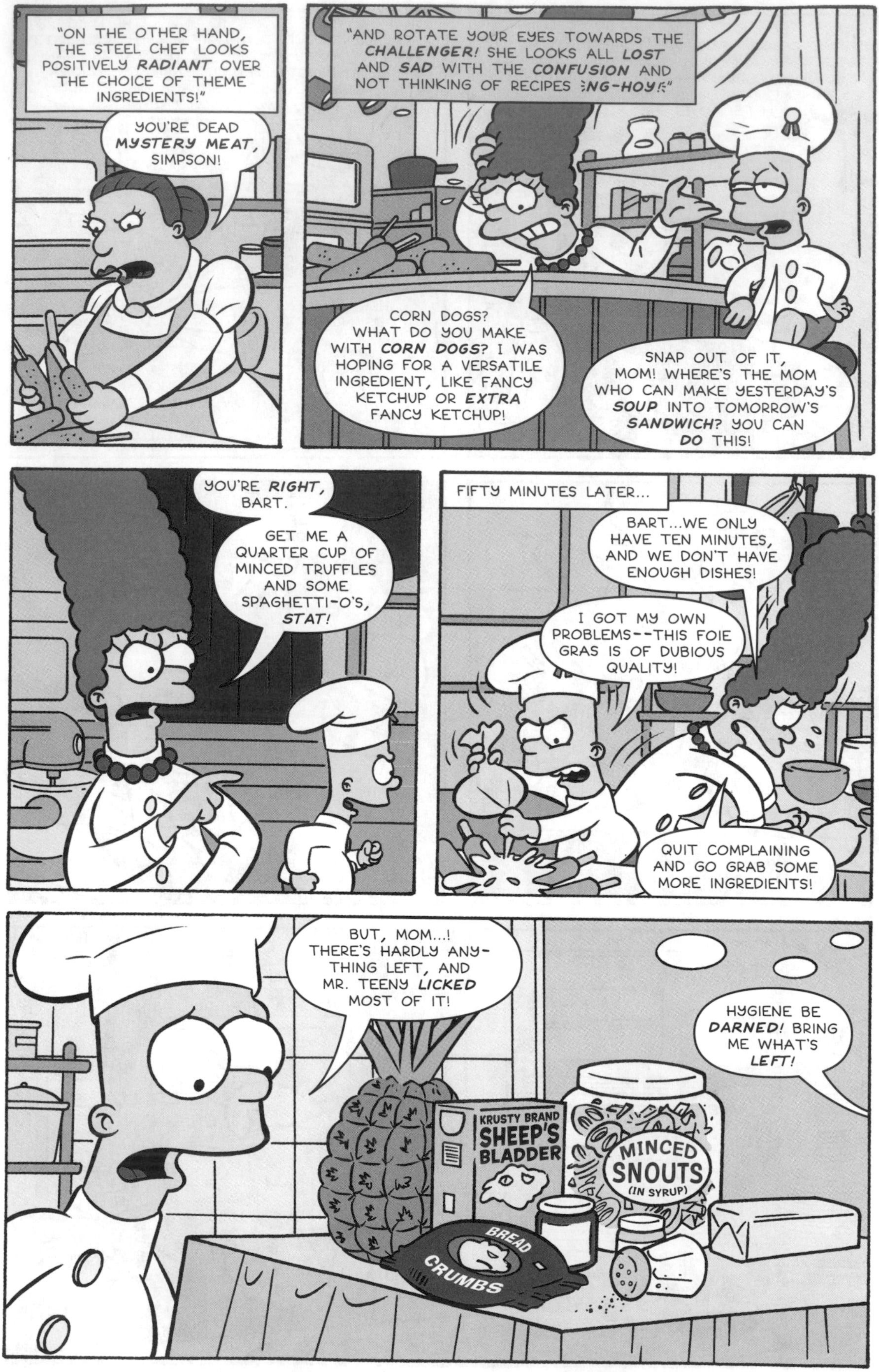
"ON THE OTHER HAND, THE STEEL CHEF LOOKS POSITIVELY RADIANT OVER THE CHOICE OF THEME INGREDIENTS!"
YOU'RE DEAD MYSTERY MEAT, SIMPSON!
"AND ROTATE YOUR EYES TOWARDS THE CHALLENGER! SHE LOOKS ALL LOST AND SAD WITH THE CONFUSION AND NOT THINKING OF RECIPES ING-HOY!"
CORN DOGS? WHAT DO YOU MAKE WITH CORN DOGS? I WAS HOPING FOR A VERSATILE INGREDIENT, LIKE FANCY KETCHUP OR EXTRA FANCY KETCHUP!
SNAP OUT OF IT, MOM! WHERE'S THE MOM WHO CAN MAKE YESTERDAY'S SOUP INTO TOMORROW'S SANDWICH? YOU CAN DO THIS!
YOU'RE RIGHT, BART.
GET ME A QUARTER CUP OF MINCED TRUFFLES AND SOME SPAGHETTI-O'S, STAT!
FIFTY MINUTES LATER...
BART...WE ONLY HAVE TEN MINUTES, AND WE DON'T HAVE ENOUGH DISHES!
I GOT MY OWN PROBLEMS--THIS FOIE GRAS IS OF DUBIOUS QUALITY!
QUIT COMPLAINING AND GO GRAB SOME MORE INGREDIENTS!
BUT, MOM...! THERE'S HARDLY ANY-THING LEFT, AND MR. TEENY LICKED MOST OF IT!
HYGIENE BE DARNED! BRING ME WHAT'S LEFT!
KRUSTY BRAND SHEEP'S BLADDER
MINCED SNOUTS (IN SYRUP)
BREAD CRUMBS

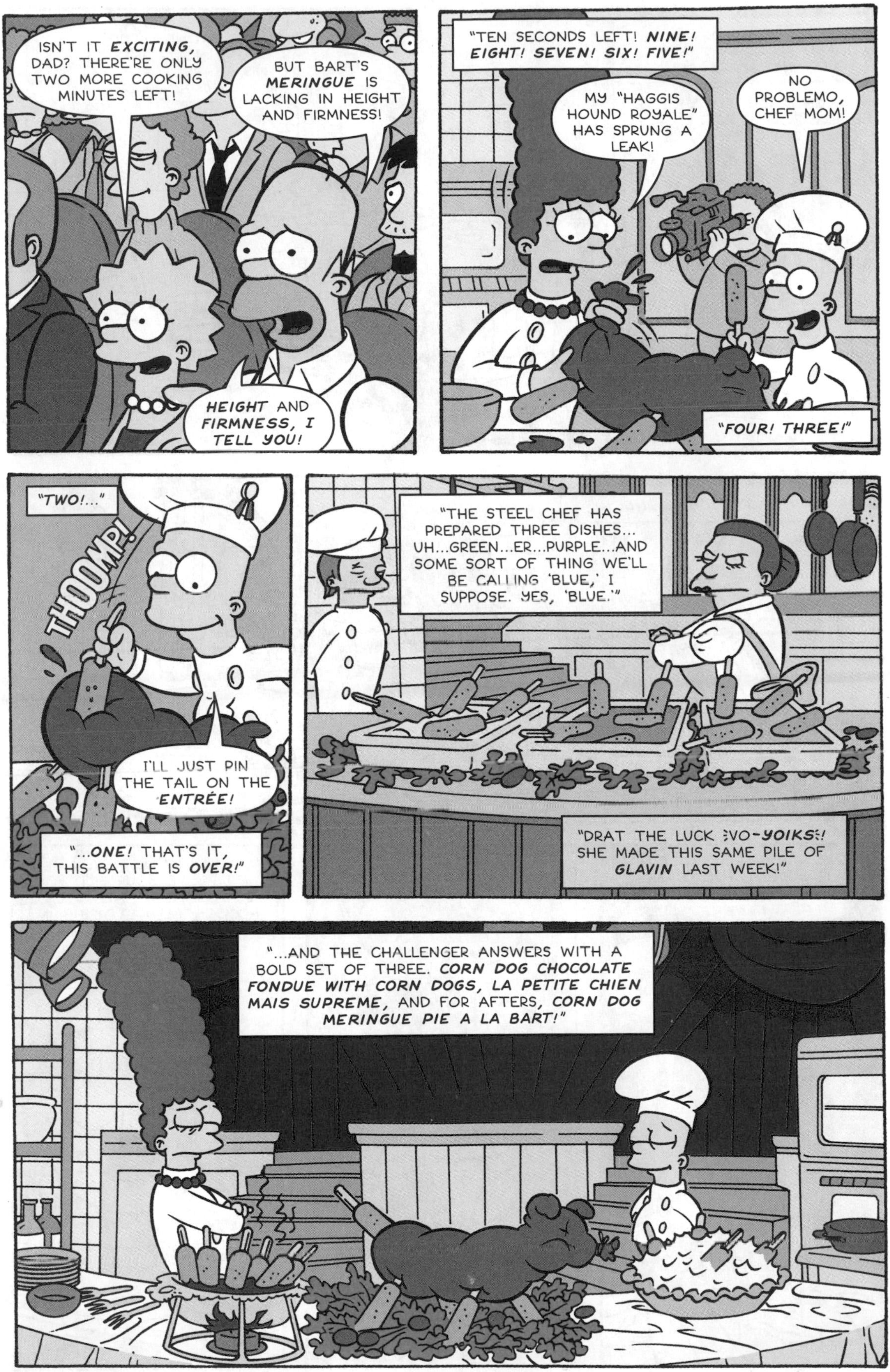
ISN'T IT *EXCITING*, DAD? THERE'RE ONLY TWO MORE COOKING MINUTES LEFT!
BUT BART'S *MERINGUE* IS LACKING IN HEIGHT AND FIRMNESS!
HEIGHT AND *FIRMNESS, I TELL YOU!*
"TEN SECONDS LEFT! *NINE! EIGHT! SEVEN! SIX! FIVE!*"
MY "HAGGIS HOUND ROYALE" HAS SPRUNG A LEAK!
NO PROBLEMO, CHEF MOM!
"*FOUR! THREE!*"
"*TWO!...*"
THOOMP!
I'LL JUST PIN THE TAIL ON THE *ENTRÉE!*
"...*ONE!* THAT'S IT, THIS BATTLE IS *OVER!*"
"THE STEEL CHEF HAS PREPARED THREE DISHES... UH...GREEN...ER...PURPLE...AND SOME SORT OF THING WE'LL BE CALLING 'BLUE,' I SUPPOSE. YES, 'BLUE.'"
"DRAT THE LUCK VO-*YOIKS*! SHE MADE THIS SAME PILE OF *GLAVIN* LAST WEEK!"
"...AND THE CHALLENGER ANSWERS WITH A BOLD SET OF THREE. *CORN DOG CHOCOLATE FONDUE WITH CORN DOGS, LA PETITE CHIEN MAIS SUPREME,* AND FOR AFTERS, *CORN DOG MERINGUE PIE A LA BART!*"

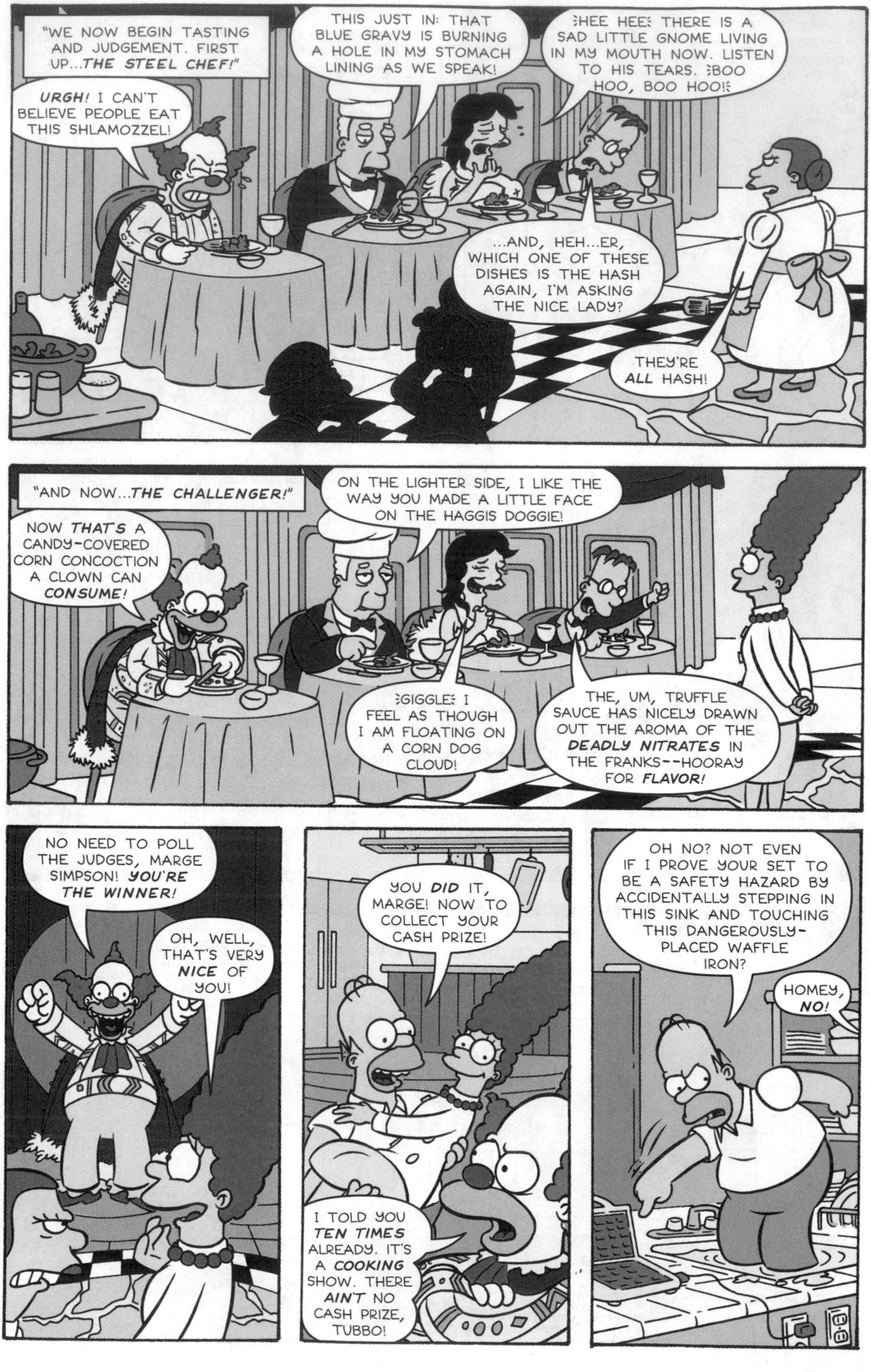
"WE NOW BEGIN TASTING AND JUDGEMENT. FIRST UP...THE STEEL CHEF!"
URGH! I CAN'T BELIEVE PEOPLE EAT THIS SHLAMOZZEL!
THIS JUST IN: THAT BLUE GRAVY IS BURNING A HOLE IN MY STOMACH LINING AS WE SPEAK!
HEE HEE THERE IS A SAD LITTLE GNOME LIVING IN MY MOUTH NOW. LISTEN TO HIS TEARS. BOO HOO, BOO HOO!
...AND, HEH...ER, WHICH ONE OF THESE DISHES IS THE HASH AGAIN, I'M ASKING THE NICE LADY?
THEY'RE ALL HASH!
"AND NOW...THE CHALLENGER!"
NOW THAT'S A CANDY-COVERED CORN CONCOCTION A CLOWN CAN CONSUME!
ON THE LIGHTER SIDE, I LIKE THE WAY YOU MADE A LITTLE FACE ON THE HAGGIS DOGGIE!
GIGGLE I FEEL AS THOUGH I AM FLOATING ON A CORN DOG CLOUD!
THE, UM, TRUFFLE SAUCE HAS NICELY DRAWN OUT THE AROMA OF THE DEADLY NITRATES IN THE FRANKS--HOORAY FOR FLAVOR!
NO NEED TO POLL THE JUDGES, MARGE SIMPSON! YOU'RE THE WINNER!
OH, WELL, THAT'S VERY NICE OF YOU!
YOU DID IT, MARGE! NOW TO COLLECT YOUR CASH PRIZE!
I TOLD YOU TEN TIMES ALREADY. IT'S A COOKING SHOW. THERE AIN'T NO CASH PRIZE, TUBBO!
OH NO? NOT EVEN IF I PROVE YOUR SET TO BE A SAFETY HAZARD BY ACCIDENTALLY STEPPING IN THIS SINK AND TOUCHING THIS DANGEROUSLY-PLACED WAFFLE IRON?
HOMEY, NO!

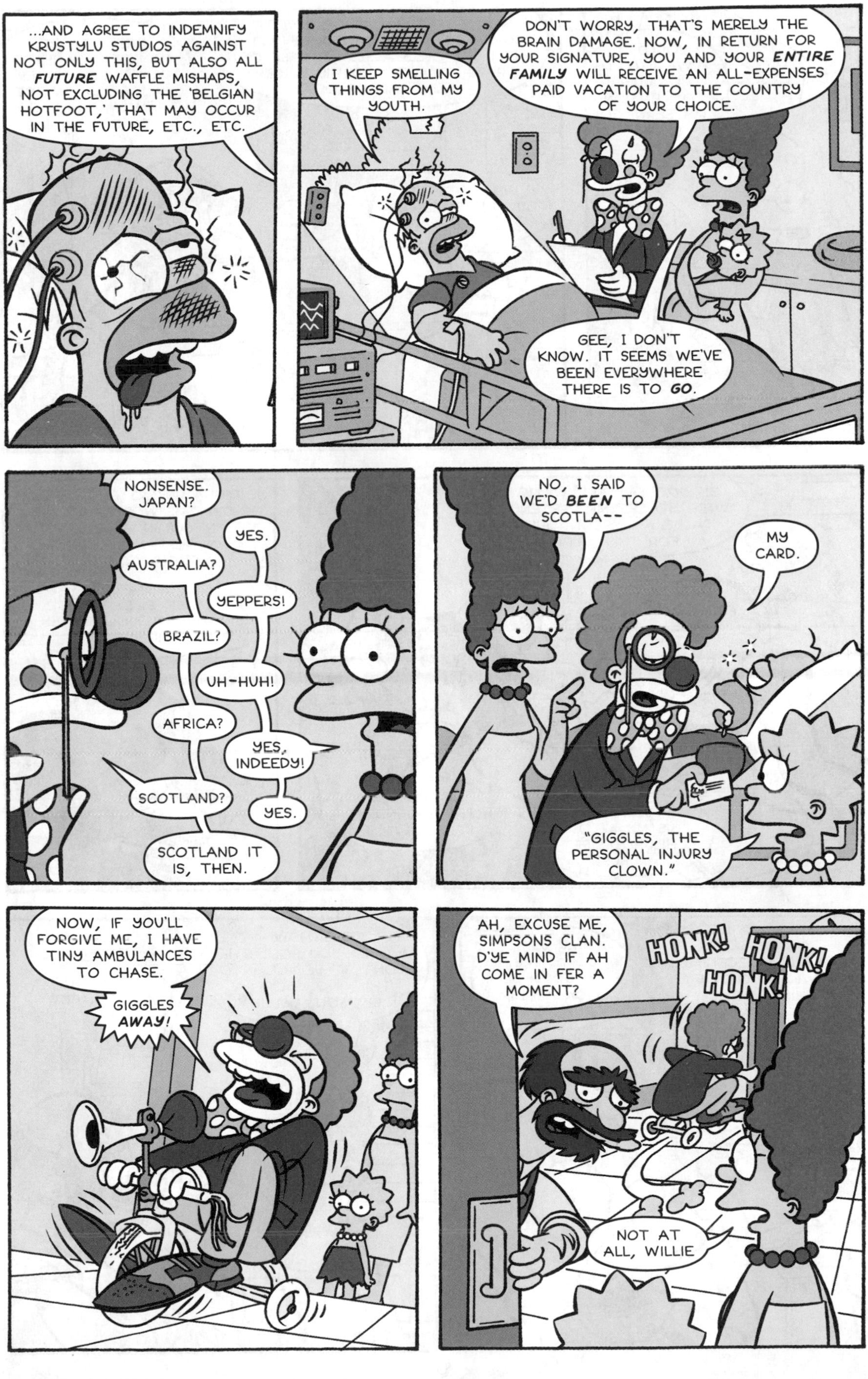
...AND AGREE TO INDEMNIFY KRUSTYLU STUDIOS AGAINST NOT ONLY THIS, BUT ALSO ALL FUTURE WAFFLE MISHAPS, NOT EXCLUDING THE 'BELGIAN HOTFOOT,' THAT MAY OCCUR IN THE FUTURE, ETC., ETC.
I KEEP SMELLING THINGS FROM MY YOUTH.
DON'T WORRY, THAT'S MERELY THE BRAIN DAMAGE. NOW, IN RETURN FOR YOUR SIGNATURE, YOU AND YOUR ENTIRE FAMILY WILL RECEIVE AN ALL-EXPENSES PAID VACATION TO THE COUNTRY OF YOUR CHOICE.
GEE, I DON'T KNOW. IT SEEMS WE'VE BEEN EVERYWHERE THERE IS TO GO.
NONSENSE. JAPAN?
YES.
AUSTRALIA?
YEPPERS!
BRAZIL?
UH-HUH!
AFRICA?
YES, INDEEDY!
SCOTLAND?
YES.
SCOTLAND IT IS, THEN.
NO, I SAID WE'D BEEN TO SCOTLA--
MY CARD.
"GIGGLES, THE PERSONAL INJURY CLOWN."
NOW, IF YOU'LL FORGIVE ME, I HAVE TINY AMBULANCES TO CHASE.
GIGGLES AWAY!
AH, EXCUSE ME, SIMPSONS CLAN. D'YE MIND IF AH COME IN FER A MOMENT?
HONK! HONK! HONK!
NOT AT ALL, WILLIE

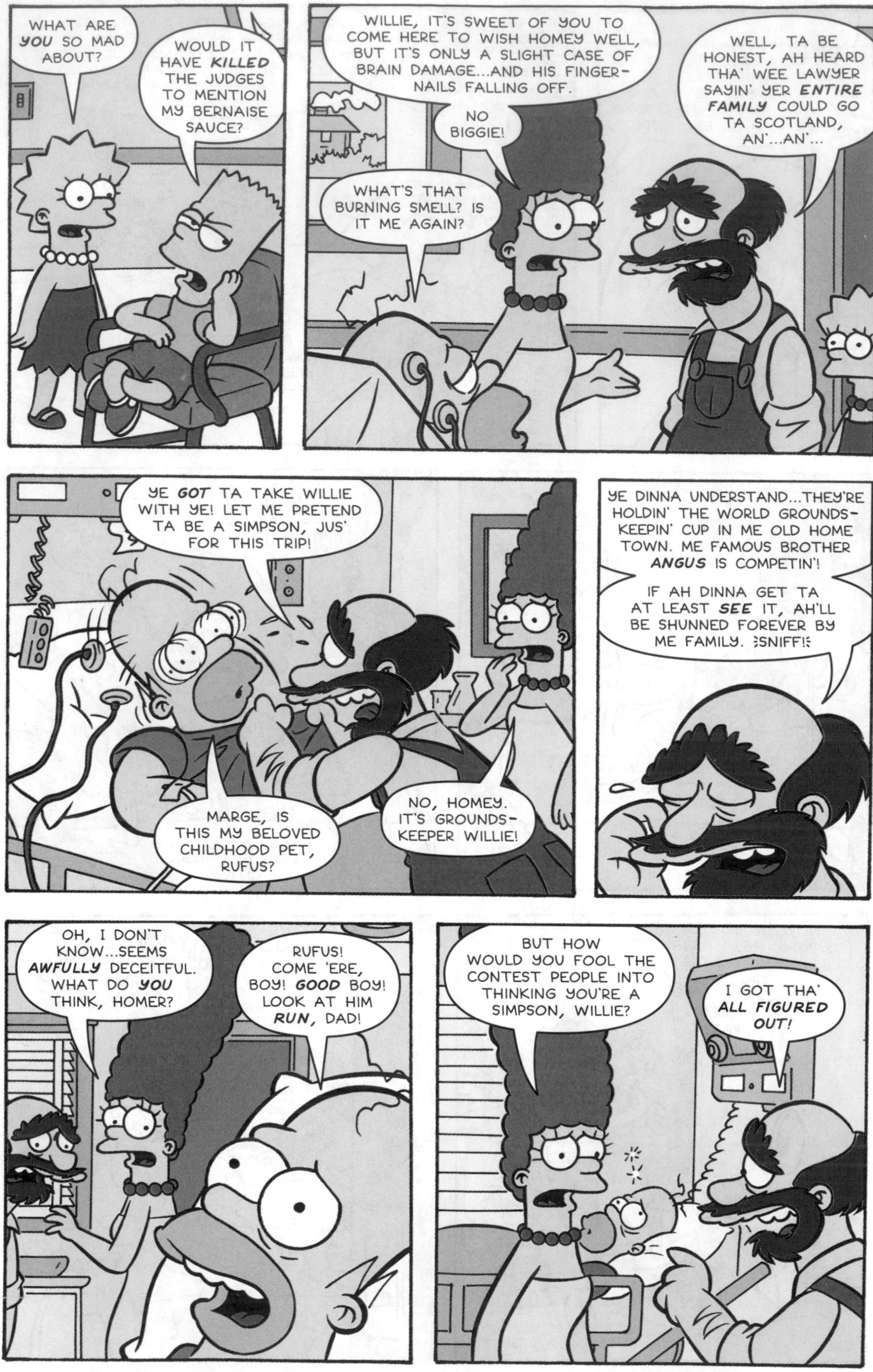
WHAT ARE YOU SO MAD ABOUT?
WOULD IT HAVE KILLED THE JUDGES TO MENTION MY BERNAISE SAUCE?
WILLIE, IT'S SWEET OF YOU TO COME HERE TO WISH HOMEY WELL, BUT IT'S ONLY A SLIGHT CASE OF BRAIN DAMAGE...AND HIS FINGER-NAILS FALLING OFF.
NO BIGGIE!
WHAT'S THAT BURNING SMELL? IS IT ME AGAIN?
WELL, TA BE HONEST, AH HEARD THA' WEE LAWYER SAYIN' YER ENTIRE FAMILY COULD GO TA SCOTLAND, AN'...AN'...
YE GOT TA TAKE WILLIE WITH YE! LET ME PRETEND TA BE A SIMPSON, JUS' FOR THIS TRIP!
MARGE, IS THIS MY BELOVED CHILDHOOD PET, RUFUS?
NO, HOMEY. IT'S GROUNDS-KEEPER WILLIE!
YE DINNA UNDERSTAND...THEY'RE HOLDIN' THE WORLD GROUNDS-KEEPIN' CUP IN ME OLD HOME TOWN. ME FAMOUS BROTHER ANGUS IS COMPETIN'!
IF AH DINNA GET TA AT LEAST SEE IT, AH'LL BE SHUNNED FOREVER BY ME FAMILY. SNIFF!
OH, I DON'T KNOW...SEEMS AWFULLY DECEITFUL. WHAT DO YOU THINK, HOMER?
RUFUS! COME 'ERE, BOY! GOOD BOY! LOOK AT HIM RUN, DAD!
BUT HOW WOULD YOU FOOL THE CONTEST PEOPLE INTO THINKING YOU'RE A SIMPSON, WILLIE?
I GOT THA' ALL FIGURED OUT!

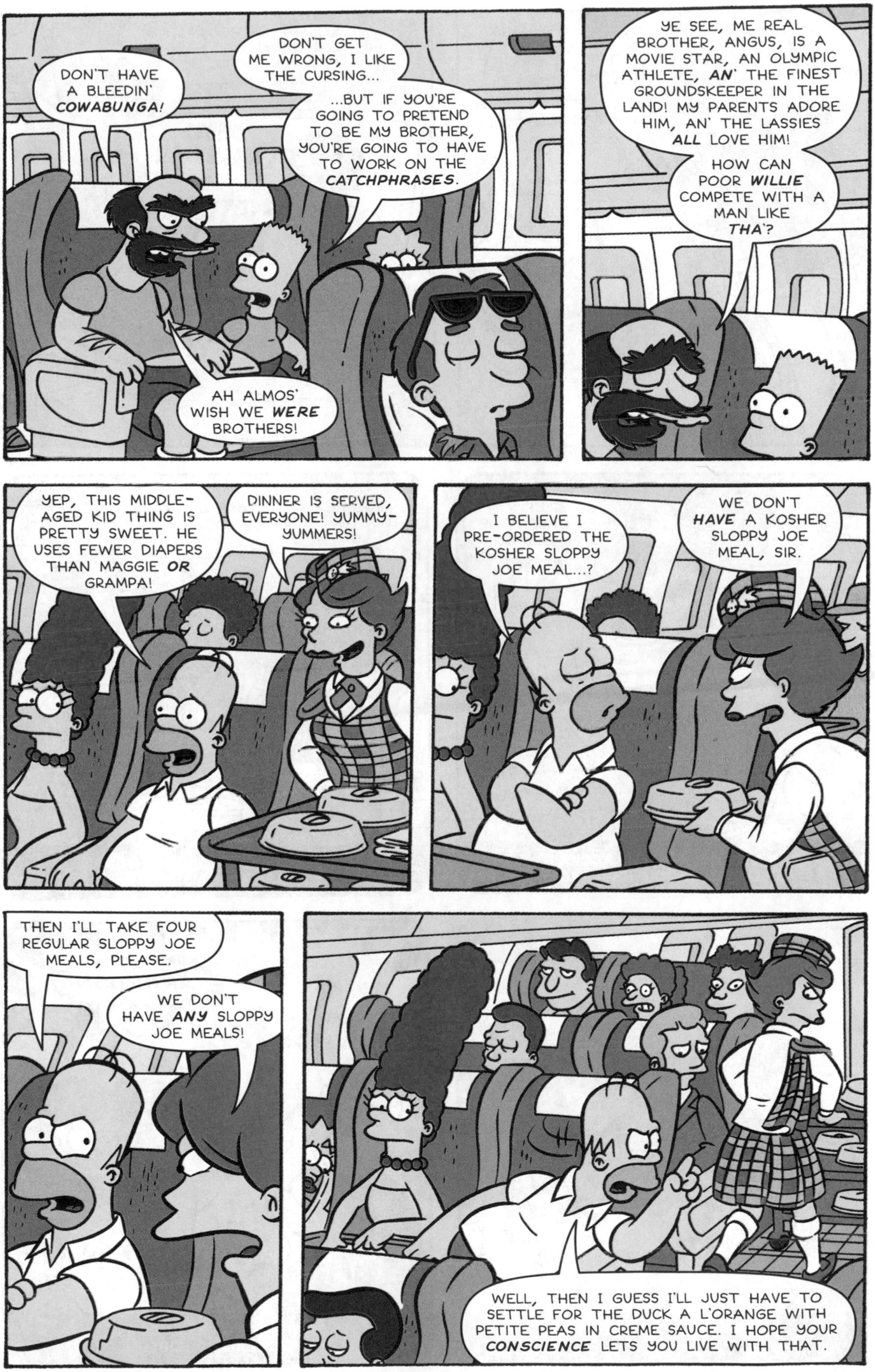
DON'T HAVE A BLEEDIN' COWABUNGA!
DON'T GET ME WRONG, I LIKE THE CURSING...
...BUT IF YOU'RE GOING TO PRETEND TO BE MY BROTHER, YOU'RE GOING TO HAVE TO WORK ON THE CATCHPHRASES.
AH ALMOS' WISH WE WERE BROTHERS!
YE SEE, ME REAL BROTHER, ANGUS, IS A MOVIE STAR, AN OLYMPIC ATHLETE, AN' THE FINEST GROUNDSKEEPER IN THE LAND! MY PARENTS ADORE HIM, AN' THE LASSIES ALL LOVE HIM!
HOW CAN POOR WILLIE COMPETE WITH A MAN LIKE THA'?
YEP, THIS MIDDLE-AGED KID THING IS PRETTY SWEET. HE USES FEWER DIAPERS THAN MAGGIE OR GRAMPA!
DINNER IS SERVED, EVERYONE! YUMMY-YUMMERS!
I BELIEVE I PRE-ORDERED THE KOSHER SLOPPY JOE MEAL...?
WE DON'T HAVE A KOSHER SLOPPY JOE MEAL, SIR.
THEN I'LL TAKE FOUR REGULAR SLOPPY JOE MEALS, PLEASE.
WE DON'T HAVE ANY SLOPPY JOE MEALS!
WELL, THEN I GUESS I'LL JUST HAVE TO SETTLE FOR THE DUCK A L'ORANGE WITH PETITE PEAS IN CREME SAUCE. I HOPE YOUR CONSCIENCE LETS YOU LIVE WITH THAT.

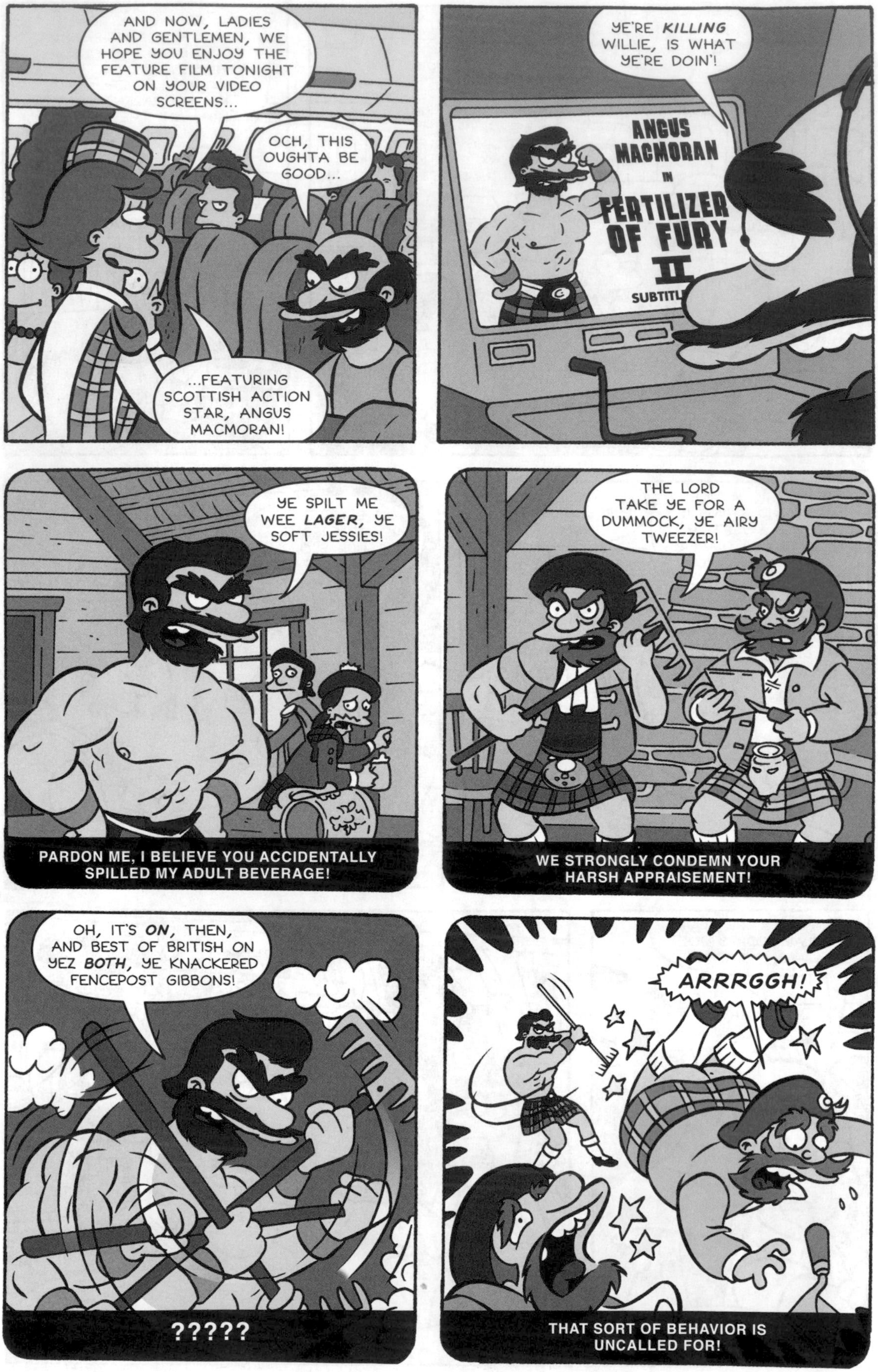
AND NOW, LADIES AND GENTLEMEN, WE HOPE YOU ENJOY THE FEATURE FILM TONIGHT ON YOUR VIDEO SCREENS...
OCH, THIS OUGHTA BE GOOD...
...FEATURING SCOTTISH ACTION STAR, ANGUS MACMORAN!
YE'RE **KILLING** WILLIE, IS WHAT YE'RE DOIN'!
ANGUS MACMORAN
IN
FERTILIZER OF FURY
II
YE SPILT ME WEE **LAGER,** YE SOFT JESSIES!
PARDON ME, I BELIEVE YOU ACCIDENTALLY SPILLED MY ADULT BEVERAGE!
THE LORD TAKE YE FOR A DUMMOCK, YE AIRY TWEEZER!
WE STRONGLY CONDEMN YOUR HARSH APPRAISEMENT!
OH, IT'S **ON**, THEN, AND BEST OF BRITISH ON YEZ **BOTH**, YE KNACKERED FENCEPOST GIBBONS!
?????
ARRRGGH!
THAT SORT OF BEHAVIOR IS UNCALLED FOR!

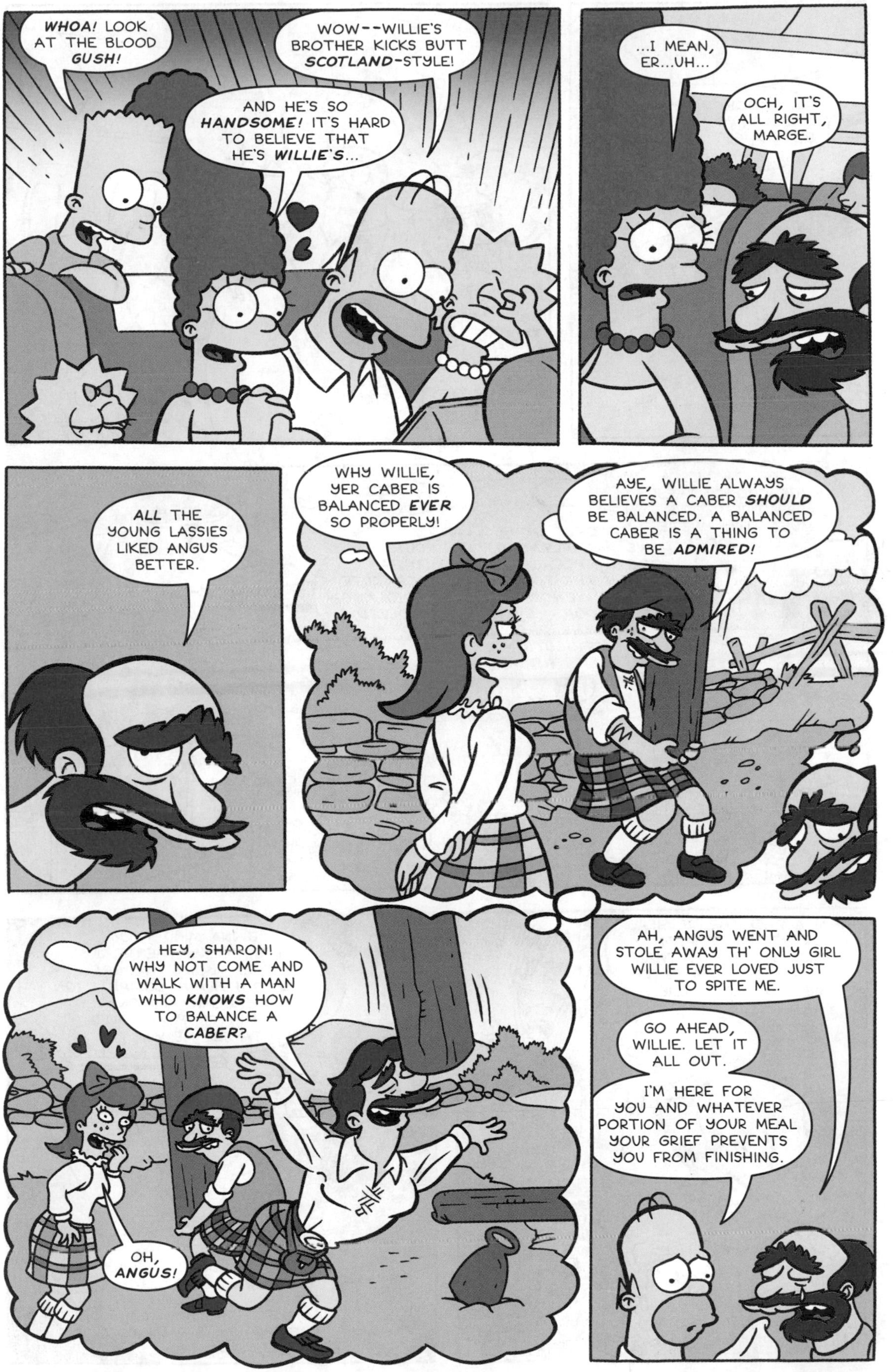
WHOA! LOOK AT THE BLOOD GUSH!
WOW--WILLIE'S BROTHER KICKS BUTT SCOTLAND-STYLE!
AND HE'S SO HANDSOME! IT'S HARD TO BELIEVE THAT HE'S WILLIE'S...
...I MEAN, ER...UH...
OCH, IT'S ALL RIGHT, MARGE.
ALL THE YOUNG LASSIES LIKED ANGUS BETTER.
WHY WILLIE, YER CABER IS BALANCED EVER SO PROPERLY!
AYE, WILLIE ALWAYS BELIEVES A CABER SHOULD BE BALANCED. A BALANCED CABER IS A THING TO BE ADMIRED!
HEY, SHARON! WHY NOT COME AND WALK WITH A MAN WHO KNOWS HOW TO BALANCE A CABER?
OH, ANGUS!
AH, ANGUS WENT AND STOLE AWAY TH' ONLY GIRL WILLIE EVER LOVED JUST TO SPITE ME.
GO AHEAD, WILLIE. LET IT ALL OUT.
I'M HERE FOR YOU AND WHATEVER PORTION OF YOUR MEAL YOUR GRIEF PREVENTS YOU FROM FINISHING.

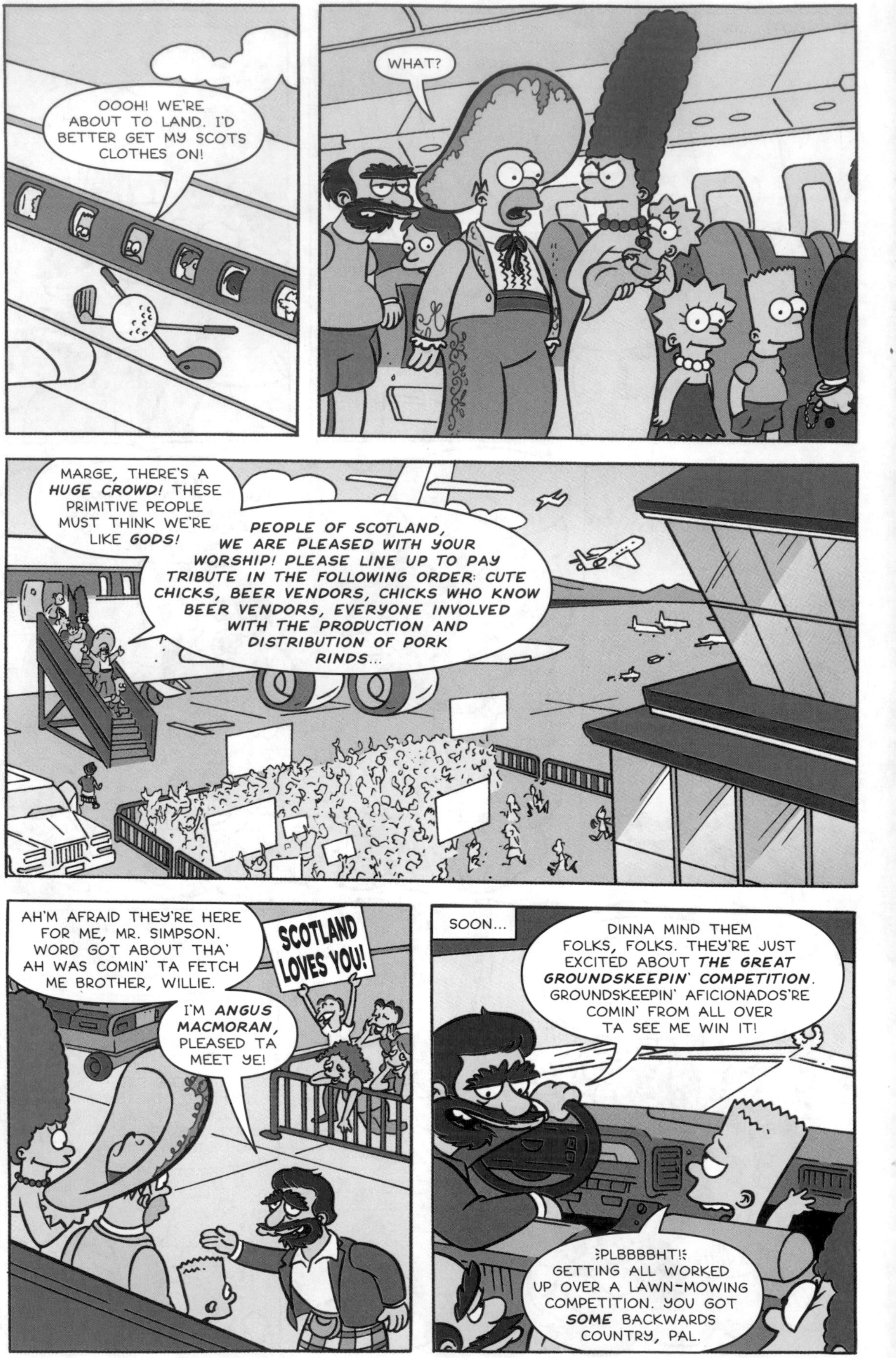
OOOH! WE'RE ABOUT TO LAND. I'D BETTER GET MY SCOTS CLOTHES ON!
WHAT?
MARGE, THERE'S A ***HUGE CROWD!*** THESE PRIMITIVE PEOPLE MUST THINK WE'RE LIKE ***GODS!***
PEOPLE OF SCOTLAND, WE ARE PLEASED WITH YOUR WORSHIP! PLEASE LINE UP TO PAY TRIBUTE IN THE FOLLOWING ORDER: CUTE CHICKS, BEER VENDORS, CHICKS WHO KNOW BEER VENDORS, EVERYONE INVOLVED WITH THE PRODUCTION AND DISTRIBUTION OF PORK RINDS...
AH'M AFRAID THEY'RE HERE FOR ME, MR. SIMPSON. WORD GOT ABOUT THA' AH WAS COMIN' TA FETCH ME BROTHER, WILLIE.
SCOTLAND LOVES YOU!
I'M ***ANGUS MACMORAN,*** PLEASED TA MEET YE!
SOON...
DINNA MIND THEM FOLKS, FOLKS. THEY'RE JUST EXCITED ABOUT ***THE GREAT GROUNDSKEEPIN' COMPETITION***. GROUNDSKEEPIN' AFICIONADOS'RE COMIN' FROM ALL OVER TA SEE ME WIN IT!
PLBBBBHT! GETTING ALL WORKED UP OVER A LAWN-MOWING COMPETITION. YOU GOT ***SOME*** BACKWARDS COUNTRY, PAL.

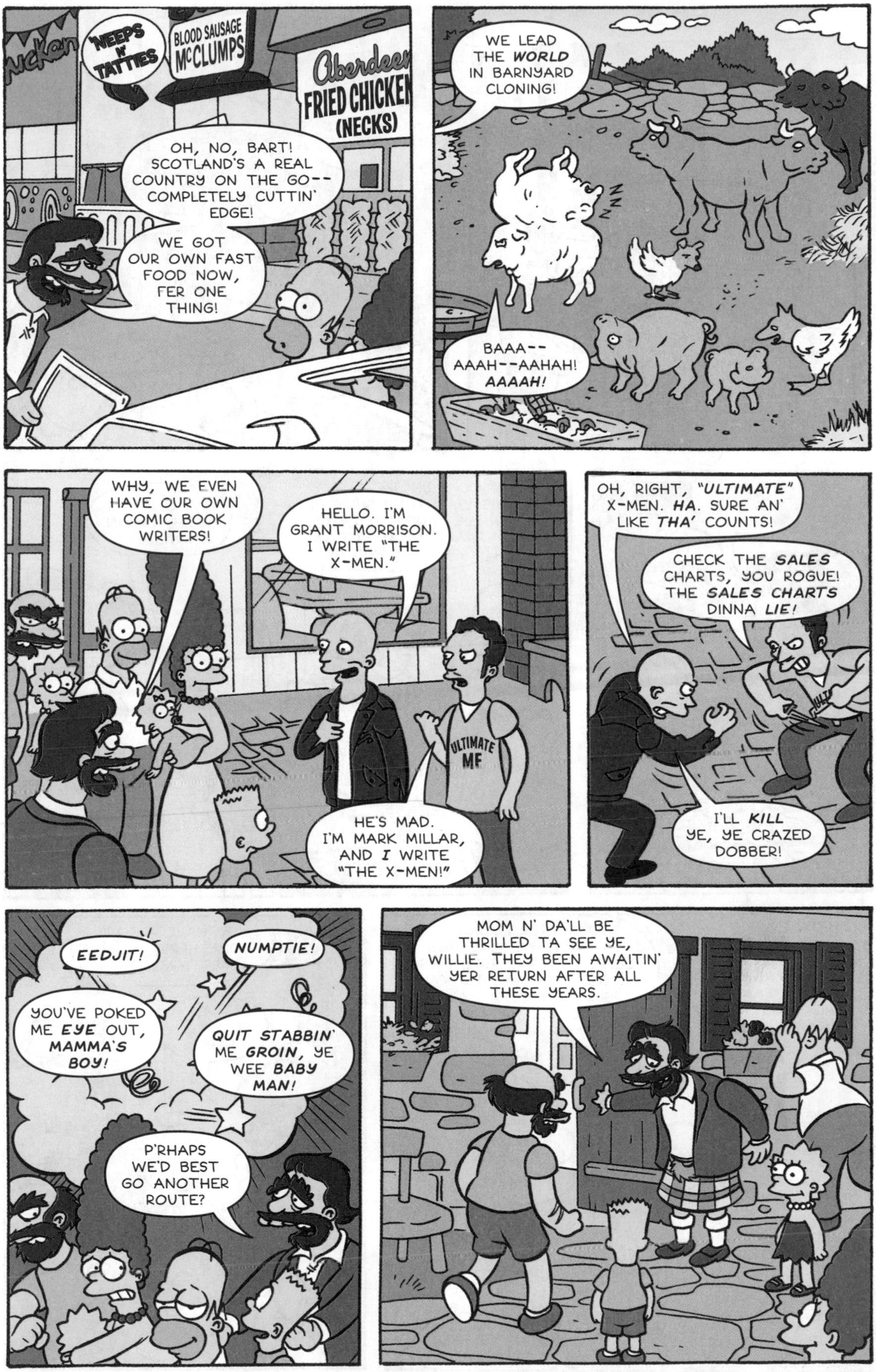
'NEEPS N' TATTIES
BLOOD SAUSAGE McCLUMPS
Aberdeen FRIED CHICKEN (NECKS)
OH, NO, BART! SCOTLAND'S A REAL COUNTRY ON THE GO--COMPLETELY CUTTIN' EDGE!
WE GOT OUR OWN FAST FOOD NOW, FER ONE THING!
WE LEAD THE WORLD IN BARNYARD CLONING!
BAAA--AAAH--AAHAH! AAAAH!
WHY, WE EVEN HAVE OUR OWN COMIC BOOK WRITERS!
HELLO. I'M GRANT MORRISON. I WRITE "THE X-MEN."
ULTIMATE ME
HE'S MAD. I'M MARK MILLAR, AND I WRITE "THE X-MEN!"
OH, RIGHT, "ULTIMATE" X-MEN. HA. SURE AN' LIKE THA' COUNTS!
CHECK THE SALES CHARTS, YOU ROGUE! THE SALES CHARTS DINNA LIE!
I'LL KILL YE, YE CRAZED DOBBER!
EEDJIT!
NUMPTIE!
YOU'VE POKED ME EYE OUT, MAMMA'S BOY!
QUIT STABBIN' ME GROIN, YE WEE BABY MAN!
P'RHAPS WE'D BEST GO ANOTHER ROUTE?
MOM N' DA'LL BE THRILLED TA SEE YE, WILLIE. THEY BEEN AWAITIN' YER RETURN AFTER ALL THESE YEARS.

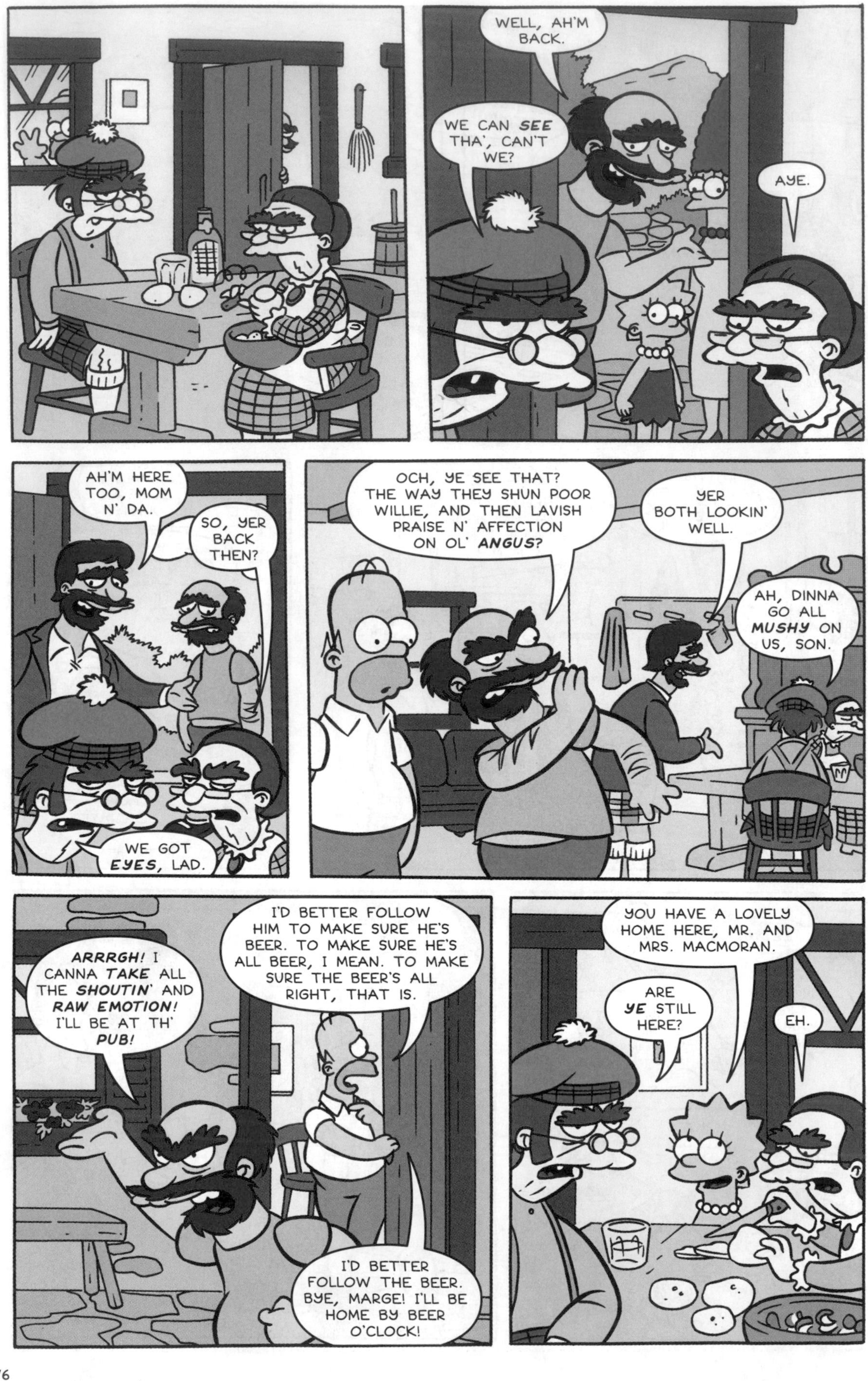
WELL, AH'M BACK.
WE CAN SEE THA', CAN'T WE?
AYE.
AH'M HERE TOO, MOM N' DA.
SO, YER BACK THEN?
WE GOT EYES, LAD.
OCH, YE SEE THAT? THE WAY THEY SHUN POOR WILLIE, AND THEN LAVISH PRAISE N' AFFECTION ON OL' ANGUS?
YER BOTH LOOKIN' WELL.
AH, DINNA GO ALL MUSHY ON US, SON.
ARRRGH! I CANNA TAKE ALL THE SHOUTIN' AND RAW EMOTION! I'LL BE AT TH' PUB!
I'D BETTER FOLLOW HIM TO MAKE SURE HE'S BEER. TO MAKE SURE HE'S ALL BEER, I MEAN. TO MAKE SURE THE BEER'S ALL RIGHT, THAT IS.
I'D BETTER FOLLOW THE BEER. BYE, MARGE! I'LL BE HOME BY BEER O'CLOCK!
YOU HAVE A LOVELY HOME HERE, MR. AND MRS. MACMORAN.
ARE YE STILL HERE?
EH.

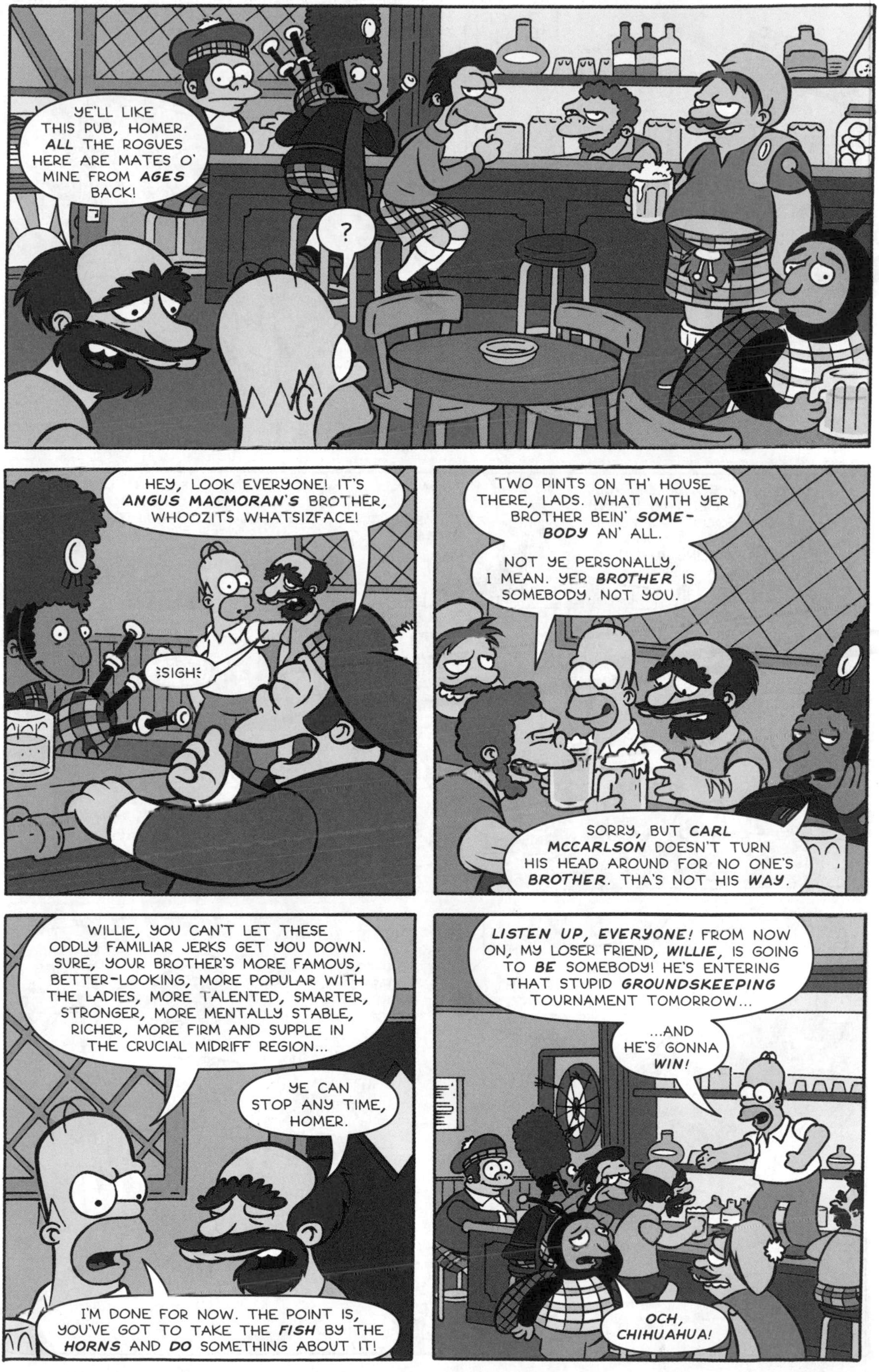
YE'LL LIKE THIS PUB, HOMER. ALL THE ROGUES HERE ARE MATES O' MINE FROM AGES BACK!
?
HEY, LOOK EVERYONE! IT'S ANGUS MACMORAN'S BROTHER, WHOOZITS WHATSIZFACE!
SIGH
TWO PINTS ON TH' HOUSE THERE, LADS. WHAT WITH YER BROTHER BEIN' SOME-BODY AN' ALL.
NOT YE PERSONALLY, I MEAN. YER BROTHER IS SOMEBODY. NOT YOU.
SORRY, BUT CARL MCCARLSON DOESN'T TURN HIS HEAD AROUND FOR NO ONE'S BROTHER. THA'S NOT HIS WAY.
WILLIE, YOU CAN'T LET THESE ODDLY FAMILIAR JERKS GET YOU DOWN. SURE, YOUR BROTHER'S MORE FAMOUS, BETTER-LOOKING, MORE POPULAR WITH THE LADIES, MORE TALENTED, SMARTER, STRONGER, MORE MENTALLY STABLE, RICHER, MORE FIRM AND SUPPLE IN THE CRUCIAL MIDRIFF REGION...
YE CAN STOP ANY TIME, HOMER.
I'M DONE FOR NOW. THE POINT IS, YOU'VE GOT TO TAKE THE FISH BY THE HORNS AND DO SOMETHING ABOUT IT!
LISTEN UP, EVERYONE! FROM NOW ON, MY LOSER FRIEND, WILLIE, IS GOING TO BE SOMEBODY! HE'S ENTERING THAT STUPID GROUNDSKEEPING TOURNAMENT TOMORROW...
...AND HE'S GONNA WIN!
OCH, CHIHUAHUA!

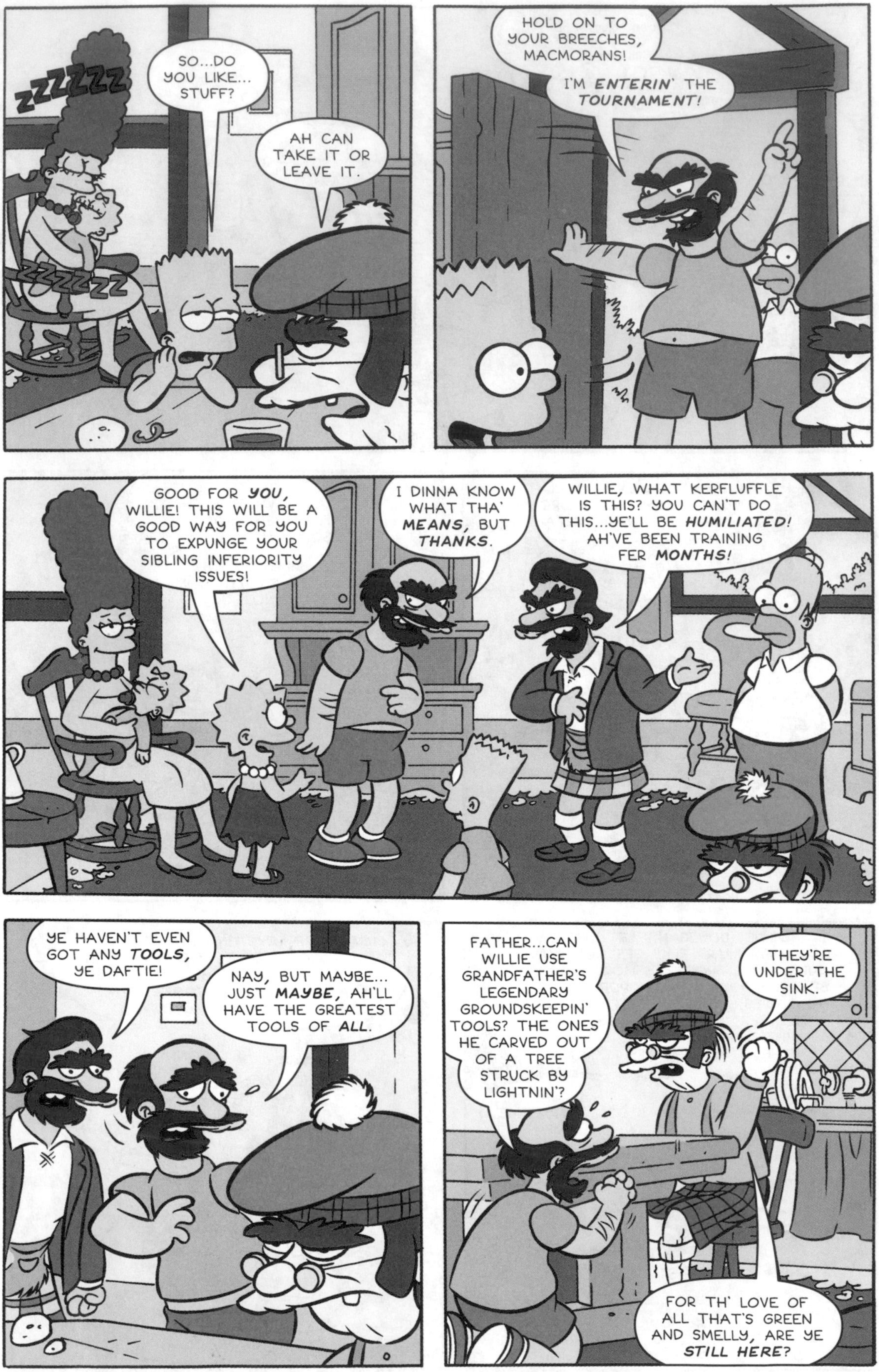
ZZZZZZ
SO...DO YOU LIKE... STUFF?
AH CAN TAKE IT OR LEAVE IT.
ZZZZZZ
HOLD ON TO YOUR BREECHES, MACMORANS!
I'M *ENTERIN'* THE *TOURNAMENT!*
GOOD FOR *YOU,* WILLIE! THIS WILL BE A GOOD WAY FOR YOU TO EXPUNGE YOUR SIBLING INFERIORITY ISSUES!
I DINNA KNOW WHAT THA' *MEANS,* BUT *THANKS.*
WILLIE, WHAT KERFLUFFLE IS THIS? YOU CAN'T DO THIS...YE'LL BE *HUMILIATED!* AH'VE BEEN TRAINING FER *MONTHS!*
YE HAVEN'T EVEN GOT ANY *TOOLS,* YE DAFTIE!
NAY, BUT MAYBE... JUST *MAYBE,* AH'LL HAVE THE GREATEST TOOLS OF *ALL.*
FATHER...CAN WILLIE USE GRANDFATHER'S LEGENDARY GROUNDSKEEPIN' TOOLS? THE ONES HE CARVED OUT OF A TREE STRUCK BY LIGHTNIN'?
THEY'RE UNDER THE SINK.
FOR TH' LOVE OF ALL THAT'S GREEN AND SMELLY, ARE YE *STILL HERE?*

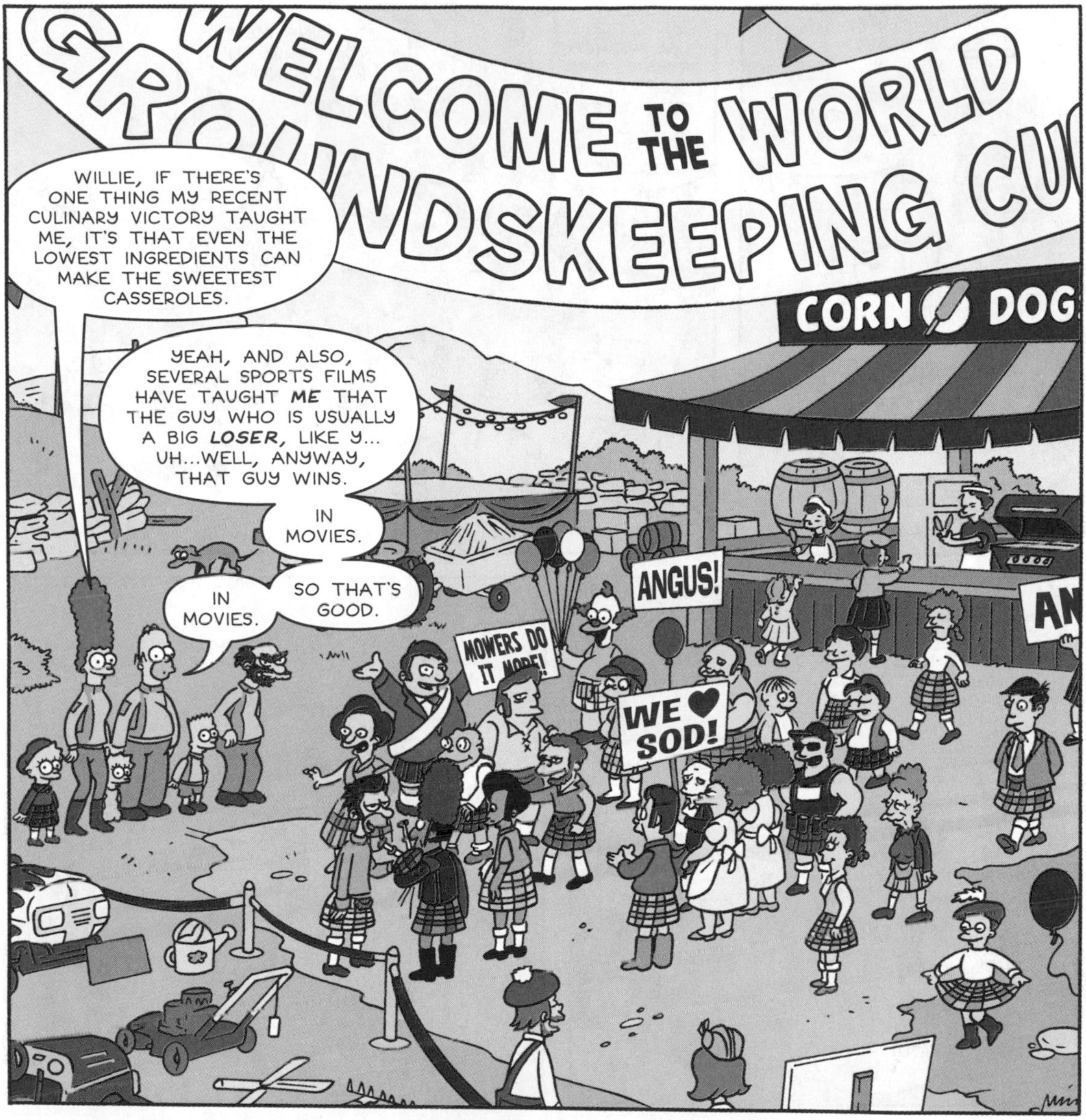
WELCOME TO THE WORLD GROUNDSKEEPING CU
CORN DOG
WILLIE, IF THERE'S ONE THING MY RECENT CULINARY VICTORY TAUGHT ME, IT'S THAT EVEN THE LOWEST INGREDIENTS CAN MAKE THE SWEETEST CASSEROLES.
YEAH, AND ALSO, SEVERAL SPORTS FILMS HAVE TAUGHT **ME** THAT THE GUY WHO IS USUALLY A BIG ***LOSER,*** LIKE Y... UH...WELL, ANYWAY, THAT GUY WINS.
IN MOVIES.
IN MOVIES.
SO THAT'S GOOD.
ANGUS!
MOWERS DO IT MORE!
WE ♥ SOD!

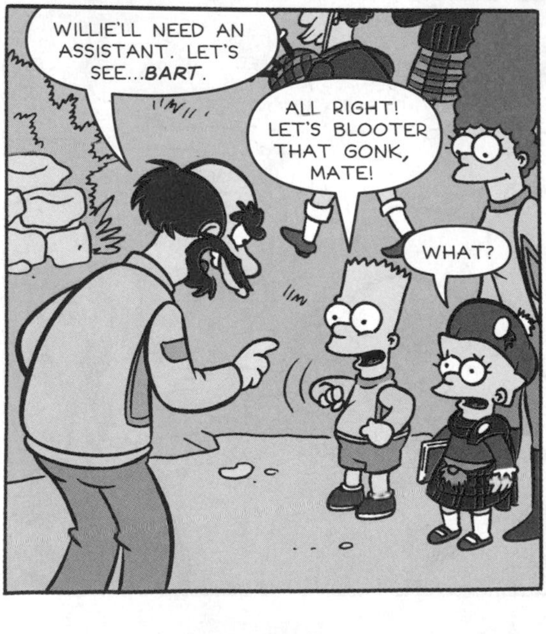
WILLIE'LL NEED AN ASSISTANT. LET'S SEE...***BART***.
ALL RIGHT! LET'S BLOOTER THAT GONK, MATE!
WHAT?

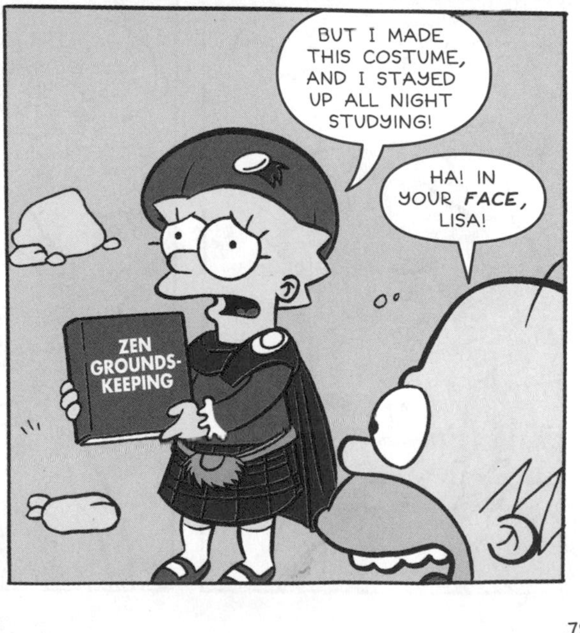
BUT I MADE THIS COSTUME, AND I STAYED UP ALL NIGHT STUDYING!
HA! IN YOUR ***FACE,*** LISA!
ZEN GROUNDS-KEEPING

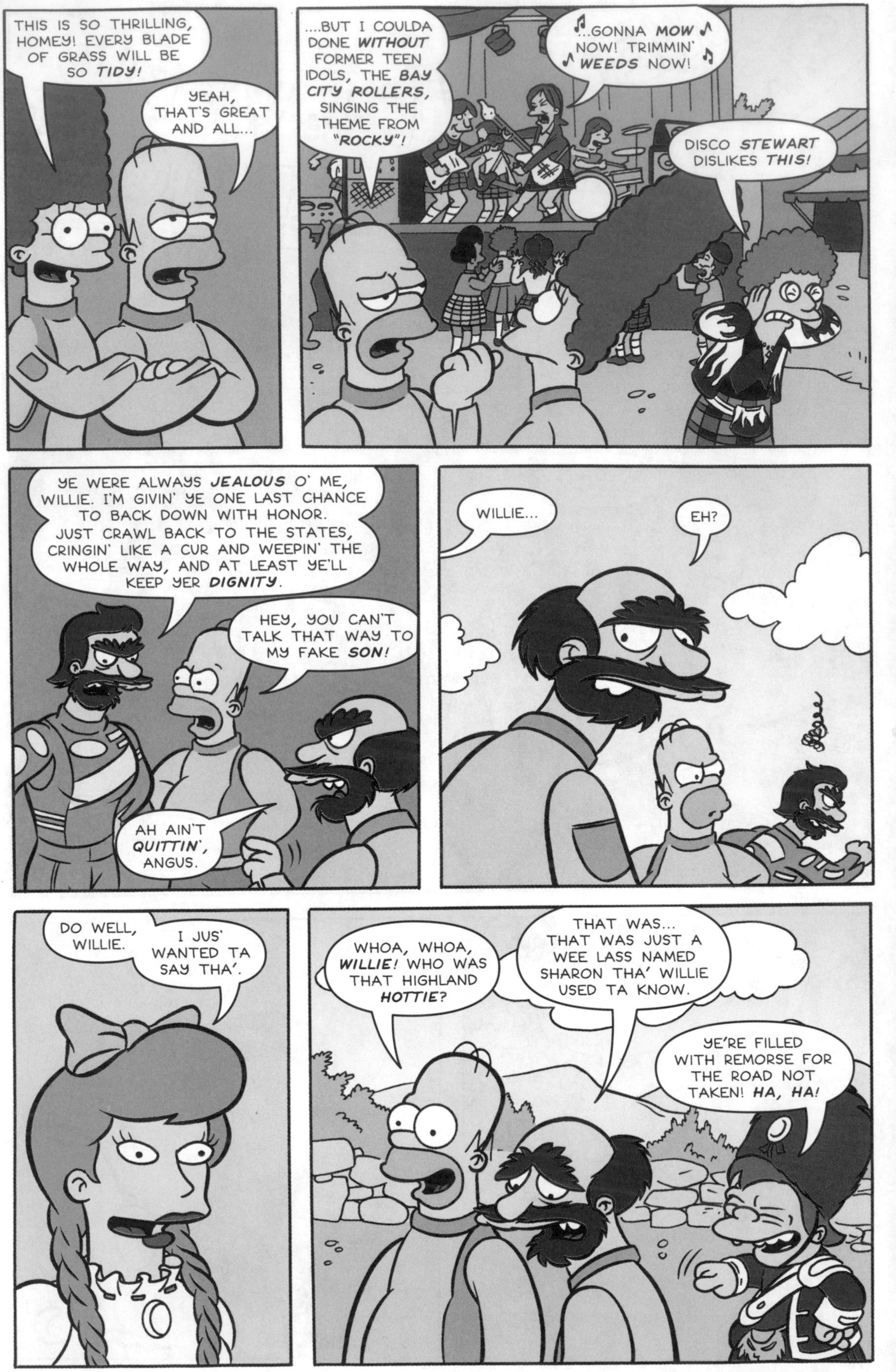
THIS IS SO THRILLING, HOMEY! EVERY BLADE OF GRASS WILL BE SO TIDY!
YEAH, THAT'S GREAT AND ALL...
....BUT I COULDA DONE WITHOUT FORMER TEEN IDOLS, THE BAY CITY ROLLERS, SINGING THE THEME FROM "ROCKY"!
♪...GONNA MOW ♪ NOW! TRIMMIN' ♪ WEEDS NOW! ♪
DISCO STEWART DISLIKES THIS!
YE WERE ALWAYS JEALOUS O' ME, WILLIE. I'M GIVIN' YE ONE LAST CHANCE TO BACK DOWN WITH HONOR. JUST CRAWL BACK TO THE STATES, CRINGIN' LIKE A CUR AND WEEPIN' THE WHOLE WAY, AND AT LEAST YE'LL KEEP YER DIGNITY.
HEY, YOU CAN'T TALK THAT WAY TO MY FAKE SON!
AH AIN'T QUITTIN', ANGUS.
WILLIE...
EH?
DO WELL, WILLIE.
I JUS' WANTED TA SAY THA'.
WHOA, WHOA, WILLIE! WHO WAS THAT HIGHLAND HOTTIE?
THAT WAS... THAT WAS JUST A WEE LASS NAMED SHARON THA' WILLIE USED TA KNOW.
YE'RE FILLED WITH REMORSE FOR THE ROAD NOT TAKEN! HA, HA!

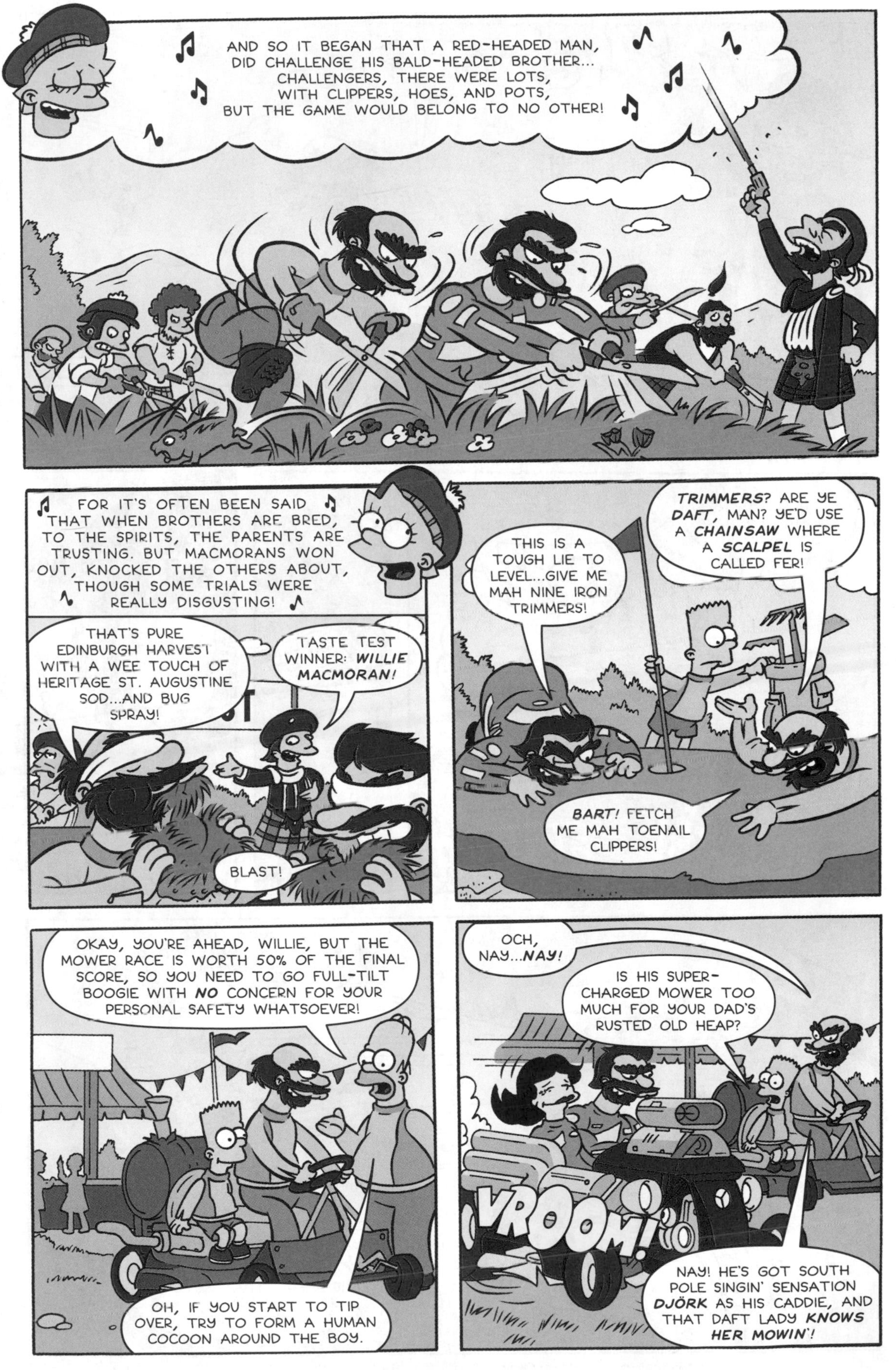
AND SO IT BEGAN THAT A RED-HEADED MAN, DID CHALLENGE HIS BALD-HEADED BROTHER... CHALLENGERS, THERE WERE LOTS, WITH CLIPPERS, HOES, AND POTS, BUT THE GAME WOULD BELONG TO NO OTHER!
FOR IT'S OFTEN BEEN SAID THAT WHEN BROTHERS ARE BRED, TO THE SPIRITS, THE PARENTS ARE TRUSTING. BUT MACMORANS WON OUT, KNOCKED THE OTHERS ABOUT, THOUGH SOME TRIALS WERE REALLY DISGUSTING!
THAT'S PURE EDINBURGH HARVEST WITH A WEE TOUCH OF HERITAGE ST. AUGUSTINE SOD...AND BUG SPRAY!
TASTE TEST WINNER: WILLIE MACMORAN!
BLAST!
THIS IS A TOUGH LIE TO LEVEL...GIVE ME MAH NINE IRON TRIMMERS!
TRIMMERS? ARE YE DAFT, MAN? YE'D USE A CHAINSAW WHERE A SCALPEL IS CALLED FER!
BART! FETCH ME MAH TOENAIL CLIPPERS!
OKAY, YOU'RE AHEAD, WILLIE, BUT THE MOWER RACE IS WORTH 50% OF THE FINAL SCORE, SO YOU NEED TO GO FULL-TILT BOOGIE WITH NO CONCERN FOR YOUR PERSONAL SAFETY WHATSOEVER!
OH, IF YOU START TO TIP OVER, TRY TO FORM A HUMAN COCOON AROUND THE BOY.
OCH, NAY...NAY!
IS HIS SUPER-CHARGED MOWER TOO MUCH FOR YOUR DAD'S RUSTED OLD HEAP?
VROOOM!
NAY! HE'S GOT SOUTH POLE SINGIN' SENSATION DJÖRK AS HIS CADDIE, AND THAT DAFT LADY KNOWS HER MOWIN'!

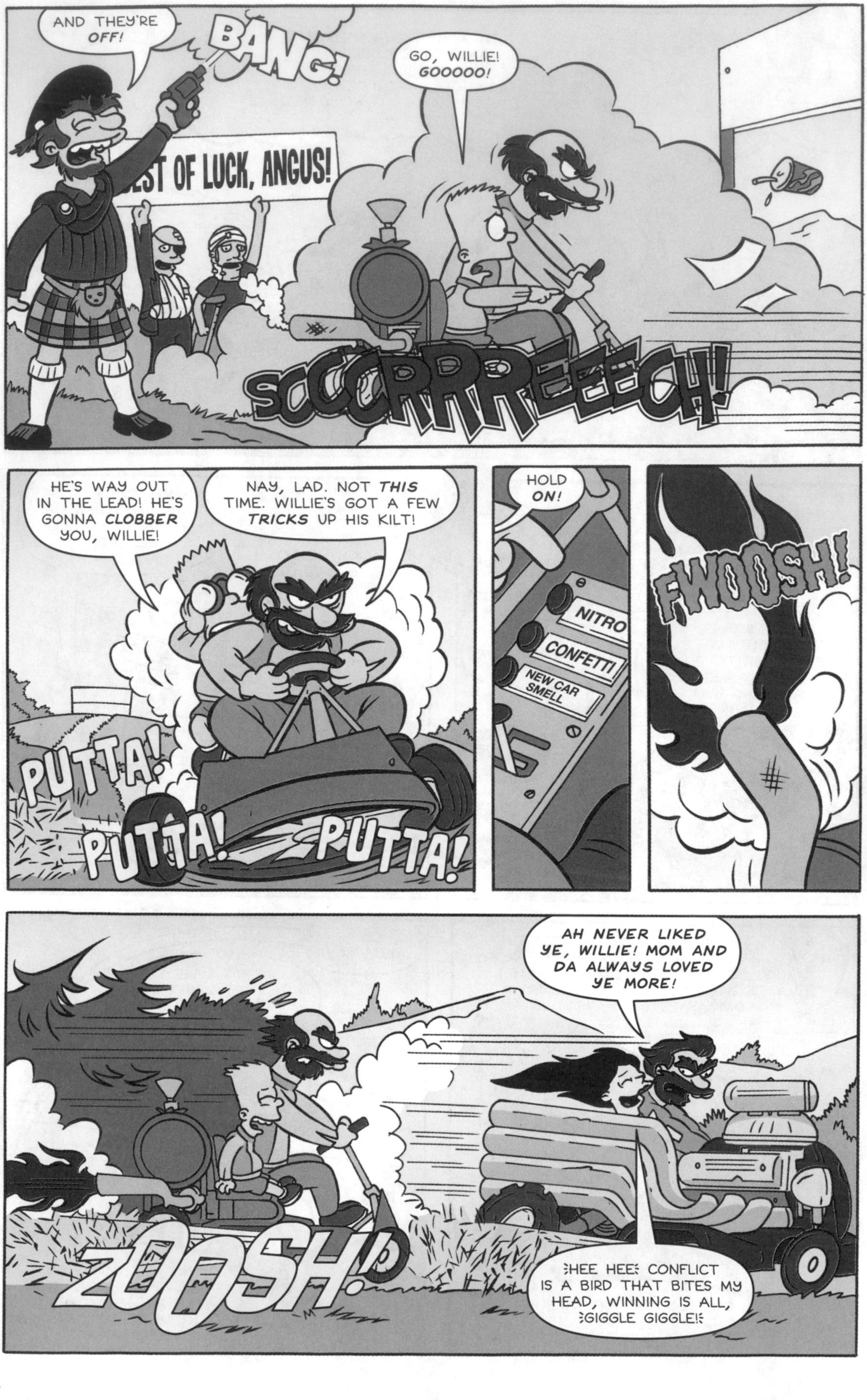
AND THEY'RE OFF!
BANG!
BEST OF LUCK, ANGUS!
GO, WILLIE! GOOOOO!
SCCCRRRREEECH!
HE'S WAY OUT IN THE LEAD! HE'S GONNA CLOBBER YOU, WILLIE!
NAY, LAD. NOT THIS TIME. WILLIE'S GOT A FEW TRICKS UP HIS KILT!
PUTTA! PUTTA! PUTTA!
HOLD ON!
NITRO
CONFETTI
NEW CAR SMELL
FWOOSH!
AH NEVER LIKED YE, WILLIE! MOM AND DA ALWAYS LOVED YE MORE!
ZOOSH!
HEE HEE CONFLICT IS A BIRD THAT BITES MY HEAD, WINNING IS ALL, GIGGLE GIGGLE!

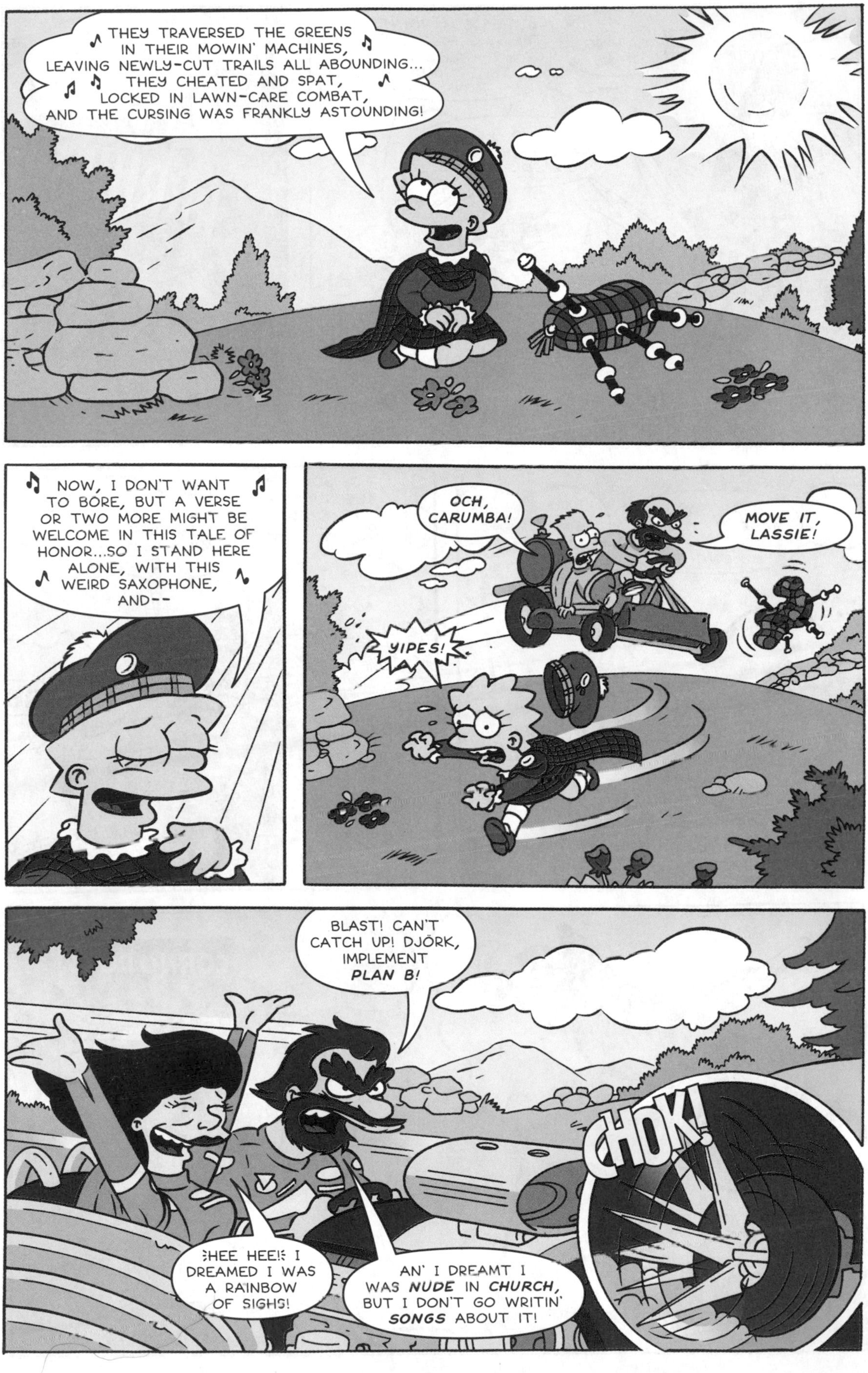
THEY TRAVERSED THE GREENS IN THEIR MOWIN' MACHINES, LEAVING NEWLY-CUT TRAILS ALL ABOUNDING... THEY CHEATED AND SPAT, LOCKED IN LAWN-CARE COMBAT, AND THE CURSING WAS FRANKLY ASTOUNDING!
NOW, I DON'T WANT TO BORE, BUT A VERSE OR TWO MORE MIGHT BE WELCOME IN THIS TALE OF HONOR...SO I STAND HERE ALONE, WITH THIS WEIRD SAXOPHONE, AND--
OCH, CARUMBA!
MOVE IT, LASSIE!
YIPES!
BLAST! CAN'T CATCH UP! DJÖRK, IMPLEMENT PLAN B!
CHOK!
HEE HEE! I DREAMED I WAS A RAINBOW OF SIGHS!
AN' I DREAMT I WAS NUDE IN CHURCH, BUT I DON'T GO WRITIN' SONGS ABOUT IT!

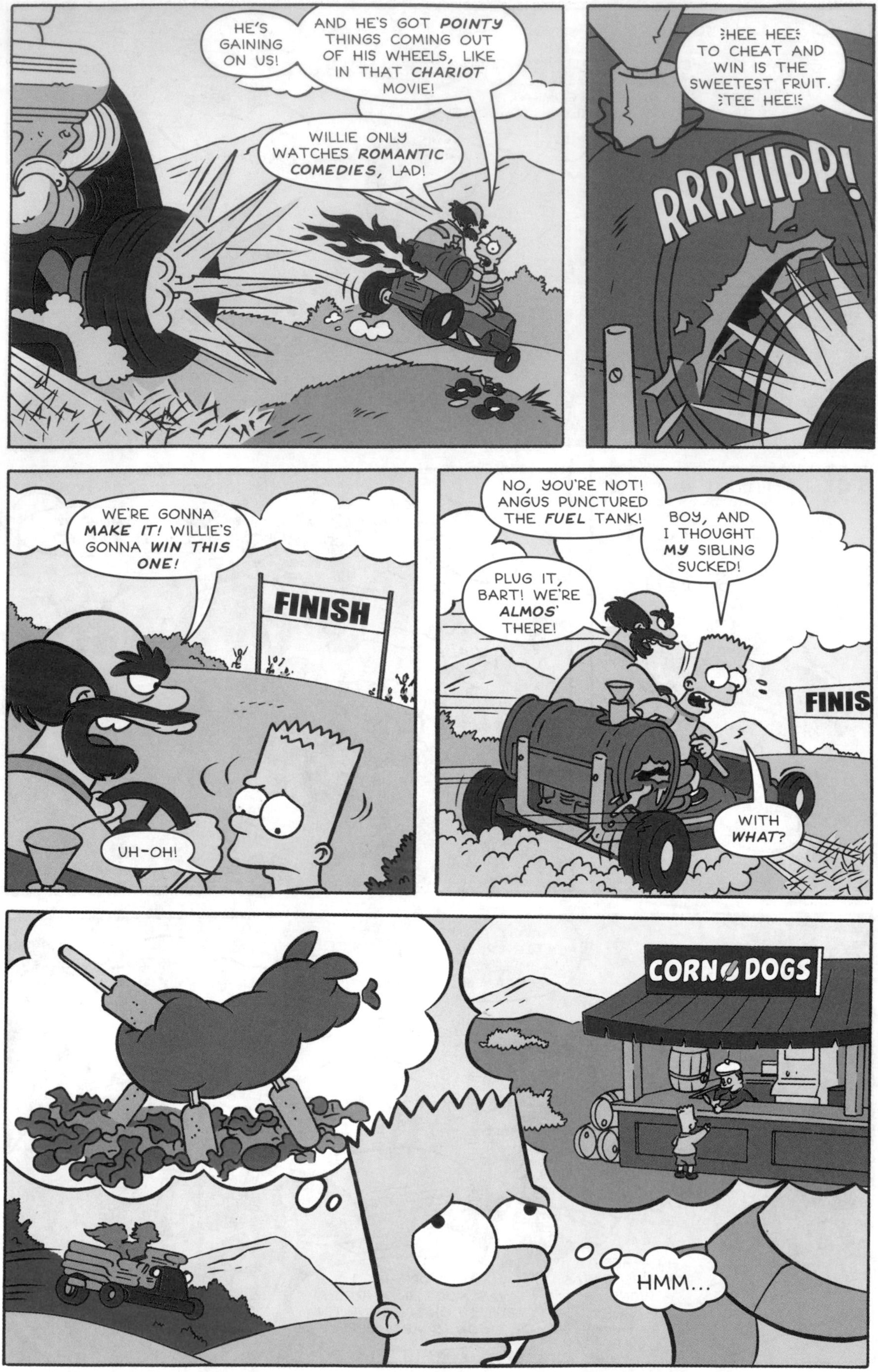
HE'S GAINING ON US!
AND HE'S GOT POINTY THINGS COMING OUT OF HIS WHEELS, LIKE IN THAT CHARIOT MOVIE!
WILLIE ONLY WATCHES ROMANTIC COMEDIES, LAD!
HEE HEE TO CHEAT AND WIN IS THE SWEETEST FRUIT. TEE HEE!
RRRIIIPP!
WE'RE GONNA MAKE IT! WILLIE'S GONNA WIN THIS ONE!
FINISH
UH-OH!
NO, YOU'RE NOT! ANGUS PUNCTURED THE FUEL TANK!
BOY, AND I THOUGHT MY SIBLING SUCKED!
PLUG IT, BART! WE'RE ALMOS' THERE!
FINIS
WITH WHAT?
CORN DOGS
HMM...

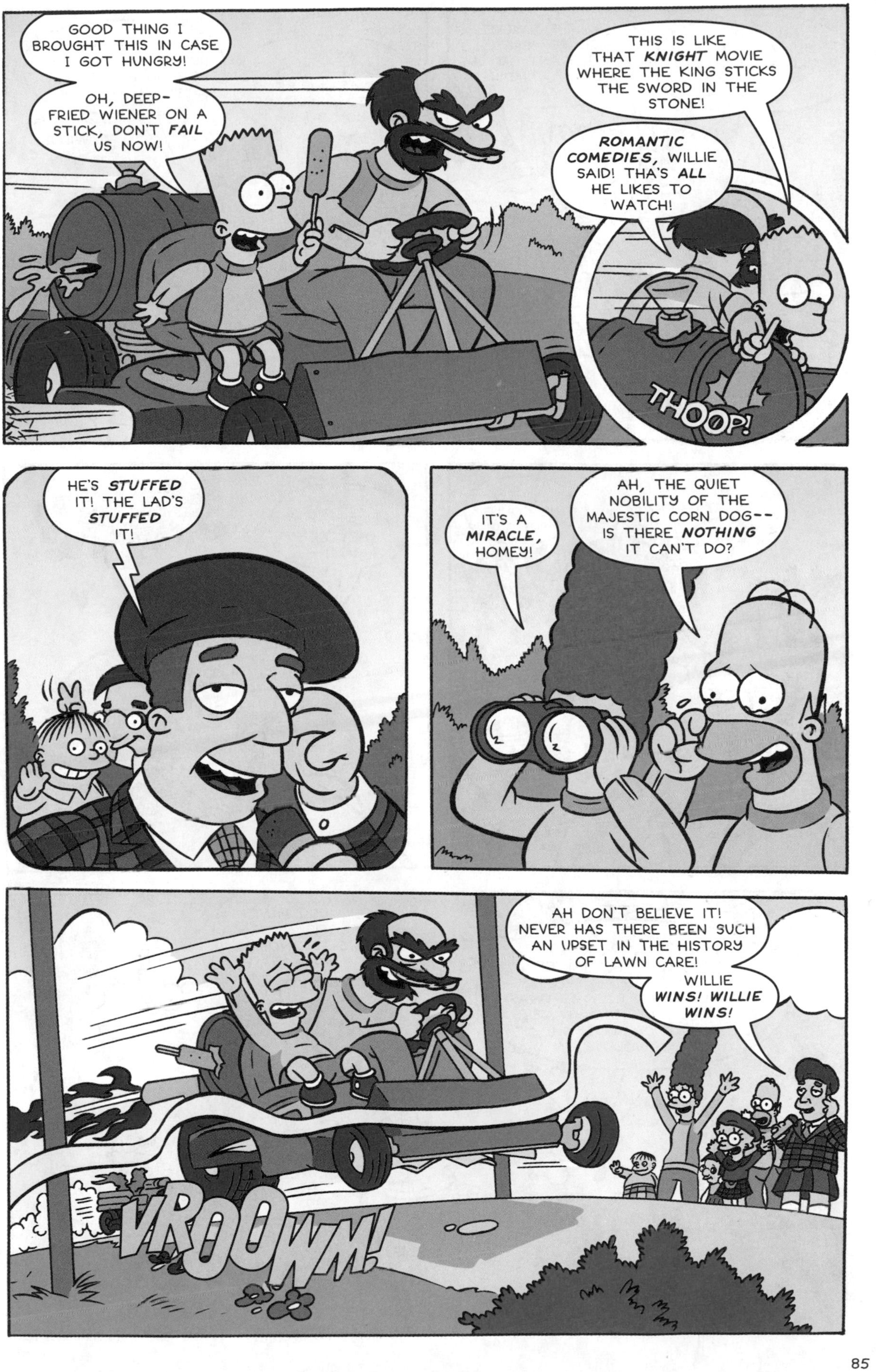
GOOD THING I BROUGHT THIS IN CASE I GOT HUNGRY!
OH, DEEP-FRIED WIENER ON A STICK, DON'T FAIL US NOW!
THIS IS LIKE THAT KNIGHT MOVIE WHERE THE KING STICKS THE SWORD IN THE STONE!
ROMANTIC COMEDIES, WILLIE SAID! THA'S ALL HE LIKES TO WATCH!
THOOP!
HE'S STUFFED IT! THE LAD'S STUFFED IT!
IT'S A MIRACLE, HOMEY!
AH, THE QUIET NOBILITY OF THE MAJESTIC CORN DOG-- IS THERE NOTHING IT CAN'T DO?
AH DON'T BELIEVE IT! NEVER HAS THERE BEEN SUCH AN UPSET IN THE HISTORY OF LAWN CARE!
WILLIE WINS! WILLIE WINS!
VROOWM!

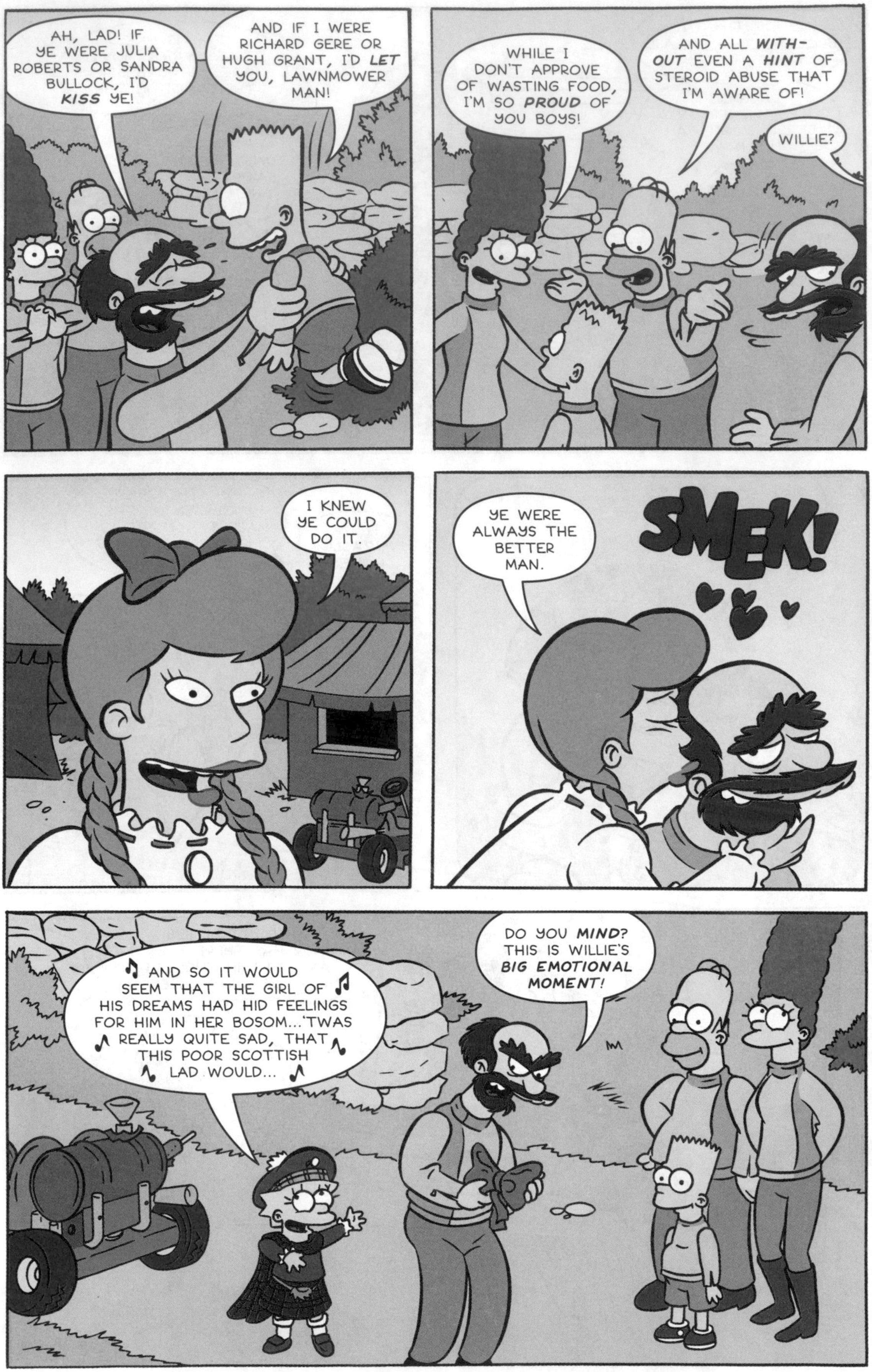
AH, LAD! IF YE WERE JULIA ROBERTS OR SANDRA BULLOCK, I'D KISS YE!
AND IF I WERE RICHARD GERE OR HUGH GRANT, I'D LET YOU, LAWNMOWER MAN!
WHILE I DON'T APPROVE OF WASTING FOOD, I'M SO PROUD OF YOU BOYS!
AND ALL WITH-OUT EVEN A HINT OF STEROID ABUSE THAT I'M AWARE OF!
WILLIE?
I KNEW YE COULD DO IT.
YE WERE ALWAYS THE BETTER MAN.
SMEK!
AND SO IT WOULD SEEM THAT THE GIRL OF HIS DREAMS HAD HID FEELINGS FOR HIM IN HER BOSOM...'TWAS REALLY QUITE SAD, THAT THIS POOR SCOTTISH LAD WOULD...
DO YOU MIND? THIS IS WILLIE'S BIG EMOTIONAL MOMENT!

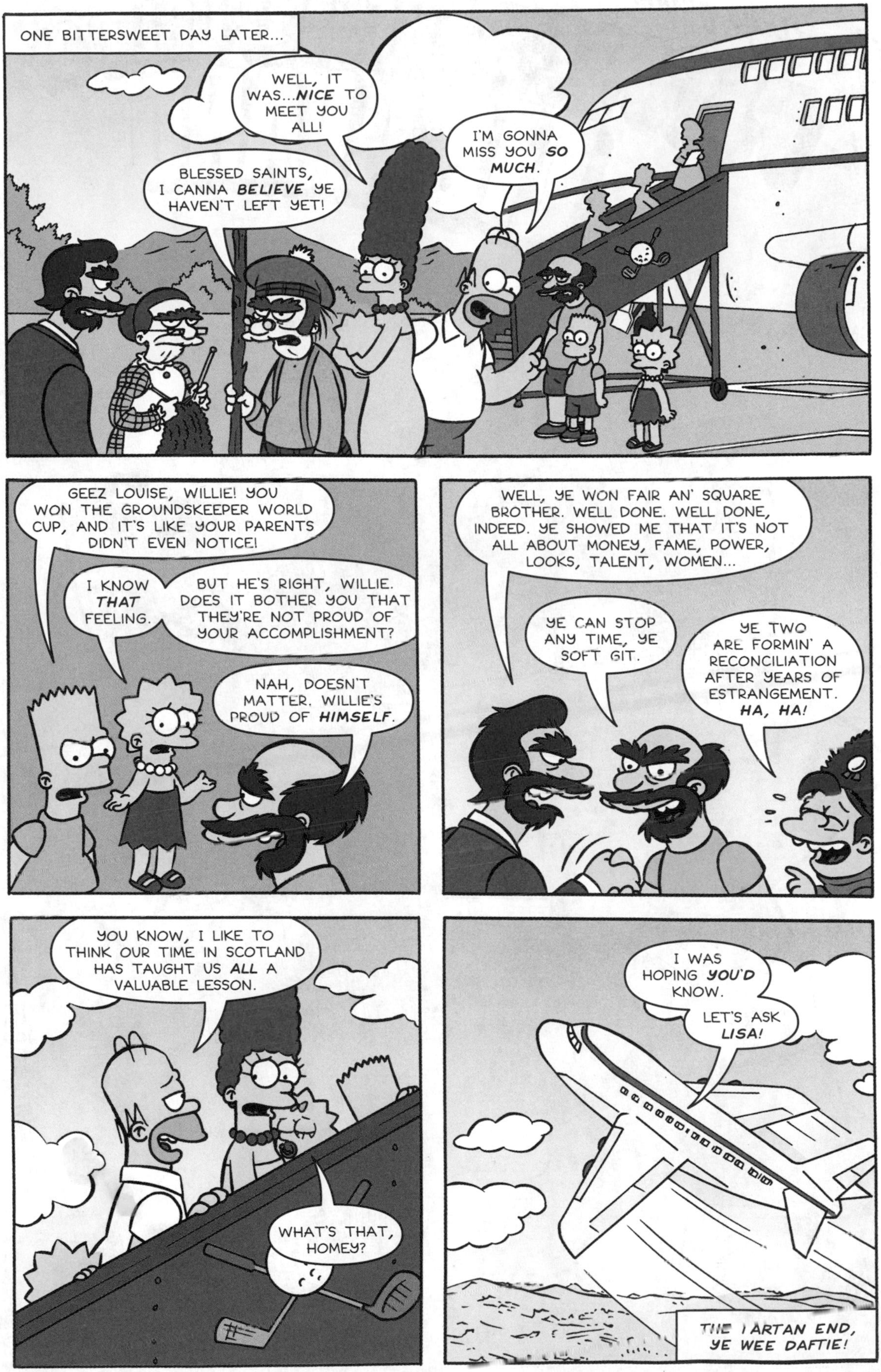
ONE BITTERSWEET DAY LATER...
BLESSED SAINTS, I CANNA BELIEVE YE HAVEN'T LEFT YET!
WELL, IT WAS...NICE TO MEET YOU ALL!
I'M GONNA MISS YOU SO MUCH.
GEEZ LOUISE, WILLIE! YOU WON THE GROUNDSKEEPER WORLD CUP, AND IT'S LIKE YOUR PARENTS DIDN'T EVEN NOTICE!
I KNOW THAT FEELING.
BUT HE'S RIGHT, WILLIE. DOES IT BOTHER YOU THAT THEY'RE NOT PROUD OF YOUR ACCOMPLISHMENT?
NAH, DOESN'T MATTER. WILLIE'S PROUD OF HIMSELF.
WELL, YE WON FAIR AN' SQUARE BROTHER. WELL DONE. WELL DONE, INDEED. YE SHOWED ME THAT IT'S NOT ALL ABOUT MONEY, FAME, POWER, LOOKS, TALENT, WOMEN...
YE CAN STOP ANY TIME, YE SOFT GIT.
YE TWO ARE FORMIN' A RECONCILIATION AFTER YEARS OF ESTRANGEMENT. HA, HA!
YOU KNOW, I LIKE TO THINK OUR TIME IN SCOTLAND HAS TAUGHT US ALL A VALUABLE LESSON.
WHAT'S THAT, HOMEY?
I WAS HOPING YOU'D KNOW.
LET'S ASK LISA!
THE TARTAN END, YE WEE DAFTIE!

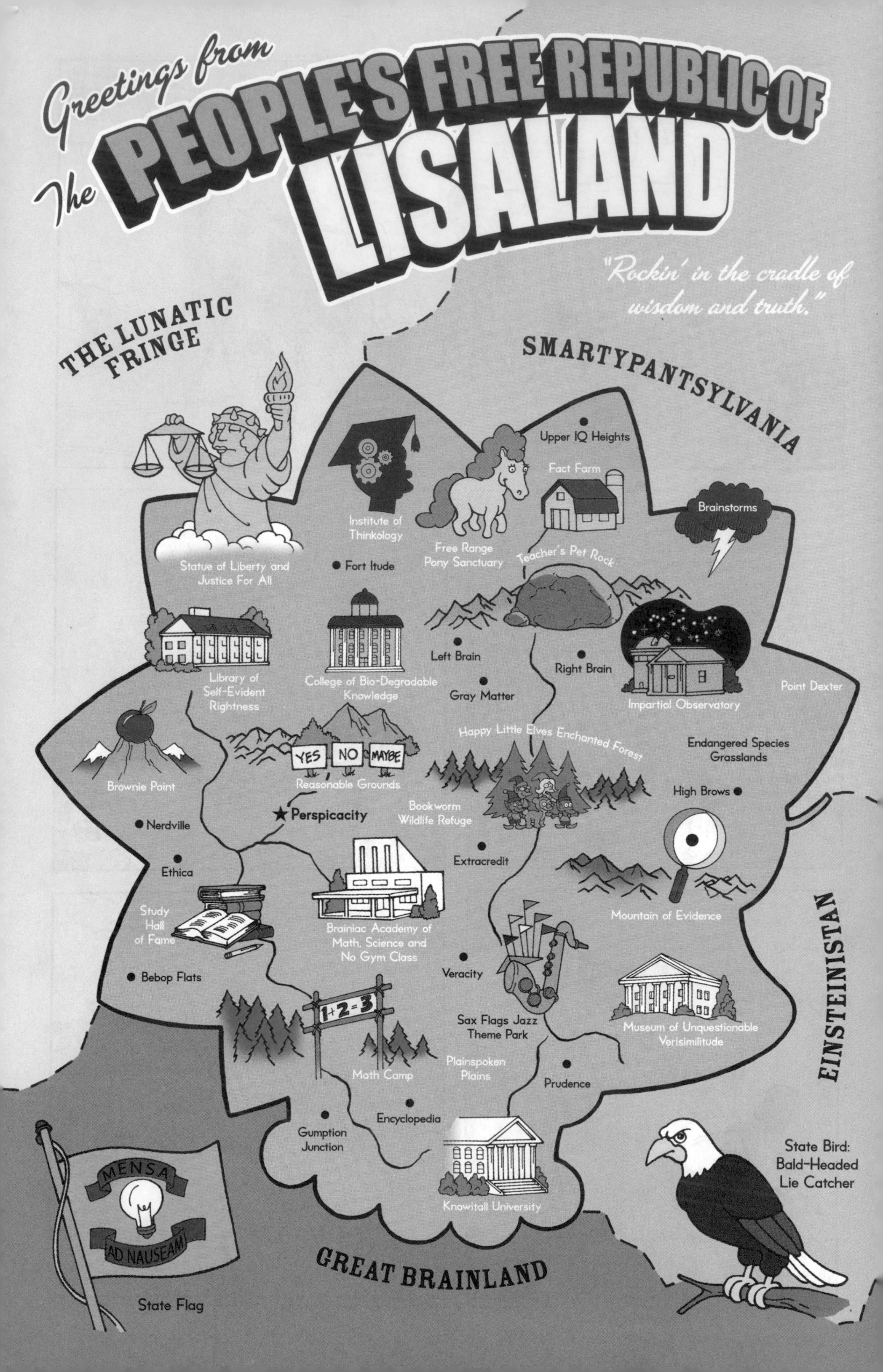
Greetings from
The PEOPLE'S FREE REPUBLIC OF
LISALAND
"Rockin' in the cradle of wisdom and truth."
THE LUNATIC FRINGE
SMARTYPANTSYLVANIA
EINSTEINISTAN
GREAT BRAINLAND
Upper IQ Heights
Fact Farm
Brainstorms
Institute of Thinkology
Free Range Pony Sanctuary
Teacher's Pet Rock
Statue of Liberty and Justice For All
Fort Itude
Library of Self-Evident Rightness
College of Bio-Degradable Knowledge
Left Brain
Right Brain
Gray Matter
Impartial Observatory
Point Dexter
Happy Little Elves Enchanted Forest
Endangered Species Grasslands
YES
NO
MAYBE
Reasonable Grounds
Brownie Point
High Brows
Bookworm Wildlife Refuge
Perspicacity
Nerdville
Ethica
Extracredit
Mountain of Evidence
Study Hall of Fame
Brainiac Academy of Math, Science and No Gym Class
Veracity
Bebop Flats
Museum of Unquestionable Verisimilitude
1+2=3
Sax Flags Jazz Theme Park
Math Camp
Plainspoken Plains
Prudence
Encyclopedia
Gumption Junction
Knowitall University
MENSA
AD NAUSEAM
State Flag
State Bird: Bald-Headed Lie Catcher

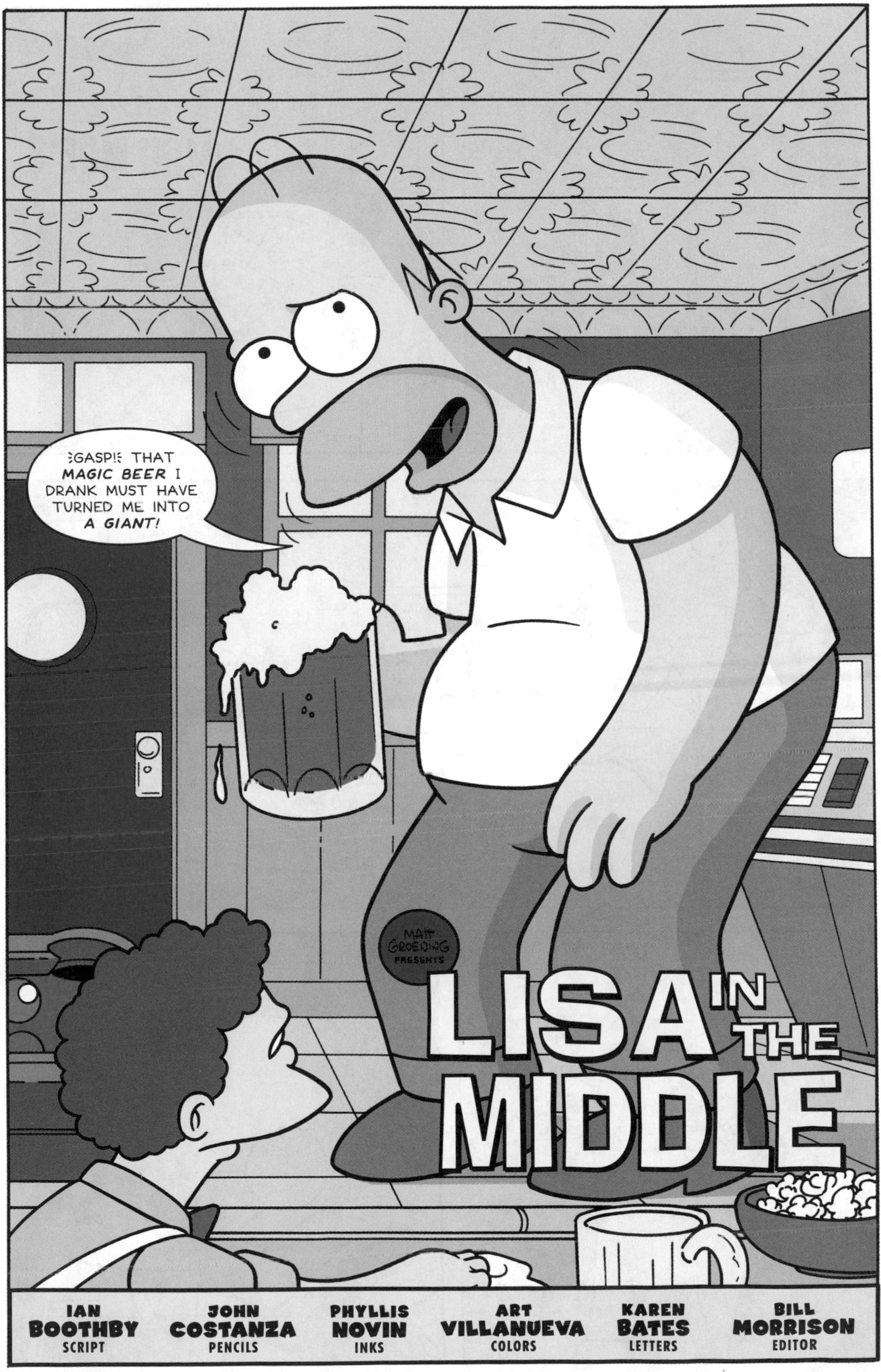
GASP! THAT MAGIC BEER I DRANK MUST HAVE TURNED ME INTO A GIANT!
MATT GROENING PRESENTS
LISA IN THE MIDDLE

IAN BOOTHBY SCRIPT
JOHN COSTANZA PENCILS
PHYLLIS NOVIN INKS
ART VILLANUEVA COLORS
KAREN BATES LETTERS
BILL MORRISON EDITOR

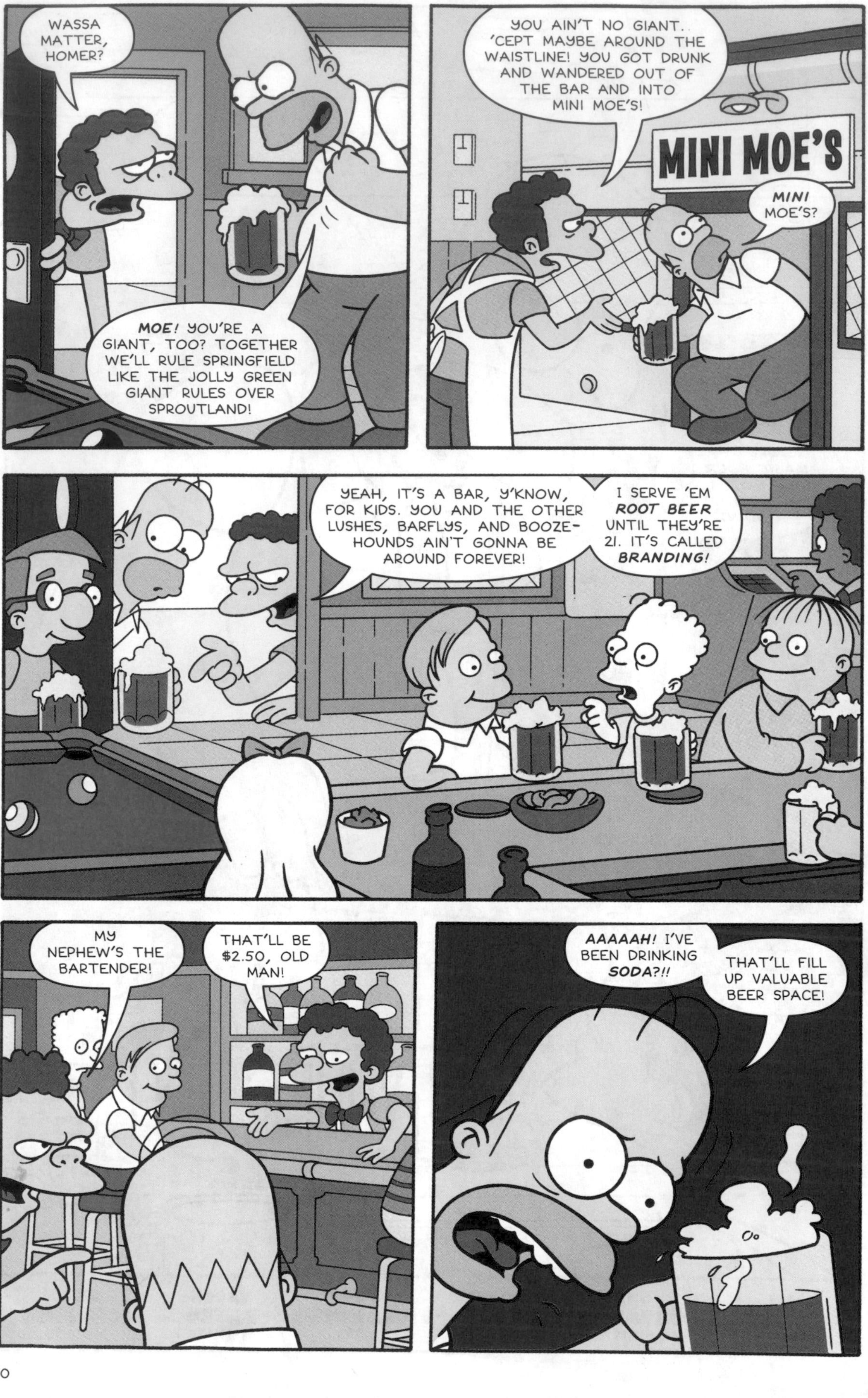
WASSA MATTER, HOMER?
MOE! YOU'RE A GIANT, TOO? TOGETHER WE'LL RULE SPRINGFIELD LIKE THE JOLLY GREEN GIANT RULES OVER SPROUTLAND!
YOU AIN'T NO GIANT.. 'CEPT MAYBE AROUND THE WAISTLINE! YOU GOT DRUNK AND WANDERED OUT OF THE BAR AND INTO MINI MOE'S!
MINI MOE'S
MINI MOE'S?
YEAH, IT'S A BAR, Y'KNOW, FOR KIDS. YOU AND THE OTHER LUSHES, BARFLYS, AND BOOZE-HOUNDS AIN'T GONNA BE AROUND FOREVER!
I SERVE 'EM ROOT BEER UNTIL THEY'RE 21. IT'S CALLED BRANDING!
MY NEPHEW'S THE BARTENDER!
THAT'LL BE $2.50, OLD MAN!
AAAAAH! I'VE BEEN DRINKING SODA?!!
THAT'LL FILL UP VALUABLE BEER SPACE!

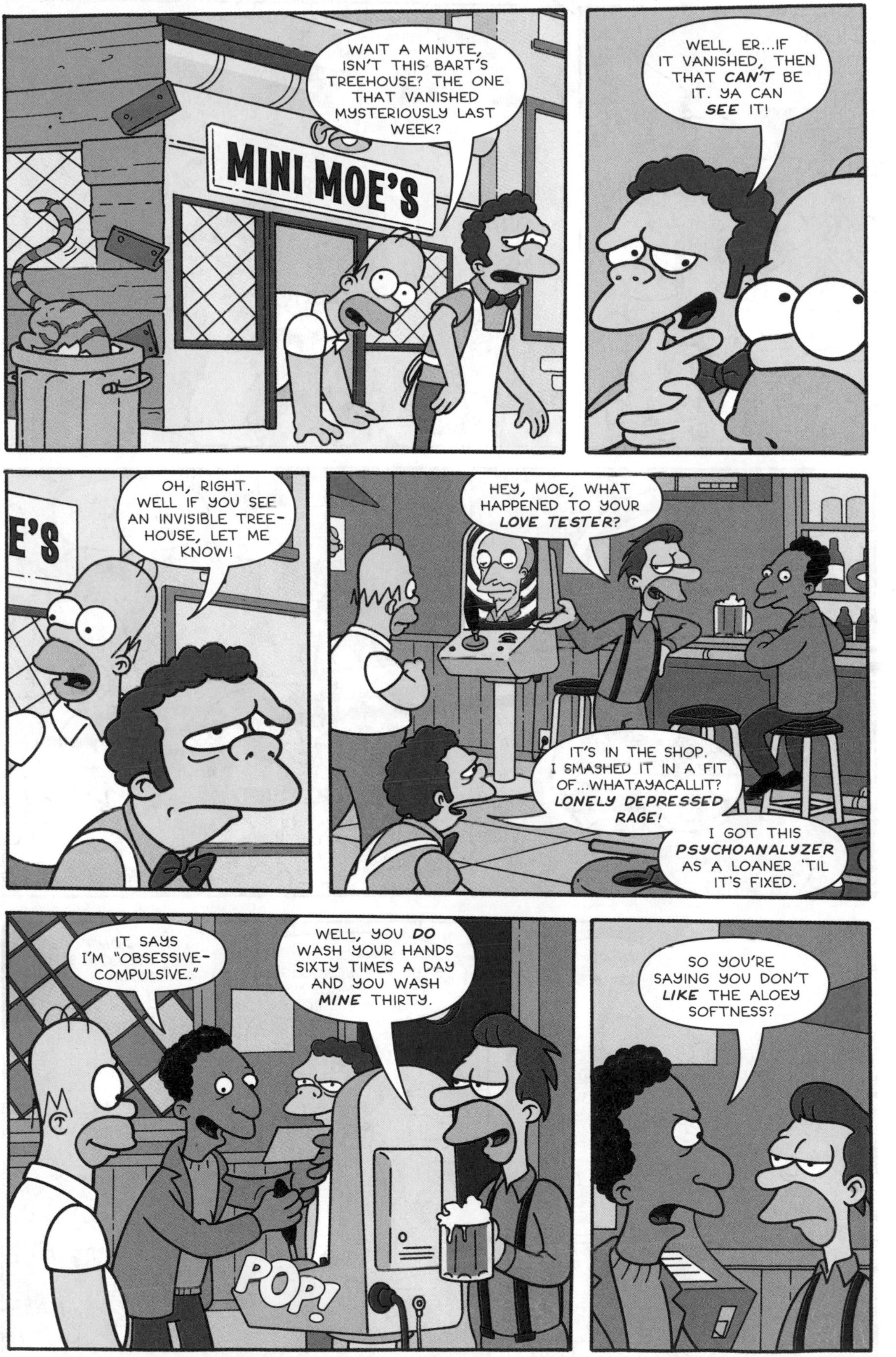
MINI MOE'S
WAIT A MINUTE, ISN'T THIS BART'S TREEHOUSE? THE ONE THAT VANISHED MYSTERIOUSLY LAST WEEK?
WELL, ER...IF IT VANISHED, THEN THAT CAN'T BE IT. YA CAN SEE IT!
OH, RIGHT. WELL IF YOU SEE AN INVISIBLE TREE-HOUSE, LET ME KNOW!
HEY, MOE, WHAT HAPPENED TO YOUR LOVE TESTER?
IT'S IN THE SHOP. I SMASHED IT IN A FIT OF...WHATAYACALLIT? LONELY DEPRESSED RAGE!
I GOT THIS PSYCHOANALYZER AS A LOANER 'TIL IT'S FIXED.
IT SAYS I'M "OBSESSIVE-COMPULSIVE."
WELL, YOU DO WASH YOUR HANDS SIXTY TIMES A DAY AND YOU WASH MINE THIRTY.
POP!
SO YOU'RE SAYING YOU DON'T LIKE THE ALOEY SOFTNESS?

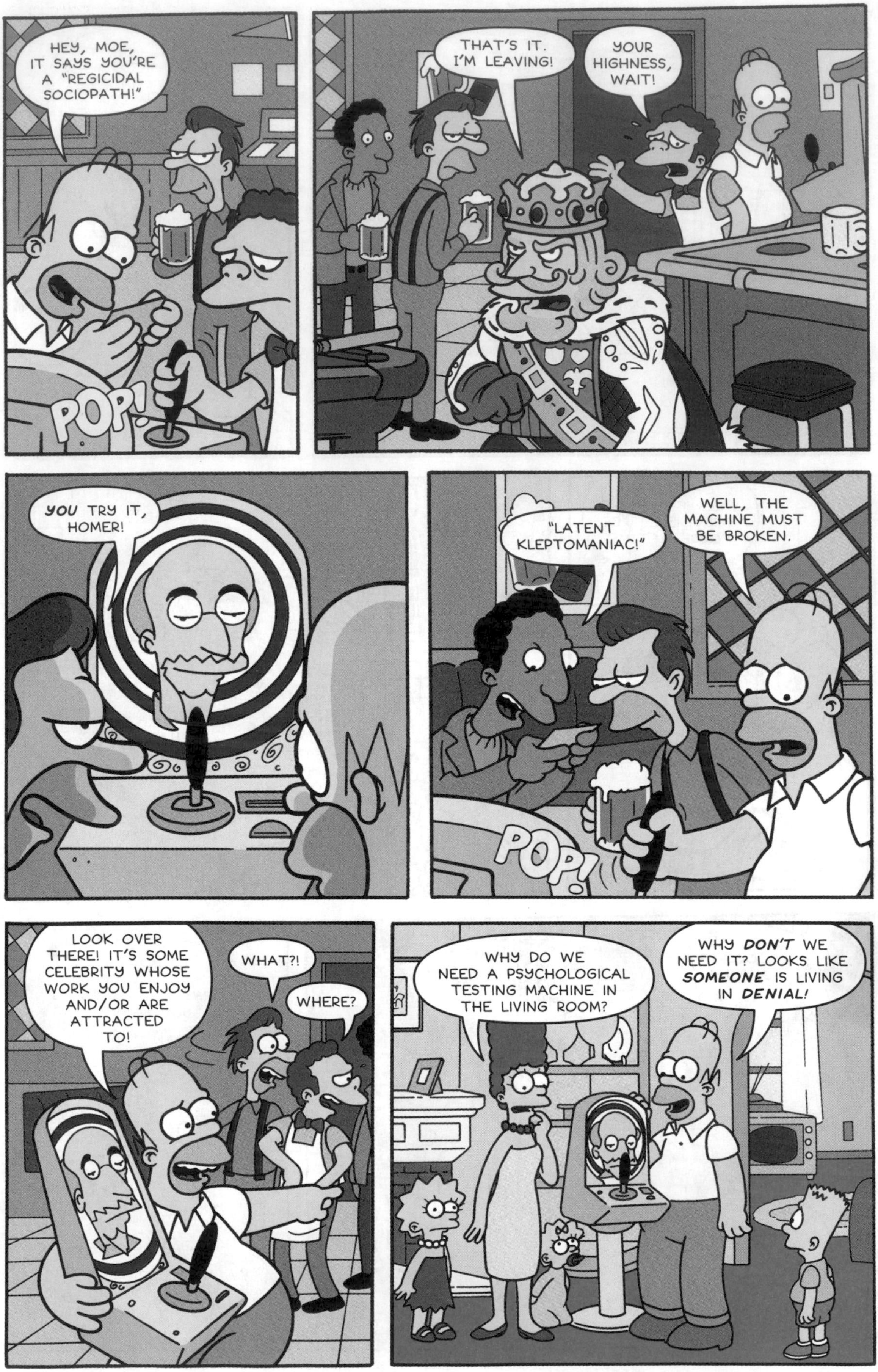
HEY, MOE, IT SAYS YOU'RE A "REGICIDAL SOCIOPATH!"
POP!
THAT'S IT. I'M LEAVING!
YOUR HIGHNESS, WAIT!
YOU TRY IT, HOMER!
"LATENT KLEPTOMANIAC!"
WELL, THE MACHINE MUST BE BROKEN.
POP!
LOOK OVER THERE! IT'S SOME CELEBRITY WHOSE WORK YOU ENJOY AND/OR ARE ATTRACTED TO!
WHAT?!
WHERE?
WHY DO WE NEED A PSYCHOLOGICAL TESTING MACHINE IN THE LIVING ROOM?
WHY DON'T WE NEED IT? LOOKS LIKE SOMEONE IS LIVING IN DENIAL!

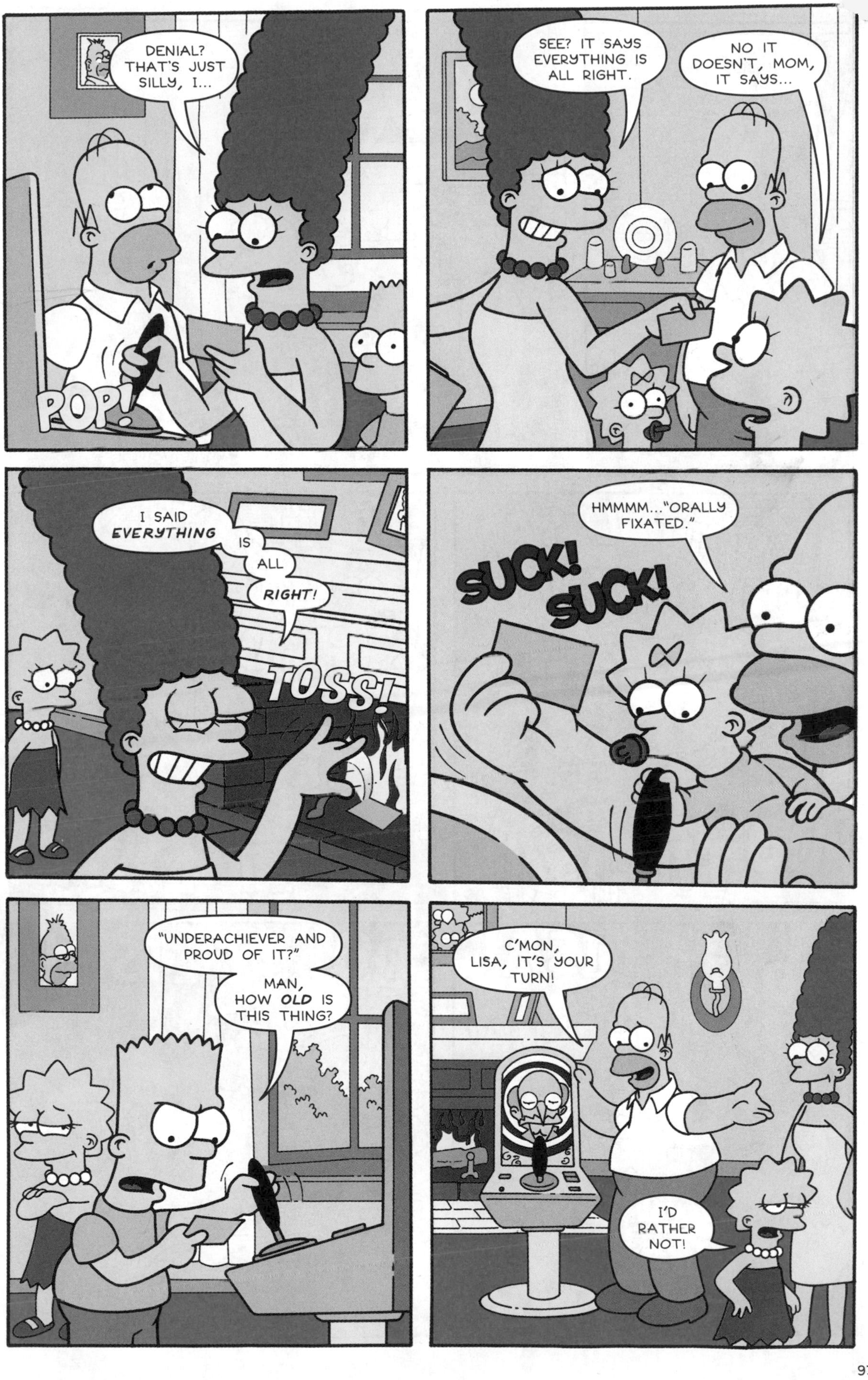
DENIAL? THAT'S JUST SILLY, I...
POP!
SEE? IT SAYS EVERYTHING IS ALL RIGHT.
NO IT DOESN'T, MOM, IT SAYS...
I SAID EVERYTHING
IS
ALL
RIGHT!
TOSS!
HMMMM..."ORALLY FIXATED."
SUCK! SUCK!
"UNDERACHIEVER AND PROUD OF IT?"
MAN, HOW OLD IS THIS THING?
C'MON, LISA, IT'S YOUR TURN!
I'D RATHER NOT!

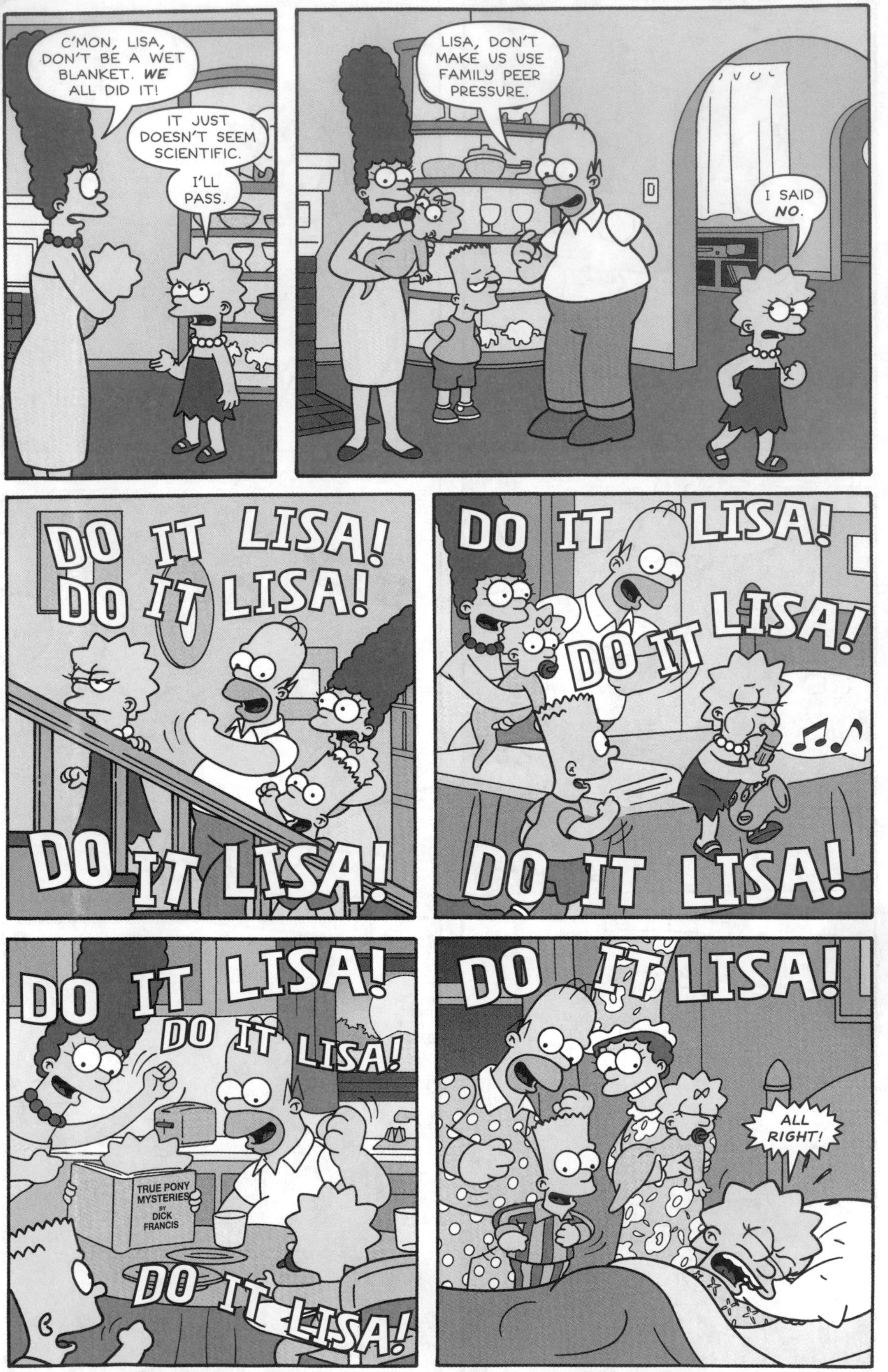
C'MON, LISA, DON'T BE A WET BLANKET. WE ALL DID IT!
IT JUST DOESN'T SEEM SCIENTIFIC.
I'LL PASS.
LISA, DON'T MAKE US USE FAMILY PEER PRESSURE.
I SAID NO.
DO IT LISA!
DO IT LISA!
DO IT LISA!
DO IT LISA!
DO IT LISA!
DO IT LISA!
DO IT LISA!
DO IT LISA!
TRUE PONY MYSTERIES BY DICK FRANCIS
DO IT LISA!
DO IT LISA!
ALL RIGHT!

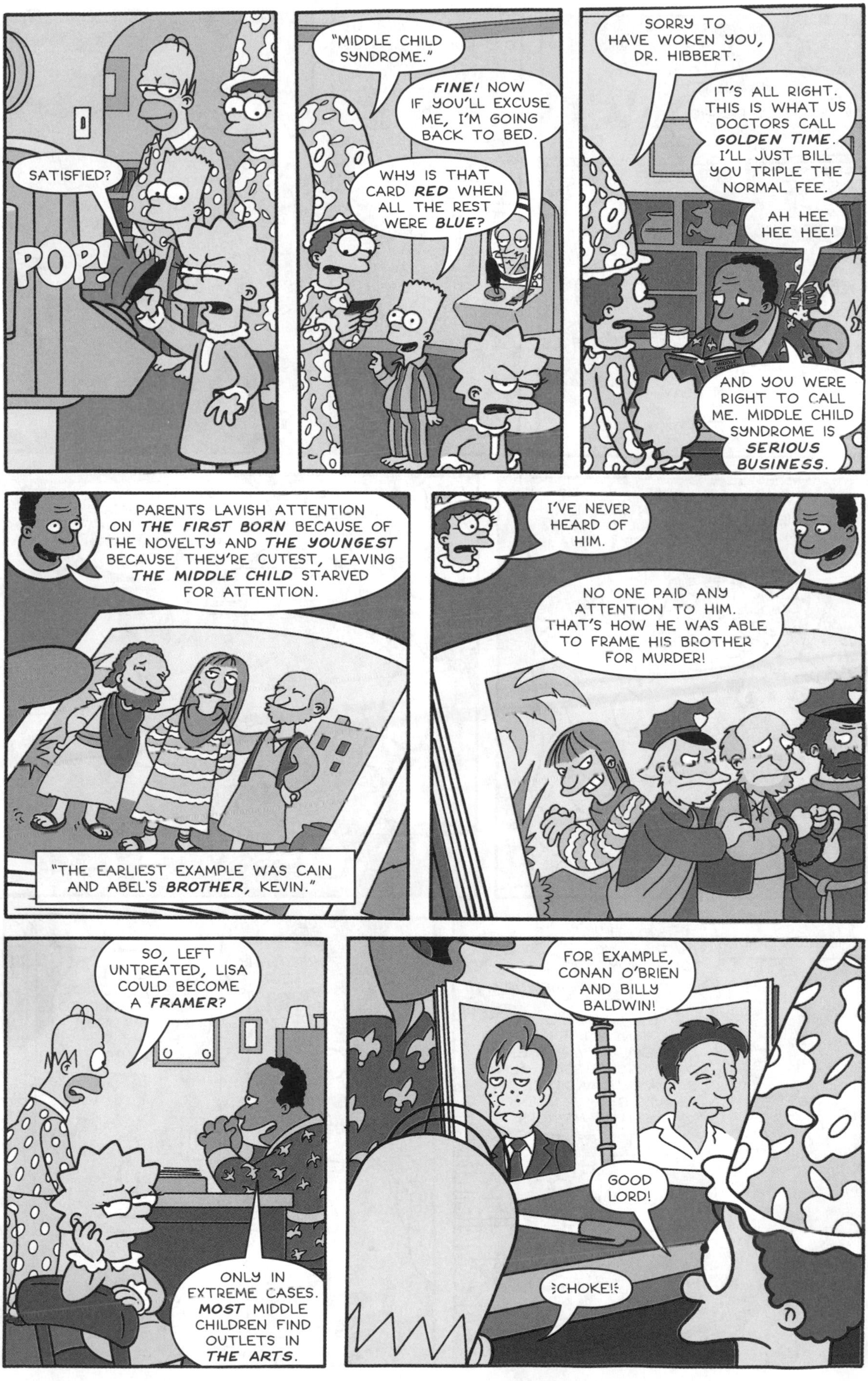
SATISFIED?
POP!
"MIDDLE CHILD SYNDROME."
FINE! NOW IF YOU'LL EXCUSE ME, I'M GOING BACK TO BED.
WHY IS THAT CARD RED WHEN ALL THE REST WERE BLUE?
SORRY TO HAVE WOKEN YOU, DR. HIBBERT.
IT'S ALL RIGHT. THIS IS WHAT US DOCTORS CALL GOLDEN TIME. I'LL JUST BILL YOU TRIPLE THE NORMAL FEE.
AH HEE HEE HEE!
AND YOU WERE RIGHT TO CALL ME. MIDDLE CHILD SYNDROME IS SERIOUS BUSINESS.
PARENTS LAVISH ATTENTION ON THE FIRST BORN BECAUSE OF THE NOVELTY AND THE YOUNGEST BECAUSE THEY'RE CUTEST, LEAVING THE MIDDLE CHILD STARVED FOR ATTENTION.
"THE EARLIEST EXAMPLE WAS CAIN AND ABEL'S BROTHER, KEVIN."
I'VE NEVER HEARD OF HIM.
NO ONE PAID ANY ATTENTION TO HIM. THAT'S HOW HE WAS ABLE TO FRAME HIS BROTHER FOR MURDER!
SO, LEFT UNTREATED, LISA COULD BECOME A FRAMER?
ONLY IN EXTREME CASES. MOST MIDDLE CHILDREN FIND OUTLETS IN THE ARTS.
FOR EXAMPLE, CONAN O'BRIEN AND BILLY BALDWIN!
GOOD LORD!
CHOKE!

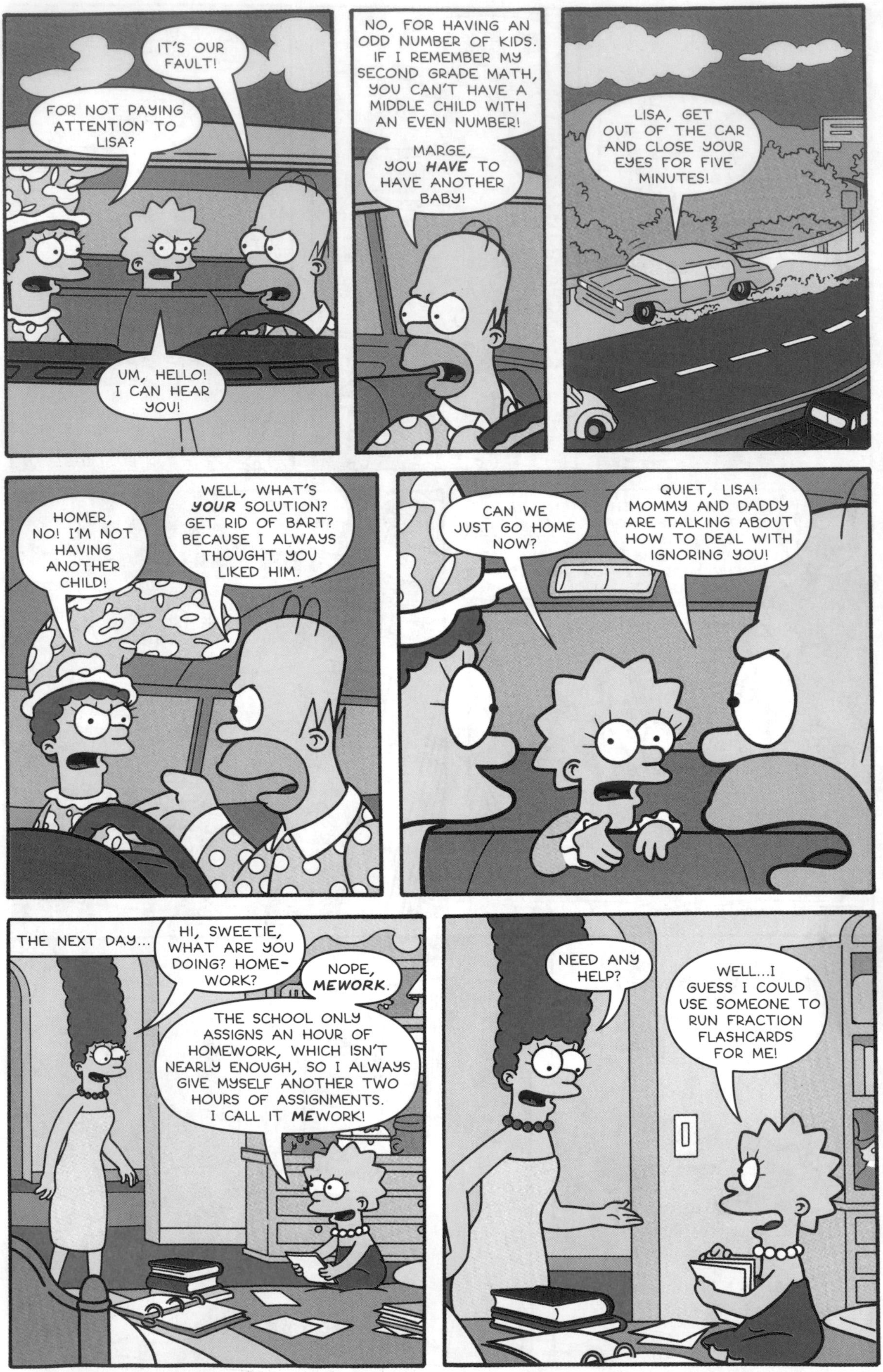
IT'S OUR FAULT!
FOR NOT PAYING ATTENTION TO LISA?
UM, HELLO! I CAN HEAR YOU!
NO, FOR HAVING AN ODD NUMBER OF KIDS. IF I REMEMBER MY SECOND GRADE MATH, YOU CAN'T HAVE A MIDDLE CHILD WITH AN EVEN NUMBER!
MARGE, YOU **HAVE** TO HAVE ANOTHER BABY!
LISA, GET OUT OF THE CAR AND CLOSE YOUR EYES FOR FIVE MINUTES!
HOMER, NO! I'M NOT HAVING ANOTHER CHILD!
WELL, WHAT'S **YOUR** SOLUTION? GET RID OF BART? BECAUSE I ALWAYS THOUGHT YOU LIKED HIM.
CAN WE JUST GO HOME NOW?
QUIET, LISA! MOMMY AND DADDY ARE TALKING ABOUT HOW TO DEAL WITH IGNORING YOU!
THE NEXT DAY...
HI, SWEETIE, WHAT ARE YOU DOING? HOME-WORK?
NOPE, **MEWORK**.
THE SCHOOL ONLY ASSIGNS AN HOUR OF HOMEWORK, WHICH ISN'T NEARLY ENOUGH, SO I ALWAYS GIVE MYSELF ANOTHER TWO HOURS OF ASSIGNMENTS. I CALL IT **ME**WORK!
NEED ANY HELP?
WELL...I GUESS I COULD USE SOMEONE TO RUN FRACTION FLASHCARDS FOR ME!

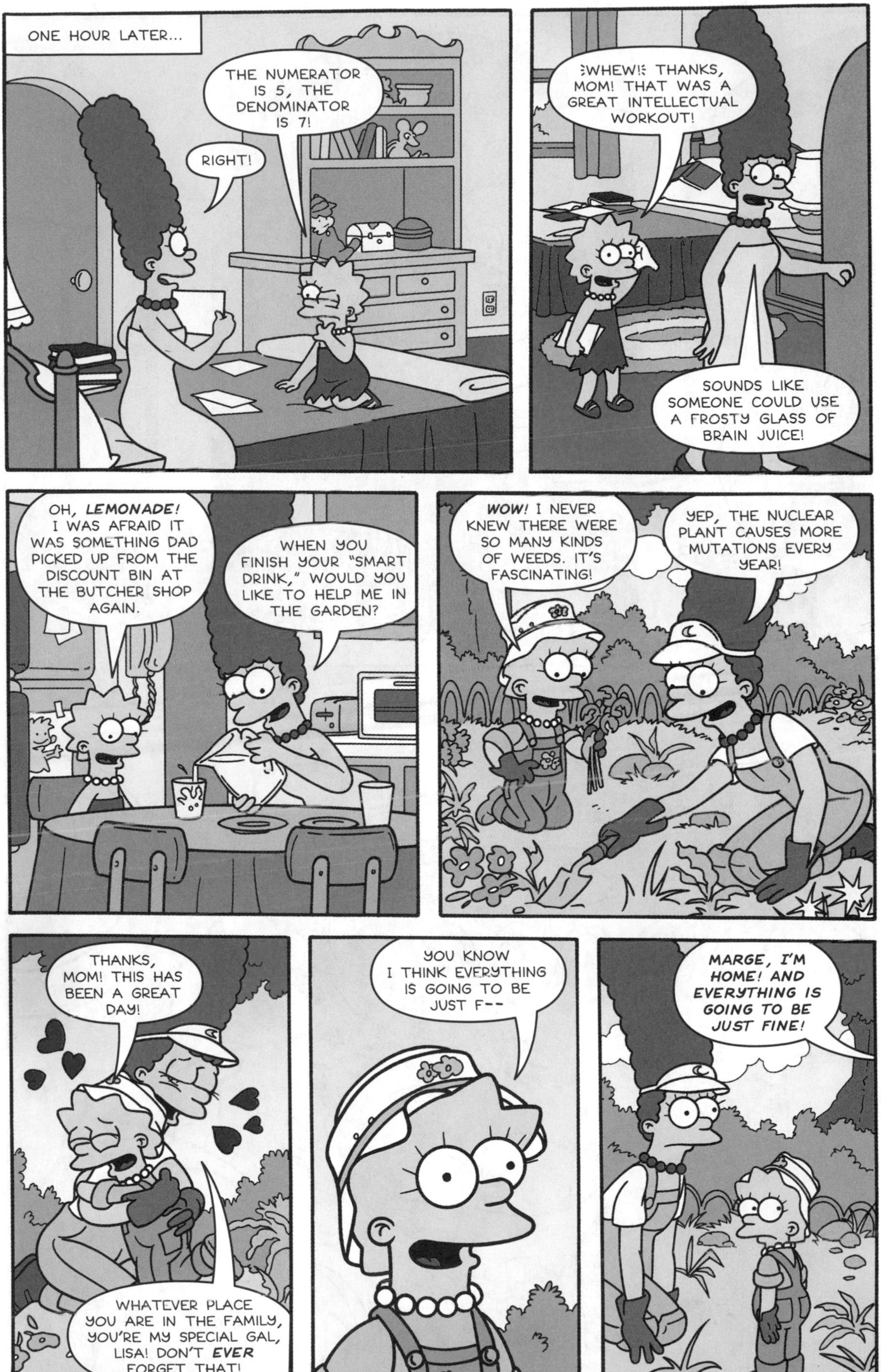
ONE HOUR LATER...
THE NUMERATOR IS 5, THE DENOMINATOR IS 7!
RIGHT!
WHEW! THANKS, MOM! THAT WAS A GREAT INTELLECTUAL WORKOUT!
SOUNDS LIKE SOMEONE COULD USE A FROSTY GLASS OF BRAIN JUICE!
OH, LEMONADE! I WAS AFRAID IT WAS SOMETHING DAD PICKED UP FROM THE DISCOUNT BIN AT THE BUTCHER SHOP AGAIN.
WHEN YOU FINISH YOUR "SMART DRINK," WOULD YOU LIKE TO HELP ME IN THE GARDEN?
WOW! I NEVER KNEW THERE WERE SO MANY KINDS OF WEEDS. IT'S FASCINATING!
YEP, THE NUCLEAR PLANT CAUSES MORE MUTATIONS EVERY YEAR!
THANKS, MOM! THIS HAS BEEN A GREAT DAY!
WHATEVER PLACE YOU ARE IN THE FAMILY, YOU'RE MY SPECIAL GAL, LISA! DON'T EVER FORGET THAT!
YOU KNOW I THINK EVERYTHING IS GOING TO BE JUST F--
MARGE, I'M HOME! AND EVERYTHING IS GOING TO BE JUST FINE!

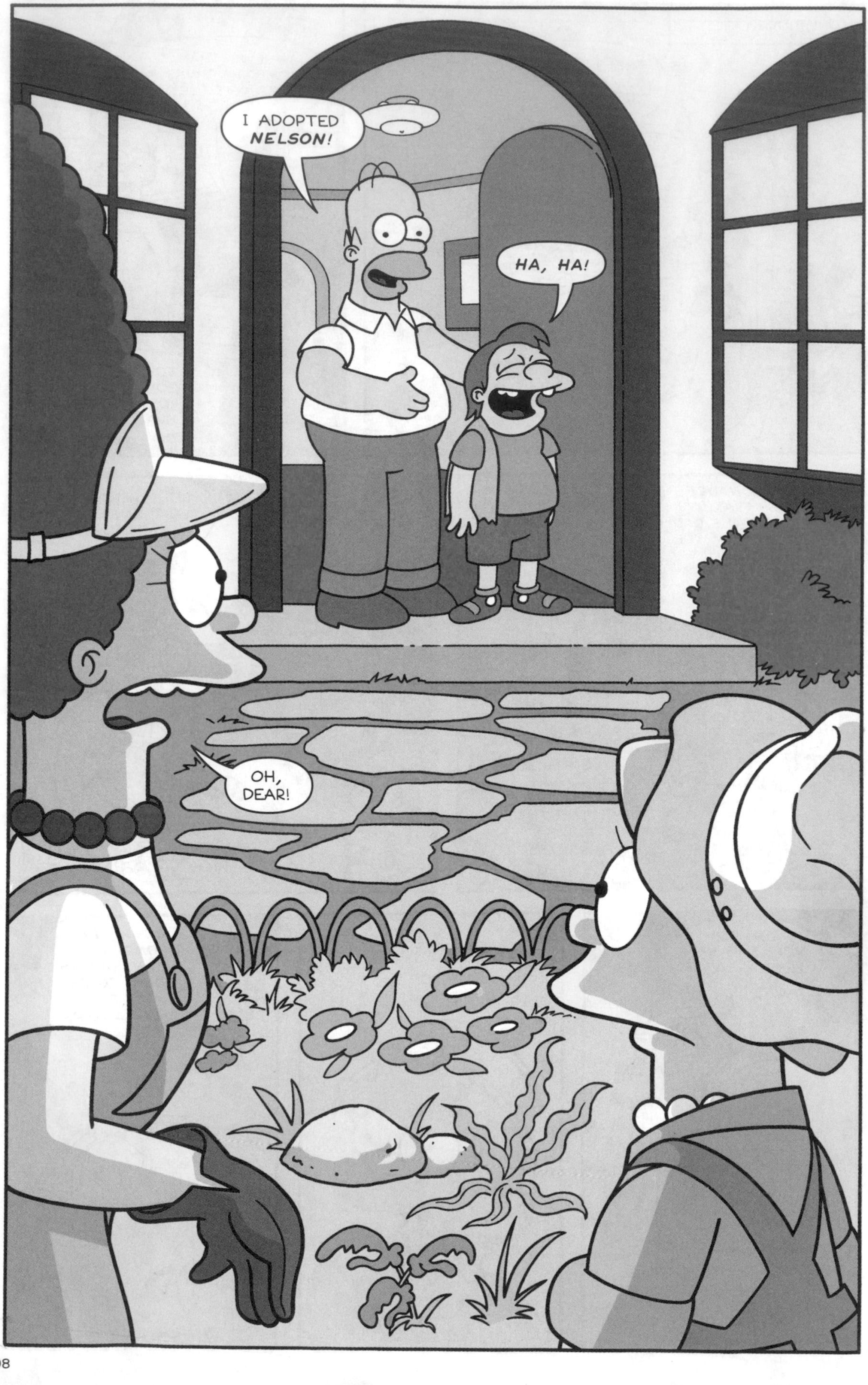
I ADOPTED **NELSON**!
HA, HA!
OH, DEAR!

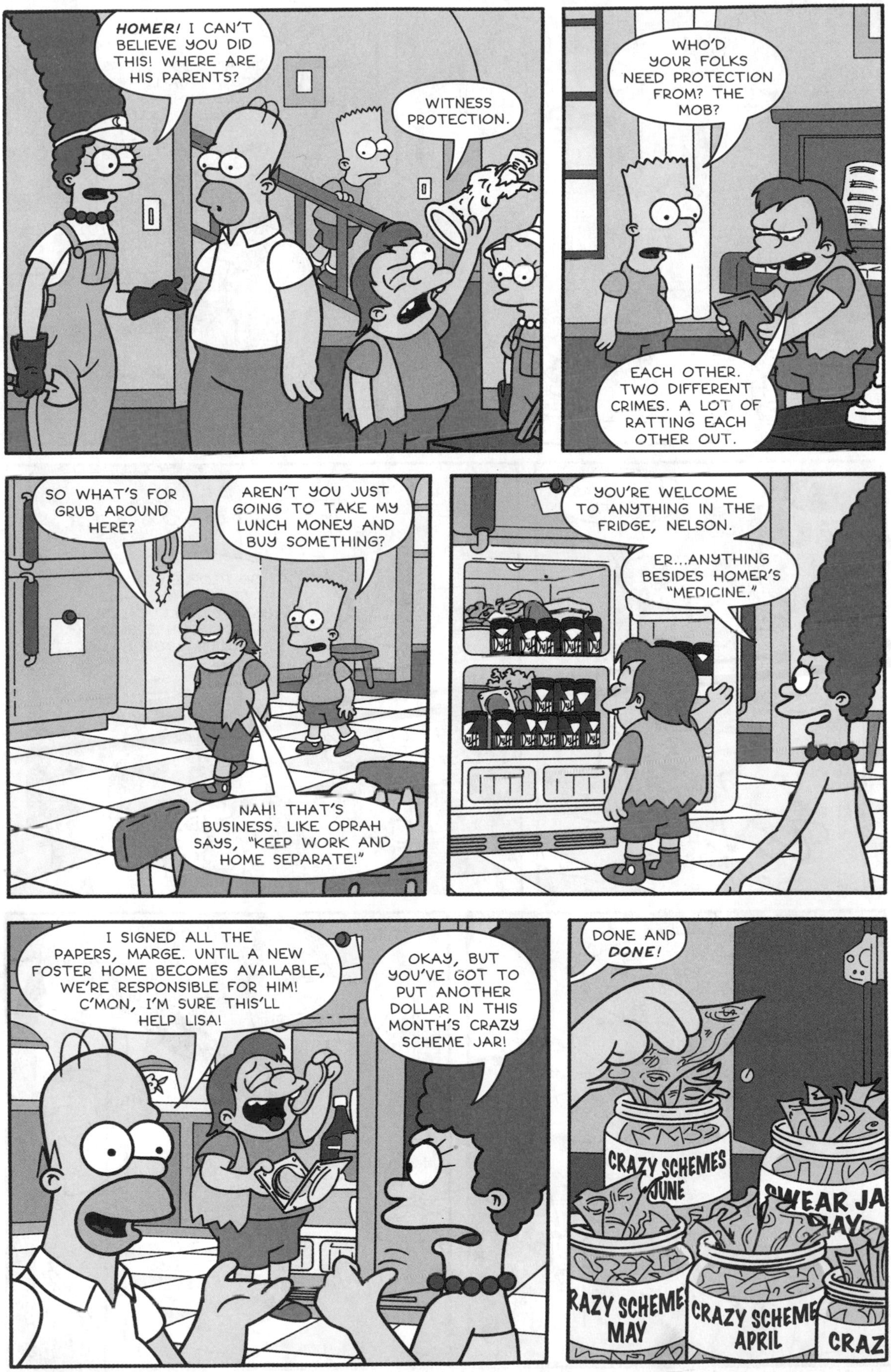
HOMER! I CAN'T BELIEVE YOU DID THIS! WHERE ARE HIS PARENTS?
WITNESS PROTECTION.
WHO'D YOUR FOLKS NEED PROTECTION FROM? THE MOB?
EACH OTHER. TWO DIFFERENT CRIMES. A LOT OF RATTING EACH OTHER OUT.
SO WHAT'S FOR GRUB AROUND HERE?
AREN'T YOU JUST GOING TO TAKE MY LUNCH MONEY AND BUY SOMETHING?
NAH! THAT'S BUSINESS. LIKE OPRAH SAYS, "KEEP WORK AND HOME SEPARATE!"
YOU'RE WELCOME TO ANYTHING IN THE FRIDGE, NELSON.
ER...ANYTHING BESIDES HOMER'S "MEDICINE."
I SIGNED ALL THE PAPERS, MARGE. UNTIL A NEW FOSTER HOME BECOMES AVAILABLE, WE'RE RESPONSIBLE FOR HIM! C'MON, I'M SURE THIS'LL HELP LISA!
OKAY, BUT YOU'VE GOT TO PUT ANOTHER DOLLAR IN THIS MONTH'S CRAZY SCHEME JAR!
DONE AND DONE!
CRAZY SCHEMES JUNE
CRAZY SCHEME MAY
CRAZY SCHEME APRIL

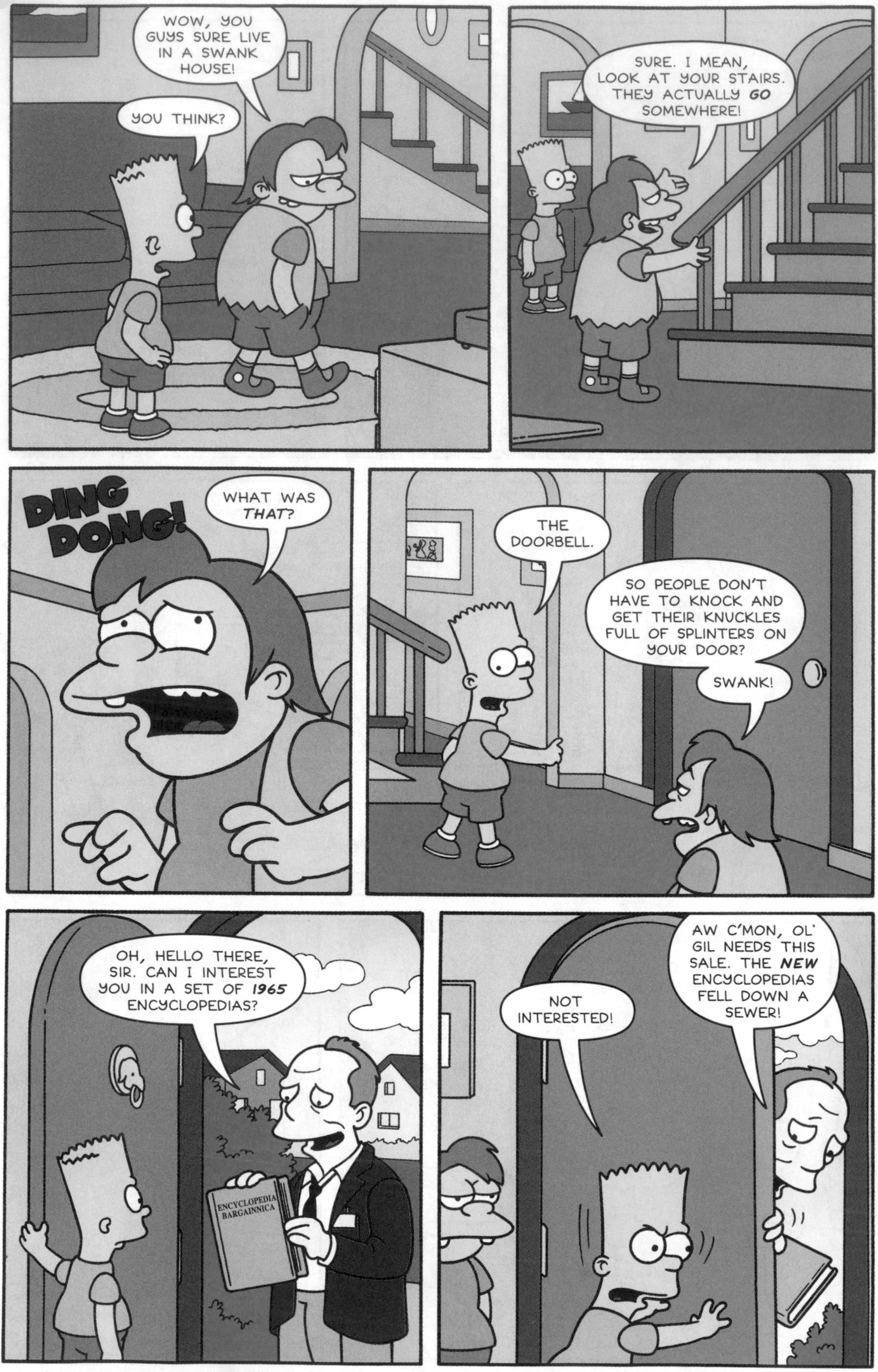
WOW, YOU GUYS SURE LIVE IN A SWANK HOUSE!
YOU THINK?
SURE. I MEAN, LOOK AT YOUR STAIRS. THEY ACTUALLY GO SOMEWHERE!
DING DONG!
WHAT WAS THAT?
THE DOORBELL.
SO PEOPLE DON'T HAVE TO KNOCK AND GET THEIR KNUCKLES FULL OF SPLINTERS ON YOUR DOOR?
SWANK!
OH, HELLO THERE, SIR. CAN I INTEREST YOU IN A SET OF 1965 ENCYCLOPEDIAS?
ENCYCLOPEDIA BARGAINNICA
NOT INTERESTED!
AW C'MON, OL' GIL NEEDS THIS SALE. THE NEW ENCYCLOPEDIAS FELL DOWN A SEWER!

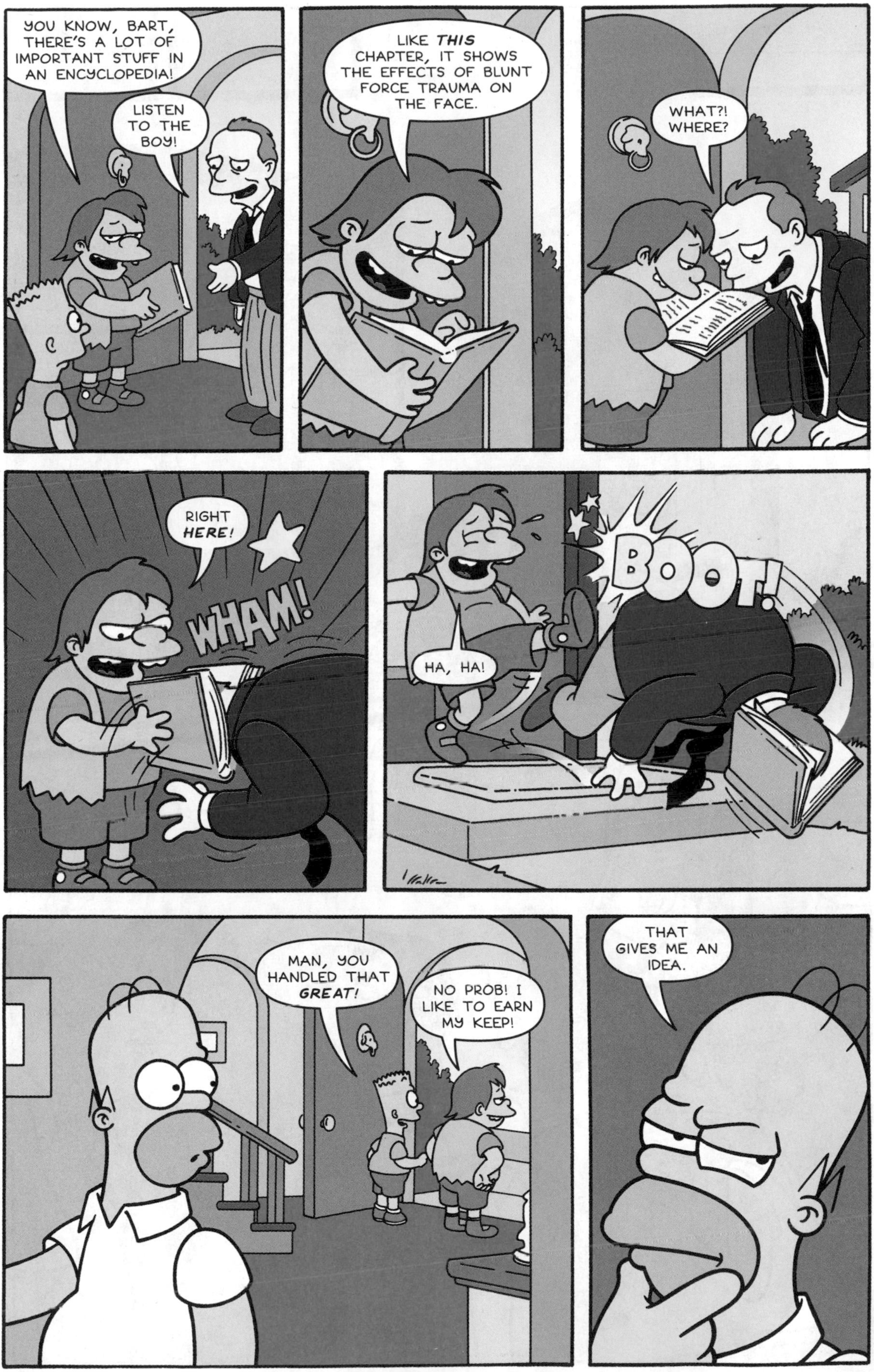
YOU KNOW, BART, THERE'S A LOT OF IMPORTANT STUFF IN AN ENCYCLOPEDIA!
LISTEN TO THE BOY!
LIKE THIS CHAPTER, IT SHOWS THE EFFECTS OF BLUNT FORCE TRAUMA ON THE FACE.
WHAT?! WHERE?
RIGHT HERE!
WHAM!
BOOT!
HA, HA!
MAN, YOU HANDLED THAT GREAT!
NO PROB! I LIKE TO EARN MY KEEP!
THAT GIVES ME AN IDEA.

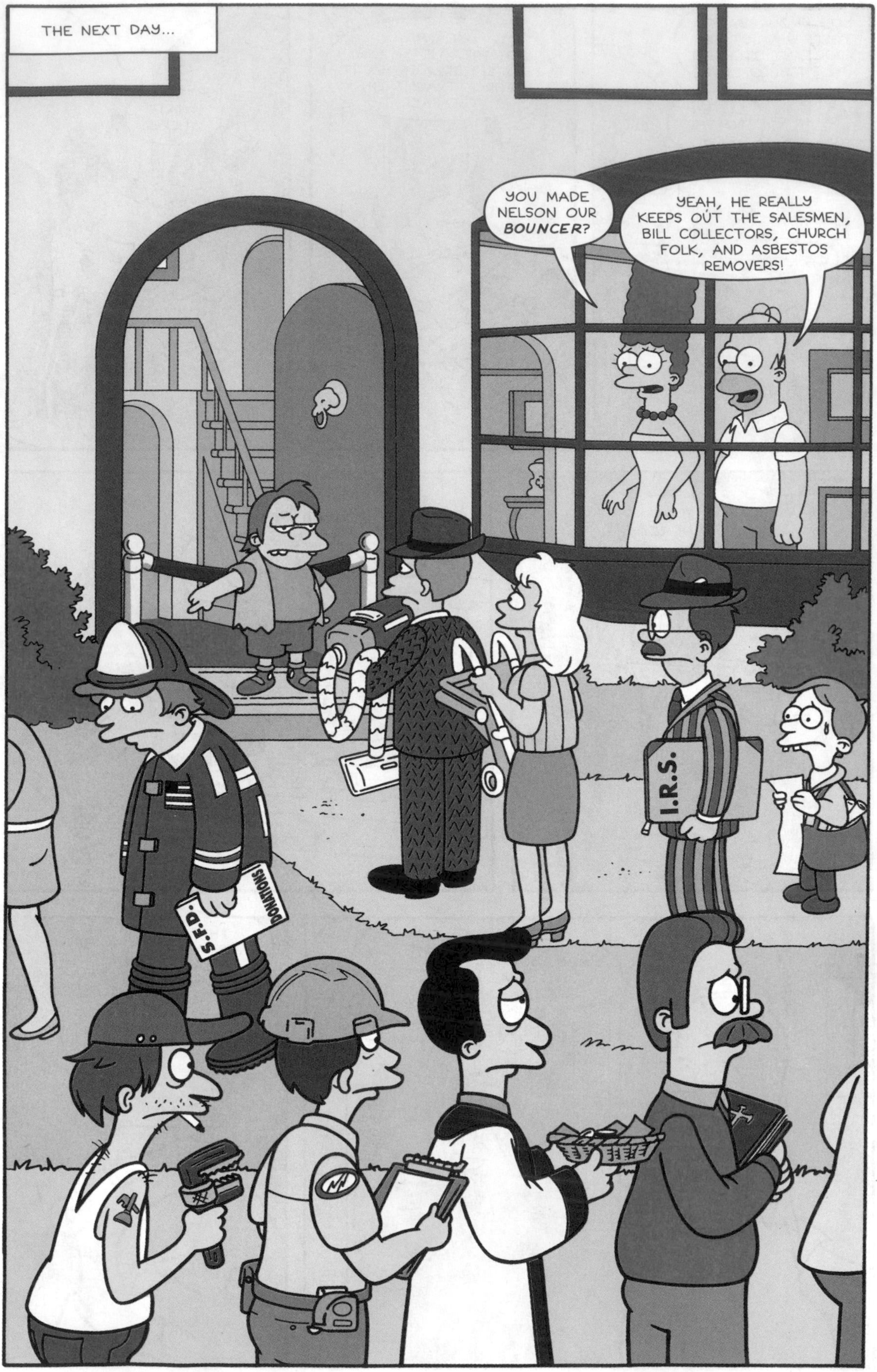
THE NEXT DAY...
YOU MADE NELSON OUR BOUNCER?
YEAH, HE REALLY KEEPS OUT THE SALESMEN, BILL COLLECTORS, CHURCH FOLK, AND ASBESTOS REMOVERS!
S.F.D.
DONATIONS
I.R.S.

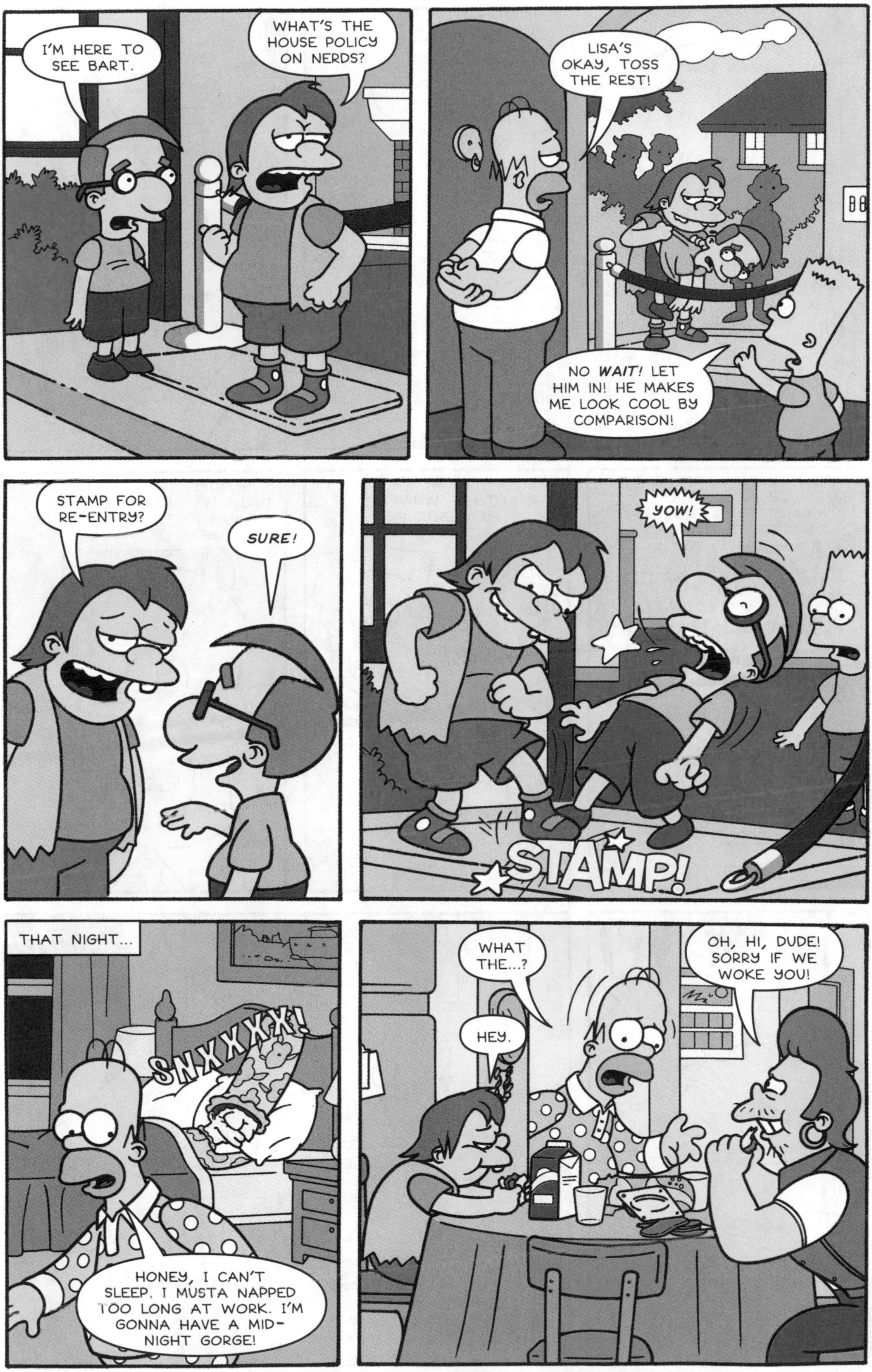
I'M HERE TO SEE BART.
WHAT'S THE HOUSE POLICY ON NERDS?
LISA'S OKAY, TOSS THE REST!
NO *WAIT!* LET HIM IN! HE MAKES ME LOOK COOL BY COMPARISON!
STAMP FOR RE-ENTRY?
SURE!
YOW!
STAMP!
THAT NIGHT...
SNXXXX!
HONEY, I CAN'T SLEEP. I MUSTA NAPPED TOO LONG AT WORK. I'M GONNA HAVE A MID-NIGHT GORGE!
WHAT THE...?
HEY.
OH, HI, DUDE! SORRY IF WE WOKE YOU!

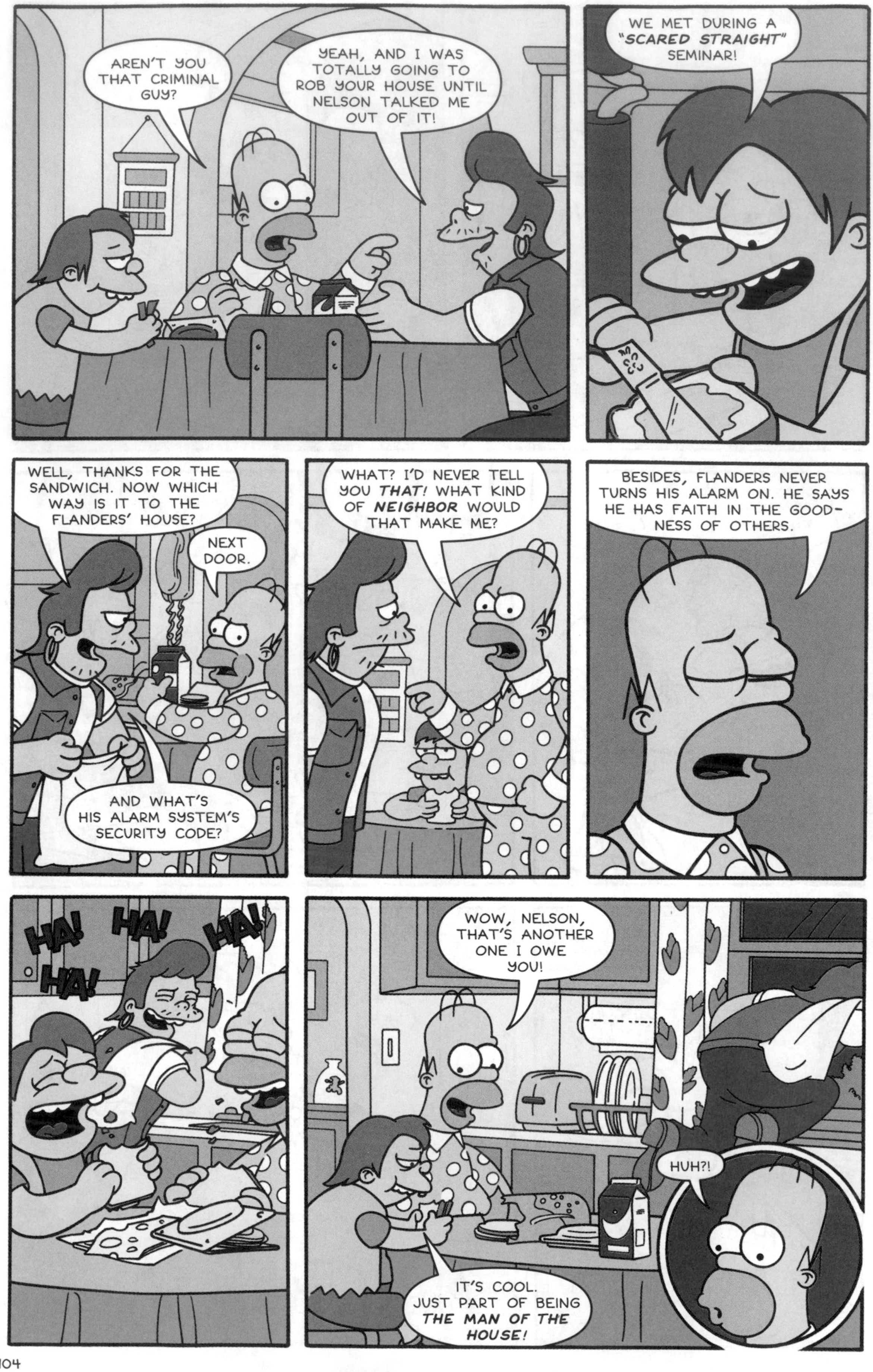
AREN'T YOU THAT CRIMINAL GUY?
YEAH, AND I WAS TOTALLY GOING TO ROB YOUR HOUSE UNTIL NELSON TALKED ME OUT OF IT!
WE MET DURING A "SCARED STRAIGHT" SEMINAR!
WELL, THANKS FOR THE SANDWICH. NOW WHICH WAY IS IT TO THE FLANDERS' HOUSE?
NEXT DOOR.
AND WHAT'S HIS ALARM SYSTEM'S SECURITY CODE?
WHAT? I'D NEVER TELL YOU THAT! WHAT KIND OF NEIGHBOR WOULD THAT MAKE ME?
BESIDES, FLANDERS NEVER TURNS HIS ALARM ON. HE SAYS HE HAS FAITH IN THE GOOD-NESS OF OTHERS.
HA! HA! HA! HA!
WOW, NELSON, THAT'S ANOTHER ONE I OWE YOU!
HUH?!
IT'S COOL. JUST PART OF BEING THE MAN OF THE HOUSE!

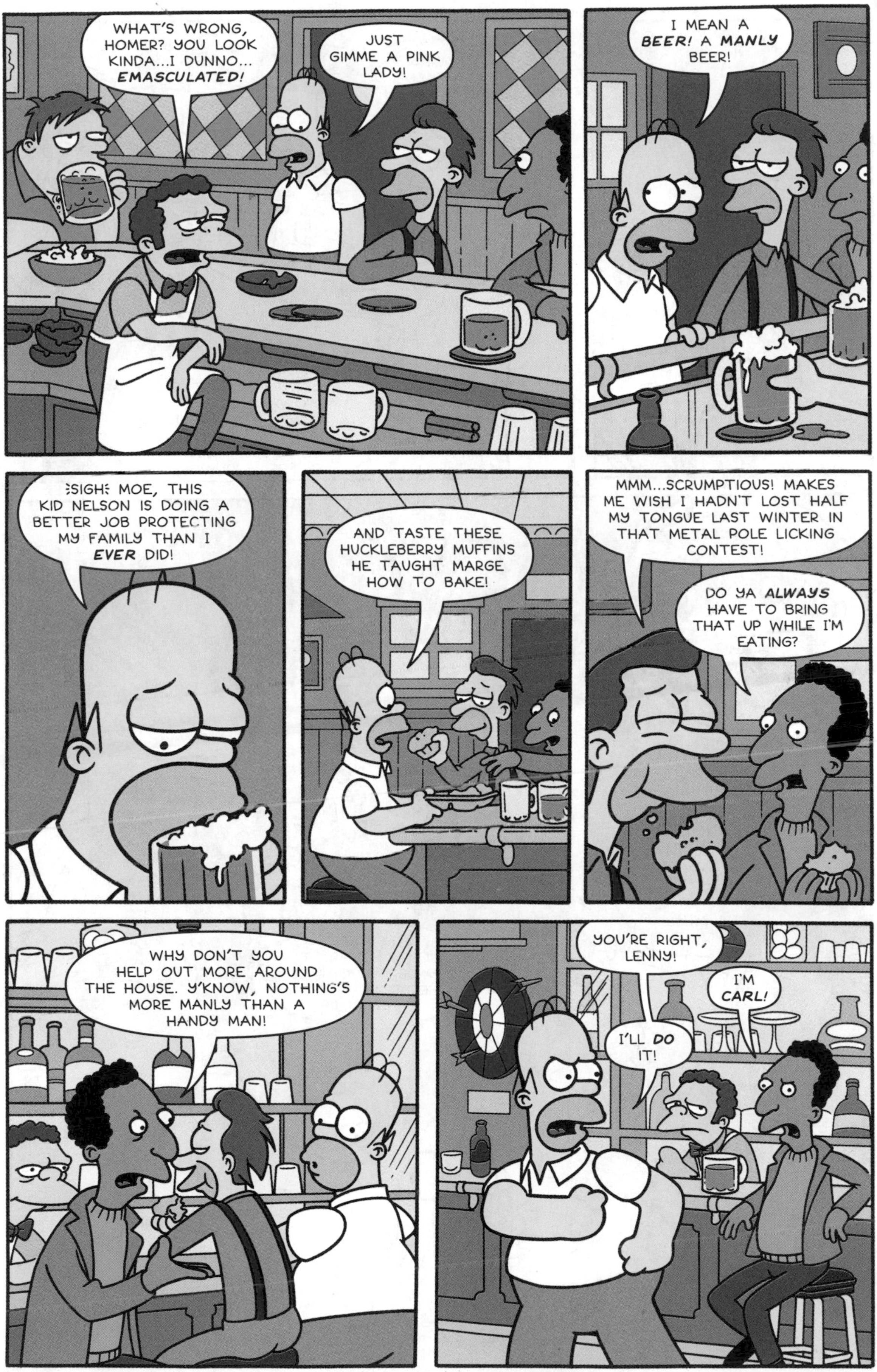
WHAT'S WRONG, HOMER? YOU LOOK KINDA...I DUNNO... **EMASCULATED!**
JUST GIMME A PINK LADY!
I MEAN A **BEER!** A **MANLY** BEER!
SIGH MOE, THIS KID NELSON IS DOING A BETTER JOB PROTECTING MY FAMILY THAN I **EVER** DID!
AND TASTE THESE HUCKLEBERRY MUFFINS HE TAUGHT MARGE HOW TO BAKE!
MMM...SCRUMPTIOUS! MAKES ME WISH I HADN'T LOST HALF MY TONGUE LAST WINTER IN THAT METAL POLE LICKING CONTEST!
DO YA **ALWAYS** HAVE TO BRING THAT UP WHILE I'M EATING?
WHY DON'T YOU HELP OUT MORE AROUND THE HOUSE. Y'KNOW, NOTHING'S MORE MANLY THAN A HANDY MAN!
YOU'RE RIGHT, LENNY!
I'M **CARL!**
I'LL **DO** IT!

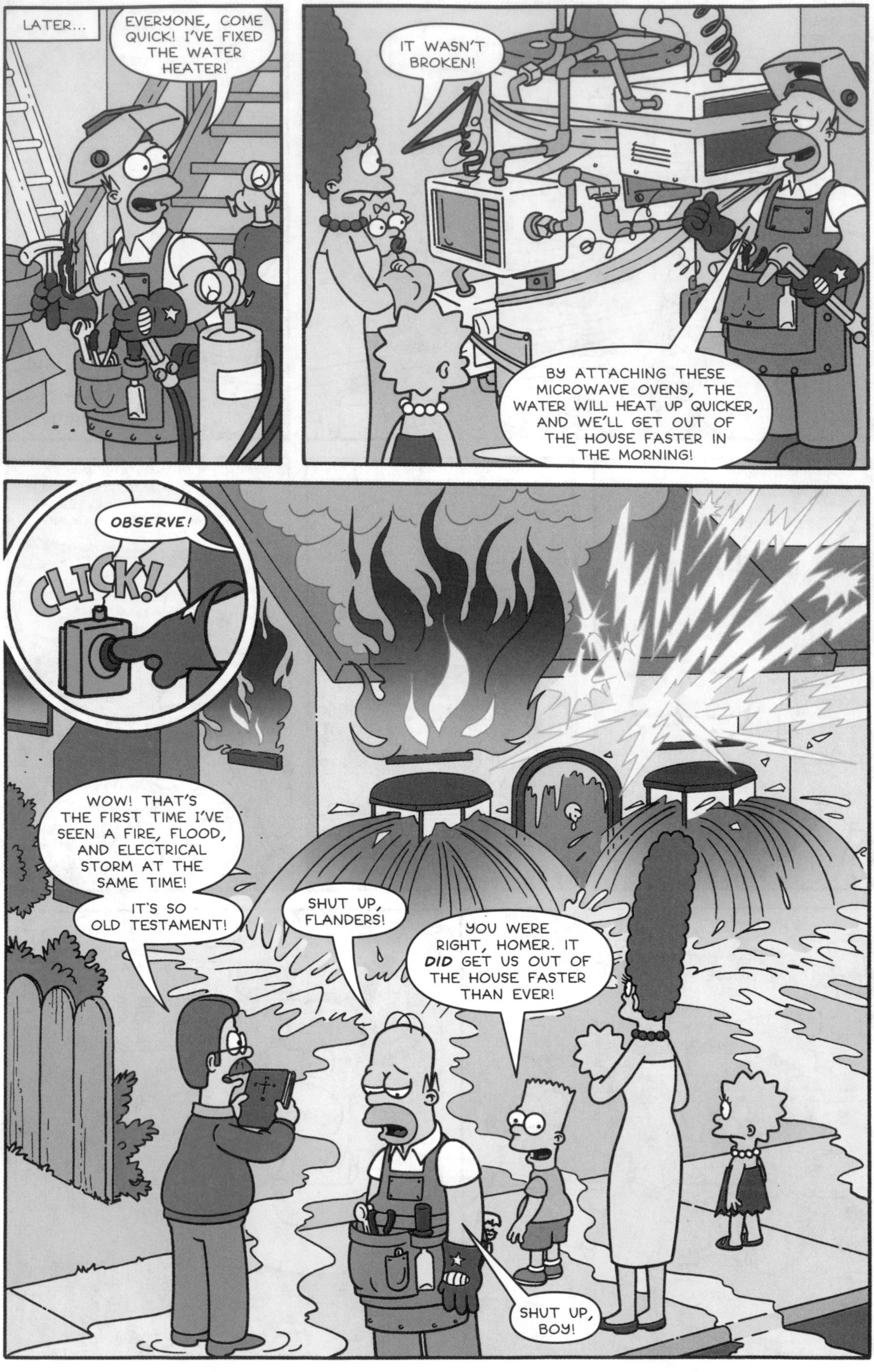

LATER...
EVERYONE, COME QUICK! I'VE FIXED THE WATER HEATER!
IT WASN'T BROKEN!
BY ATTACHING THESE MICROWAVE OVENS, THE WATER WILL HEAT UP QUICKER, AND WE'LL GET OUT OF THE HOUSE FASTER IN THE MORNING!
OBSERVE!
CLICK!
WOW! THAT'S THE FIRST TIME I'VE SEEN A FIRE, FLOOD, AND ELECTRICAL STORM AT THE SAME TIME!
IT'S SO OLD TESTAMENT!
SHUT UP, FLANDERS!
YOU WERE RIGHT, HOMER. IT *DID* GET US OUT OF THE HOUSE FASTER THAN EVER!
SHUT UP, BOY!

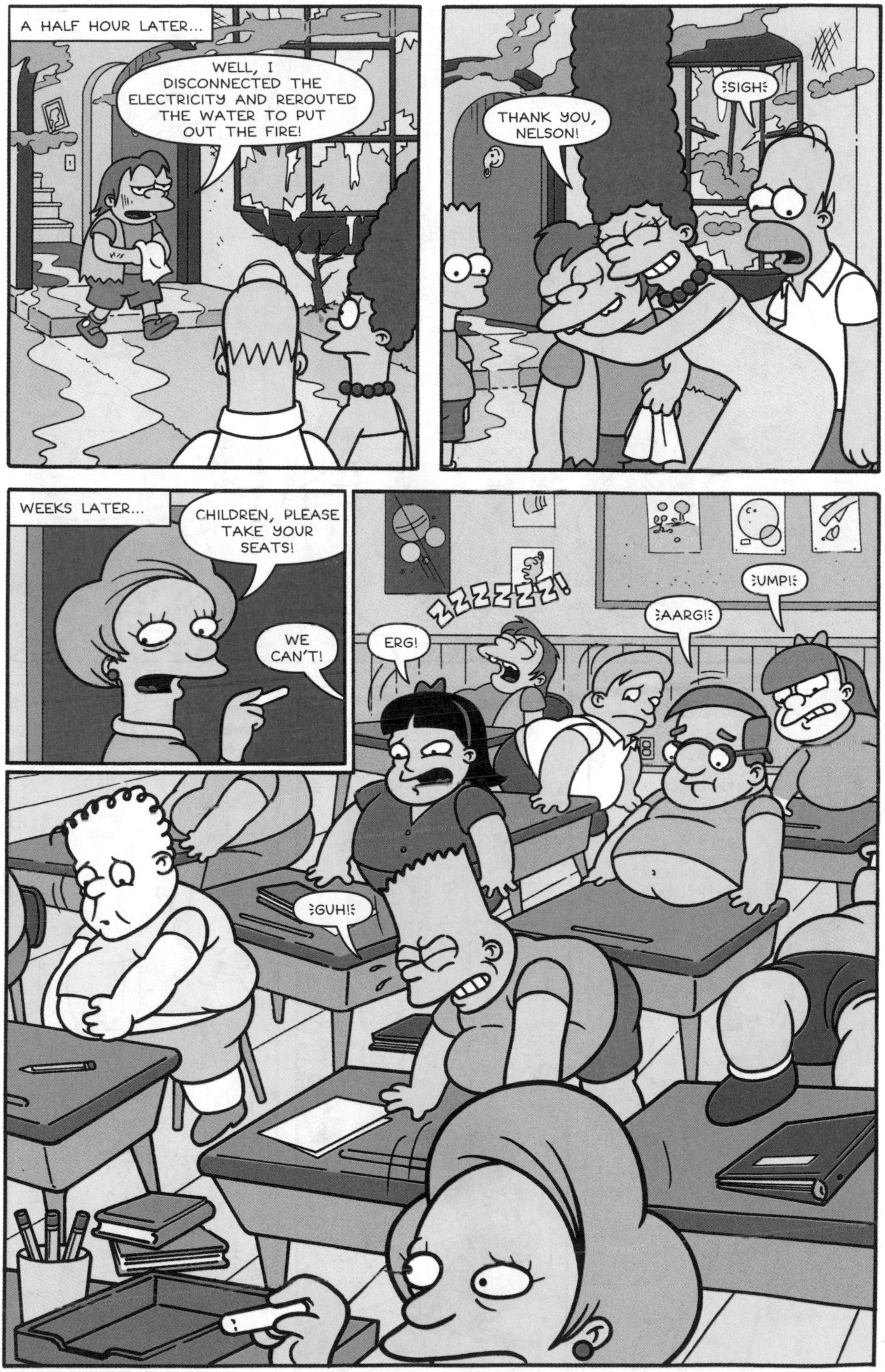
A HALF HOUR LATER...
WELL, I DISCONNECTED THE ELECTRICITY AND REROUTED THE WATER TO PUT OUT THE FIRE!
THANK YOU, NELSON!
SIGH
WEEKS LATER...
CHILDREN, PLEASE TAKE YOUR SEATS!
WE CAN'T!
ZZZZZZZ!
ERG!
AARG!
UMP!
GUH!

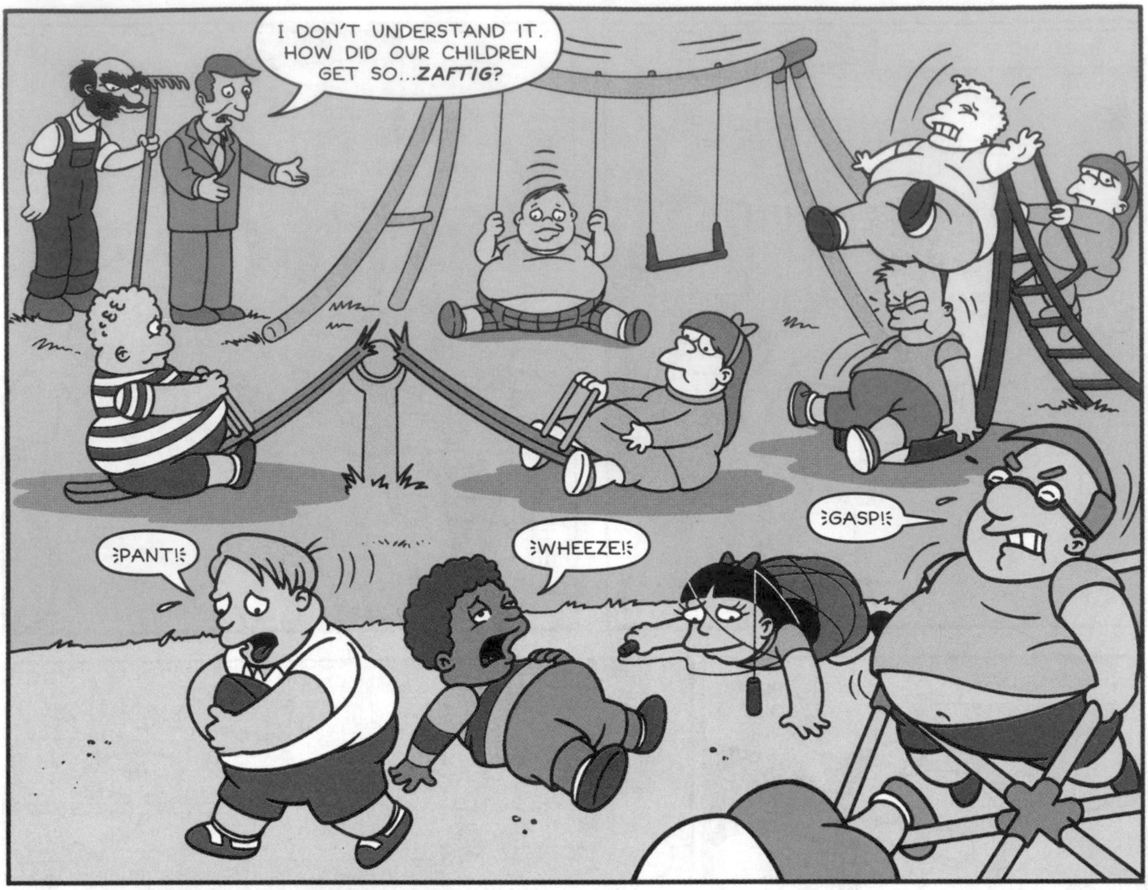
I DON'T UNDERSTAND IT. HOW DID OUR CHILDREN GET SO...*ZAFTIG*?
PANT!
WHEEZE!
GASP!

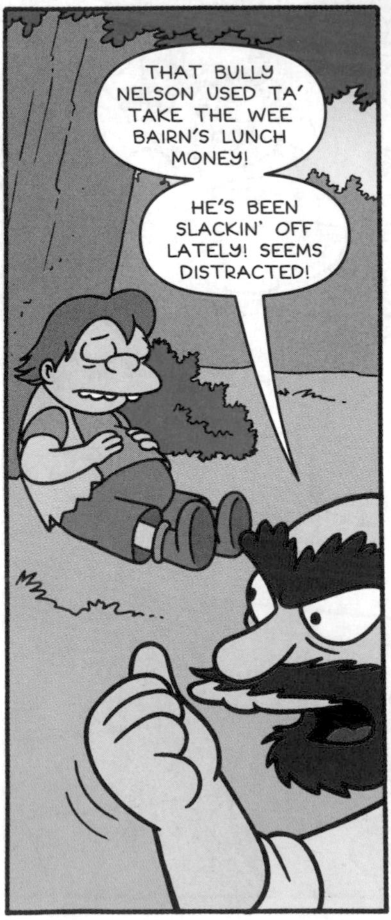
THAT BULLY NELSON USED TA' TAKE THE WEE BAIRN'S LUNCH MONEY!
HE'S BEEN SLACKIN' OFF LATELY! SEEMS DISTRACTED!

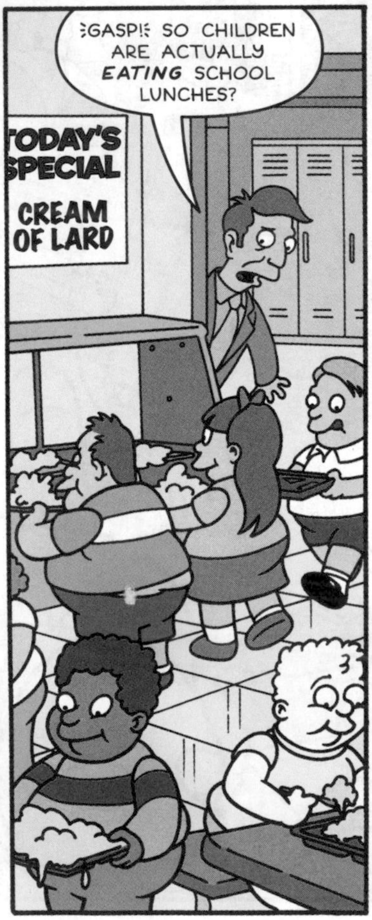
GASP! SO CHILDREN ARE ACTUALLY *EATING* SCHOOL LUNCHES?
TODAY'S SPECIAL
CREAM OF LARD

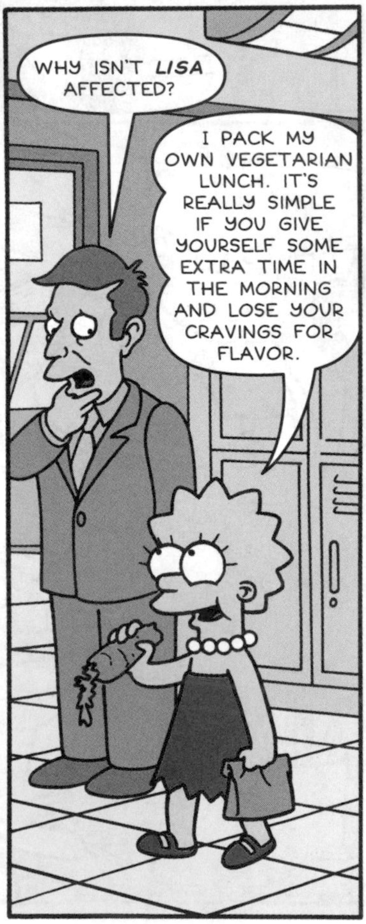
WHY ISN'T *LISA* AFFECTED?
I PACK MY OWN VEGETARIAN LUNCH. IT'S REALLY SIMPLE IF YOU GIVE YOURSELF SOME EXTRA TIME IN THE MORNING AND LOSE YOUR CRAVINGS FOR FLAVOR.

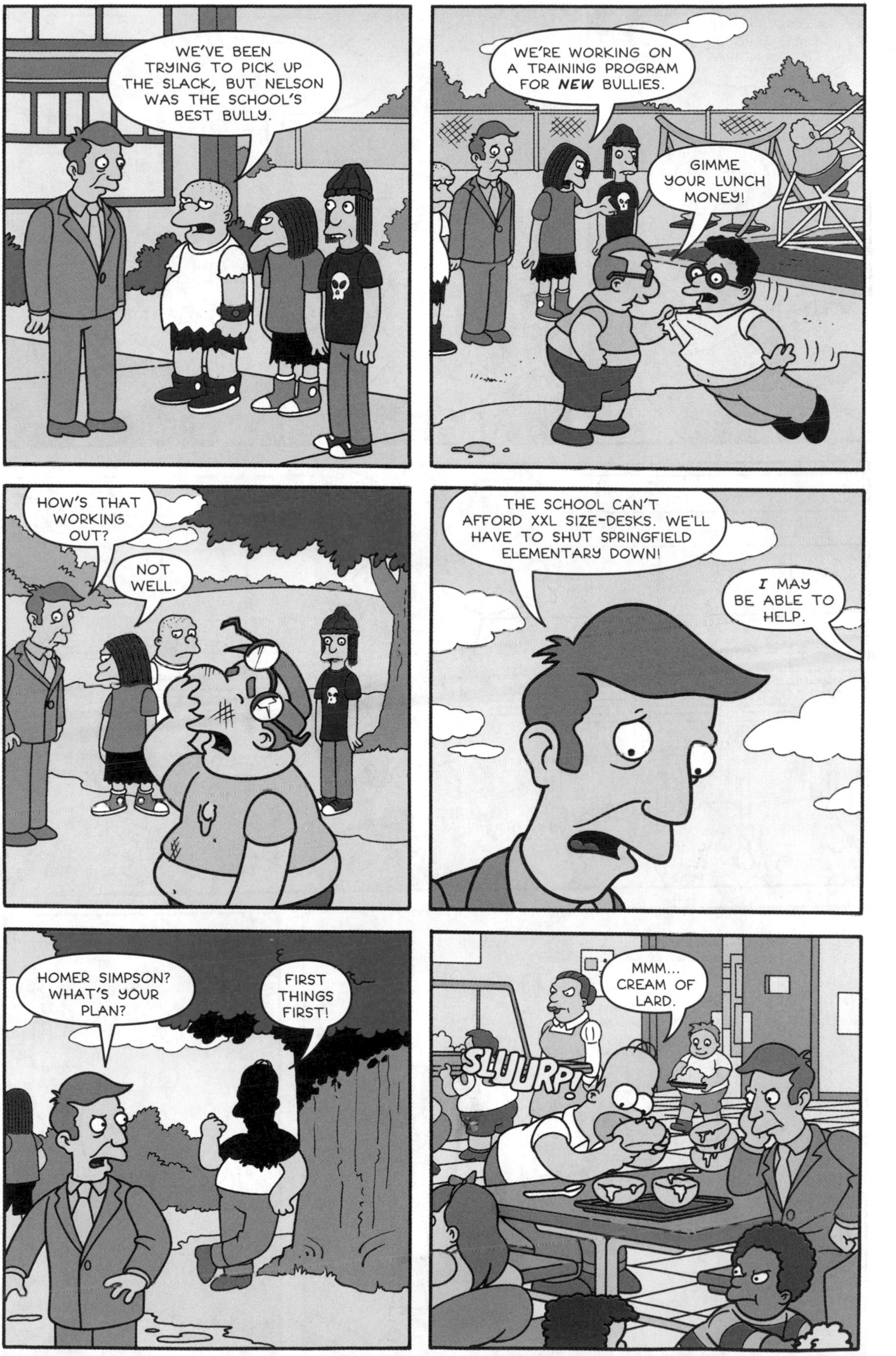
WE'VE BEEN TRYING TO PICK UP THE SLACK, BUT NELSON WAS THE SCHOOL'S BEST BULLY.
WE'RE WORKING ON A TRAINING PROGRAM FOR NEW BULLIES.
GIMME YOUR LUNCH MONEY!
HOW'S THAT WORKING OUT?
NOT WELL.
THE SCHOOL CAN'T AFFORD XXL SIZE-DESKS. WE'LL HAVE TO SHUT SPRINGFIELD ELEMENTARY DOWN!
I MAY BE ABLE TO HELP.
HOMER SIMPSON? WHAT'S YOUR PLAN?
FIRST THINGS FIRST!
MMM... CREAM OF LARD.
SLUURP!

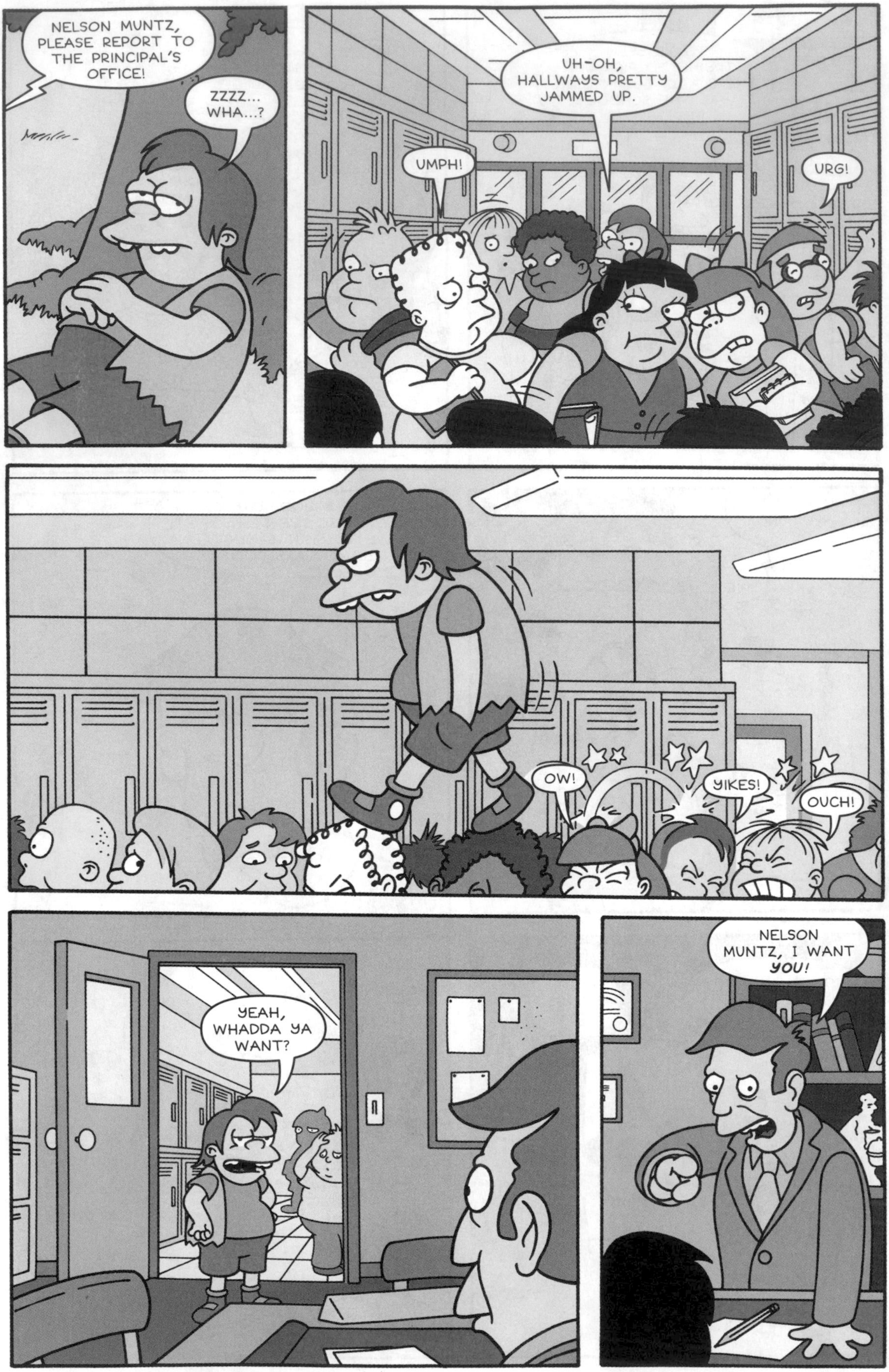
NELSON MUNTZ, PLEASE REPORT TO THE PRINCIPAL'S OFFICE!
ZZZZ... WHA...?
UH-OH, HALLWAYS PRETTY JAMMED UP.
UMPH!
URG!
OW!
YIKES!
OUCH!
YEAH, WHADDA YA WANT?
NELSON MUNTZ, I WANT *YOU*!

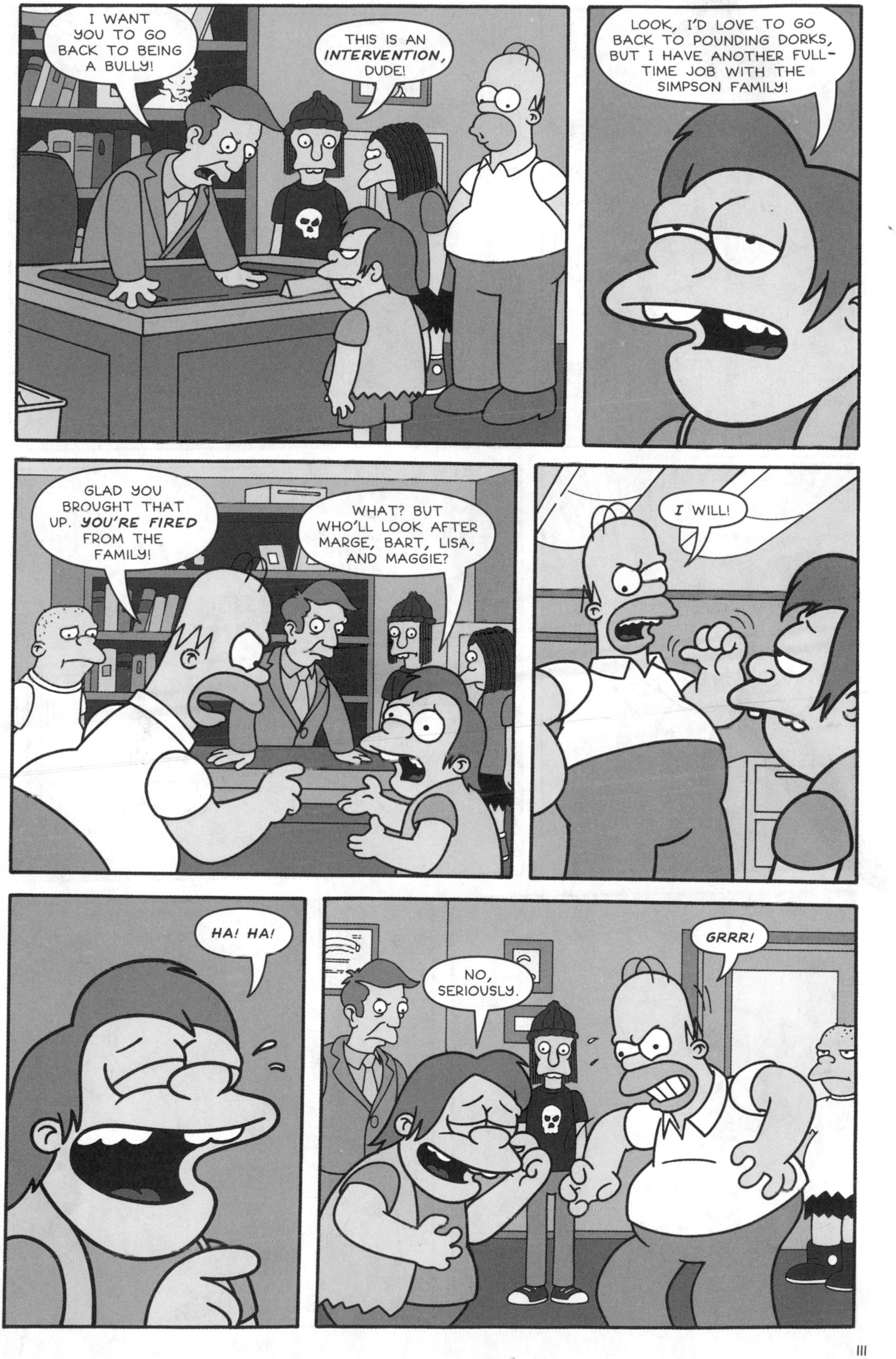

I WANT YOU TO GO BACK TO BEING A BULLY!
THIS IS AN *INTERVENTION*, DUDE!
LOOK, I'D LOVE TO GO BACK TO POUNDING DORKS, BUT I HAVE ANOTHER FULL-TIME JOB WITH THE SIMPSON FAMILY!
GLAD YOU BROUGHT THAT UP. *YOU'RE FIRED* FROM THE FAMILY!
WHAT? BUT WHO'LL LOOK AFTER MARGE, BART, LISA, AND MAGGIE?
I WILL!
HA! HA!
NO, SERIOUSLY.
GRRR!

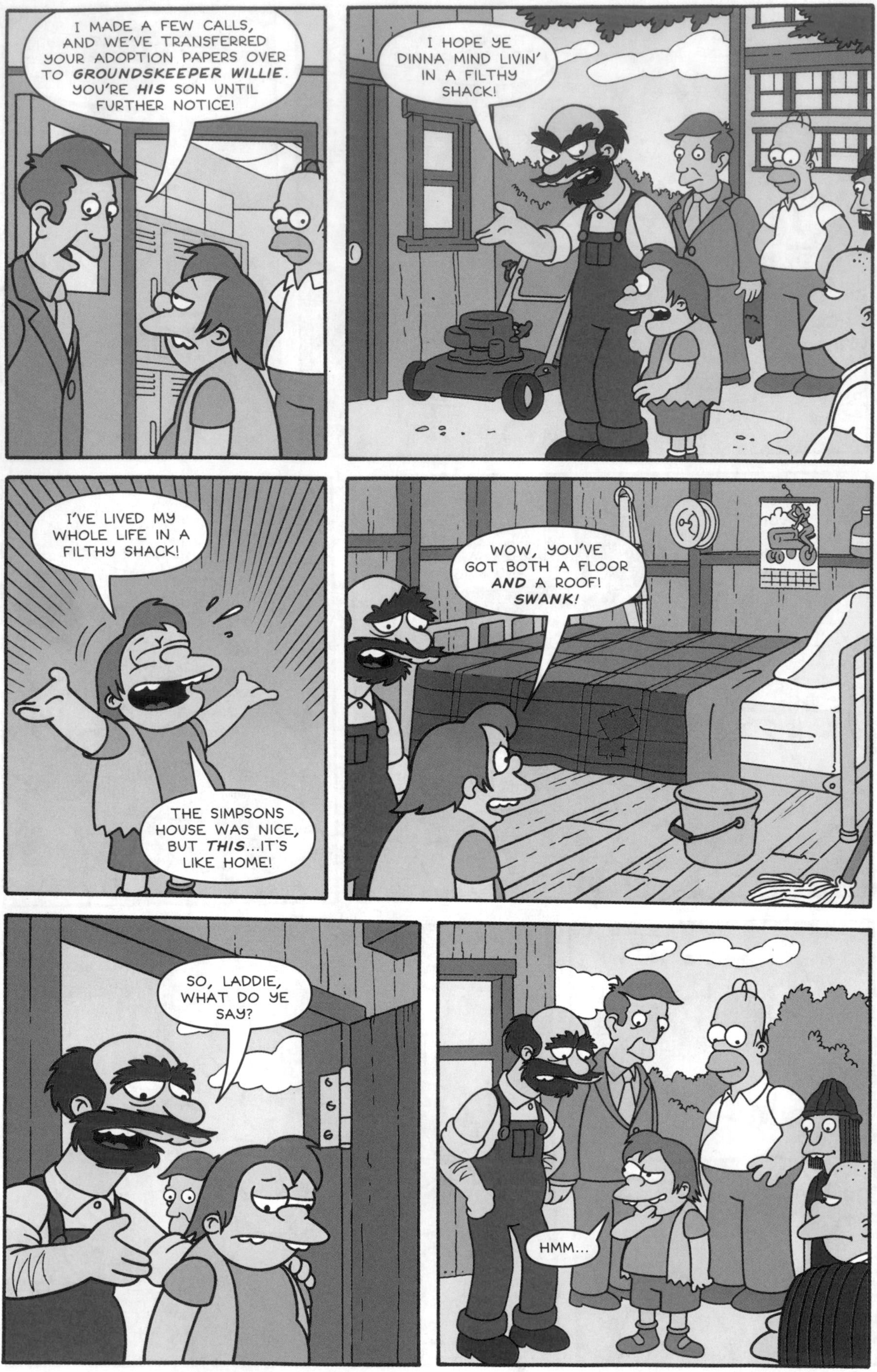

I MADE A FEW CALLS, AND WE'VE TRANSFERRED YOUR ADOPTION PAPERS OVER TO **GROUNDSKEEPER WILLIE**. YOU'RE **HIS** SON UNTIL FURTHER NOTICE!
I HOPE YE DINNA MIND LIVIN' IN A FILTHY SHACK!
I'VE LIVED MY WHOLE LIFE IN A FILTHY SHACK!
THE SIMPSONS HOUSE WAS NICE, BUT **THIS**...IT'S LIKE HOME!
WOW, YOU'VE GOT BOTH A FLOOR **AND** A ROOF! **SWANK!**
SO, LADDIE, WHAT DO YE SAY?
HMM...

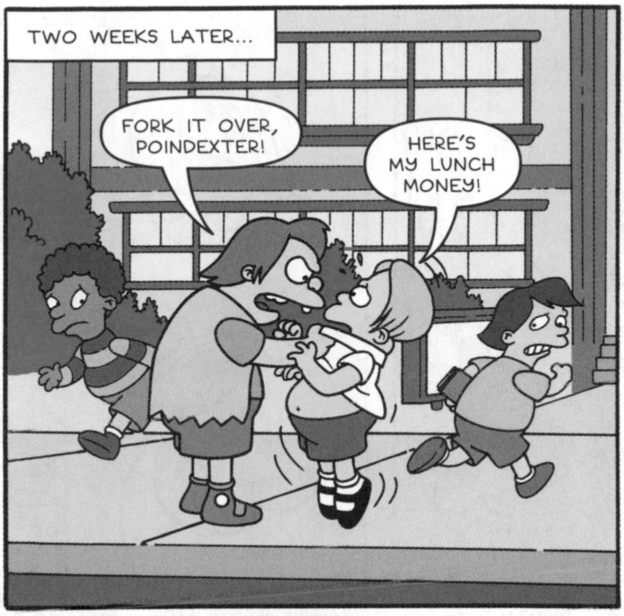
TWO WEEKS LATER...
FORK IT OVER, POINDEXTER!
HERE'S MY LUNCH MONEY!

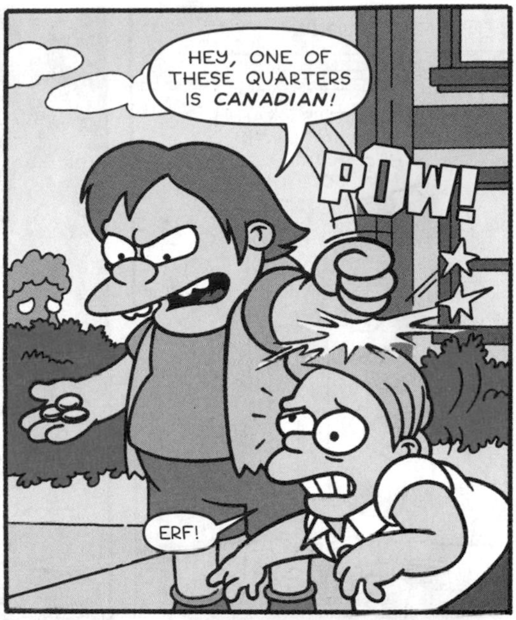
HEY, ONE OF THESE QUARTERS IS CANADIAN!
POW!
ERF!

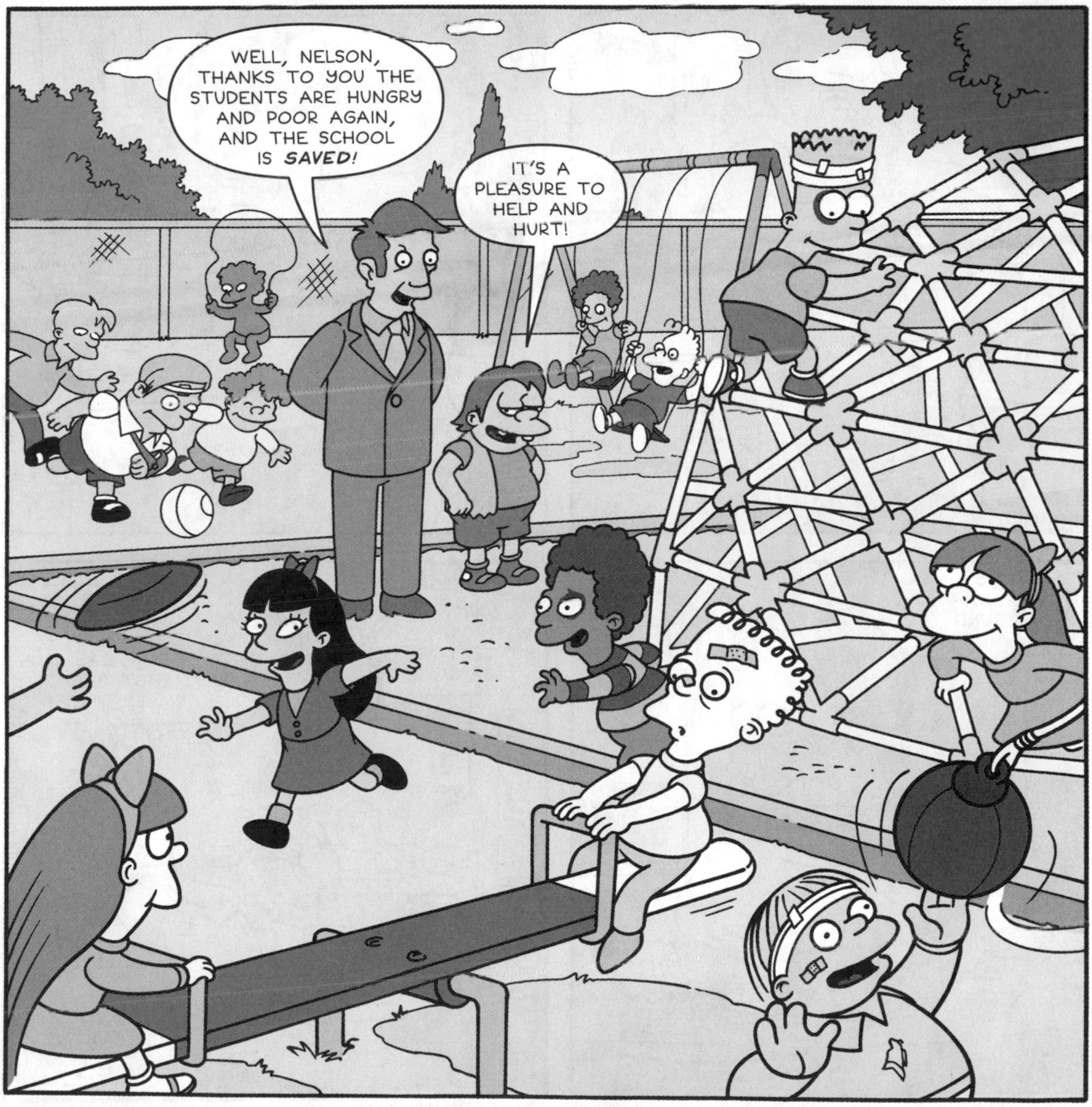
WELL, NELSON, THANKS TO YOU THE STUDENTS ARE HUNGRY AND POOR AGAIN, AND THE SCHOOL IS SAVED!
IT'S A PLEASURE TO HELP AND HURT!

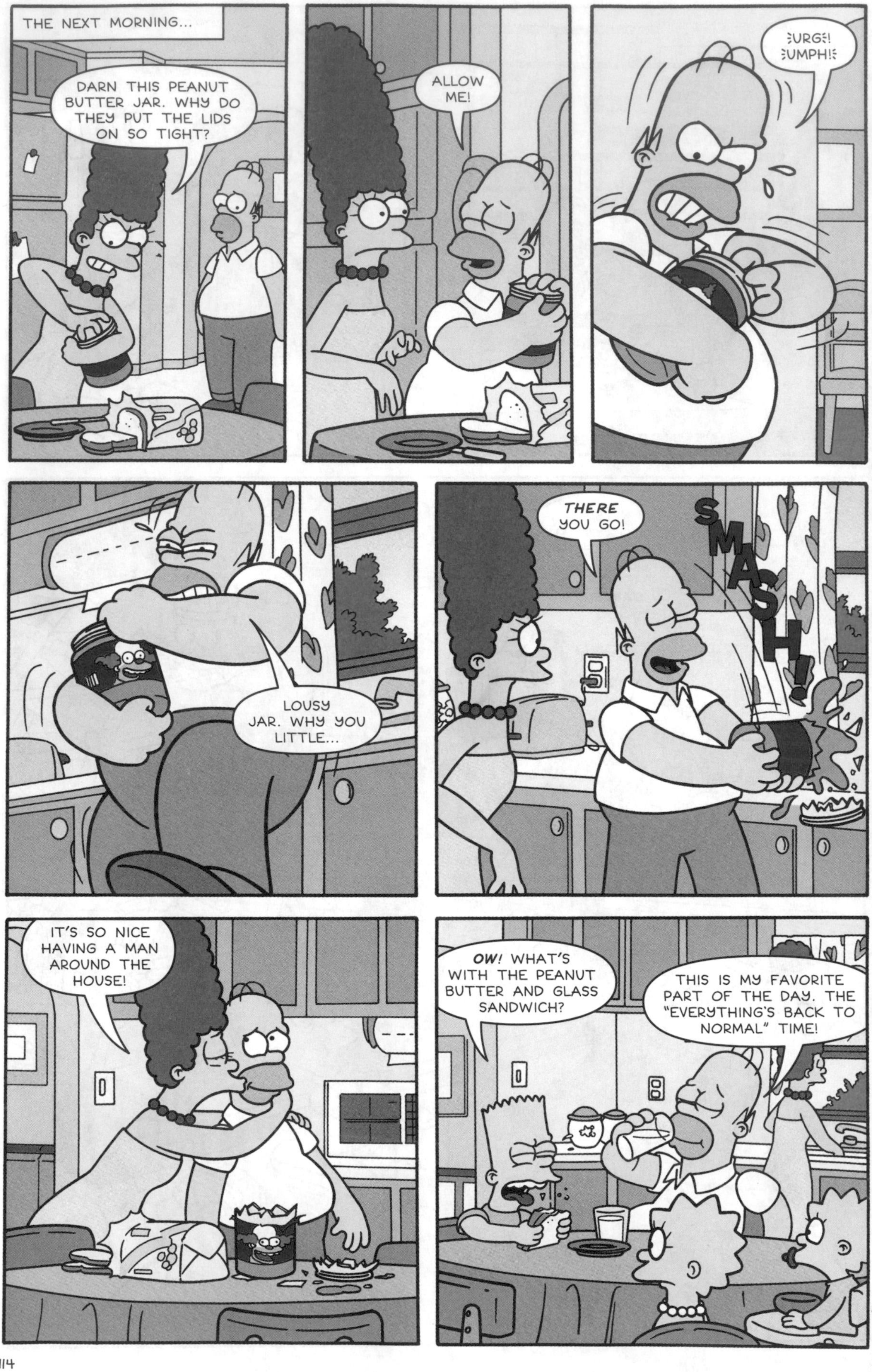

THE NEXT MORNING...
DARN THIS PEANUT BUTTER JAR. WHY DO THEY PUT THE LIDS ON SO TIGHT?
ALLOW ME!
URG! UMPH!
LOUSY JAR. WHY YOU LITTLE...
THERE YOU GO!
SMASH!
IT'S SO NICE HAVING A MAN AROUND THE HOUSE!
OW! WHAT'S WITH THE PEANUT BUTTER AND GLASS SANDWICH?
THIS IS MY FAVORITE PART OF THE DAY. THE "EVERYTHING'S BACK TO NORMAL" TIME!

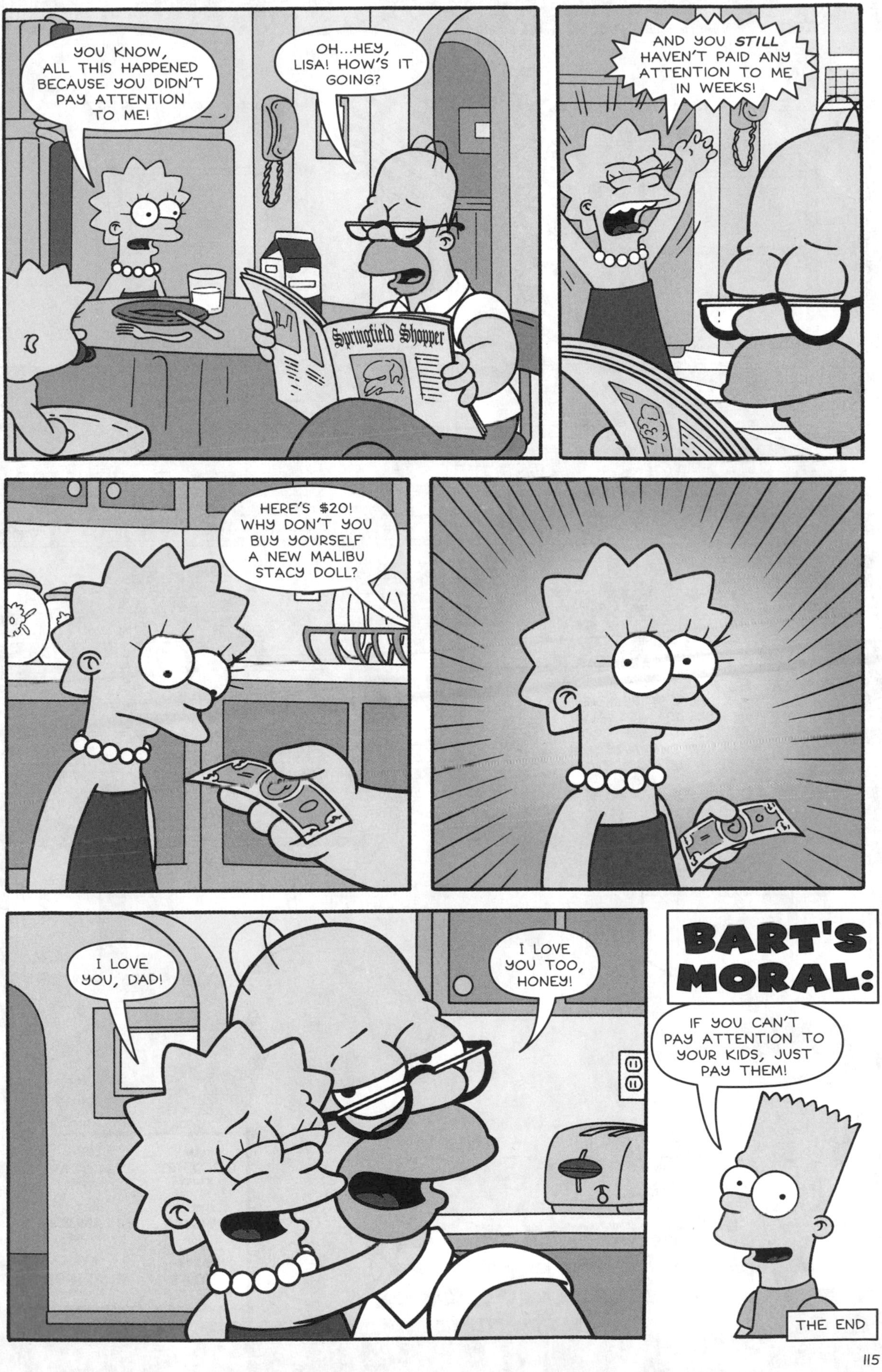
YOU KNOW, ALL THIS HAPPENED BECAUSE YOU DIDN'T PAY ATTENTION TO ME!
OH...HEY, LISA! HOW'S IT GOING?
Springfield Shopper
AND YOU STILL HAVEN'T PAID ANY ATTENTION TO ME IN WEEKS!
HERE'S $20! WHY DON'T YOU BUY YOURSELF A NEW MALIBU STACY DOLL?
I LOVE YOU, DAD!
I LOVE YOU TOO, HONEY!
BART'S MORAL:
IF YOU CAN'T PAY ATTENTION TO YOUR KIDS, JUST PAY THEM!
THE END

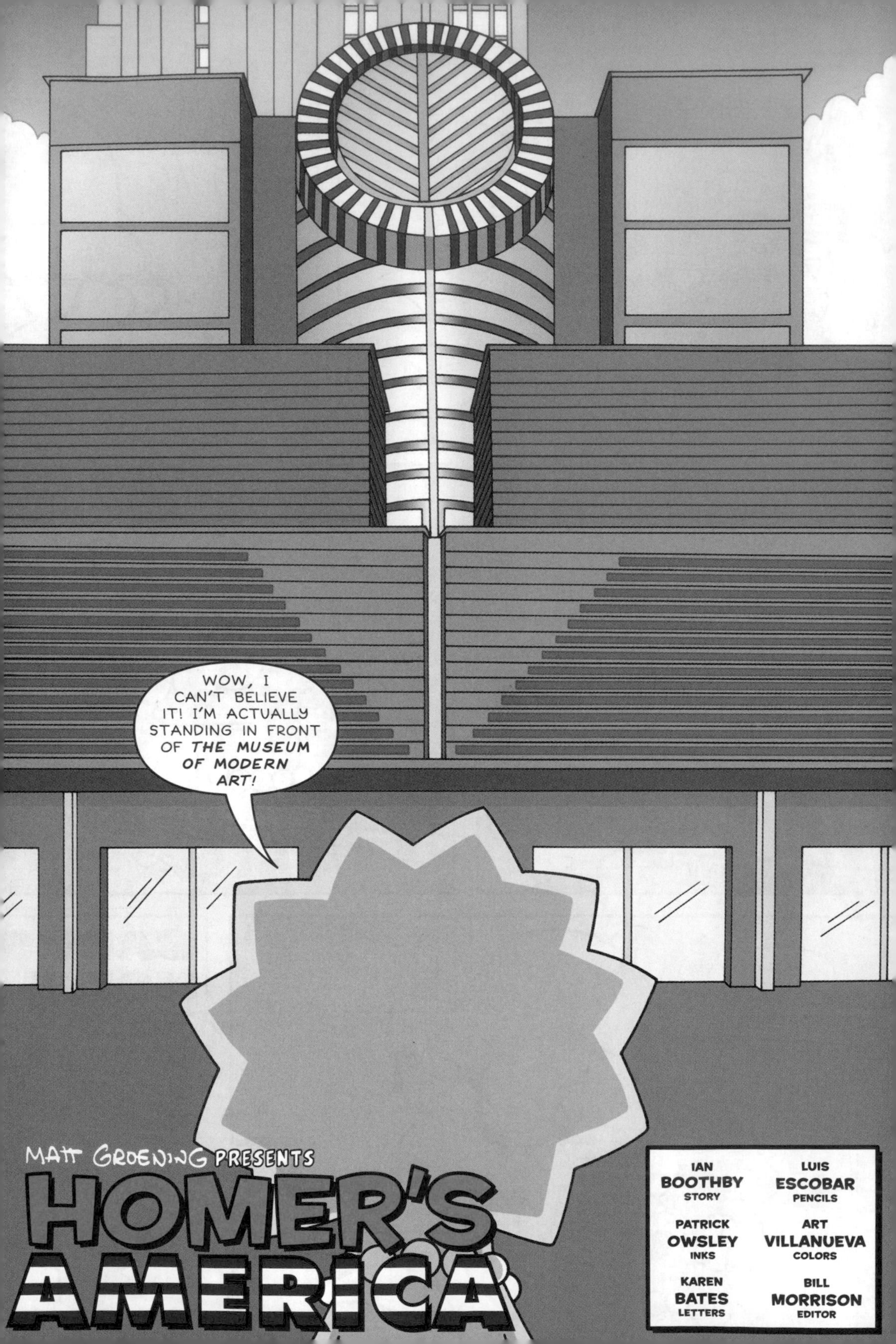
WOW, I CAN'T BELIEVE IT! I'M ACTUALLY STANDING IN FRONT OF THE MUSEUM OF MODERN ART!
MATT GROENING PRESENTS
HOMER'S AMERICA
IAN BOOTHBY STORY
LUIS ESCOBAR PENCILS
PATRICK OWSLEY INKS
ART VILLANUEVA COLORS
KAREN BATES LETTERS
BILL MORRISON EDITOR

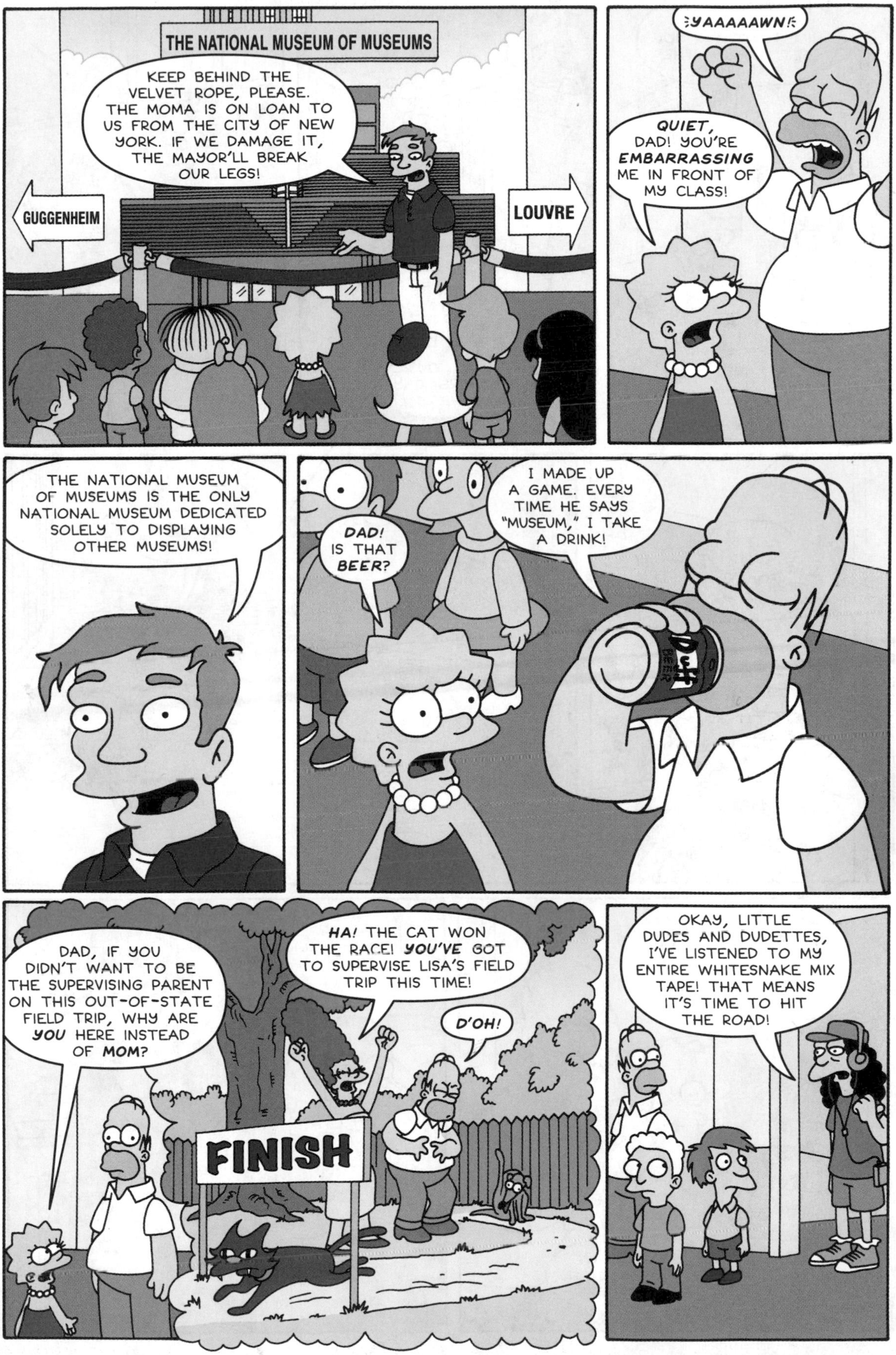
THE NATIONAL MUSEUM OF MUSEUMS
KEEP BEHIND THE VELVET ROPE, PLEASE. THE MOMA IS ON LOAN TO US FROM THE CITY OF NEW YORK. IF WE DAMAGE IT, THE MAYOR'LL BREAK OUR LEGS!
GUGGENHEIM
LOUVRE
YAAAAAWN!
QUIET, DAD! YOU'RE EMBARRASSING ME IN FRONT OF MY CLASS!
THE NATIONAL MUSEUM OF MUSEUMS IS THE ONLY NATIONAL MUSEUM DEDICATED SOLELY TO DISPLAYING OTHER MUSEUMS!
DAD! IS THAT BEER?
I MADE UP A GAME. EVERY TIME HE SAYS "MUSEUM," I TAKE A DRINK!
Duff BEER
DAD, IF YOU DIDN'T WANT TO BE THE SUPERVISING PARENT ON THIS OUT-OF-STATE FIELD TRIP, WHY ARE YOU HERE INSTEAD OF MOM?
HA! THE CAT WON THE RACE! YOU'VE GOT TO SUPERVISE LISA'S FIELD TRIP THIS TIME!
D'OH!
FINISH
OKAY, LITTLE DUDES AND DUDETTES, I'VE LISTENED TO MY ENTIRE WHITESNAKE MIX TAPE! THAT MEANS IT'S TIME TO HIT THE ROAD!

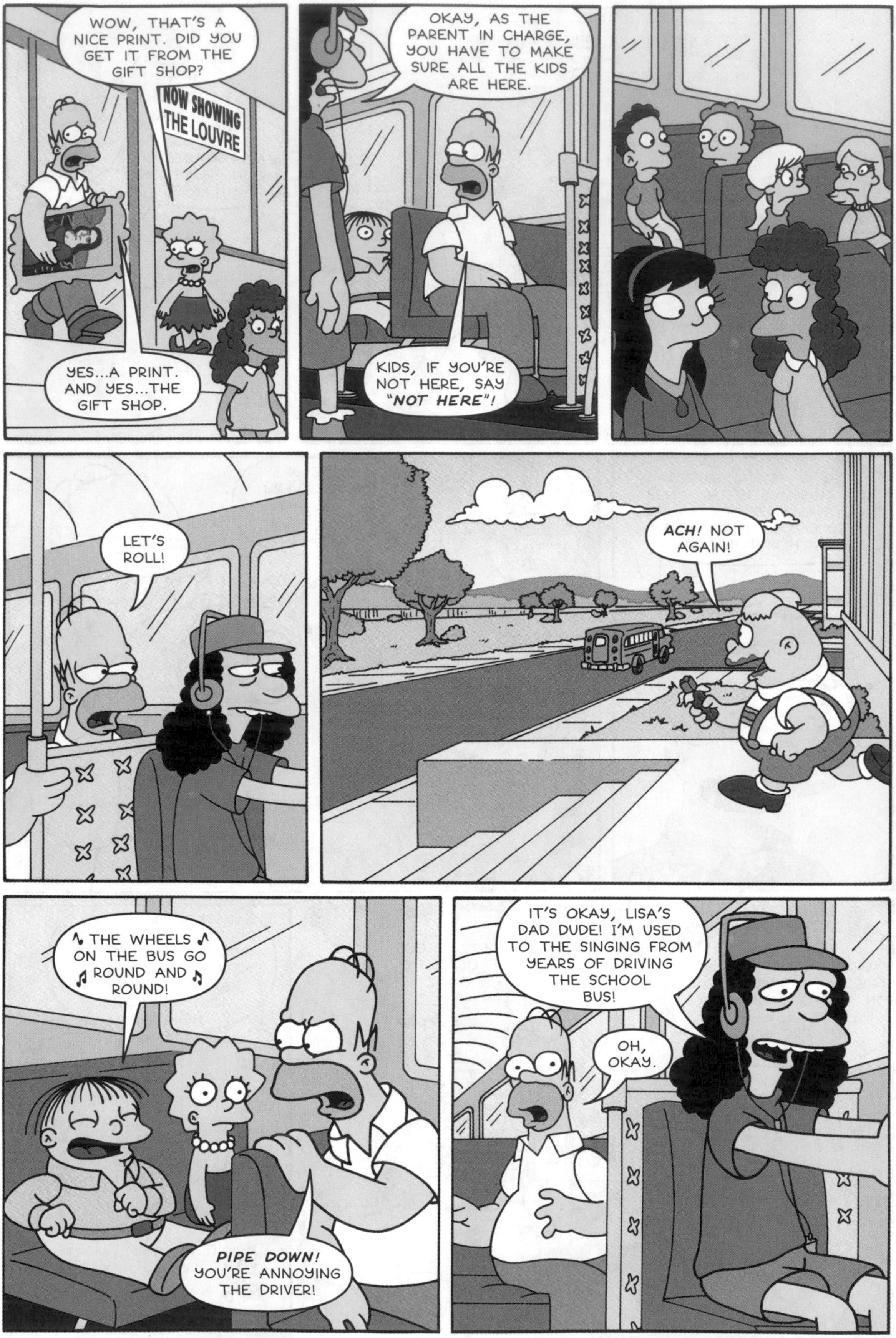
WOW, THAT'S A NICE PRINT. DID YOU GET IT FROM THE GIFT SHOP?
NOW SHOWING THE LOUVRE
YES...A PRINT. AND YES...THE GIFT SHOP.
OKAY, AS THE PARENT IN CHARGE, YOU HAVE TO MAKE SURE ALL THE KIDS ARE HERE.
KIDS, IF YOU'RE NOT HERE, SAY "NOT HERE"!
LET'S ROLL!
ACH! NOT AGAIN!
♪ THE WHEELS ON THE BUS GO ROUND AND ROUND! ♪
PIPE DOWN! YOU'RE ANNOYING THE DRIVER!
IT'S OKAY, LISA'S DAD DUDE! I'M USED TO THE SINGING FROM YEARS OF DRIVING THE SCHOOL BUS!
OH, OKAY.

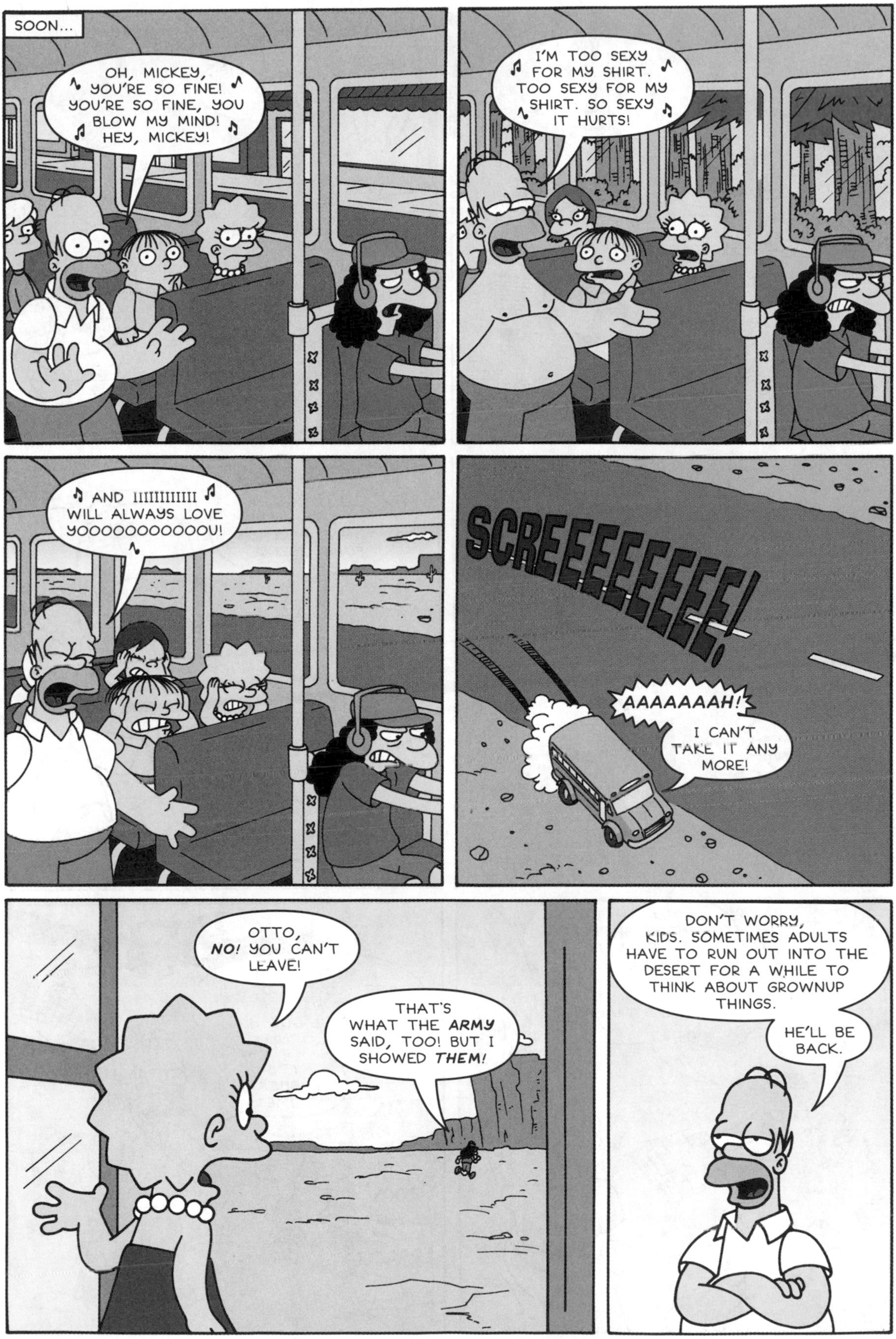
SOON...
OH, MICKEY, YOU'RE SO FINE! YOU'RE SO FINE, YOU BLOW MY MIND! HEY, MICKEY!
I'M TOO SEXY FOR MY SHIRT. TOO SEXY FOR MY SHIRT. SO SEXY IT HURTS!
AND IIIIIIIIIII WILL ALWAYS LOVE YOOOOOOOOOOOU!
SCREEEEEEEEE!
AAAAAAAH!
I CAN'T TAKE IT ANY MORE!
OTTO, NO! YOU CAN'T LEAVE!
THAT'S WHAT THE ARMY SAID, TOO! BUT I SHOWED THEM!
DON'T WORRY, KIDS. SOMETIMES ADULTS HAVE TO RUN OUT INTO THE DESERT FOR A WHILE TO THINK ABOUT GROWNUP THINGS.
HE'LL BE BACK.

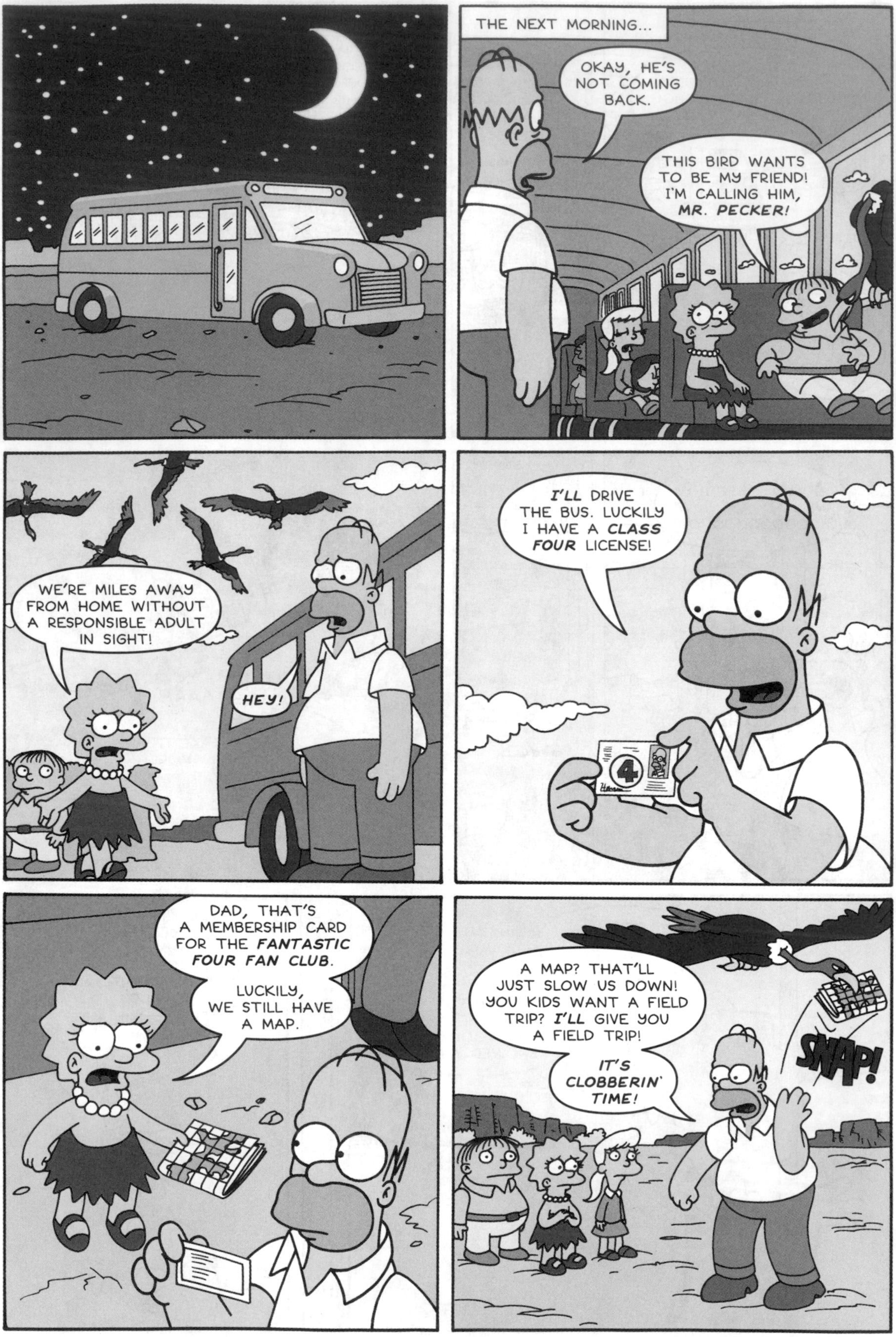
THE NEXT MORNING...
OKAY, HE'S NOT COMING BACK.
THIS BIRD WANTS TO BE MY FRIEND! I'M CALLING HIM, MR. PECKER!
WE'RE MILES AWAY FROM HOME WITHOUT A RESPONSIBLE ADULT IN SIGHT!
HEY!
I'LL DRIVE THE BUS. LUCKILY I HAVE A CLASS FOUR LICENSE!
DAD, THAT'S A MEMBERSHIP CARD FOR THE FANTASTIC FOUR FAN CLUB.
LUCKILY, WE STILL HAVE A MAP.
A MAP? THAT'LL JUST SLOW US DOWN! YOU KIDS WANT A FIELD TRIP? I'LL GIVE YOU A FIELD TRIP!
IT'S CLOBBERIN' TIME!
SNAP!

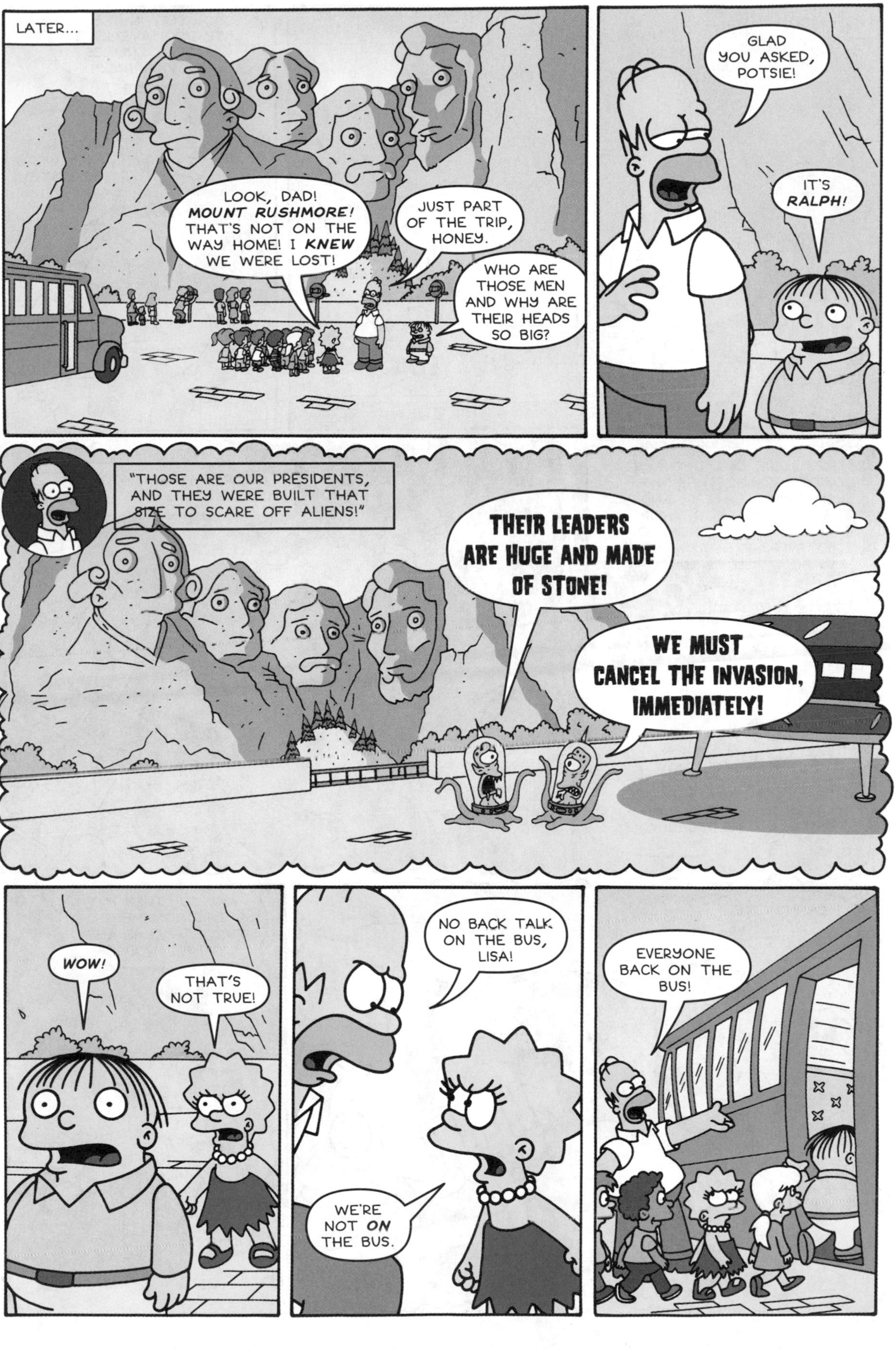
LATER...
LOOK, DAD! MOUNT RUSHMORE! THAT'S NOT ON THE WAY HOME! I KNEW WE WERE LOST!
JUST PART OF THE TRIP, HONEY.
WHO ARE THOSE MEN AND WHY ARE THEIR HEADS SO BIG?
GLAD YOU ASKED, POTSIE!
IT'S RALPH!
"THOSE ARE OUR PRESIDENTS, AND THEY WERE BUILT THAT SIZE TO SCARE OFF ALIENS!"
THEIR LEADERS ARE HUGE AND MADE OF STONE!
WE MUST CANCEL THE INVASION, IMMEDIATELY!
WOW!
THAT'S NOT TRUE!
NO BACK TALK ON THE BUS, LISA!
WE'RE NOT ON THE BUS.
EVERYONE BACK ON THE BUS!

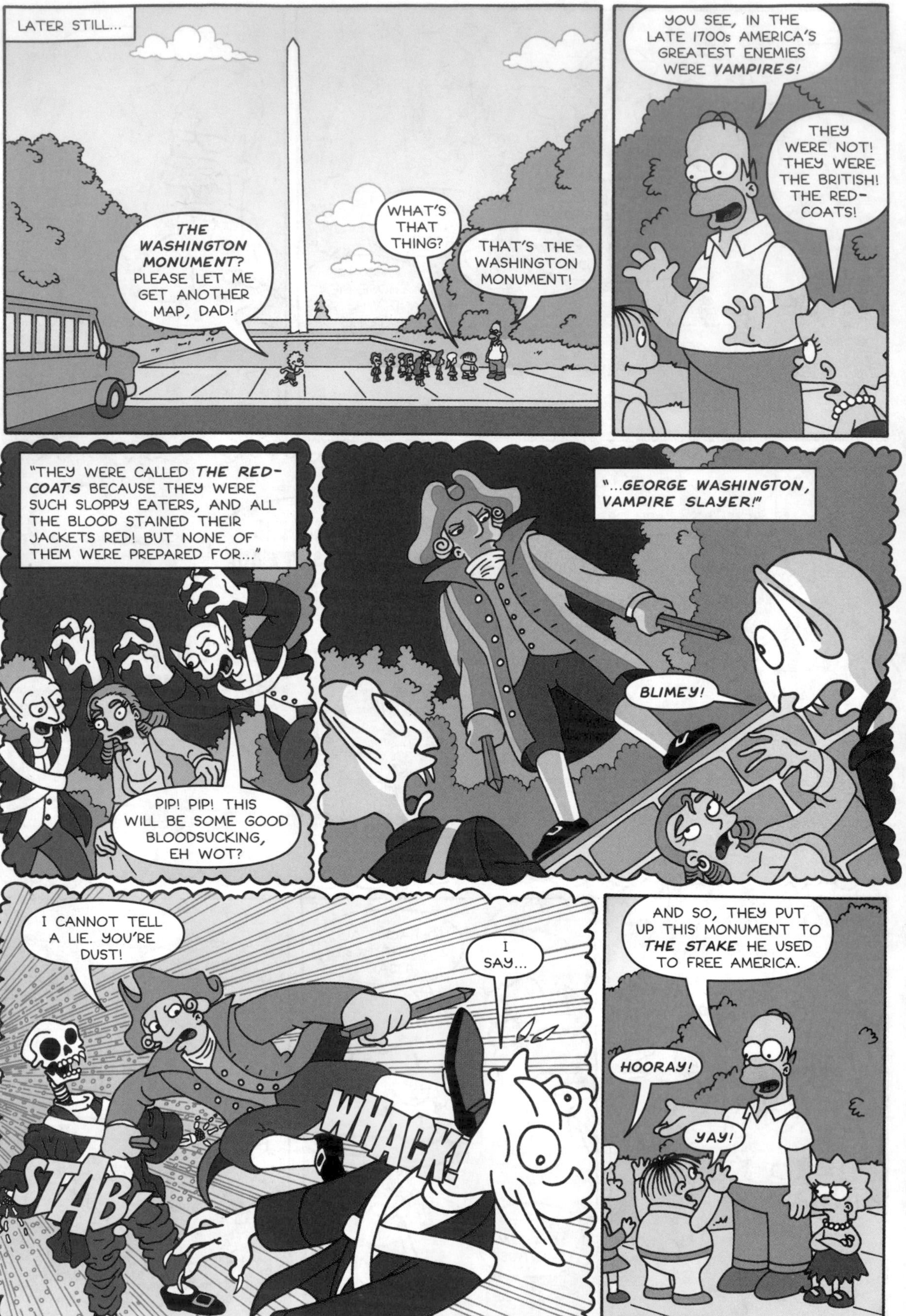
LATER STILL...
THE WASHINGTON MONUMENT? PLEASE LET ME GET ANOTHER MAP, DAD!
WHAT'S THAT THING?
THAT'S THE WASHINGTON MONUMENT!
YOU SEE, IN THE LATE 1700s AMERICA'S GREATEST ENEMIES WERE VAMPIRES!
THEY WERE NOT! THEY WERE THE BRITISH! THE RED-COATS!
"THEY WERE CALLED THE RED-COATS BECAUSE THEY WERE SUCH SLOPPY EATERS, AND ALL THE BLOOD STAINED THEIR JACKETS RED! BUT NONE OF THEM WERE PREPARED FOR..."
PIP! PIP! THIS WILL BE SOME GOOD BLOODSUCKING, EH WOT?
"...GEORGE WASHINGTON, VAMPIRE SLAYER!"
BLIMEY!
I CANNOT TELL A LIE. YOU'RE DUST!
I SAY...
WHACK!
STAB!
AND SO, THEY PUT UP THIS MONUMENT TO THE STAKE HE USED TO FREE AMERICA.
HOORAY!
YAY!

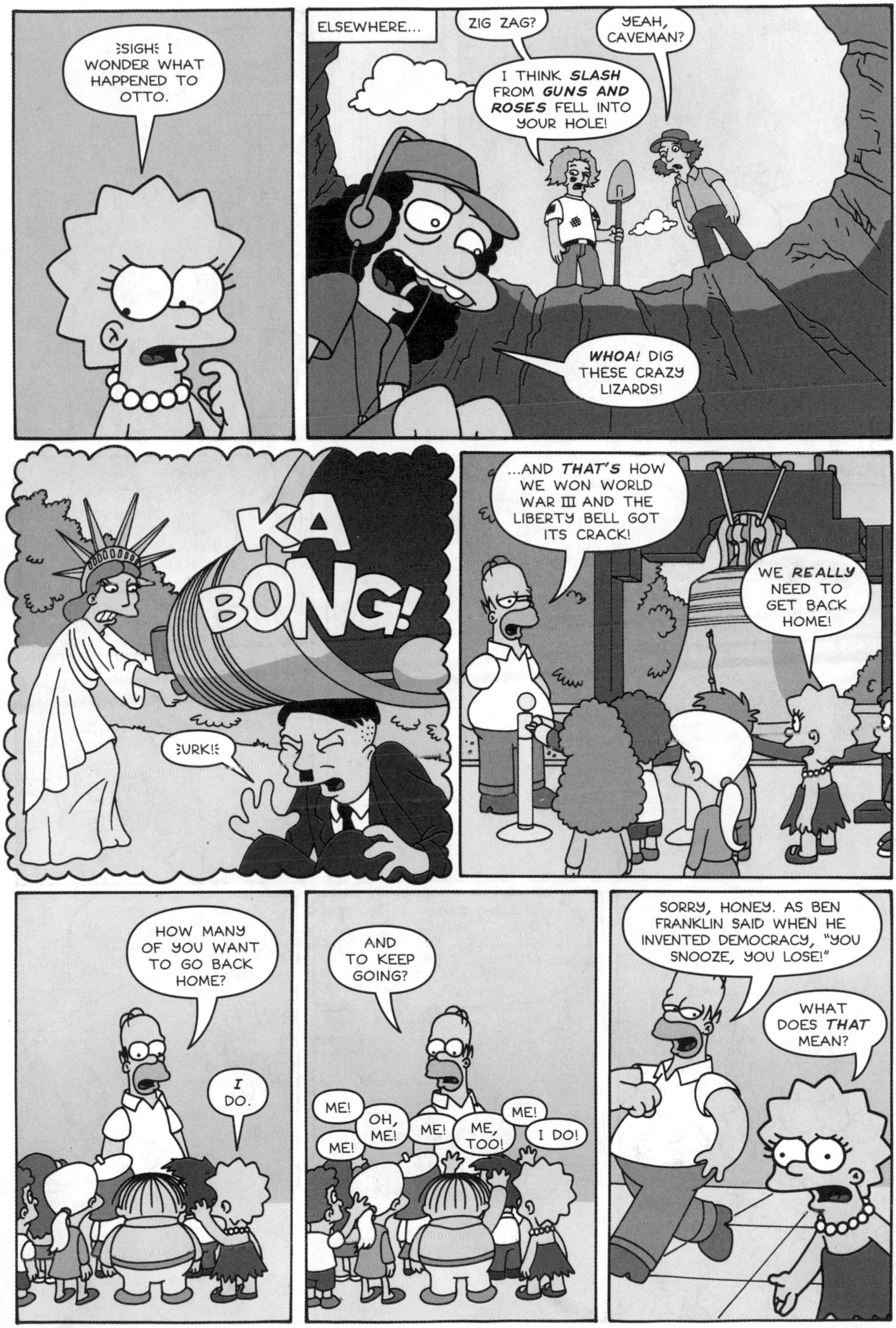

⁝SIGH⁝ I WONDER WHAT HAPPENED TO OTTO.
ELSEWHERE...
ZIG ZAG?
YEAH, CAVEMAN?
I THINK SLASH FROM GUNS AND ROSES FELL INTO YOUR HOLE!
WHOA! DIG THESE CRAZY LIZARDS!
KA BONG!
⁝URK!⁝
...AND THAT'S HOW WE WON WORLD WAR III AND THE LIBERTY BELL GOT ITS CRACK!
WE REALLY NEED TO GET BACK HOME!
HOW MANY OF YOU WANT TO GO BACK HOME?
I DO.
AND TO KEEP GOING?
ME!
ME!
OH, ME!
ME!
ME, TOO!
ME!
I DO!
SORRY, HONEY. AS BEN FRANKLIN SAID WHEN HE INVENTED DEMOCRACY, "YOU SNOOZE, YOU LOSE!"
WHAT DOES THAT MEAN?

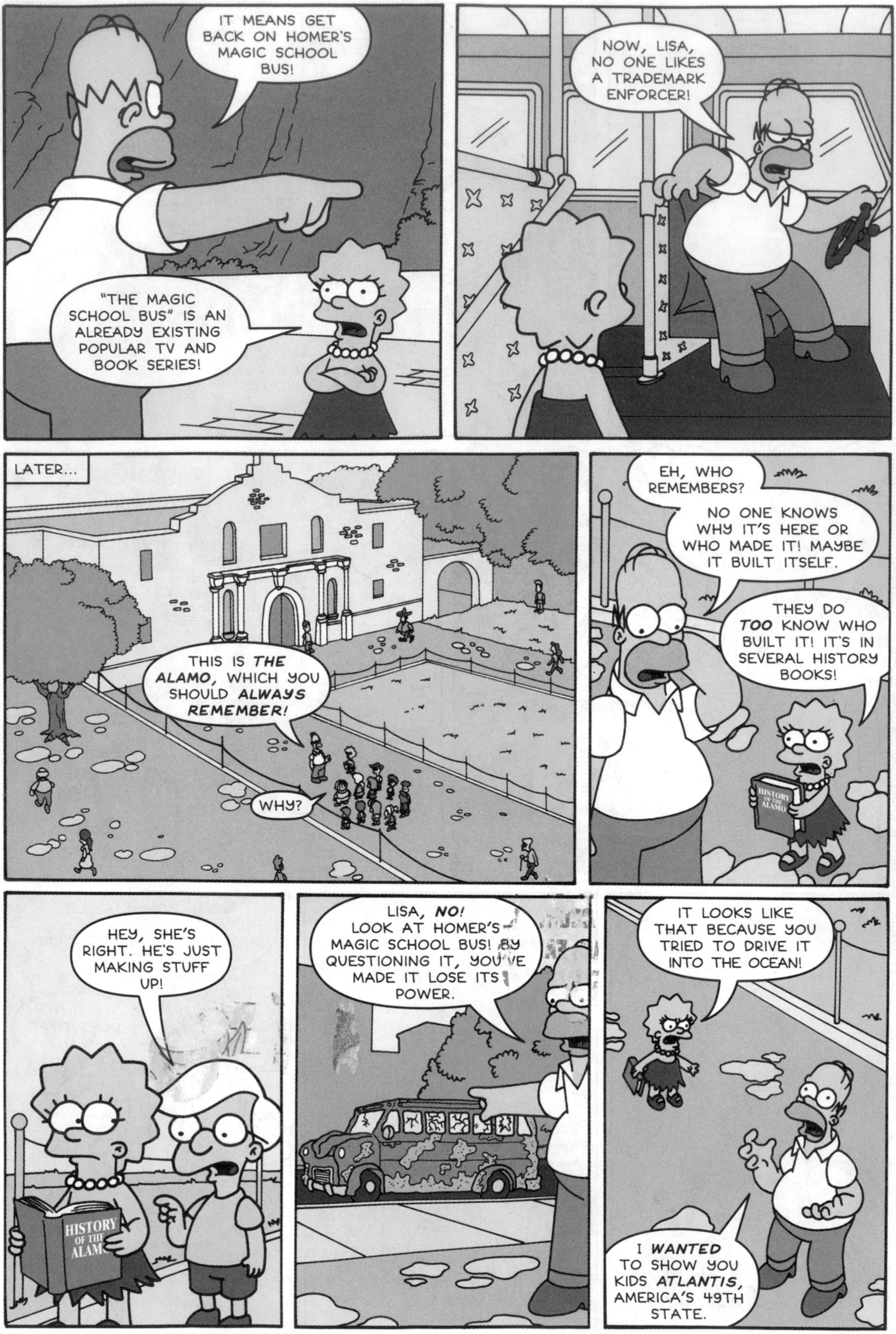

IT MEANS GET BACK ON HOMER'S MAGIC SCHOOL BUS!
"THE MAGIC SCHOOL BUS" IS AN ALREADY EXISTING POPULAR TV AND BOOK SERIES!
NOW, LISA, NO ONE LIKES A TRADEMARK ENFORCER!
LATER...
THIS IS ***THE ALAMO,*** WHICH YOU SHOULD ***ALWAYS REMEMBER!***
WHY?
EH, WHO REMEMBERS?
NO ONE KNOWS WHY IT'S HERE OR WHO MADE IT! MAYBE IT BUILT ITSELF.
THEY DO ***TOO*** KNOW WHO BUILT IT! IT'S IN SEVERAL HISTORY BOOKS!
HISTORY OF THE ALAMO
HEY, SHE'S RIGHT. HE'S JUST MAKING STUFF UP!
LISA, ***NO!*** LOOK AT HOMER'S MAGIC SCHOOL BUS! BY QUESTIONING IT, YOU'VE MADE IT LOSE ITS POWER.
IT LOOKS LIKE THAT BECAUSE YOU TRIED TO DRIVE IT INTO THE OCEAN!
I ***WANTED*** TO SHOW YOU KIDS ***ATLANTIS,*** AMERICA'S 49TH STATE.

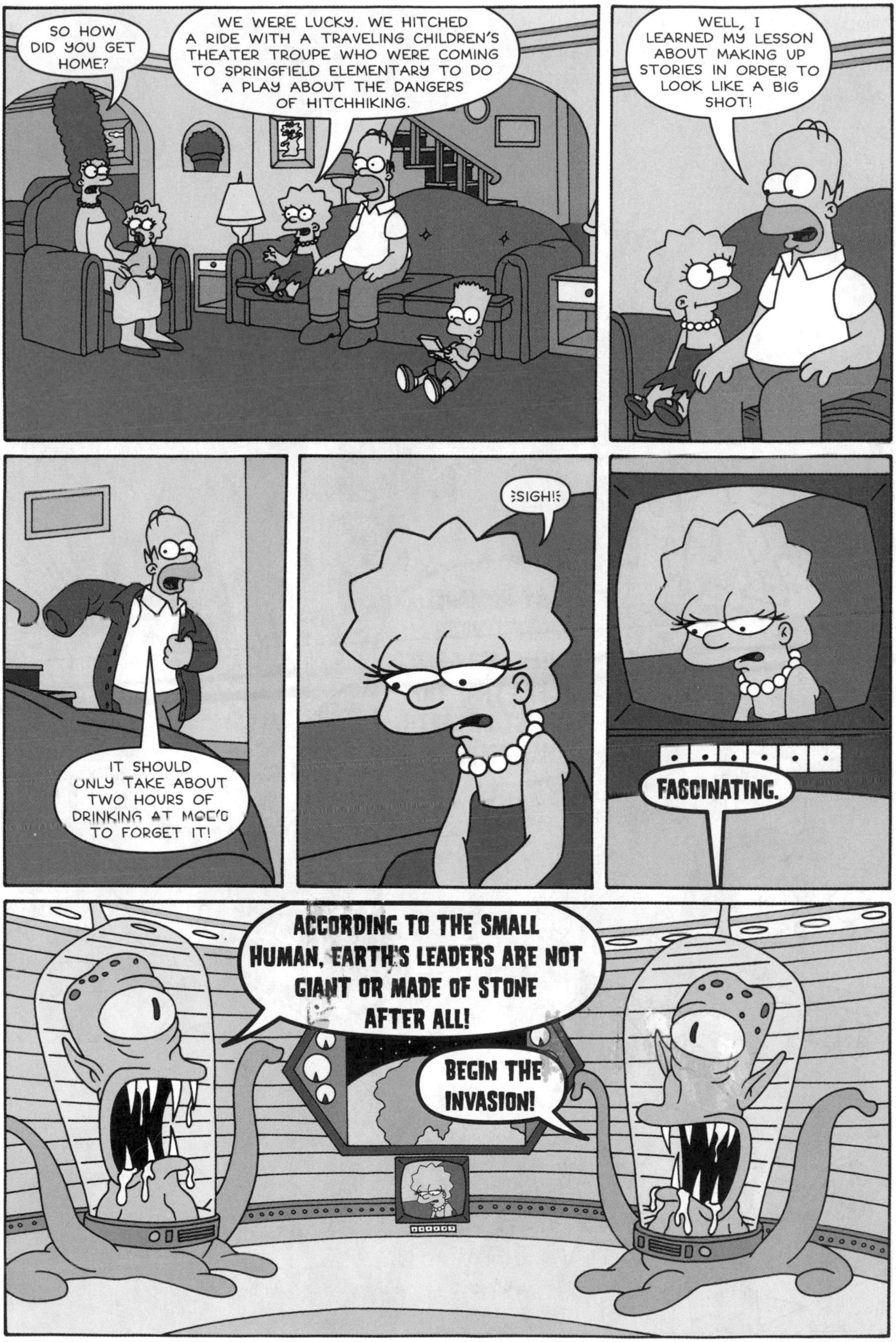
SO HOW DID YOU GET HOME?
WE WERE LUCKY. WE HITCHED A RIDE WITH A TRAVELING CHILDREN'S THEATER TROUPE WHO WERE COMING TO SPRINGFIELD ELEMENTARY TO DO A PLAY ABOUT THE DANGERS OF HITCHHIKING.
WELL, I LEARNED MY LESSON ABOUT MAKING UP STORIES IN ORDER TO LOOK LIKE A BIG SHOT!
IT SHOULD ONLY TAKE ABOUT TWO HOURS OF DRINKING AT MOE'S TO FORGET IT!
SIGH!
FASCINATING.
ACCORDING TO THE SMALL HUMAN, EARTH'S LEADERS ARE NOT GIANT OR MADE OF STONE AFTER ALL!
BEGIN THE INVASION!

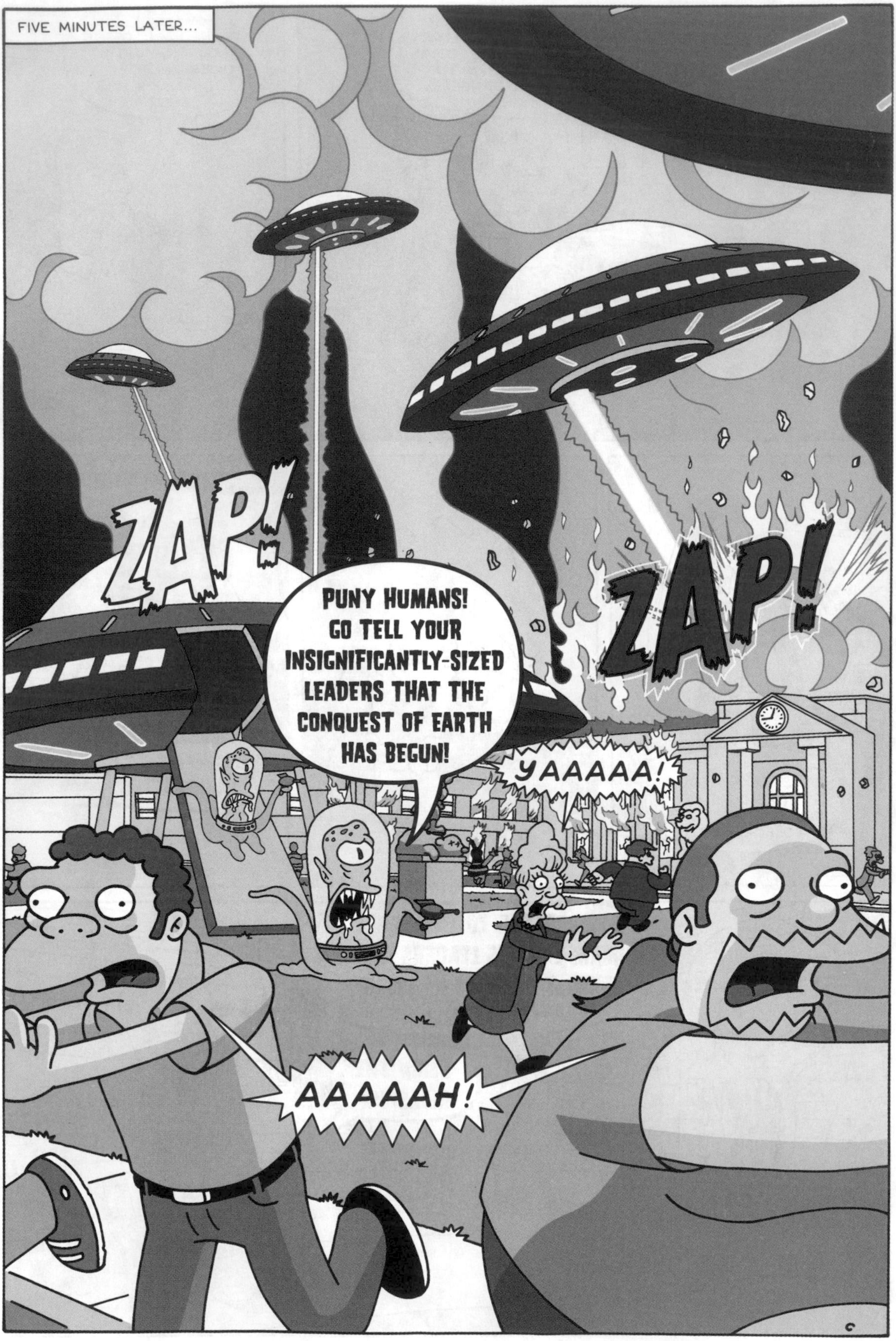
FIVE MINUTES LATER...
ZAP!
PUNY HUMANS! GO TELL YOUR INSIGNIFICANTLY-SIZED LEADERS THAT THE CONQUEST OF EARTH HAS BEGUN!
ZAP!
YAAAAA!
AAAAAH!

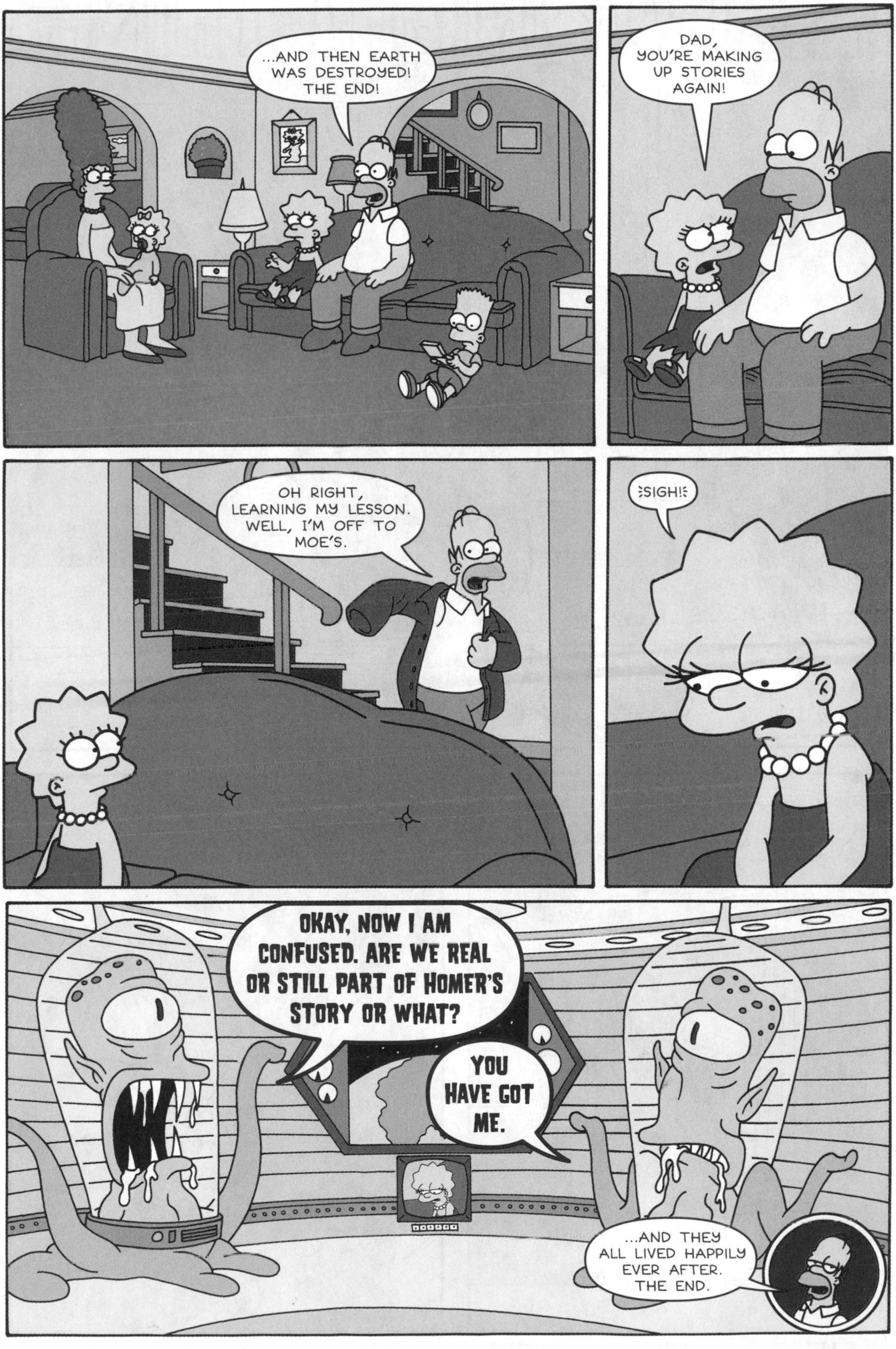
...AND THEN EARTH WAS DESTROYED! THE END!
DAD, YOU'RE MAKING UP STORIES AGAIN!
OH RIGHT, LEARNING MY LESSON. WELL, I'M OFF TO MOE'S.
SIGH!
OKAY, NOW I AM CONFUSED. ARE WE REAL OR STILL PART OF HOMER'S STORY OR WHAT?
YOU HAVE GOT ME.
...AND THEY ALL LIVED HAPPILY EVER AFTER. THE END.

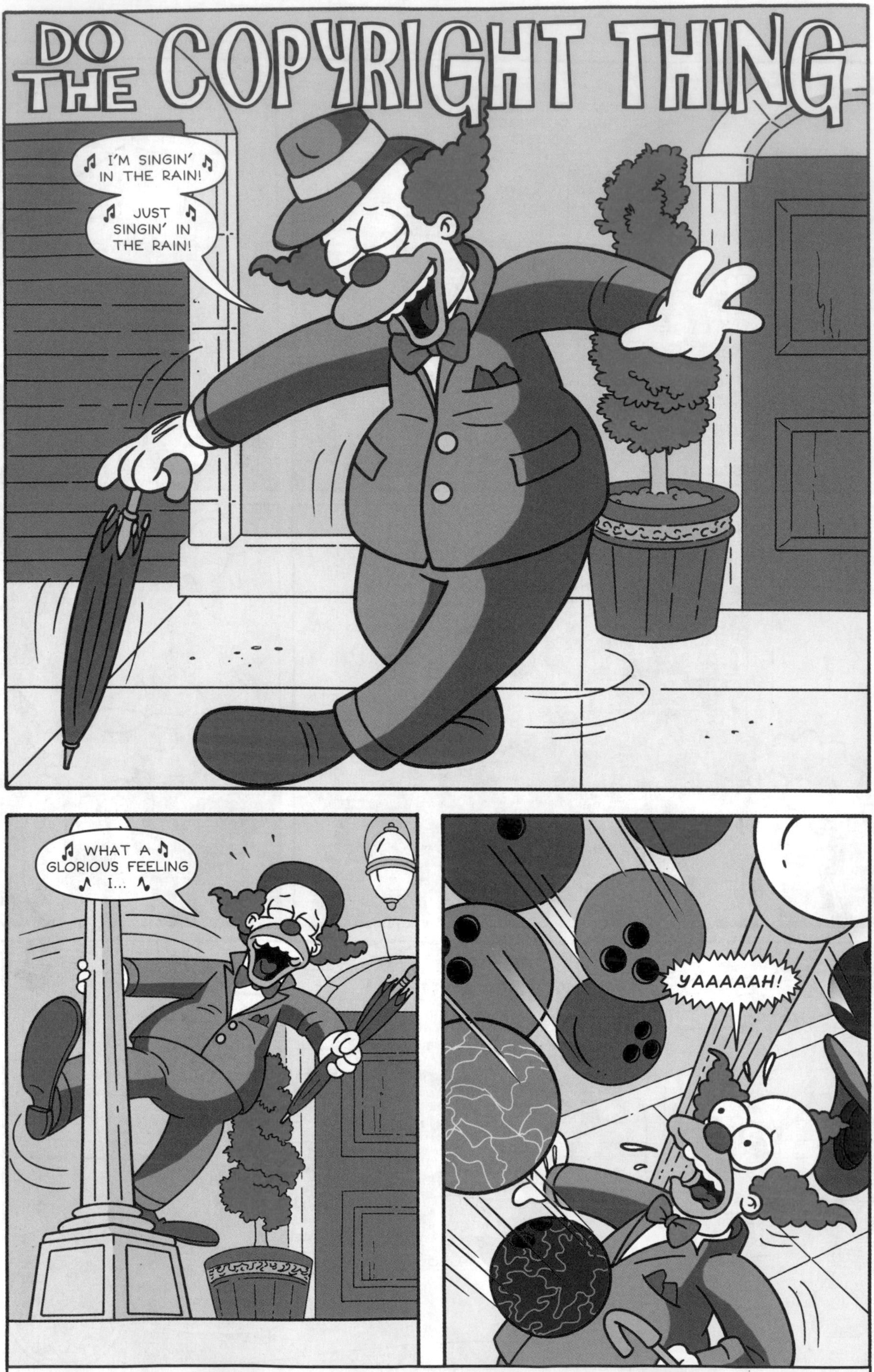
DO THE COPYRIGHT THING
♫ I'M SINGIN' ♫ IN THE RAIN!
♫ JUST ♫ SINGIN' IN THE RAIN!
♫ WHAT A ♫ GLORIOUS FEELING I...
YAAAAAH!

IAN **BOOTHBY** STORY	JOHN **COSTANZA** PENCILS	PHYLLIS **NOVIN** INKS	ART **VILLANUEVA** COLORS	KAREN **BATES** LETTERS	BILL **MORRISON** EDITOR

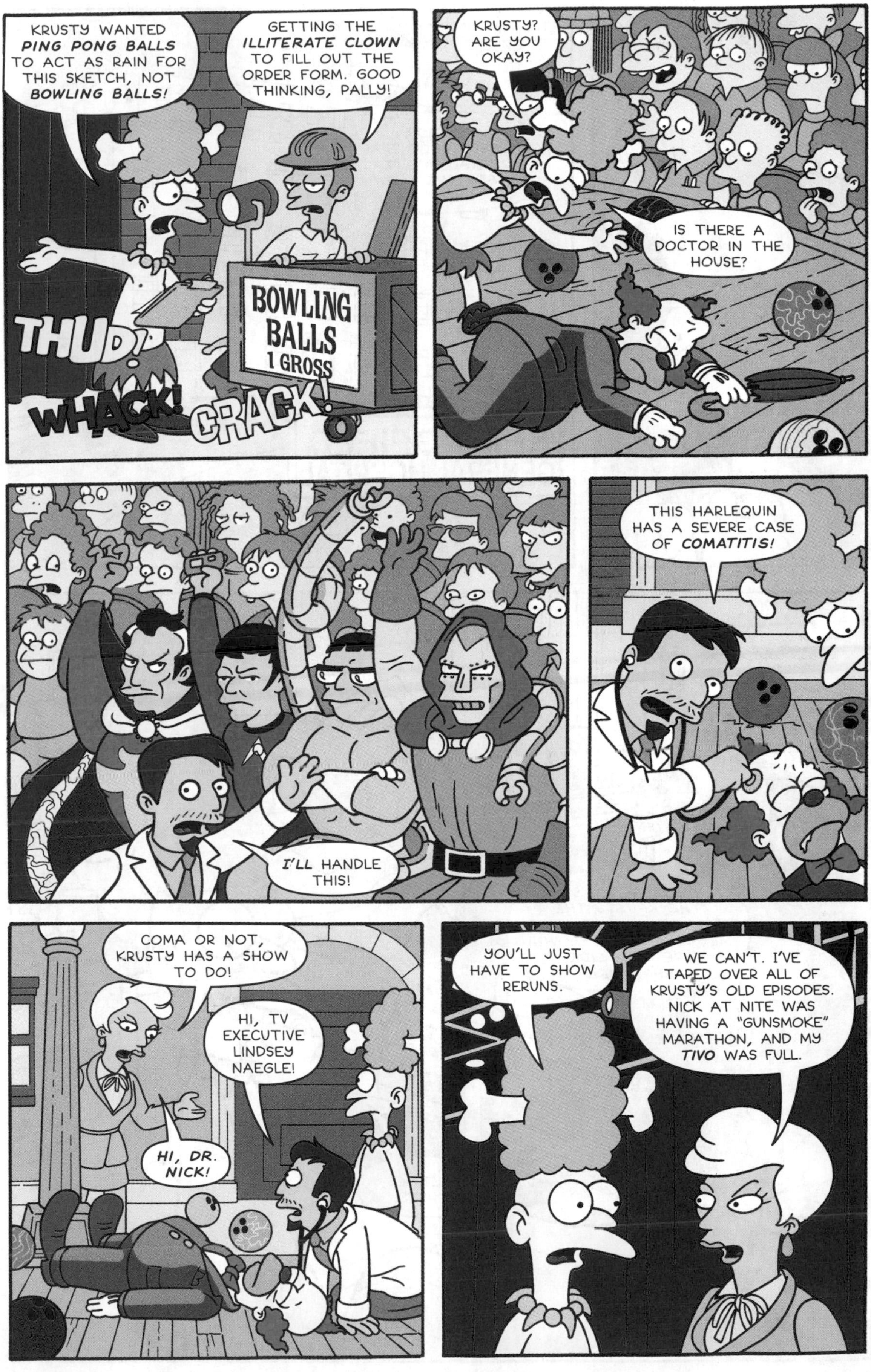
KRUSTY WANTED PING PONG BALLS TO ACT AS RAIN FOR THIS SKETCH, NOT BOWLING BALLS!
GETTING THE ILLITERATE CLOWN TO FILL OUT THE ORDER FORM. GOOD THINKING, PALLY!
BOWLING BALLS 1 GROSS
THUD!
WHACK!
CRACK!
KRUSTY? ARE YOU OKAY?
IS THERE A DOCTOR IN THE HOUSE?
I'LL HANDLE THIS!
THIS HARLEQUIN HAS A SEVERE CASE OF COMATITIS!
COMA OR NOT, KRUSTY HAS A SHOW TO DO!
HI, TV EXECUTIVE LINDSEY NAEGLE!
HI, DR. NICK!
YOU'LL JUST HAVE TO SHOW RERUNS.
WE CAN'T. I'VE TAPED OVER ALL OF KRUSTY'S OLD EPISODES. NICK AT NITE WAS HAVING A "GUNSMOKE" MARATHON, AND MY TIVO WAS FULL.

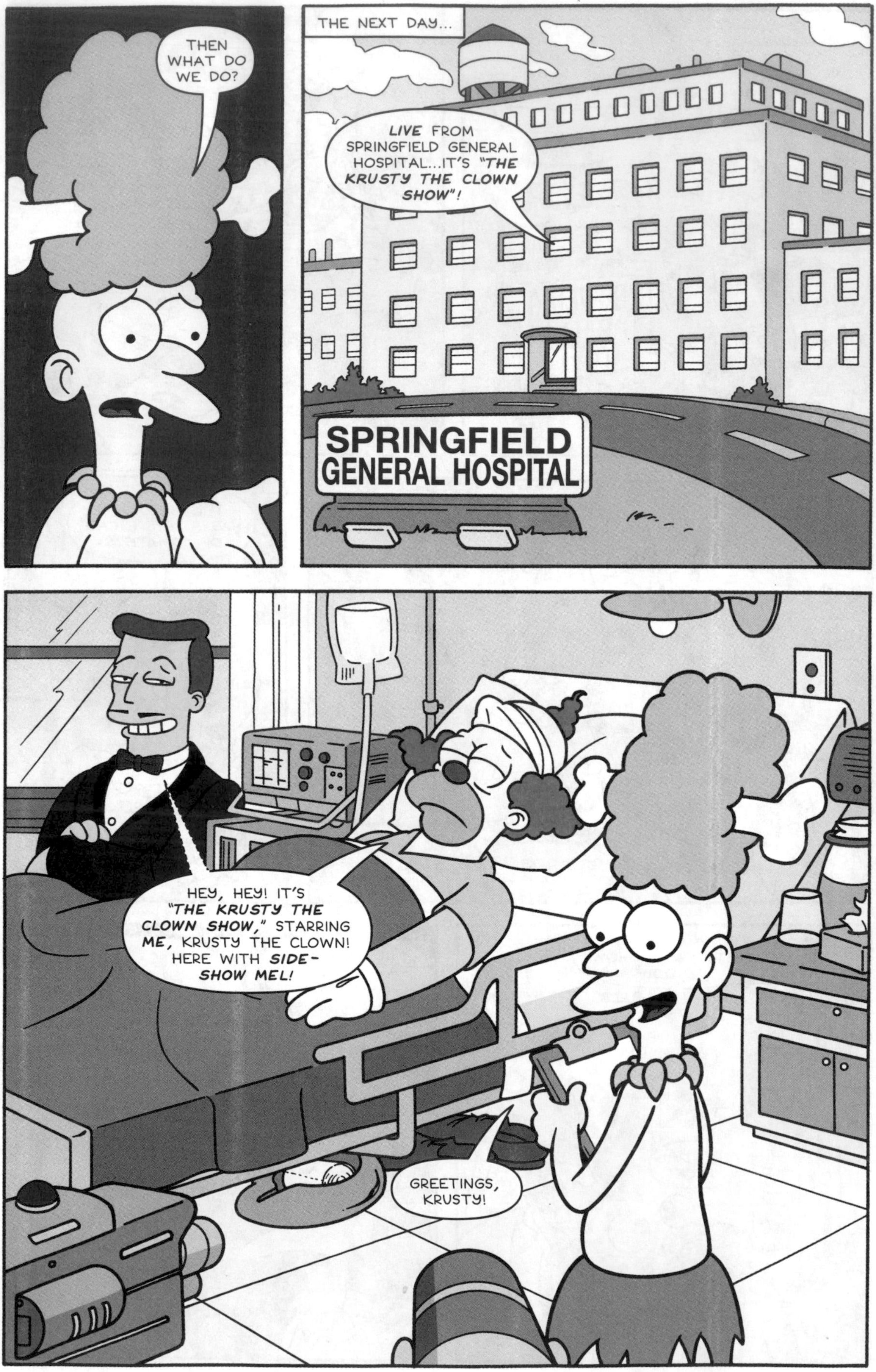
THEN WHAT DO WE DO?
THE NEXT DAY...
LIVE FROM SPRINGFIELD GENERAL HOSPITAL...IT'S "THE KRUSTY THE CLOWN SHOW"!
SPRINGFIELD GENERAL HOSPITAL
HEY, HEY! IT'S "THE KRUSTY THE CLOWN SHOW," STARRING ME, KRUSTY THE CLOWN! HERE WITH SIDE-SHOW MEL!
GREETINGS, KRUSTY!

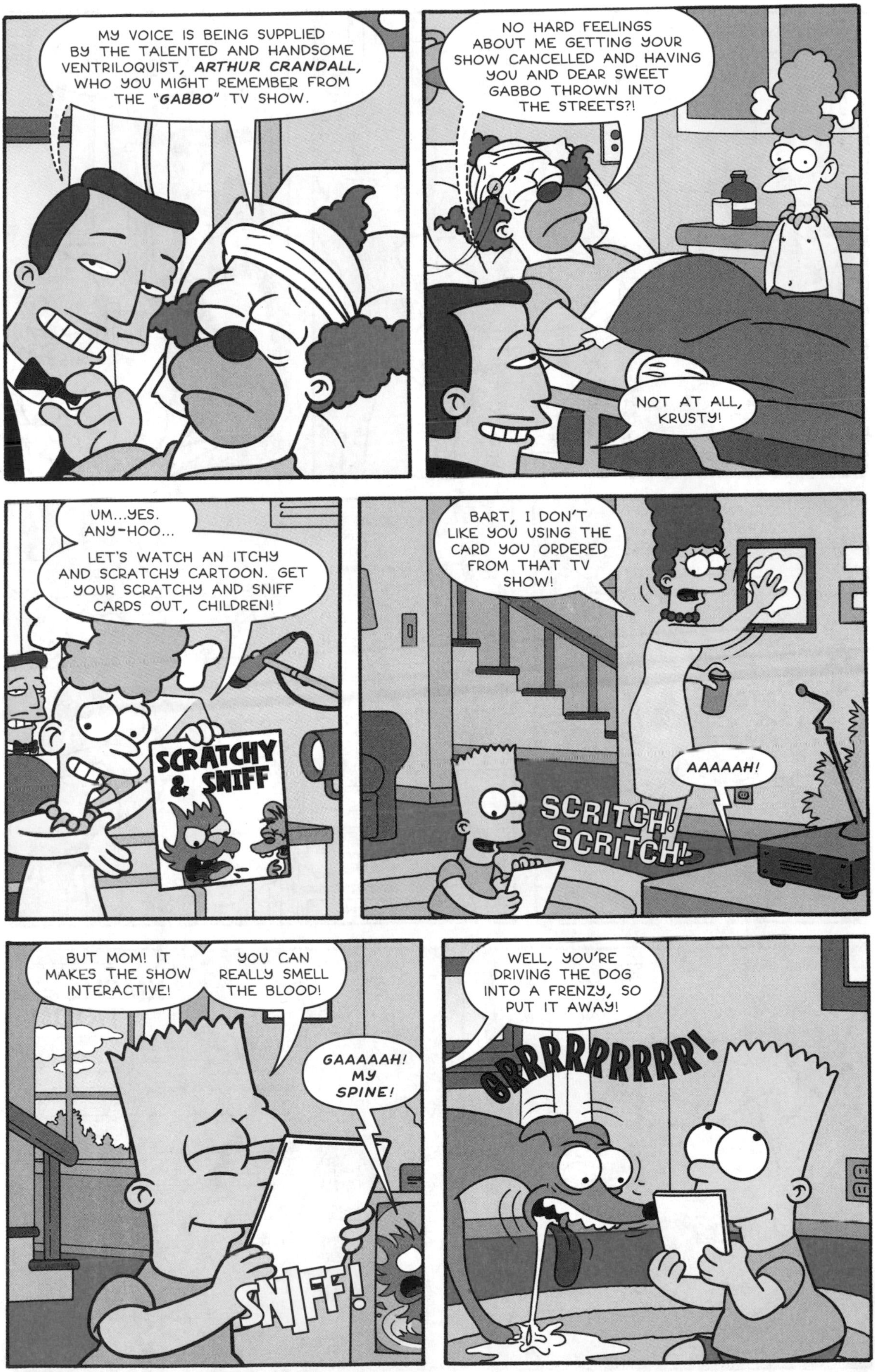
MY VOICE IS BEING SUPPLIED BY THE TALENTED AND HANDSOME VENTRILOQUIST, ARTHUR CRANDALL, WHO YOU MIGHT REMEMBER FROM THE "GABBO" TV SHOW.
NO HARD FEELINGS ABOUT ME GETTING YOUR SHOW CANCELLED AND HAVING YOU AND DEAR SWEET GABBO THROWN INTO THE STREETS?!
NOT AT ALL, KRUSTY!
UM...YES. ANY-HOO...
LET'S WATCH AN ITCHY AND SCRATCHY CARTOON. GET YOUR SCRATCHY AND SNIFF CARDS OUT, CHILDREN!
SCRATCHY & SNIFF
BART, I DON'T LIKE YOU USING THE CARD YOU ORDERED FROM THAT TV SHOW!
AAAAAH!
SCRITCH! SCRITCH!
BUT MOM! IT MAKES THE SHOW INTERACTIVE!
YOU CAN REALLY SMELL THE BLOOD!
GAAAAAH! MY SPINE!
SNIFF!
WELL, YOU'RE DRIVING THE DOG INTO A FRENZY, SO PUT IT AWAY!
GRRRRRRRRRR!

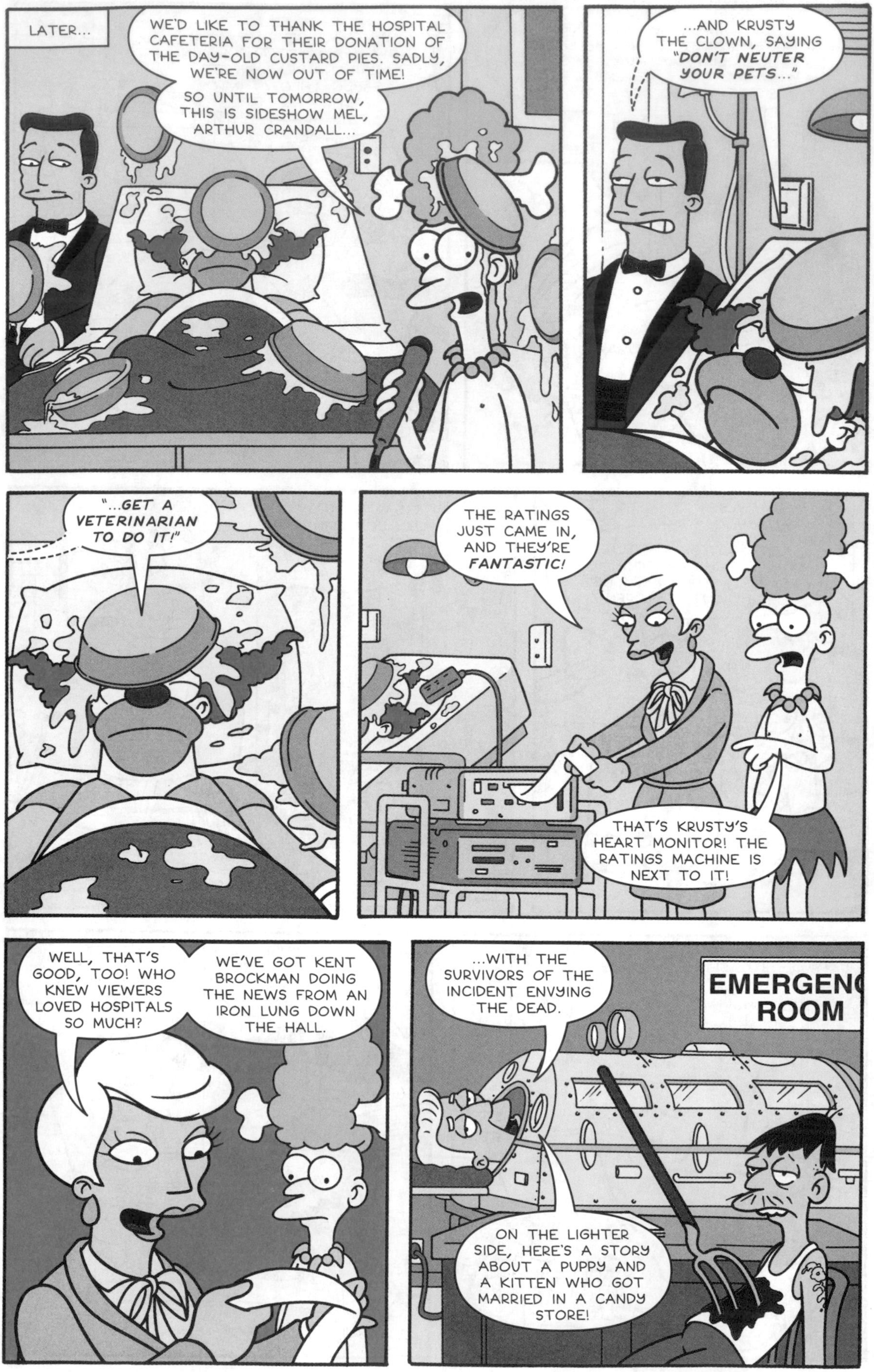
LATER...
WE'D LIKE TO THANK THE HOSPITAL CAFETERIA FOR THEIR DONATION OF THE DAY-OLD CUSTARD PIES. SADLY, WE'RE NOW OUT OF TIME!
SO UNTIL TOMORROW, THIS IS SIDESHOW MEL, ARTHUR CRANDALL...
...AND KRUSTY THE CLOWN, SAYING "DON'T NEUTER YOUR PETS..."
"...GET A VETERINARIAN TO DO IT!"
THE RATINGS JUST CAME IN, AND THEY'RE FANTASTIC!
THAT'S KRUSTY'S HEART MONITOR! THE RATINGS MACHINE IS NEXT TO IT!
WELL, THAT'S GOOD, TOO! WHO KNEW VIEWERS LOVED HOSPITALS SO MUCH?
WE'VE GOT KENT BROCKMAN DOING THE NEWS FROM AN IRON LUNG DOWN THE HALL.
EMERGENC
ROOM
...WITH THE SURVIVORS OF THE INCIDENT ENVYING THE DEAD.
ON THE LIGHTER SIDE, HERE'S A STORY ABOUT A PUPPY AND A KITTEN WHO GOT MARRIED IN A CANDY STORE!

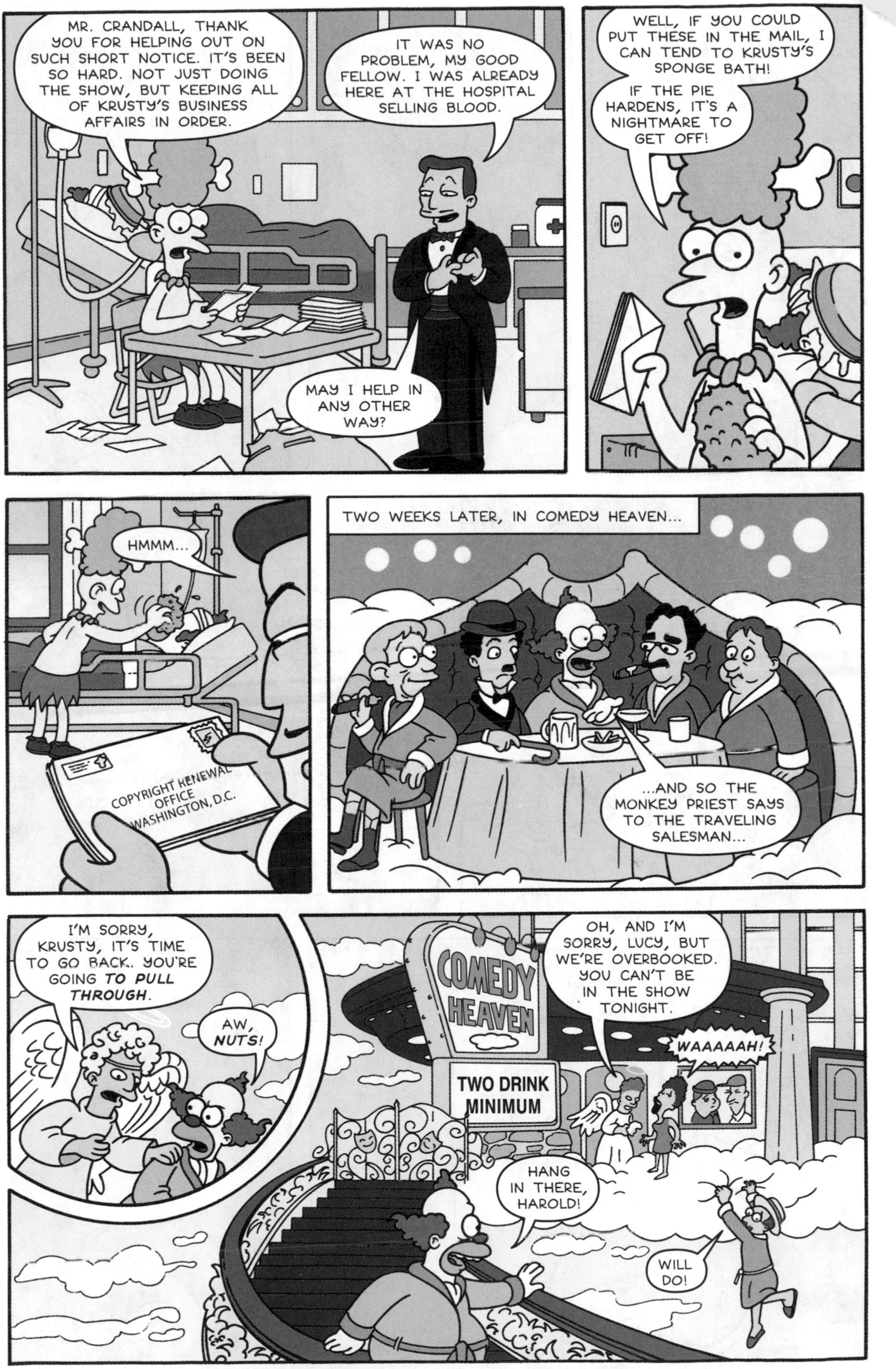
MR. CRANDALL, THANK YOU FOR HELPING OUT ON SUCH SHORT NOTICE. IT'S BEEN SO HARD. NOT JUST DOING THE SHOW, BUT KEEPING ALL OF KRUSTY'S BUSINESS AFFAIRS IN ORDER.
IT WAS NO PROBLEM, MY GOOD FELLOW. I WAS ALREADY HERE AT THE HOSPITAL SELLING BLOOD.
MAY I HELP IN ANY OTHER WAY?
WELL, IF YOU COULD PUT THESE IN THE MAIL, I CAN TEND TO KRUSTY'S SPONGE BATH!
IF THE PIE HARDENS, IT'S A NIGHTMARE TO GET OFF!
HMMM...
COPYRIGHT RENEWAL OFFICE WASHINGTON, D.C.
TWO WEEKS LATER, IN COMEDY HEAVEN...
...AND SO THE MONKEY PRIEST SAYS TO THE TRAVELING SALESMAN...
I'M SORRY, KRUSTY, IT'S TIME TO GO BACK.. YOU'RE GOING TO PULL THROUGH.
AW, NUTS!
COMEDY HEAVEN
OH, AND I'M SORRY, LUCY, BUT WE'RE OVERBOOKED. YOU CAN'T BE IN THE SHOW TONIGHT.
WAAAAAH!
TWO DRINK MINIMUM
HANG IN THERE, HAROLD!
WILL DO!

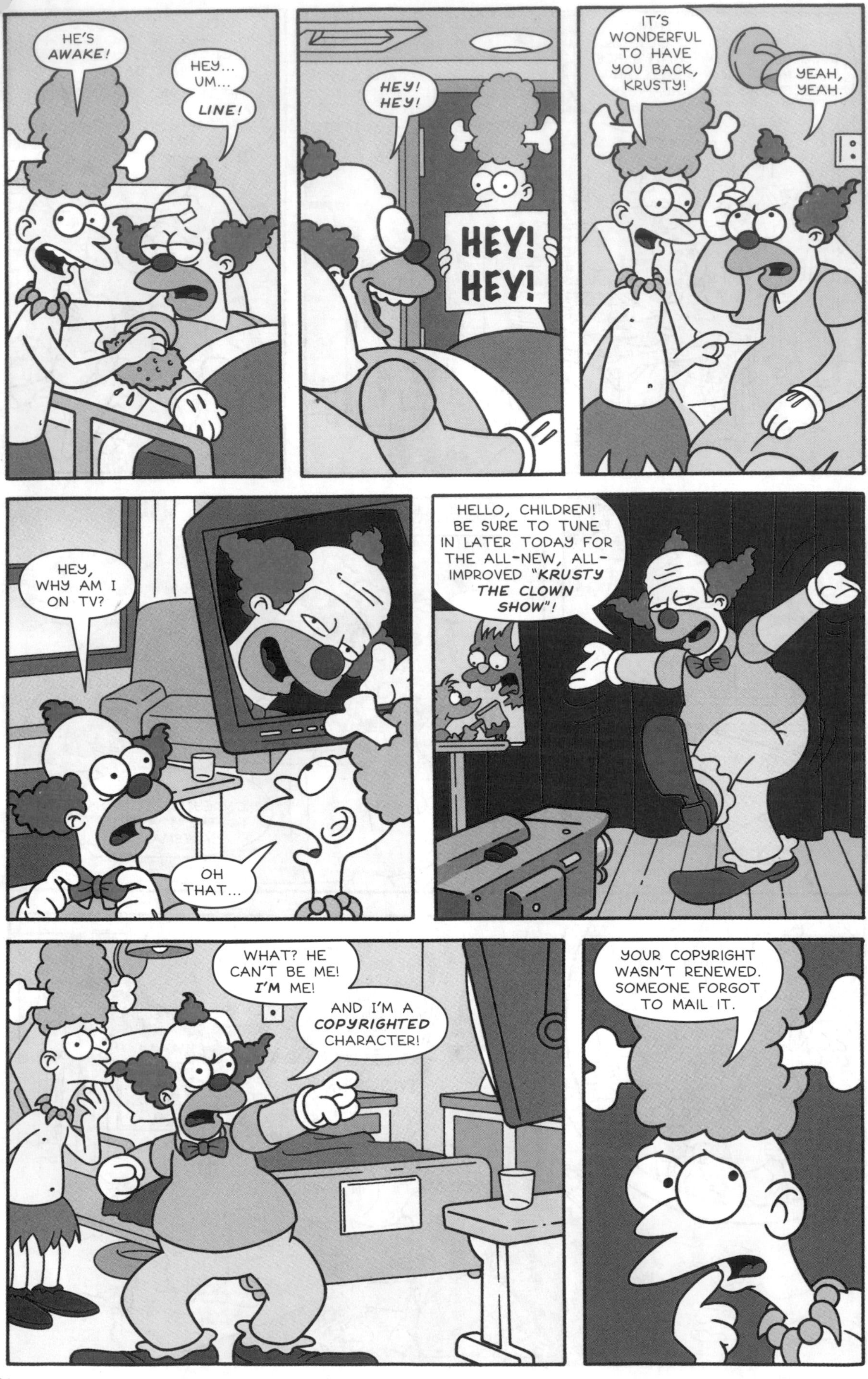
HE'S AWAKE!
HEY... UM... LINE!
HEY! HEY!
HEY! HEY!
IT'S WONDERFUL TO HAVE YOU BACK, KRUSTY!
YEAH, YEAH.
HEY, WHY AM I ON TV?
OH THAT...
HELLO, CHILDREN! BE SURE TO TUNE IN LATER TODAY FOR THE ALL-NEW, ALL-IMPROVED "KRUSTY THE CLOWN SHOW"!
WHAT? HE CAN'T BE ME! I'M ME!
AND I'M A COPYRIGHTED CHARACTER!
YOUR COPYRIGHT WASN'T RENEWED. SOMEONE FORGOT TO MAIL IT.

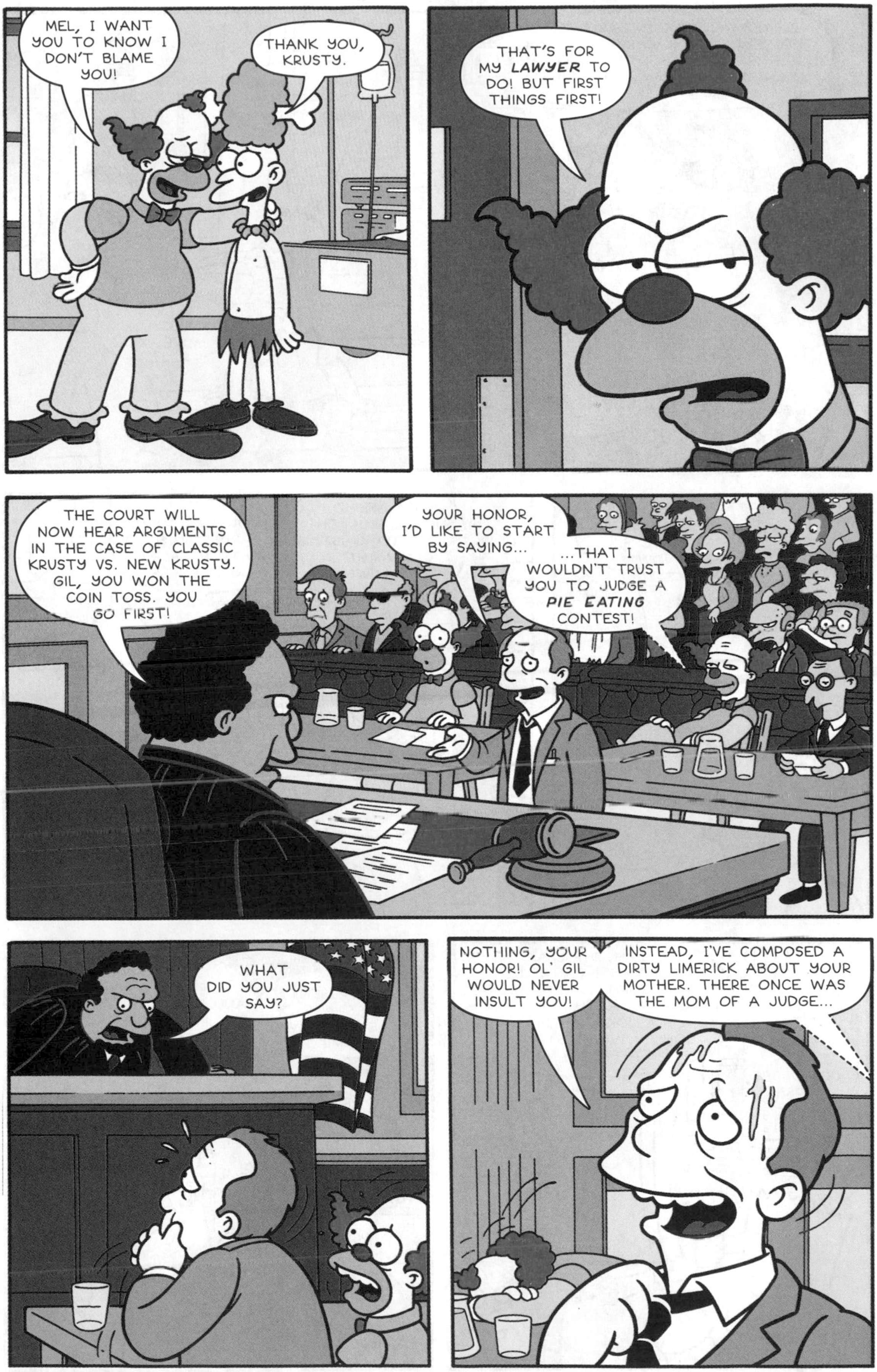
MEL, I WANT YOU TO KNOW I DON'T BLAME YOU!
THANK YOU, KRUSTY.
THAT'S FOR MY LAWYER TO DO! BUT FIRST THINGS FIRST!
THE COURT WILL NOW HEAR ARGUMENTS IN THE CASE OF CLASSIC KRUSTY VS. NEW KRUSTY. GIL, YOU WON THE COIN TOSS. YOU GO FIRST!
YOUR HONOR, I'D LIKE TO START BY SAYING...
...THAT I WOULDN'T TRUST YOU TO JUDGE A PIE EATING CONTEST!
WHAT DID YOU JUST SAY?
NOTHING, YOUR HONOR! OL' GIL WOULD NEVER INSULT YOU!
INSTEAD, I'VE COMPOSED A DIRTY LIMERICK ABOUT YOUR MOTHER. THERE ONCE WAS THE MOM OF A JUDGE...

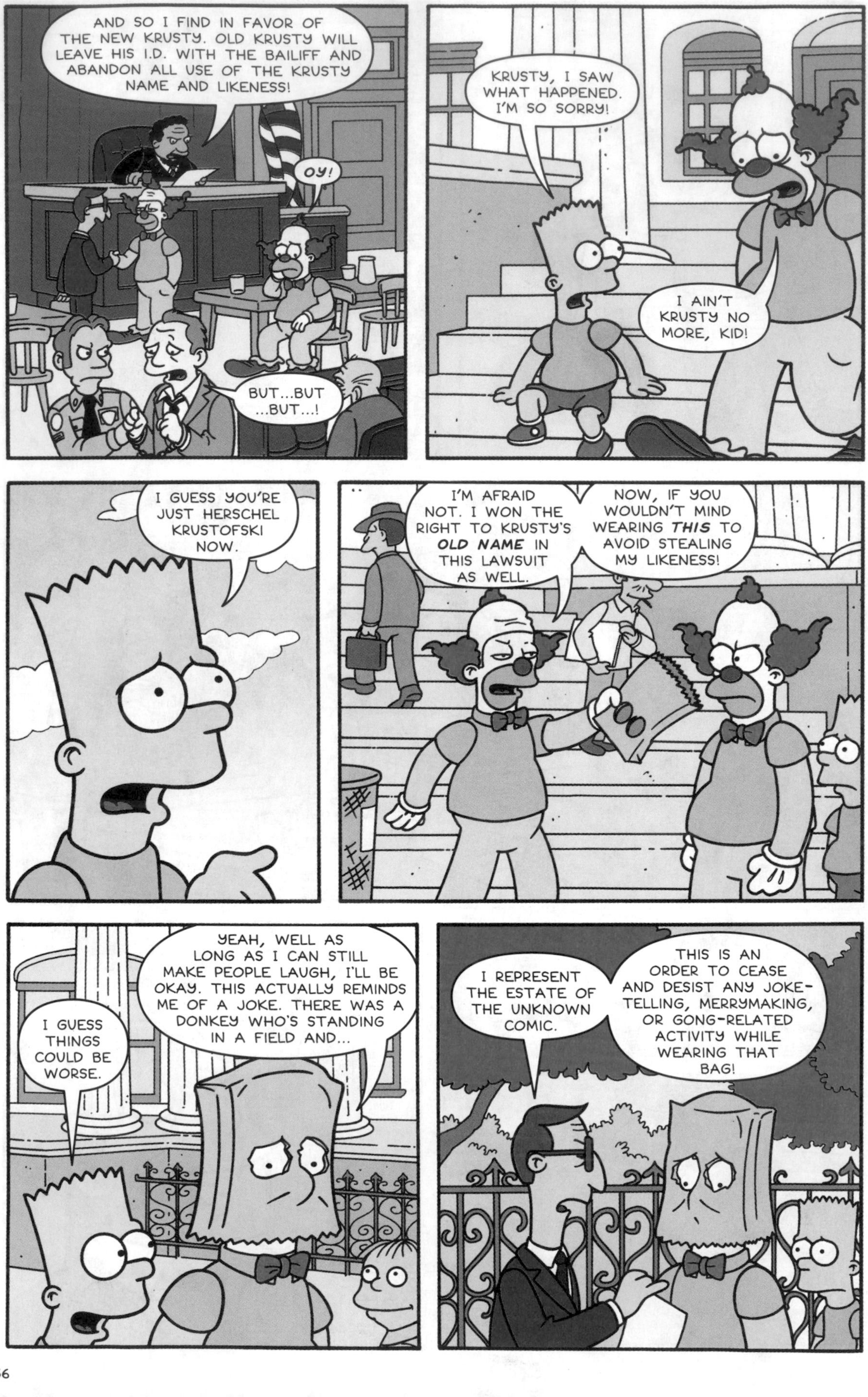
AND SO I FIND IN FAVOR OF THE NEW KRUSTY. OLD KRUSTY WILL LEAVE HIS I.D. WITH THE BAILIFF AND ABANDON ALL USE OF THE KRUSTY NAME AND LIKENESS!
OY!
BUT...BUT ...BUT...!
KRUSTY, I SAW WHAT HAPPENED. I'M SO SORRY!
I AIN'T KRUSTY NO MORE, KID!
I GUESS YOU'RE JUST HERSCHEL KRUSTOFSKI NOW.
I'M AFRAID NOT. I WON THE RIGHT TO KRUSTY'S OLD NAME IN THIS LAWSUIT AS WELL.
NOW, IF YOU WOULDN'T MIND WEARING THIS TO AVOID STEALING MY LIKENESS!
I GUESS THINGS COULD BE WORSE.
YEAH, WELL AS LONG AS I CAN STILL MAKE PEOPLE LAUGH, I'LL BE OKAY. THIS ACTUALLY REMINDS ME OF A JOKE. THERE WAS A DONKEY WHO'S STANDING IN A FIELD AND...
I REPRESENT THE ESTATE OF THE UNKNOWN COMIC.
THIS IS AN ORDER TO CEASE AND DESIST ANY JOKE-TELLING, MERRYMAKING, OR GONG-RELATED ACTIVITY WHILE WEARING THAT BAG!

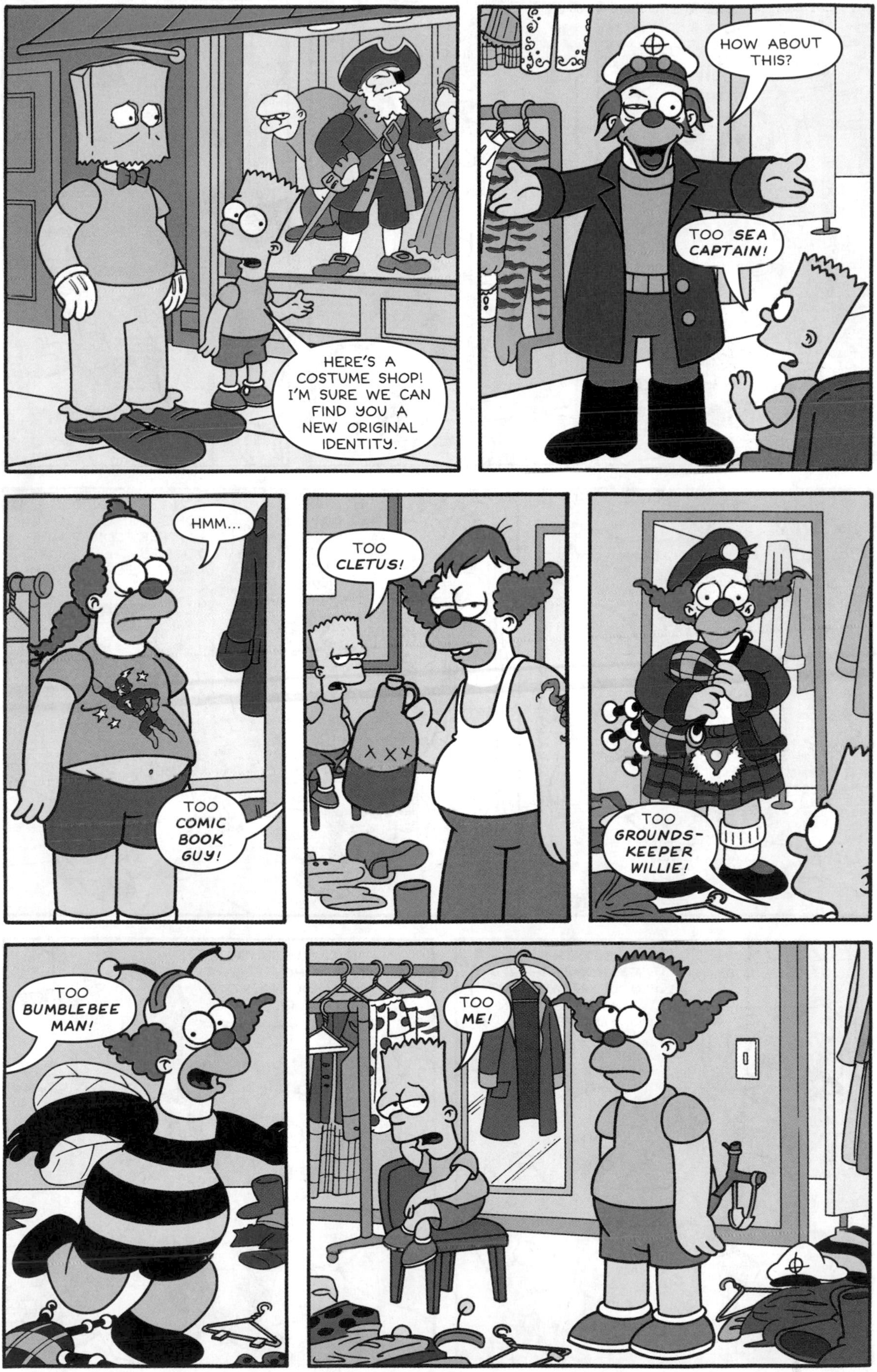
HERE'S A COSTUME SHOP! I'M SURE WE CAN FIND YOU A NEW ORIGINAL IDENTITY.
HOW ABOUT THIS?
TOO SEA CAPTAIN!
HMM...
TOO COMIC BOOK GUY!
TOO CLETUS!
TOO GROUNDS-KEEPER WILLIE!
TOO BUMBLEBEE MAN!
TOO ME!

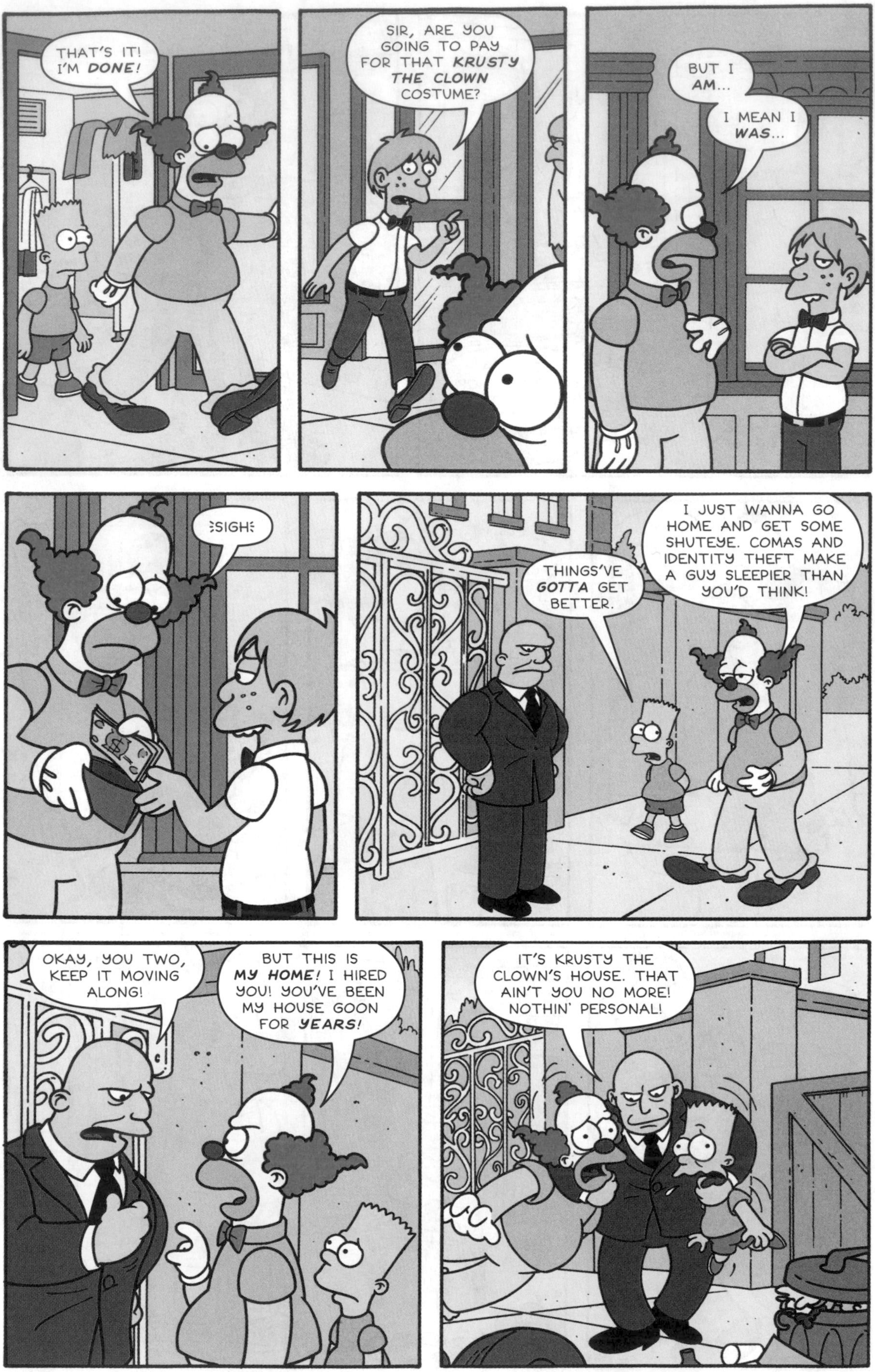
THAT'S IT! I'M **DONE!**
SIR, ARE YOU GOING TO PAY FOR THAT **KRUSTY THE CLOWN** COSTUME?
BUT I **AM**...
I MEAN I **WAS**...
:SIGH:
THINGS'VE **GOTTA** GET BETTER.
I JUST WANNA GO HOME AND GET SOME SHUTEYE. COMAS AND IDENTITY THEFT MAKE A GUY SLEEPIER THAN YOU'D THINK!
OKAY, YOU TWO, KEEP IT MOVING ALONG!
BUT THIS IS **MY HOME!** I HIRED YOU! YOU'VE BEEN MY HOUSE GOON FOR **YEARS!**
IT'S KRUSTY THE CLOWN'S HOUSE. THAT AIN'T YOU NO MORE! NOTHIN' PERSONAL!

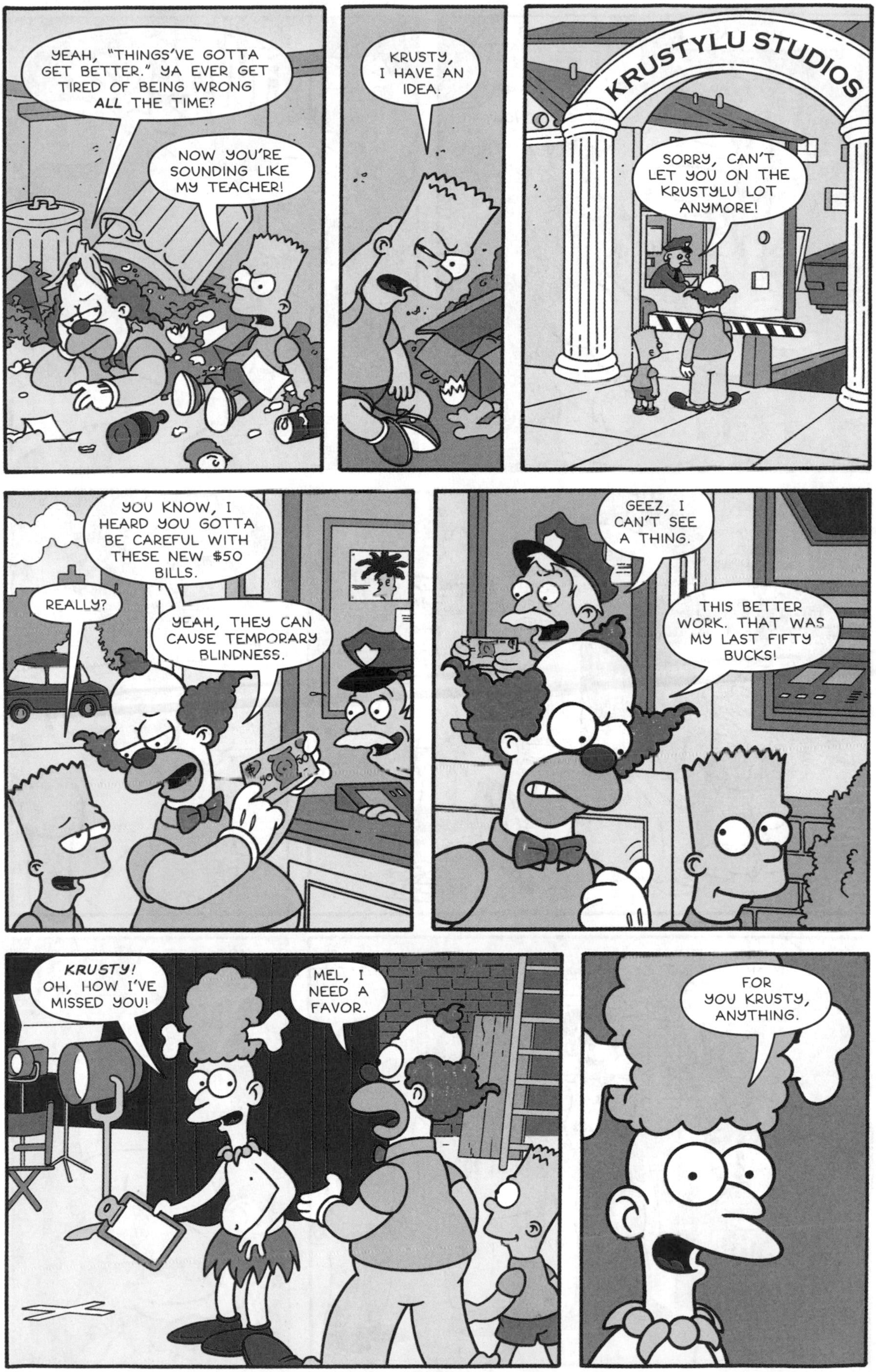
YEAH, "THINGS'VE GOTTA GET BETTER." YA EVER GET TIRED OF BEING WRONG ALL THE TIME?
NOW YOU'RE SOUNDING LIKE MY TEACHER!
KRUSTY, I HAVE AN IDEA.
KRUSTYLU STUDIOS
SORRY, CAN'T LET YOU ON THE KRUSTYLU LOT ANYMORE!
YOU KNOW, I HEARD YOU GOTTA BE CAREFUL WITH THESE NEW $50 BILLS.
REALLY?
YEAH, THEY CAN CAUSE TEMPORARY BLINDNESS.
GEEZ, I CAN'T SEE A THING.
THIS BETTER WORK. THAT WAS MY LAST FIFTY BUCKS!
KRUSTY! OH, HOW I'VE MISSED YOU!
MEL, I NEED A FAVOR.
FOR YOU KRUSTY, ANYTHING.

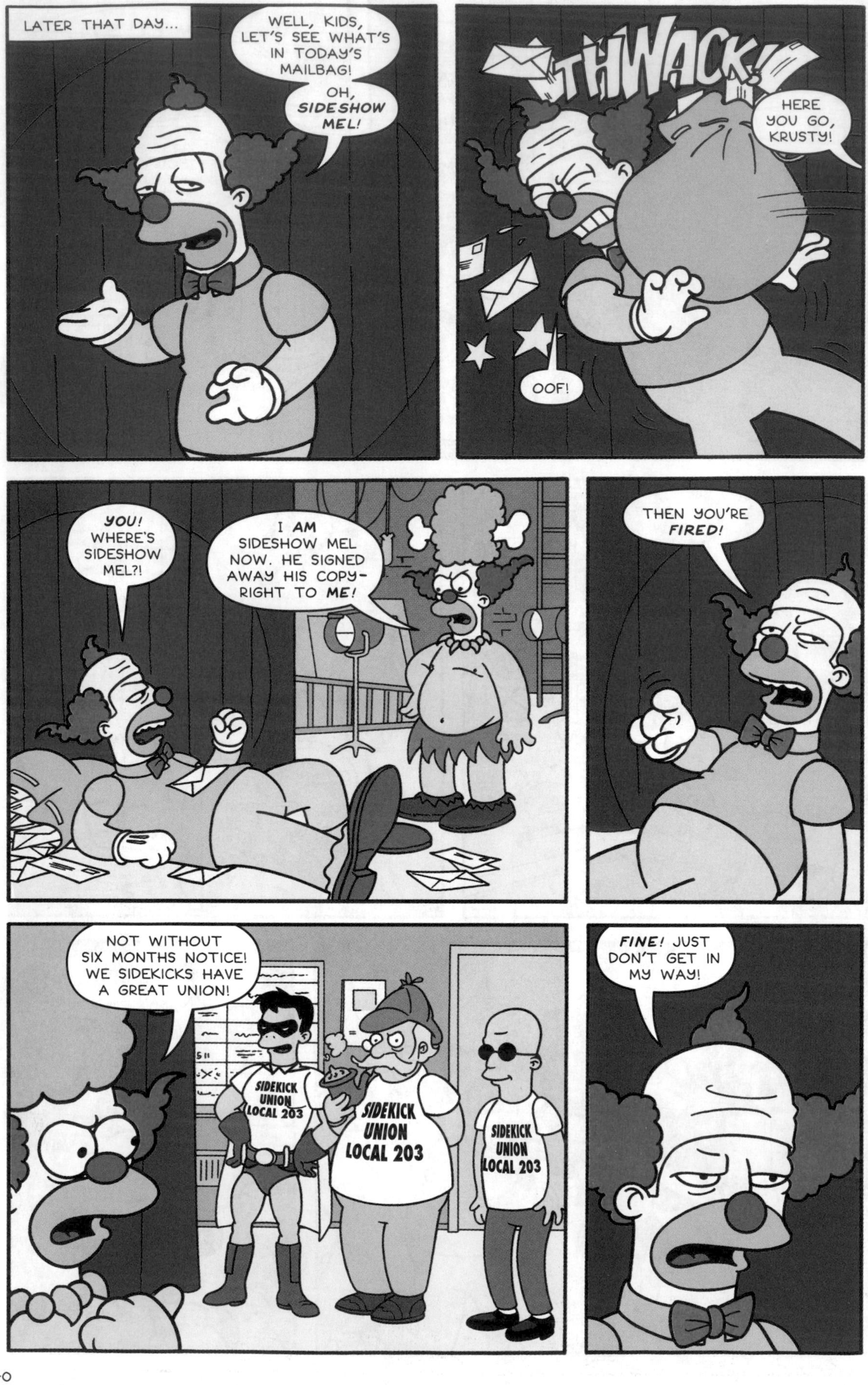
LATER THAT DAY...
WELL, KIDS, LET'S SEE WHAT'S IN TODAY'S MAILBAG!
OH, SIDESHOW MEL!
THWACK!
HERE YOU GO, KRUSTY!
OOF!
YOU! WHERE'S SIDESHOW MEL?!
I AM SIDESHOW MEL NOW. HE SIGNED AWAY HIS COPY-RIGHT TO ME!
THEN YOU'RE FIRED!
NOT WITHOUT SIX MONTHS NOTICE! WE SIDEKICKS HAVE A GREAT UNION!
SIDEKICK UNION LOCAL 203
SIDEKICK UNION LOCAL 203
SIDEKICK UNION LOCAL 203
FINE! JUST DON'T GET IN MY WAY!

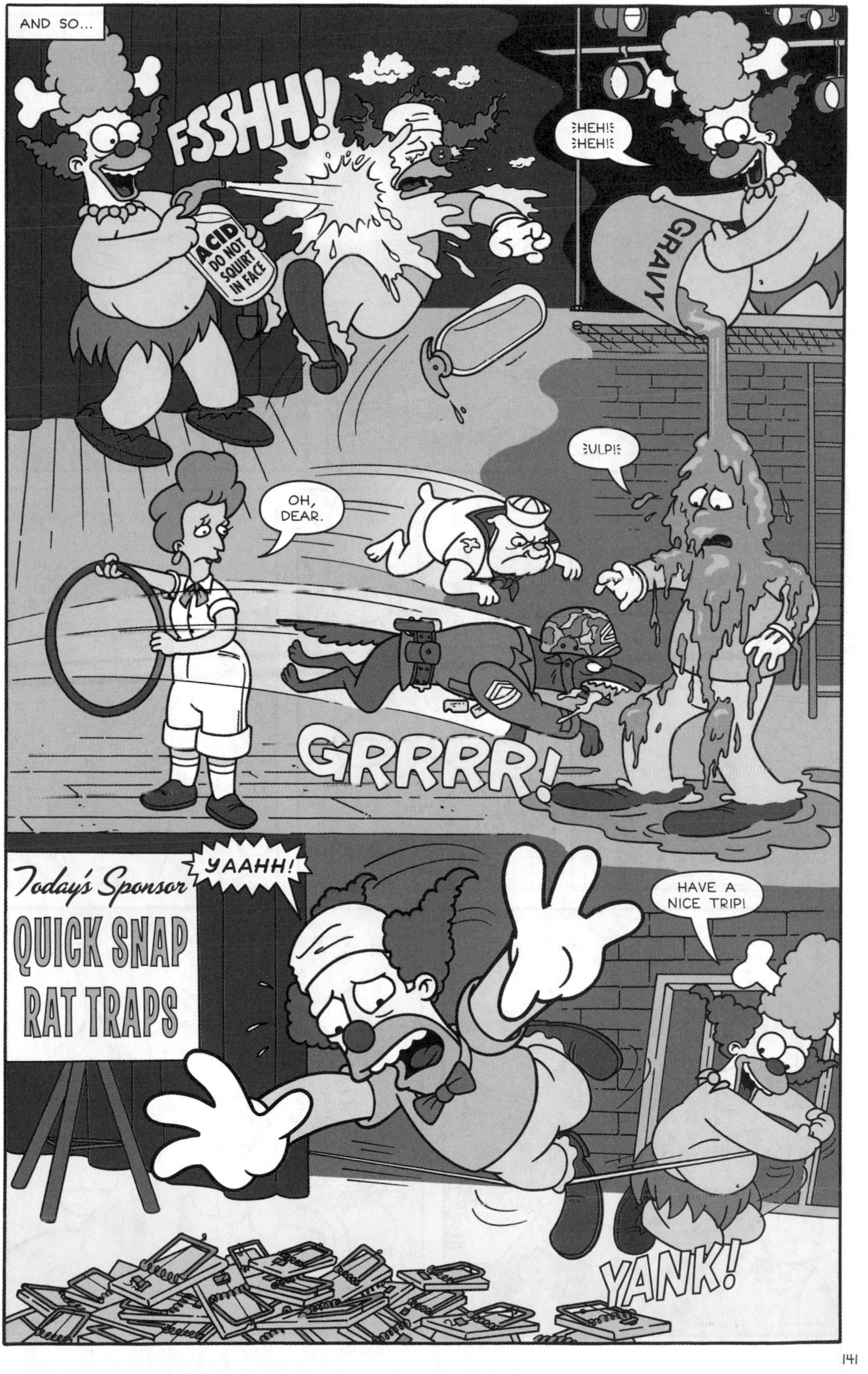
AND SO...
FSSHH!
ACID DO NOT SQUIRT IN FACE
HEH! HEH!
GRAVY
ULP!
OH, DEAR.
GRRRR!
Today's Sponsor
QUICK SNAP RAT TRAPS
YAAHH!
HAVE A NICE TRIP!
YANK!

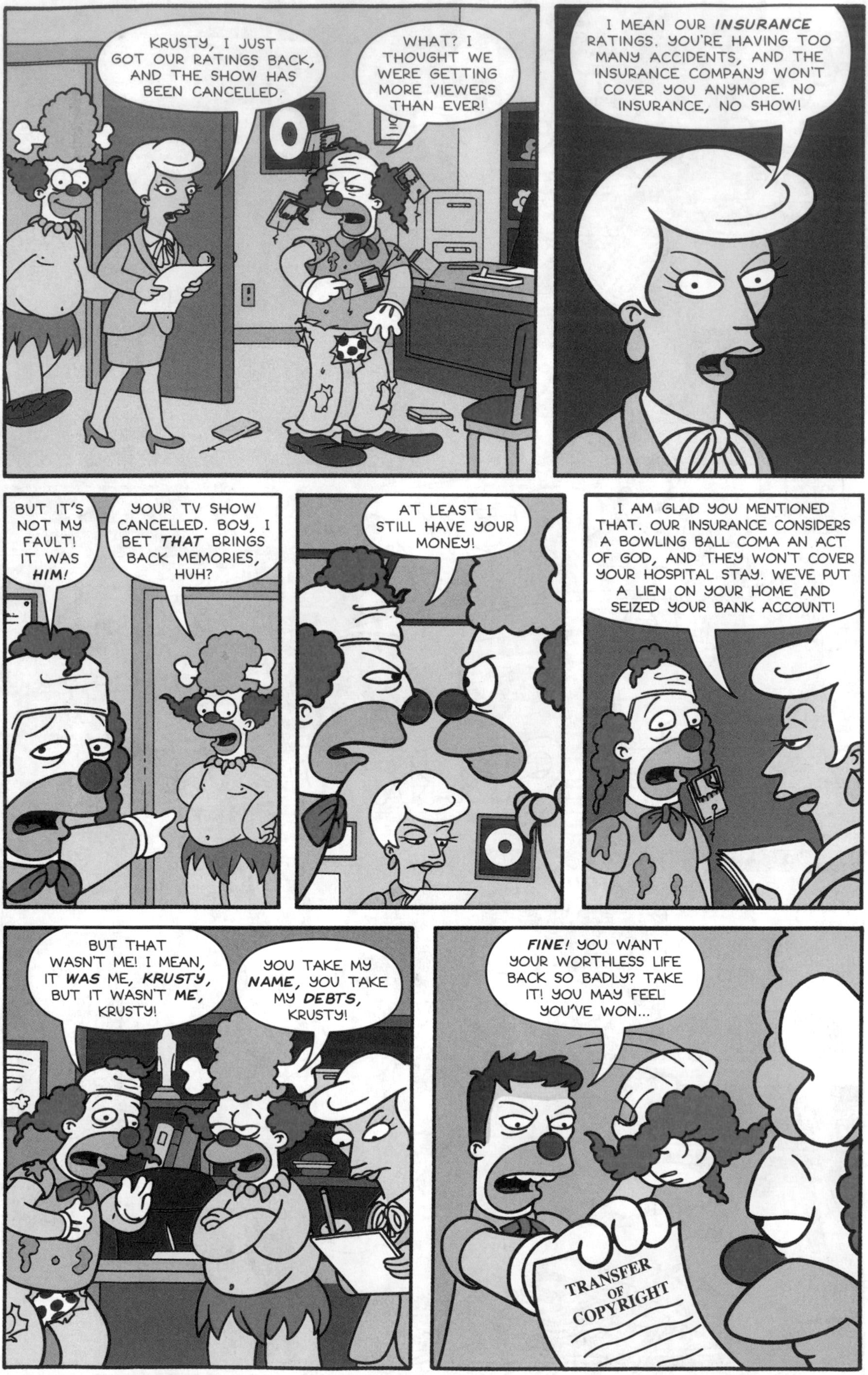
KRUSTY, I JUST GOT OUR RATINGS BACK, AND THE SHOW HAS BEEN CANCELLED.
WHAT? I THOUGHT WE WERE GETTING MORE VIEWERS THAN EVER!
I MEAN OUR ***INSURANCE*** RATINGS. YOU'RE HAVING TOO MANY ACCIDENTS, AND THE INSURANCE COMPANY WON'T COVER YOU ANYMORE. NO INSURANCE, NO SHOW!
BUT IT'S NOT MY FAULT! IT WAS ***HIM!***
YOUR TV SHOW CANCELLED. BOY, I BET ***THAT*** BRINGS BACK MEMORIES, HUH?
AT LEAST I STILL HAVE YOUR MONEY!
I AM GLAD YOU MENTIONED THAT. OUR INSURANCE CONSIDERS A BOWLING BALL COMA AN ACT OF GOD, AND THEY WON'T COVER YOUR HOSPITAL STAY. WE'VE PUT A LIEN ON YOUR HOME AND SEIZED YOUR BANK ACCOUNT!
BUT THAT WASN'T ME! I MEAN, IT ***WAS*** ME, ***KRUSTY,*** BUT IT WASN'T ***ME,*** KRUSTY!
YOU TAKE MY ***NAME,*** YOU TAKE MY ***DEBTS,*** KRUSTY!
FINE! YOU WANT YOUR WORTHLESS LIFE BACK SO BADLY? TAKE IT! YOU MAY FEEL YOU'VE WON...
TRANSFER OF COPYRIGHT

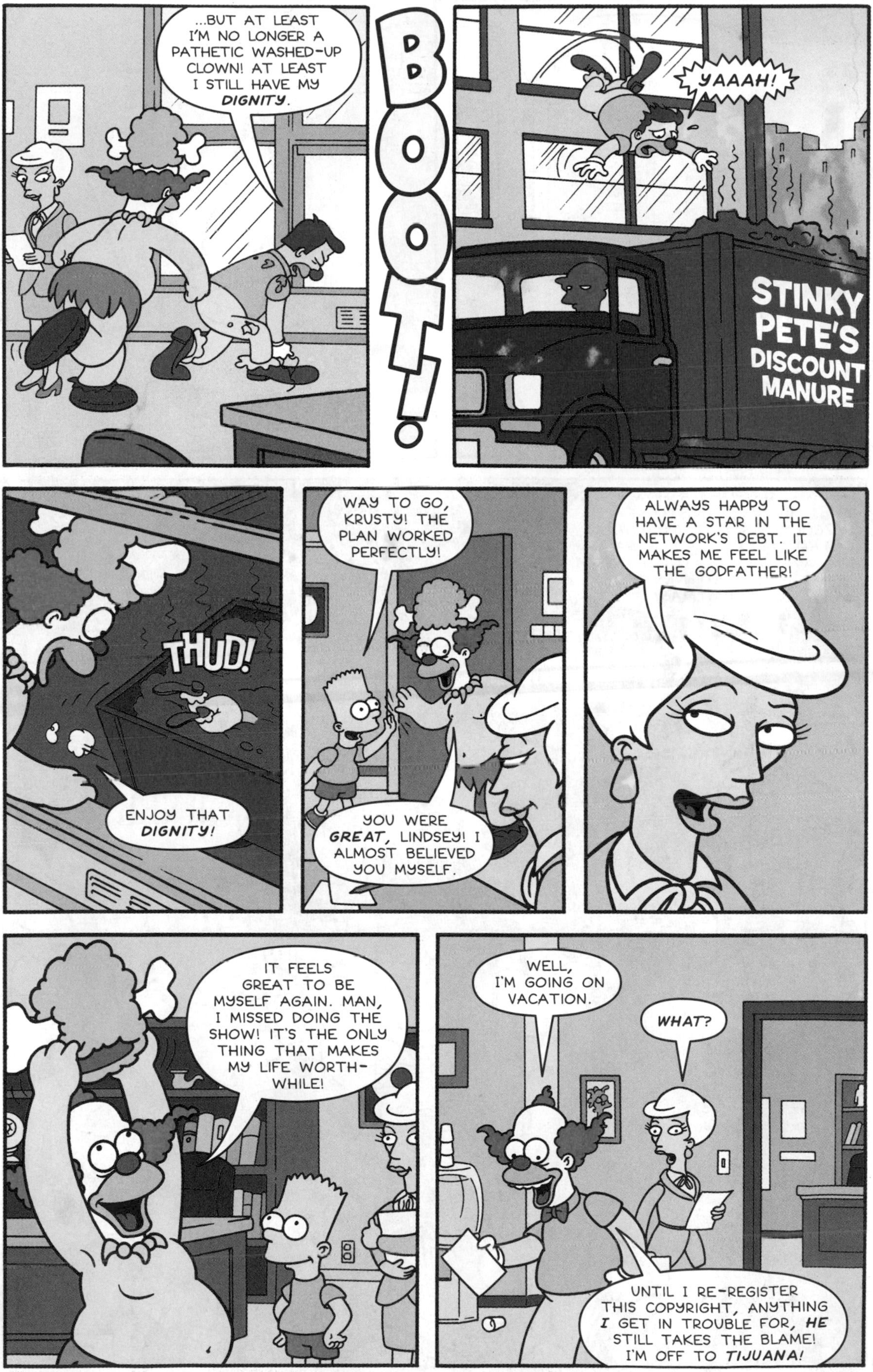
...BUT AT LEAST I'M NO LONGER A PATHETIC WASHED-UP CLOWN! AT LEAST I STILL HAVE MY DIGNITY.
BOOT!
YAAAH!
STINKY PETE'S DISCOUNT MANURE
THUD!
ENJOY THAT DIGNITY!
WAY TO GO, KRUSTY! THE PLAN WORKED PERFECTLY!
YOU WERE GREAT, LINDSEY! I ALMOST BELIEVED YOU MYSELF.
ALWAYS HAPPY TO HAVE A STAR IN THE NETWORK'S DEBT. IT MAKES ME FEEL LIKE THE GODFATHER!
IT FEELS GREAT TO BE MYSELF AGAIN. MAN, I MISSED DOING THE SHOW! IT'S THE ONLY THING THAT MAKES MY LIFE WORTH-WHILE!
WELL, I'M GOING ON VACATION.
WHAT?
UNTIL I RE-REGISTER THIS COPYRIGHT, ANYTHING I GET IN TROUBLE FOR, HE STILL TAKES THE BLAME! I'M OFF TO TIJUANA!

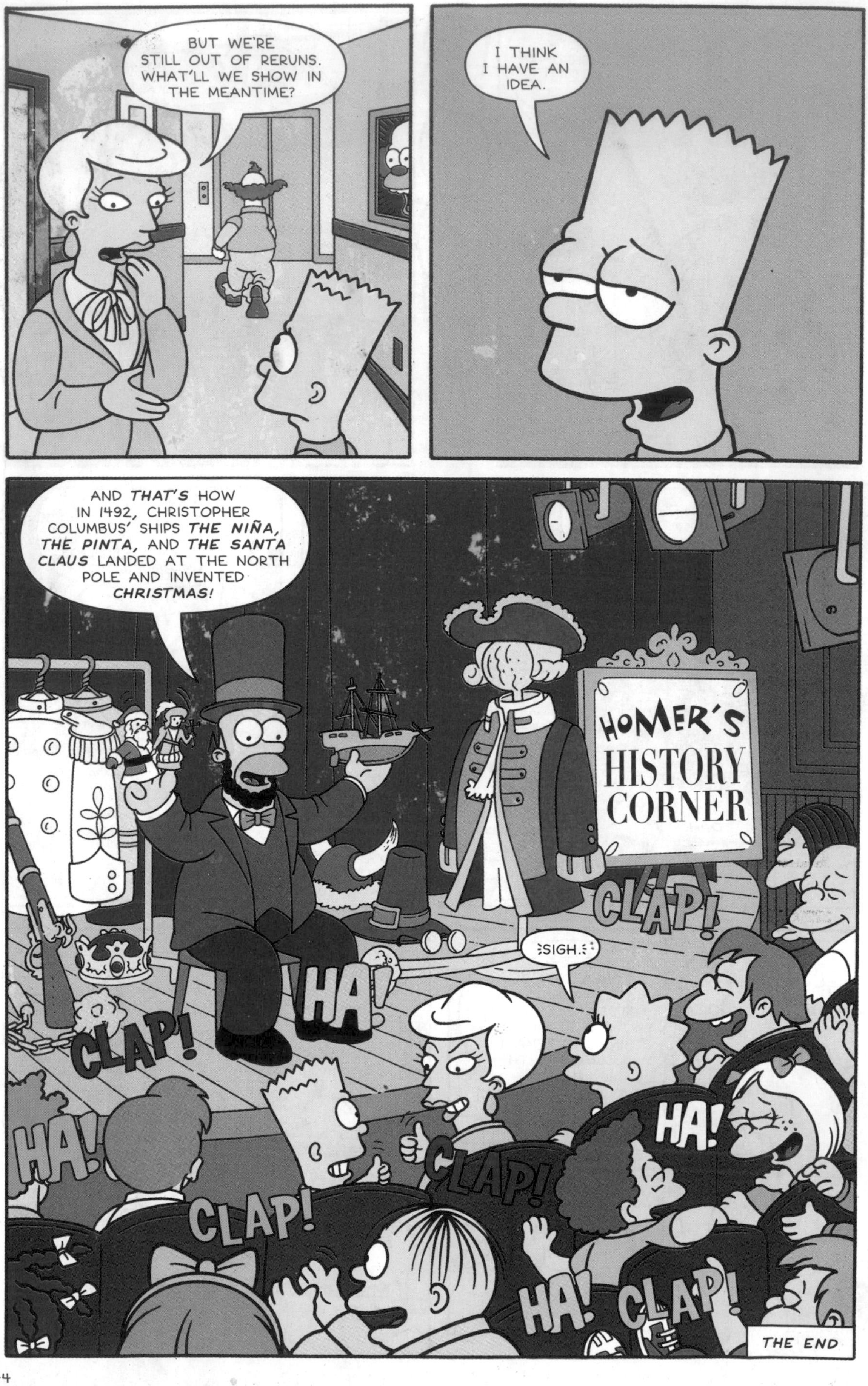
BUT WE'RE STILL OUT OF RERUNS. WHAT'LL WE SHOW IN THE MEANTIME?
I THINK I HAVE AN IDEA.
AND THAT'S HOW IN 1492, CHRISTOPHER COLUMBUS' SHIPS THE NIÑA, THE PINTA, AND THE SANTA CLAUS LANDED AT THE NORTH POLE AND INVENTED CHRISTMAS!
HOMER'S HISTORY CORNER
CLAP!
SIGH.
HA!
CLAP!
HA!
HA!
CLAP!
CLAP!
HA!
CLAP!
THE END